Lecture Notes in Computer Science 4915

Commenced Publication in 1973
Founding and Former Series Editors:
Gerhard Goos, Juris Hartmanis, and Jan van Leeuwen

T0223305

Andy King (Ed.)

Logic-Based Program Synthesis and Transformation

17th International Symposium, LOPSTR 2007
Kongens Lyngby, Denmark, August 23-24, 2007
Revised Selected Papers

 Springer

Volume Editor

Andy King
Computing Laboratory
University of Kent
Canterbury, UK
E-mail: a.m.king@kent.ac.uk

Library of Congress Control Number: 2008922726

CR Subject Classification (1998): F.3.1, D.1.1, D.1.6, D.2.4, I.2.2, F.4.1

LNCS Sublibrary: SL 1 – Theoretical Computer Science and General Issues

ISSN   0302-9743
ISBN-10   3-540-78768-2 Springer Berlin Heidelberg New York
ISBN-13   978-3-540-78768-6 Springer Berlin Heidelberg New York

Springer is a part of Springer Science+Business Media

springer.com

© Springer-Verlag Berlin Heidelberg 2008
Printed in Germany

Typesetting: Camera-ready by author, data conversion by Scientific Publishing Services, Chennai, India
Printed on acid-free paper   SPIN: 12245710   06/3180   5 4 3 2 1 0

Preface

This volume contains a selection of the the papers presented at the 17th International Symposium on Logic-Based Program Synthesis and Transformation, that was held in Kongens Lyngby, Denmark, August 23–24, 2007. Previous LOPSTR symposia were held in Venice (2007 and 1999), London (2005 and 2000), Verona (2004), Uppsala (2003), Madrid (2002), Paphos (2001), Manchester (1998, 1992 and 1991), Leuven (1997), Stockholm (1996), Arhhem (1995), Pisa (1994) and Louvain-la-Neuve (1993).

The aim of the LOPSTR series is to stimulate and promote international research and collaboration on logic-based program development. LOPSTR thus traditionally solicits papers in the areas of: specification, synthesis, verification, transformation, analysis, optimization, composition, security, reuse, applications and tools, component-based software development, software architectures, agent-based software development and program refinement. Formal proceedings are produced only after the symposium, so that authors can incorporate this feedback in the published papers. Thirty submissions were received and each paper, in turn, received at least three reviews. The Committee decided to accept seven full papers for presentation and for immediate inclusion in the final post-conference proceedings. Nine extended abstracts were also selected for presentation, of which six papers were accepted for publication in this volume, after revision and another round of reviewing. Michael Codish contributed a paper to the proceedings to accompany his invited talk.

I am very grateful to the Program Committee and the reviewers for their invaluable help and expertise. The Steering Committee and, in particular Germán Puebla, generously shared their experience. I would like to thank Andrei Voronkov for his excellent EasyChair paper submission and reviewing system; Michael Hanus for his guidance in using EasyChair; and Andreas Matthias for his pdf-pages LATEX package which simplified the production of the pre-conference LOPSTR proceedings.

LOPSTR 2007 was co-located with SAS 2007 and my warmest thanks go to Christian W. Probst (Local Chair), who was always willing to help in every aspect of the organization of LOPSTR 2007. Special thanks also go Hanne Riis Nielson, Flemming Nielson (Treasurer), Sebastian Nanz, Terkel K. Tolstrup, Eva Bing, and Elsebeth Strøm, who, together with Christian, took care of the overall planning and local organization of LOPSTR 2007.

December 2007   Andy King

Organization

Program Committee

Elvira Albert	Universidad Complutense Madrid, Spain
John Gallagher	University of Roskilde, Denmark
Michael Hanus	Christian-Albrechts-Universität zu Kiel, Germany
Jacob Howe	City University, UK
Andy King	(Program Chair) University of Kent, UK
Michael Leuschel	Heinrich-Heine-Universität Düsseldorf, Germany
Mario Ornaghi	Università degli Studi di Milano, Italy
Étienne Payet	Université de La Réunion, France
Alberto Pettorossi	Università di Roma Tor Vergata, Italy
Carla Piazza	Università degli Studi di Udine, Italy
C. R. Ramakrishnan	SUNY Stony Brook, USA
Abhik Roychoudhury	National University of Singapore, Singapore
Peter Schneider-Kamp	RWTH Aachen, Germany
Alexander Serebrenik	(Publicity Chair) Technische Universiteit Eindhoven
Josep Silva	Technical University of Valencia, Spain
Wim Vanhoof	University of Namur, Belgium

Steering Committee

Alberto Pettorossi	Università di Roma Tor Vergata, Italy
Michael Leuschel	Heinrich-Heine-Universität Düsseldorf, Germany
Maurice Bruynooghe	Katholieke Universiteit Leuven, Belgium
Sandro Etalle	Universiteit Twente, Netherlands
Patricia Hill	University of Leeds, UK
German Puebla	Technical University of Madrid, Spain
Andy King	University of Kent, UK

Local Organization Committee

Christian W. Probst	(Local Chair) Technical University of Denmark
Sebastian Nanz	Technical University of Denmark
Terkel K. Tolstrup	Technical University of Denmark
Eva Bing	Technical University of Denmark
Elsebeth Strøm	Technical University of Denmark
Hanne Riis Nielson	Technical University of Denmark
Flemming Nielson	(Treasurer) Technical University of Denmark

Additional Referees

Slim Abdennadher
Armin Biere
Davide Bresolin
Maurice Bruynooghe
Manuel Carro
Alberto Casagrande
Agostino Dovier
Camillo Fiorentini
Andrea Formisano
Ankit Goel
Gopal Gupta
Frank Huch

Lunjin Lu
Salvador Lucas
Fred Mesnard
Eric Monfroy
José Morales
Rafael Navarro
Alessandro Dal Palu'
David Pearce
Maurizio Proietti
Arend Rensink
Jaime Sanchez
Beata Sarna-Starosta

Valerio Senni
Andrew Sentosa
Jaroslav Sevcik
Axel Simon
Jan-Georg Smaus
Fausto Spoto
German Vidal
Marc Voorhoeve
Tao Wang
Jan Martijn van der Werf

Table of Contents

Software Engineering

Proving Termination with (Boolean) Satisfaction

Michael Codish*

Department of Computer Science
Ben-Gurion University of the Negev
Beer-Sheva, Israel
mcodish@cs.bgu.ac.il

1 Introduction

At some point there was the Davis-Putnam-Logemann-Loveland (DPLL) algorithm [6]. Forty v e years later, research on Boolean satisfiability (SAT) is still ceaselessly generating even better SAT solvers capable of handling even larger SAT instances. Remarkably, the majority of these tools still bear the hallmark of the DPLL algorithm. In sync with the availability of progressively stronger SAT solvers is an accumulating number of applications which demonstrate that real world problems can often be solved by encoding them into SAT. When successful, this circumvents the need to redevelop complex search algorithms from scratch.

This presentation is about the application of Boolean SAT solvers to the problem of determining program termination. Proving termination is all about the search for suitable ranking functions. The key idea in this work is to encode the search for particular forms of ranking functions to Boolean statements which are satisfiable if and only if such ranking functions exist. In this way, proving termination can be performed using a state-of-the-art Boolean satisfaction solver.

2 Encoding Lexicographic Path Orders

In [3] we describe a propositional encoding for lexicographic path orders (LPOs) [15,8] and the corresponding LPO-termination property of term rewrite systems. In brief, a term rewrite system (TRS) is a set of rules of the form $\ell \to r$ where ℓ and r are terms constructed from given sets of symbols and variables. A lexicographic path order is an order $\succ_{lpo}$ on terms, induced from a partial order $>$ on the symbols occurring in the terms (a so-called *precedence*). A term rewrite system is LPO-terminating if and only if there exists a partial order on the symbols such that the induced LPO orients all of the rules in the system. Namely such that $\ell \succ_{lpo} r$ for each rule $\ell \to r$.

There are two variants of LPO-termination: "strict" and "quasi" depending on if we restrict the precedence to be strict or not. Both imply termination of

---

* Supported by the Frankel Center for Computer Sciences at Ben-Gurion University.

King, A. (Ed.): LOPSTR 2007, LNCS 4915, pp. 1–7, 2008.

the corresponding term rewrite system. Quasi-LPO-termination is typically the harder problem as the search for a non-strict precedence is more extensive than that for a strict precedence. Both of the corresponding decision problems, strict- and quasi- LPO-termination, are decidable and NP complete [16].

We encode an LPO-termination problem to SAT in two steps: first, a *partial order constraint* on the symbols in the system is derived; then this constraint is solved through an encoding to SAT obtained by viewing each symbol as an integer value corresponding to its index in the partial order. Partial order constraints are propositional formula in which the atoms are statements about a partial order on a finite set of symbols and can be seen as an instance of the more general formulae of separation logic (sometimes called difference logic) described in [23].

Consider an example. To orient a rule $not(or(A, B)) \rightarrow and(not(A), not(B))$, is reduced to solving the following partial order constraint on the symbols $\{or, and, not\}$:

$$((or > and) \wedge (or > not)) \vee (not > and).$$

We encode each of the three symbols as an integer in two bits, and each atom in the partial order constraint as a comparison on a pair of integers in bit representation. For instance, numbering the bits with subscripts on the symbols, the encoding of the atom $(or > and)$ works out to:

$$(((\underbrace{or_{[2]} \wedge \neg and_{[2]}}_{or_{[2]} > and_{[2]}}) \vee (\underbrace{or_{[2]} \leftrightarrow and_{[2]}}_{or_{[2]} = and_{[2]}} \wedge \underbrace{or_{[1]} \wedge \neg and_{[1]}}_{or_{[1]} > and_{[1]}}))$$

The experimental results presented in [3] are unequivocal. Our SAT based implementation of LPO-termination surpasses in orders of magnitude the performance of previous implementations such as those provided at the time by the termination proving tools TTT [13] and APROVE [12].

3   Encoding Argument Filterings

Lexicographic path orders on their own are too weak for many interesting termination problems and hence are typically combined with more sophisticated termination proving techniques. One of the most popular and powerful such techniques is the *dependency pair* (DP) method [1]. A main advantage is that this allows the application of *argument filterings* which specify parts of terms that should be ignored when comparing terms. It can be viewed like this: given a set of pairs of terms to orient with an LPO, first decide which parts of the terms to filter away and then orient the filtered pairs in an LPO. The argument filtering specifies for each function symbol f if subterms of the form $f(s_1, \ldots, s_n)$ should be *collapsed* to their i^{th} argument; or if some of the argument positions should be filtered away. Filtering terms can simplify considerably the partial order constraints that need be solved to find an LPO. However, argument filterings represent also a severe bottleneck for the automation of dependency pairs, as the search space for argument filterings is enormous (exponential in the sum of the arities of the symbols).

In [5] we introduce a propositional encoding which combines the search for an LPO with the search for an argument filtering. The key idea is to introduce a small number of additional Boolean variables: one for each symbol to indicate if it is collapsed, and one for each argument position of a symbol to indicate if it is filtered. Then the encoding of LPO is enhanced to consider these new variables. So, there exist an argument filtering and an LPO which orient a set of inequalities if and only if the encoding of the inequalities is satisfiable. Moreover, each model of the encoding corresponds to a suitable argument filtering and a suitable LPO which orient the inequalities. Once again experimental results [5] indicate speedups in orders of magnitude.

4   Encoding Recursive Path Orders

In [22] we introduce two additional extensions which together lead to an encoding of the so-called recursive path order with status (RPO). In the first extension, the lexicographic path order is extended to consider the lexicographic extension, not just from left-to-right, but rather with respect to any fixed order. It can be viewed like this: given a permutation for each symbol in a term rewrite system, first reorder the arguments of every subterm as prescribed by the permutation for its root symbol. Then check if the resulting system is LPO-terminating. So, now to orient a set of rules we seek a partial order on the symbols as well as permutations for each symbol. For the encoding, we introduce a small number of additional Boolean variables to represent for each symbol the order its arguments are permuted to. Then the encoding of LPO is enhanced to consider this order (in terms of these new variables). In the second extension, we consider an encoding of the the multiset path order (MPO) [7] where term arguments are compared with the multiset ordering. Also, in this case, with a small number of additional Boolean variables we can model the multiset order in the encoding. For RPO, each symbol in the system is associated with a *status* (one more Boolean variable per symbol in the encoding) indicating if its arguments are to be compared with a multiset extension or with a lexicographic extension modulo some permutation. By now the reader will not be surprised that we simply encode all of the components for RPO to SAT to obtain an implementation using a SAT solver. The results presented in [22] again leave no doubt that encoding to SAT is the way to go.

5   Experimental Results

Throughout this work we have found Prolog a convenient language for expressing the various encodings to SAT. Prototype analyzers were written in SWI Prolog [25] applying the MiniSAT solver [20] through its Prolog interface described in [4]. Subsequently the approach has been integrated within the termination analyzer AProVE [11], using the SAT4J solver [21].

In [22] we report the following results for the various analyses described in this paper. We tested the implementation on all 865 TRSs from the TPDB [24]. The

TPDB is the collection of examples used in the annual *International Termination Competition* [19]. The experiments were run under AProVE on a 2.2 GHz AMD Athlon 64 with a time-out of 60 seconds (as in the *International Termination Competition* [19]).

In the table below, the first two rows compare our SAT-based approach for application of the various path orders to the previous dedicated solvers for path orders in AProVE 1.2 which did not use SAT solving. The last two rows give a similar comparison for the path orders in combination with the dependency pairs method and argument filterings. The columns contain the data for LPO with strict and non-strict precedence (denoted *lpo/qlpo*), for LPO with permutations (*lpos/qlpos*), for MPO (*mpo/qmpo*), and for RPO with status (*rpo/qrpo*). For each encoding we give the number of TRSs which could be proved terminating (with the number of time-outs in brackets) and the analysis time (in seconds) for the full collection (including time-outs). For the SAT based implementation, checking the full collection of 865 TRSs for strict-RPO termination with argument filterings requires about 100 seconds. Allowing non-strict orders takes about 3 times longer.

	Solver	*lpo*	*qlpo*	*lpos*	*qlpos*	*mpo*	*qmpo*	*rpo*	*qrpo*
1	SAT-based (direct)	123 (0)	127 (0)	141 (0)	155 (0)	92 (0)	98 (0)	146 (0)	162 (0)
		31.0	44.7	26.1	40.6	49.4	74.2	50.0	85.3
2	dedicated (direct)	123 (5)	127(16)	141 (6)	154(45)	92 (7)	98(31)	145(10)	158 (65)
		334.4	1426.3	460.4	3291.7	653.2	2669.1	908.6	4708.2
3	SAT-based (arg. filt.)	357 (0)	389 (0)	362 (0)	395 (2)	369 (0)	408 (1)	375 (0)	416 (2)
		79.3	199.6	69.0	261.1	110.9	267.8	108.8	331.4
4	dedicated (arg. filt.)	350(55)	374(79)	355(57)	380(92)	359(69)	391(82)	364(74)	394(102)
		4039.6	5469.4	4522.8	6476.5	5169.7	5839.5	5536.6	7186.1

The table shows that with our SAT encodings, performance improves by orders of magnitude over existing solvers both for direct analysis with path orders and for the combination of path orders and argument filterings in the DP framework. Note that without a time-out, this effect would be intensified. By using SAT, the number of time-outs reduces dramatically from up to 102 to at most 2. The two remaining SAT examples with time-out have function symbols of high arity and can only be shown terminating by further sophisticated termination techniques in addition to RPO. Apart from these two, for SAT, there are only 15 examples that take longer than two seconds and only 3 of these take longer than 10 seconds. The table also shows that the use of RPO instead of LPO increases the proving power substantially, while in the SAT-based setting, run-times increase only mildly.

6   Other SAT Based Termination Analyses

The first encoding of a termination problem into propositional logic is presented in [17]. The encoding is different than the one we consider and adopts a BDD-based representation. It does not provide competitive results. However, it makes an important step. Another BDD-based encoding, this one for size-change termination [18], is described in [2]. Here, sets of size change graphs are viewed as partial order constraints, similar to those considered in this paper for term rewrite systems.

In the past year, several additional papers [9,10,14,26] have illustrated the huge potential in applying SAT solvers for other types of termination proving techniques for term rewrite systems. A common theme in all of these works is to represent (finite domain) integer variables as binary numbers in bit representation and to encode arithmetic constraints as Boolean functions on these representations. Results indicate uniformly that the SAT based approach to proving termination is very attractive.

7 Summary

Lexicographic- and multiset- path orders are about lifting a base order on terms to consider the arguments of terms as sequences or as multisets with corresponding lexicographic or multiset orders. We have introduced a new kind of propositional encoding for reasoning about termination of term rewrite systems based on variants of these path orders. Our results have had a direct impact on the design of several major termination analyzers for term rewrite systems.

Of particular and general interest are the encoding techniques which enable to refine a search algorithm to consider a property of interest for all subsets of objects, instead of for the full set of objects; or to check if a property holds when considering a sequence of objects in any order, instead of in the fixed left-to-right order. The common theme is to represent with a small number of additional Boolean variables the large number of cases which need be considered. For the extensions of LPO-termination considered in this work, the additional cost in analysis time is minor in comparison to the increase in the size of the search space.

Acknowledgment. The author has been lucky to work on this research with friends, old and new. Thankyou coauthors of [3], [5], and [22]: Elena Annov, Jürgen Giesl, Vitaly Lagoon, Peter Schneider–Kamp, Peter J. Stuckey, and René Thiemann.

References

1. Arts, T., Giesl, J.: Termination of term rewriting using dependency pairs. Theoretical Computer Science 236(1-2), 133–178 (2000)
2. Codish, M., Lagoon, V., Schachte, P., Stuckey, P.J.: Size-Change Termination Analysis in k-Bits. In: Sestoft, P. (ed.) ESOP 2006 and ETAPS 2006. LNCS, vol. 3924, pp. 230–245. Springer, Heidelberg (2006)
3. Stuckey, P.J., Codish, M., Lagoon, V.: Solving Partial Order Constraints for LPO Termination. In: Pfenning, F. (ed.) RTA 2006. LNCS, vol. 4098, pp. 4–18. Springer, Heidelberg (2006)

4. Codish, M., Lagoon, V., Stuckey, P.J.: Logic programming with satisfiability. The Journal of Theory and Practice of Logic Programming 8(1) (2008), http://arxiv.org/pdf/cs.PL/0702072

5. Codish, M., Schneider-Kamp, P., Lagoon, V., Thiemann, R., Giesl, J.: SAT Solving for Argument Filterings. In: Hermann, M., Voronkov, A. (eds.) LPAR 2006. LNCS (LNAI), vol. 4246, pp. 30–44. Springer, Heidelberg (2006)

6. Davis, M., Logemann, G., Loveland, D.W.: A machine program for theorem-proving. Commun. ACM 5(7), 394–397 (1962)

7. Dershowitz, N.: Orderings for term-rewriting systems. Theoretical Computer Science 17, 279–301 (1982)

8. Dershowitz, N.: Termination of rewriting. Journal of Symbolic Computation 3(1/2), 69–116 (1987)

9. Waldmann, J., Zantema, H., Endrullis, J.: Matrix Interpretations for Proving Termination of Term Rewriting. In: Furbach, U., Shankar, N. (eds.) IJCAR 2006. LNCS (LNAI), vol. 4130, pp. 574–588. Springer, Heidelberg (2006)

10. Fuhs, C., Giesl, J., Middeldorp, A., Schneider-Kamp, P., Thiemann, R., Zankl, H.: SAT solving for termination analysis with polynomial interpretations. In: Marques-Silva, J., Sakallah, K.A. (eds.) SAT 2007. LNCS, vol. 4501, pp. 340–354. Springer, Heidelberg (2007)

11. Giesl, J., Schneider-Kamp, P., Thiemann, R.: AProVE 1.2. In: Furbach, U., Shankar, N. (eds.) IJCAR 2006. LNCS (LNAI), vol. 4130, pp. 281–286. Springer, Heidelberg (2006)

12. Giesl, J., Thiemann, R., Schneider-Kamp, P., Falke, S.: Automated Termination Proofs with AProVE. In: van Oostrom, V. (ed.) RTA 2004. LNCS, vol. 3091, pp. 210–220. Springer, Heidelberg (2004)

13. Middeldorp, A., Hirokawa, N.: Tyrolean Termination Tool. In: Giesl, J. (ed.) RTA 2005. LNCS, vol. 3467, pp. 175–184. Springer, Heidelberg (2005)

14. Waldmann, J., Hofbauer, D.: Termination of String Rewriting with Matrix Interpretations. In: Pfenning, F. (ed.) RTA 2006. LNCS, vol. 4098, pp. 328–342. Springer, Heidelberg (2006)

15. Kamin, S., Levy, J.-J.: Two generalizations of the recursive path ordering. In: Department of Computer Science, University of Illinois, Urbana, IL (viewed December 2005) (1980), http://www.ens-lyon.fr/LIP/REWRITING/OLD_PUBLICATIONS_ON_TERMINATION

16. Krishnamoorthy, M., Narendran, P.: On recursive path ordering. Theoretical Computer Science 40, 323–328 (1985)

17. Kurihara, M., Kondo, H.: Efficient BDD Encodings for Partial Order Constraints with Application to Expert Systems in Software Verification. In: Orchard, B., Yang, C., Ali, M. (eds.) IEA/AIE 2004. LNCS (LNAI), vol. 3029, pp. 827–837. Springer, Heidelberg (2004)

18. Lee, C.S., Jones, N.D., Ben-Amram, A.M.: The size-change principle for program termination. ACM SIGPLAN Notices, Proceedings of POPL 2001 36(3), 81–92 (2001)

19. Marché, C., Zantema, H.: The Termination Competition. In: Baader, F. (ed.) RTA 2007. LNCS, vol. 4533, pp. 303–313. Springer, Heidelberg (2007) (To appear)

20. MiniSAT solver. Viewed(December 2005), http://www.cs.chalmers.se/Cs/Research/FormalMethods/MiniSat

21. SAT4J satisfiability library for Java, http://www.sat4j.org

22. Schneider-Kamp, P., Thiemann, R., Annov, E., Codish, M., Giesl, J.: Proving Termination Using Recursive Path Orders and SAT Solving. In: Konev, B., Wolter, F. (eds.) FroCos 2007. LNCS (LNAI), vol. 4720, pp. 267–282. Springer, Heidelberg (2007)
23. Talupur, M., Sinha, N., Strichman, O., Pnueli, A.: Range allocation for separation logic. In: CAV, pp. 148–161 (2004)
24. The termination problem data base, `http://www.lri.fr/~marche/tpdb/`
25. Wielemaker, J.: An overview of the SWI-Prolog programming environment. In: Mesnard, F., Serebenik, A. (eds.) Proceedings of the 13th International Workshop on Logic Programming Environments, Katholieke Universiteit Leuven. CW 371, (December 2003) pp. 1–16. (2003)
26. Middeldorp, A., Zankl, H.: Satisfying KBO Constraints. In: Baader, F. (ed.) RTA 2007. LNCS, vol. 4533, pp. 389–403. Springer, Heidelberg (2007)

Termination Analysis of Logic Programs Based on Dependency Graphs

Manh Thang Nguyen[1], Jürgen Giesl[2], Peter Schneider-Kamp[2],
and Danny De Schreye[1]

[1] Department of Computer Science, K. U. Leuven, Belgium
{ManhThang.Nguyen,Danny.DeSchreye}@cs.kuleuven.be
[2] LuFG Informatik 2, RWTH Aachen, Germany
{giesl,psk}@informatik.rwth-aachen.de

Abstract. This paper introduces a modular framework for termination analysis of logic programming. To this end, we adapt the notions of dependency pairs and dependency graphs (which were developed for term rewriting) to the logic programming domain. The main idea of the approach is that termination conditions for a program are established based on the decomposition of its dependency graph into its strongly connected components. These conditions can then be analysed separately by possibly different well-founded orders. We propose a constraint-based approach for automating the framework. Then, for example, termination techniques based on polynomial interpretations can be plugged in as a component to generate well-founded orders.

1 Introduction

Termination analysis in logic programming (LP) traditionally aims at proving that a given logic program terminates w.r.t. a specific set of queries. Termination proofs are usually done by finding ranking functions that map the states of the program to a sequence of elements of a well-founded domain such that the sequence is decreasing w.r.t. the well-founded order of the domain. Practically, it is sufficient to consider only the states that are involved in loops of the program.

Techniques in termination analysis of LPs can be divided into two groups: the global versus the local approach [4,6,5,8,10,12,26]. In the global approach, one wants to find only **one ranking function** for all loops [8,10,26]. In contrast, techniques in the local approach apply **different ranking functions** for different loops [4,5,12]. Some automated techniques in the global approach are based on a constraint-based framework to search for a suitable ranking function. This is done by first generating a set of symbolic constraints from all termination conditions. Then, a constraint solver is used to solve the set of constraints, yielding a suitable ranking function for the proof. In the local approach, most techniques use a given small set of norms, and try to prove that (a combination of) these norms can be applied for the termination proof of the program. It is unclear at this stage whether a search for arbitrary norms in the local approach could also be automated using a constraint-based technique like [10].

King, A. (Ed.): LOPSTR 2007, LNCS 4915, pp. 8–22, 2008.

While the constraint-based global approach is very suitable for automation, it has some drawbacks. Since it generates the constraints for all termination conditions and solves them at once, it may be very time-consuming, especially for non-terminating programs. This is because the time for solving a set of constraints often increases exponentially with its size. Moreover, if a complex well-founded order is needed for the termination proof (e.g., a lexicographical order), it is often difficult to find such an order using the constraint-based global approach.

Example 1 (ack). Consider a logic program P computing the Ackermann function. We used a variant with a predecessor predicate $p/2$ in order to illustrate how our technique handles local variables. We want to prove termination of this program w.r.t. the set of queries $S = \{ack(t_1, t_2, t_3) \mid t_1 \text{ and } t_2 \text{ are ground terms}, t_3 \text{ is an arbitrary term}\}$.

$$p(s(X), X).$$
$$ack(0, X, s(X)).$$
$$ack(X, 0, Z) :\!- p(X, Y), ack(Y, s(0), Z).$$
$$ack(s(X), s(Y), Z) :\!- ack(s(X), Y, Z'), ack(X, Z', Z).$$

Proving termination of this example based on the local approach involves two ranking functions: The first one measures the size of the first argument and the other measures the size of the second argument of the predicate $ack/3$. However, with the constraint-based global approach, it is impossible to find a single ranking function for the termination proof (if one is restricted to ranking functions based on polynomial interpretations). As a matter of fact, both tools cTI *[25] and* Polytool *[26,27] fail to prove termination of this example.*

In addition to the local and global approaches which work *directly* on logic programs, there are also several *transformational* approaches which transform logic programs to *term rewrite systems* (TRSs). One of the most recent techniques in this line of work is [31]. However, as demonstrated in [31], it turned out that there remain many LPs whose termination can currently only be proved by tools working with direct approaches. (An example is the *"der"*-program from [9,26].) On the other hand, there are also many LPs where currently only transformational tools succeed (e.g., the example *"LP/SGST06-shuffle"* from the *Termination Problem Data Base* (TPDB) [32] that is used in the annual *International Competition of Termination Tools* [24]). The present paper tries to solve this problem by porting TRS-techniques so that they can be applied to LPs directly. In this way, we intend to combine the advantages of direct and transformational approaches. Indeed, a first prototypical implementation shows that the new approach of the present paper can handle both the examples *"der"* and *"shuffle"* above as well as other examples that could not be handled by *any* tool up to now (e.g., *"LP/SGST06-snake"* from the TPDB).

More precisely, in this paper we introduce a modular framework for termination analysis of LPs. To this end, the dependency pair technique for termination analysis of TRSs introduced in [1] is adapted to the LP context. With this new technique, termination analysis of programs like Ex. 1 can be done by decomposing it into several simple sub-problems. Each of them can be solved independently by using any suitable well-founded order.

We also propose a constraint-based approach for automating the approach in which termination techniques based on polynomial interpretations can be plugged in as a component to search for well-founded orders.

The paper is organised as follows. In Sect. 2, we provide some preliminaries. In Sect. 3, we introduce a modular framework for proving termination of LPs based on dependency graphs. In Sect. 4, we present a constraint-based approach to automate the framework. Finally, we end with a conclusion in Sect. 5.

2   Preliminaries

A *quasi-order* on a set S is a reflexive and transitive binary relation $\succsim$ defined on elements of S. In this paper, we use quasi-orders comparing atoms with each other and comparing terms with each other. We define the *associated equivalence relation* $\approx$ as $s \approx t$ iff $s \succsim t$ and $t \succsim s$. A *well-founded order* on S is a transitive relation $\succ$ where there is no infinite sequence $s_0 \succ s_1 \succ \ldots$ with $s_i \in S$. A *reduction pair* $(\succsim, \succ)$ consists of a quasi-order $\succsim$ and a well-founded order $\succ$ that are *compatible* (i.e., $t_1 \succsim t_2 \succ t_3$ implies $t_1 \succ t_3$).[1]

We assume familiarity with standard notions of logic programs. In the paper, P denotes a pure logic program and $Term_P$, $Atom_P$ denote the sets of terms and atoms constructed from P respectively. Given an atom A, $rel(A)$ is the predicate occurring in A. Given two atoms A and B, we denote by $mgu(A, B)$ their most general unifier. A *query* Q is a finite sequence of atoms. We consider termination of P w.r.t. Q using the left-to-right selection rule that is commonly used in implementations of logic programming.[2]

Let S be a set of atomic queries. The call set, $Call(P, S)$, is the set of all atoms A, such that a variant of A is the selected atom in some derivation for (P, Q), for some $Q \in S$. In this paper, we use ranking functions and reduction pairs built from norms and level mappings [3]. A *norm* is a mapping $\| \cdot \| : Term_P \to \mathbb{N}$. A *level mapping* is a mapping $| \cdot | : Atom_P \to \mathbb{N}$. An *interargument relation* for a predicate p/n is a relation $R_{p/n} = \{p(t_1, \ldots, t_n) \mid t_i \in Term_P \wedge \varphi_p(t_1, \ldots, t_n)\}$, where (1) $\varphi_p(t_1, \ldots, t_n)$ is a formula of an arbitrary boolean combination of inequalities, and (2) each inequality in φ_p is either $s_i \succsim s_j$ or $s_i \succ s_j$, where s_i, s_j are constructed from $t_1, \ldots, t_n$ by applying function symbols of P. $R_{p/n}$ is *valid* iff for every $p(t_1, \ldots, t_n) \in Atom_P$: $P \models p(t_1, \ldots, t_n)$ implies $p(t_1, \ldots, t_n) \in R_{p/n}$. A reduction pair $(\succsim, \succ)$ is *rigid* on a term or an atom A if

---

[1] In contrast to the definition of "reduction pairs" in term rewriting [21], for the theoretical results in Sect. 3 we do not require $\succsim$ and $\succ$ to be closed under substitutions. But to automate our method, in Sect. 4 we choose relations $\succsim$ and $\succ$ that result from polynomial interpretations and that are closed under substitutions.

[2] By fixing the selection rule, methods for termination analysis can exploit this and become much stronger. This is similar to termination analysis of term rewriting (in particular, when using dependency pairs). Here, termination of *innermost* rewriting is easier to show than termination of full rewriting.

for all substitutions σ, we have $A \approx A\sigma$. A reduction pair $(\succsim, \succ)$ is rigid on a set of terms or atoms if it is rigid on all its elements.

Example 2 (call set, norm, and level mapping for ack). We again regard the program P and the set of queries S in Ex. 1. Then we have $Call(P, S) = S \cup \{ p(t_1, t_2) \mid t_1 \text{ is a ground term, } t_2 \text{ is a variable} \}$. Consider the reduction pair $(\succsim, \succ)$ which is induced[3] by a norm $\|0\| = 0$, $\|s(t)\| = 1 + \|t\|$, $\|X\| = 0$ for all variables X, and by an associated level mapping $|p(t_1, t_2)| = 0$ and $|ack(t_1, t_2, t_3)| = \|t_1\|$. Thus, we have $s(0) \succ 0$, $ack(s(0), X, Y) \succ ack(0, X, Y)$, and $ack(0, X, Y) \approx ack(0, 0, 0)$. Note that $(\succsim, \succ)$ is rigid on $Call(P, S)$. An example for a valid interargument relation w.r.t. $(\succsim, \succ)$ is $R_{p/2} = \{ p(t_1, t_2) \mid t_1 \succ t_2 \}$.

3 Dependency Graphs in Logic Programming

Def. 3 adapts the notion of *dependency pairs* [1] from TRSs to the LP setting.

Definition 3 (dependency triple). *A dependency triple is a tuple of three elements $\langle H, I, B \rangle$ in which H and B are atoms and I is a list of atoms. For a logic program P, we define the set $DT(P)$ of all dependency triples as $DT(P) = \{\langle H, I, B \rangle \mid H :- I, B, \ldots \in P\}$.*

Given a program, the number of its dependency triples is finite.

Example 4 (dependency triples of ack). Reconsider the program from Ex. 1. The dependency triples $DT(P)$ of the program are:

$$\langle ack(X, 0, Z), [\,], p(X, Y) \rangle \tag{1}$$
$$\langle ack(X, 0, Z), [p(X, Y)], ack(Y, s(0), Z) \rangle \tag{2}$$
$$\langle ack(s(X), s(Y), Z), [\,], ack(s(X), Y, Z') \rangle \tag{3}$$
$$\langle ack(s(X), s(Y), Z), [ack(s(X), Y, Z')], ack(X, Z', Z) \rangle \tag{4}$$

Now we adapt the notion of the (estimated) *dependency graph* [1] from TRSs to LPs.[4] While "dependency triples" are related to the "binary clauses" of [5], our notion of dependency graphs for LPs is similar to the "atom dependency graph" of [12]. But in contrast to [12], we use dependency graphs to modularize termination proofs such that *several different* reduction pairs can be used in the termination proof of one program.

The nodes of the dependency graph are the dependency triples and there must be an arc from a dependency triple N to a dependency triple M whenever an attempt to solve the "proof goal" N could load to the "proof goal" M. To estimate this, we use the notion of *connectivity*.

---

[3] So for terms t_1, t_2 we define $t_1 \underset{(\succsim)}{} t_2$ iff $\|t_1\| \underset{(\geq)}{} \|t_2\|$ and for atoms A_1, A_2 we define $A_1 \underset{(\succsim)}{} A_2$ iff $|A_1| \underset{(\geq)}{} |A_2|$.

[4] Our notion should not be confused with the notion of the "(predicate) dependency graph" from [2,12,28] that simply represents the dependencies between different predicate symbols.

Definition 5 (connectivity). *Let $\langle H_1, I_1, B_1 \rangle$ and $\langle H_2, I_2, B_2 \rangle$ be two dependency triples. $\langle H_1, I_1, B_1 \rangle$ is connectable to $\langle H_2, I_2, B_2 \rangle$ iff B_1 unifies with a renamed apart variant of H_2.*

Example 6 (connectivity for ack's dependency triples). In Ex. 1, dependency triple (2) is connectable to (3) and (4), and both dependency triples (3) and (4) are connectable to all dependency triples (1), (2), (3), and (4).

Definition 7 (dependency graph). *Let DT be a set of dependency triples. The dependency graph associated with DT is a directed graph whose vertices are the dependency triples DT and there is an arc from a vertex N to a vertex M iff N is connectable to M. Let P be a logic program. The dependency graph associated with $DT(P)$ is called the dependency graph of P, denoted as $DG(P)$.*

Example 8 (dependency graph for ack). Fig. 1 shows the dependency graph for the ack-program in Ex. 1.

Now every infinite execution of the program corresponds to a cycle in the dependency graph. In our setting, a set $\mathcal{C} \neq \emptyset$ of dependency triples is called a *cycle* if for all $N, M \in \mathcal{C}$ there is a non-empty path from N to M in the graph which only traverses dependency triples of $\mathcal{C}$. A cycle $\mathcal{C}$ is a *strongly connected component* (SCC) if $\mathcal{C}$ is not a proper subset of another cycle.

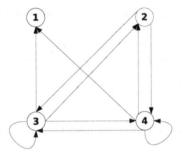

Fig. 1. The dependency graph for the *ack*-program

Note that in standard graph terminology, a path $N_0 \rightarrow N_1 \rightarrow \ldots \rightarrow N_k$ in a directed graph forms a cycle if $N_0 = N_k$ and $k \geq 1$. In our context we identify cycles with the *set* of elements that occur in it, i.e., we call $\{N_0, N_1, \ldots, N_{k-1}\}$ a cycle, cf. [15]. Since a set never contains multiple occurrences of an element, this results in several cycling paths being identified with the same set. Similarly, an SCC is a graph in standard graph terminology, whereas we identify an SCC with the set of elements occurring in it. Then indeed, SCCs are the same as maximal cycles.

Example 9 (cycles and SCCs for ack). The dependency graph in Fig. 1 has six cycles $\mathcal{C}_1 = \{(3)\}$, $\mathcal{C}_2 = \{(4)\}$, $\mathcal{C}_3 = \{(2), (3)\}$, $\mathcal{C}_4 = \{(2), (4)\}$, $\mathcal{C}_5 = \{(3), (4)\}$, $\mathcal{C}_6 = \{(2), (3), (4)\}$, and one strongly connected component $\mathcal{C}_6 = \{(2), (3), (4)\}$.

Note that each vertex in the dependency graph corresponds to a possible transition from one state to another state in the computational execution of the program. Each loop of the execution corresponds to a cycle in the graph. Intuitively, a program is terminating if there is no cycle in the graph which is traversed infinitely many times.

To use dependency graphs for termination proofs, we proceed as in [1,16,19]. The idea is to inspect each SCC of the dependency graph separately and to find a reduction pair $(\succsim, \succ)$ such that *some* dependency triples of the SCC are *strictly* decreasing (w.r.t. $\succ$) and all others are *weakly* decreasing (w.r.t. $\succsim$). The following definition formalizes when a dependency triple is considered to be "decreasing". It relies on interargument relations for the predicates of the program. Sect. 4 explains how to synthesize such interargument relations and how to find reduction pairs automatically that make dependency triples "decreasing".

Definition 10 (decreasing dependency triples). *Let P be a program. Let $(\succsim, \succ)$ be a reduction pair and $R = \{R_{p_1}, \ldots, R_{p_k}\}$ be a set of interargument relations based on $(\succsim, \succ)$ for the predicates $p_1, \ldots, p_k$ defined in P. Let $N = \langle H, [I_1, \ldots, I_n], B \rangle$ be a dependency triple in $DT(P)$. N is weakly decreasing (denoted $(\succsim, R) \models N$) if $H\sigma \succsim B\sigma$ holds for any substitution σ where $(\succsim, \succ)$ is rigid on $H\sigma$ and where $I_1\sigma \in R_{rel(I_1)}, \ldots, I_n\sigma \in R_{rel(I_n)}$. Analogously, N is strictly decreasing (denoted $(\succ, R) \models N$) if $H\sigma \succ B\sigma$ holds for any such σ.*

Example 11 (decreasing dependency triples for ack). Consider the reduction pair $(\succsim, \succ)$ from Ex. 2. Let R be the set of valid interargument relations where $R_{ack/3} = \{ack(t_1, t_2, t_3) \mid t_1, t_2, t_3 \in Term_P\}$ and where $R_{p/2}$ is defined as in Ex. 2. Then we have $(\succ, R) \models (2)$. The reason is that for any substitution σ where $(\succsim, \succ)$ is rigid on $ack(X, 0, Z)\sigma$ (i.e., where $X\sigma$ is a ground term) and where $p(X, Y)\sigma \in R_{p/2}$ (i.e., where $X\sigma \succ Y\sigma$), we have $ack(X, 0, Z)\sigma \succ ack(Y, s(0), Z)\sigma$. Similarly, we also have $(\succsim, R) \models (3)$ and $(\succ, R) \models (4)$.

Note that we can restrict ourselves to those SCCs of the dependency graph that can be invoked by calls from $Call(P, S)$. The reason is that only those SCCs can be involved in loops of the execution of the program P, when starting with a query from S. Therefore, we define which SCCs are *reachable* from $Call(P, S)$.

Definition 12 (reachable SCCs). *Let P be a program, S be a set of atomic queries, and $N = \langle H, [I_1, \ldots, I_n], B \rangle$ be a dependency triple. N is reachable from $Call(P, S)$ if there is an $A \in Call(P, S)$ such that A unifies with a renamed apart variant of H. An SCC $\mathcal{C}$ in $DG(P)$ is reachable from $Call(P, S)$ if there is an $N \in \mathcal{C}$ which is reachable from $Call(P, S)$.*

In the *ack*-example, the only SCC in the dependency graph is reachable from the set $Call(P, S)$ of Ex. 2. But if the *ack*-program contained another clause "$q :- q$", then the SCC with the resulting dependency triple $\langle q, [], q \rangle$ would not be reachable from the call set of Ex. 2. Since it suffices to prove absence of infinite loops only for the *reachable* SCCs, one could then still prove termination of all queries from S. But if one had to regard *all* SCCs, then the termination proof would fail, since the SCC with the dependency triple $\langle q, [], q \rangle$ gives rise to an infinite loop. The set of reachable SCCs can easily be (over-)approximated automatically as soon as one has an (over-)approximation of $Call(P, S)$, cf. Sect. 4.

To prove termination, we select an arbitrary reachable SCC $\mathcal{C}$ of the dependency graph. Then, we try to find a reduction pair $(\succsim, \succ)$ such that some dependency triples $\mathcal{C}_\succ \subseteq \mathcal{C}$ are strictly decreasing and all other dependency triples (from $C \setminus C_{\succ}$) are weakly decreasing. This means that the strictly decreasing dependency triples from $C_{\succ}$ can never "occur" *infinitely often* in any execution of the program. Thus, we remove the vertices $C_{\succ}$ (and all edges originating or ending in these vertices) from the dependency graph. Afterwards the procedure is repeated (with a possibly different reduction pair). If one finally ends up with a graph without reachable SCCs, then termination of the program is proved.

In this way, our method can use different reduction pairs for different SCCs of the dependency graph. Moreover, one can also use several different reduction pairs in the termination analysis of one single SCC, since SCCs are handled in an incremental way by removing one dependency triple after the other.

However, in our approach we may only use reduction pairs $(\succsim, \succ)$ that are rigid on $Call(P, S)$. This prevents an increase of atoms and terms due to further instantiations in subsequent derivation steps. For details, we refer to [26].

Definition 13 (acceptability). *Let P be a program and S be a set of atomic queries. A subgraph G of the dependency graph $DG(P)$ is called* acceptable *w.r.t. S iff either G has no SCC reachable from $Call(P, S)$ or else, G has such an SCC C and there is a reduction pair $(\succsim, \succ)$ and a set of valid interargument relations $R = \{R_{p_1}, \ldots, R_{p_k}\}$ based on $(\succsim, \succ)$ for the predicates $p_1, \ldots, p_k$ in P, such that*

- *$(\succsim, \succ)$ is rigid on $Call(P, S)$,*
- *there is a non-empty subset $C_{\succ} \subseteq C$ such that $(\succ, R) \models N$ for all $N \in C_{\succ}$ and $(\succsim, R) \models N$ for all $N \in C \setminus C_{\succ}$, and*
- *the graph resulting from G by removing all vertices in $C_{\succ}$ is also acceptable.*

Example 14 (termination of ack). The dependency graph of the *ack*-program in Fig. 1 has only one SCC. First, we select a reduction pair $(\succsim, \succ)$. We re-use the reduction pair from Ex. 2 and the valid interargument relations R from Ex. 11. As shown in Ex. 11, then (2) and (4) are strictly decreasing, whereas (3) is only weakly decreasing. Thus, we remove (2) and (4) from the dependency graph.

The remaining graph has only one vertex (3) and an edge from (3) to itself. Thus, now the only SCC is $\{(3)\}$. We select another reduction pair $(\succsim', \succ')$ which is defined by the same norm $\| \cdot \|$ as in Ex. 2 and by a new level mapping with $|ack(t_1, t_2, t_3)| = \|t_2\|$. Now we have $(\succ', R) \models (3)$, i.e., (3) can be removed.

The remaining graph is empty and thus, it has no SCC. Hence, termination of the *ack*-program is proved.

The following theorem states the soundness of our approach.[5]

Theorem 15 (soundness). *A program P is terminating w.r.t. a set of atomic queries S if its dependency graph $DG(P)$ is acceptable w.r.t. S.*

Proof. If P is not terminating w.r.t. S, then there is an $A \in Call(P, S)$, an infinite sequence of (variable renamed) dependency triples $N_0, N_1, \ldots$ with $N_i = \langle H_i, [I_{i1}, \ldots, I_{in_i}], B_i \rangle$, and substitutions $\theta_0, \theta_1, \ldots$ and $\sigma_0, \sigma_1, \ldots$ such that

---

[5] Note that the proof of Thm. 15 is similar to the one for the dependency pair method in [1]. So in contrast to the "local approaches" [4,5,12] for logic programs and the size-change-based methods [23,29,33] for other programming paradigms, Thm. 15 does not rely on Ramsey's theorem [6,30].

- $\theta_0 = mgu(A, H_0)$
- σ_i is a computed answer substitution for the query $(I_{i1}, \ldots, I_{in_i})\theta_i$
- $\theta_{i+1} = mgu(B_i\theta_i\sigma_i, H_{i+1})$

Since there is an edge from N_i to N_{i+1} for all i in the dependency graph, the sequence $N_0, N_1, \ldots$ contains an infinite tail which traverses a cycle of the dependency graph infinitely often.

For any subgraph G of the dependency graph, we show that if this infinite tail is contained in G, then G cannot be acceptable. We use induction on the number of vertices in G. The claim is obviously true if G does not contain any SCC reachable from $Call(P, S)$. Thus, let G contain a reachable SCC $\mathcal{C}$ as in Def. 13. If the infinite tail is still contained in the acceptable subgraph resulting from removing all vertices from $\mathcal{C}_{\succ}$, the claim follows from the induction hypothesis.

It remains to regard the case where the infinite tail $N_i, N_{i+1}, \ldots$ only traverses dependency triples from $\mathcal{C}$ and where a dependency triple from $\mathcal{C}_{\succ}$ is traversed infinitely often. Thus, we obtain an infinite sequence

$$
\begin{aligned}
H_i\theta_i &\approx \text{(by rigidity, since } H_i\theta_i = B_{i-1}\theta_{i-1}\sigma_{i-1}\theta_i \\
&\qquad \text{and } B_{i-1}\theta_{i-1}\sigma_{i-1} \in Call(P, S)) \\
H_i\theta_i\sigma_i\theta_{i+1} &\succsim \\
B_i\theta_i\sigma_i\theta_{i+1} &= \\
H_{i+1}\theta_{i+1} &\approx \text{(by rigidity, since } H_{i+1}\theta_{i+1} = B_i\theta_i\sigma_i\theta_{i+1} \\
&\qquad \text{and } B_i\theta_i\sigma_i \in Call(P, S)) \\
H_{i+1}\theta_{i+1}\sigma_{i+1}\theta_{i+2} &\succsim \\
B_{i+1}\theta_{i+1}\sigma_{i+1}\theta_{i+2} &= \\
\ldots
\end{aligned}
$$

where infinitely many $\succsim$-steps are "strict" (i.e., we can replace infinitely many $\succsim$-steps by "$\succ$"). This is a contradiction to the well-foundedness of $\succ$.   □

Thm. 15 can be considered an extension of Thm. 1 in [9], where a strict decrease is required for every (mutually) recursive clause of the program, instead of a decrease on the SCCs as in our theorem above. In particular, Ex. 1 cannot be solved using Thm. 1 of [9].

The converse direction of Thm. 15 does not hold since "acceptability" requires the reduction pair to be rigid on $Call(P, S)$. Hence, the program with the two clauses "$p(X) :\!- q(X, Y), p(Y)$" and "$q(a, b)$" and the set of queries $S = \{p(X)\}$ from [9] is a counterexample to the completeness direction of Thm. 15.

4   Toward Automation

Now we discuss how to automate our approach. In Sect. 4.1, we present a general algorithm to mechanize the technique of Def. 13 and Thm. 15. Then, in Sect. 4.2 we show how to plug in existing approaches for the generation of polynomial interpretations in order to synthesize suitable reduction pairs automatically.

4.1   A General Framework

Def. 13 and Thm. 15 provide a method to detect termination of a program P w.r.t. a set of queries S. The method can be automated as follows:

1. Compute the dependency graph $DG(P)$ and remove all vertices which are not reachable from $Call(P, S)$. Decompose the remaining graph into its SCCs.
2. If the set of SCCs is empty, stop with "success" (the program is terminating). Otherwise, select one SCC from the set.
3. If the selected SCC cannot be proved to be acceptable, we stop with "fail" (the program may be non-terminating). If the SCC is acceptable, we delete the strictly decreasing vertices from it and decompose the remaining graph into its SCCs. We add this set of SCCs to the remaining set of SCCs and continue with Step 2.

Step 1 guarantees that all remaining vertices and hence, also all remaining SCCs are reachable from $Call(P, S)$. Therefore, it is obvious that all SCCs decomposed later in Step 3 are also reachable from $Call(P, S)$.

Fig. 2 shows an algorithm based on Step 1-3. In the figure, $reach(G)$ removes all dependency triples from the dependency graph G which are not reachable from $Call(P, S)$, $gcc(G)$ computes the set of SCCs of a graph G, $select(S)$ returns an element selected from the set S, $minus(S_1, S_2)$ returns a set containing all elements that are in the set S_1 but not in S_2, ":=" is the assignment and "=" is the comparison operator. The function $exist(G, O)$ checks if there exists a reduction pair and a set of interargument relations such that G is acceptable. If yes, then the reduction pair is assigned to O. The function $induce(G, O)$ returns a graph which results from G by removing all vertices N where $(\succ, R) \models N$ and their related arcs. Finally, $union(S_1, S_2)$ returns a set that is the union of the sets S_1 and S_2.

Since $Call(P, S)$ can be infinite in general, it is undecidable whether a dependency triple is reachable from $Call(P, S)$. Heuristically, it can be done by first abstracting $Call(P, S)$ to a finite set of call patterns and then checking if there exists a call pattern which unifies with the vertex [26,27].

The function $exist(G, O)$ is the core of the algorithm. Interestingly, it does not force us to use a fixed type of orders. Therefore,

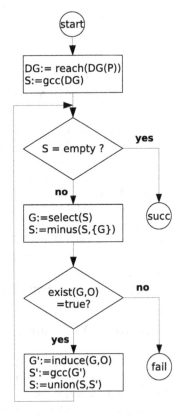

Fig. 2. Our algorithm to verify termination of programs

the algorithm can be considered a framework where different termination techniques for finding well-founded orders can be plugged in to support the function $exist(G, O)$. In Sect. 4.2, we discuss how the termination analysis technique based on polynomial interpretations from [26,27] can be applied to the framework.

4.2 Generating Well-Founded Orders

Since arbitrary techniques can be applied to search for reduction pairs required in the function $exist(G, O)$, an obvious option is to use polynomial interpretations, one of the most powerful techniques in termination analysis of logic programming and term rewriting systems [7,14,20,22,26,27].[6] The main idea of the technique is to map each function and predicate symbol to a polynomial, under a polynomial interpretation $|\cdot|_I$. The polynomials are considered as functions of type $\mathbb{N} \times \ldots \times \mathbb{N} \to \mathbb{N}$, and the coefficients of the polynomials are also in $\mathbb{N}$. In this way, terms and atoms are mapped to polynomials as well.

Example 16 (polynomial interpretation for ack). The norm and level mapping of Ex. 2 correspond to the polynomial interpretation $|0|_I = 0$, $|s(X)|_I = 1 + X$, $|p(X,Y)|_I = 0$, $|ack(X,Y,Z)|_I = X$. So we have $|ack(s(X), s(Y), Z)|_I = |s(X)|_I = 1 + X$ and $|ack(X, Z', Z)|_I = |X|_I = X$.

For any polynomial interpretation I, we define a quasi-order $\succsim_I$ on terms and atoms: $t_1 \succsim_I t_2$ iff $|t_1|_I \geq |t_2|_I$ holds for all instantiations of the variables in the polynomials $|t_1|_I$ and $|t_2|_I$ by natural numbers. (It suffices to regard only natural numbers n where $n \geq |c|_I$ for all (constant) function symbols $c/0$ of P.) Similarly, the well-founded order $\succ_I$ is defined as $t_1 \succ_I t_2$ iff $|t_1|_I > |t_2|_I$ holds for all instantiations of the variables in the polynomials $|t_1|_I$ and $|t_2|_I$ by such natural numbers. Obviously, $(\succsim_I, \succ_I)$ is always a reduction pair. Moreover, a term or atom t is rigid w.r.t. $(\succsim_I, \succ_I)$ iff $|t|_I$ contains no variables.

Now, all conditions in Def. 13 can be stated as constraints on polynomials. A reduction pair $(\succsim_I, \succ_I)$ satisfies the conditions in Def. 13 iff the polynomial interpretation $|\cdot|_I$ satisfies the resulting constraints on the polynomials.

Of course, we do not choose a particular polynomial interpretation. Instead, we want to *search* for a suitable one automatically. In the philosophy of the constraint-based approach in [10,27], we introduce a general symbolic form for the polynomial associated with each predicate and function symbol, and for interargument relations. Since there is no finite symbolic representation for all possible polynomials, we restrict ourselves to fixed types of polynomials. For example, each function and predicate symbol can be associated with a linear polynomial and each interargument relation for a predicate can be expressed in linear form as follows.[7] Here, f_i, p_i^L, and p_i^R are "abstract" symbolic coefficients.

---

[6] Other possible options would be recursive path orders [11], matrix orders [13], etc.

[7] As already observed for term rewriting, in the vast majority of examples, *linear* polynomial interpretations are already sufficient if they are used in connection with the dependency pair method. But of course, our approach also permits the use of polynomials with higher degree.

In order to complete the termination proof, one has to find suitable instantiations of these coefficients with natural numbers.

- $|f(X_1,\ldots,X_n)|_I = f_0 + \sum_{i=1}^n f_i X_i,$
- $R_{p/n} = \{\, p(t_1,\ldots,t_n) \mid p_0^L + \sum_{i=1}^n p_i^L |t_i|_I \geq p_0^R + \sum_{i=1}^n p_i^R |t_i|_I \,\}.$

Based on the symbolic forms for polynomial interpretations and interargument relations, all termination conditions expressed in Def. 13 can also be reformulated symbolically. Specifically, the conditions for the function $exist(G,O)$ (which checks whether G is acceptable) are expressed as a set of polynomial constraints with symbolic coefficients (e.g. $f_i, p_i^L, p_i^R, \ldots$). The central question is how to search for an instantiation of these symbolic coefficients such that the set of constraints is satisfied. In [27], we introduced a transformational approach to transform all constraints into a sufficient set of Diophantine constraints on natural numbers where all unknown symbolic coefficients become variables (cf. also [20]). A solution for the Diophantine constraints gives a suitable reduction pair $(\succsim_I, \succ_I)$ and a set of valid interargument relations based on the reduction pair. Finding such a solution can be done by using any available Diophantine constraint solver, e.g. [7,14]. Finally, the rigidity condition can be symbolised based on the *rigid type graph*. For more details, we refer to [26,27].

Example 17 (symbolic termination conditions for ack). Reconsider Ex. 1. We define an "abstract" symbolic polynomial interpretation as $|0|_I = c$, $|s(X)|_I = s_0 + s_1 X$, $|p(X,Y)|_I = p_0 + p_1 X + p_2 Y$, $|ack(X,Y,Z)|_I = a_0 + a_1 X + a_2 Y + a_3 Z$, and a set of interargument relations $R = \{R_{p/2}, R_{ack/3}\}$ with

$$
\begin{aligned}
R_{p/2} &= \{ p(t_1,t_2) & \mid & \; p_0^L + p_1^L |t_1|_I + p_2^L |t_2|_I \geq \\
& & & \; p_0^R + p_1^R |t_1|_I + p_2^R |t_2|_I \quad \} \\
R_{ack/3} &= \{ ack(t_1,t_2,t_3) & \mid & \; a_0^L + a_1^L |t_1|_I + a_2^L |t_2|_I + a_3^L |t_3|_I \geq \\
& & & \; a_0^R + a_1^R |t_1|_I + a_2^R |t_2|_I + a_3^R |t_3|_I \quad \}.
\end{aligned}
$$

The conditions for acceptability of the dependency graph can be reformulated as follows:

1. *For any dependency triple $N \in \{(2),(3),(4)\}$, we require $(\succsim_I, R) \models N$:*

$$
\begin{aligned}
\forall X,Y,Z\,[\quad & p_0^L + p_1^L X + p_2^L Y \geq p_0^R + p_1^R X + p_2^R Y \\
& \Rightarrow a_0 + a_1 X + a_2 c + a_3 Z \geq a_0 + a_1 Y + a_2(s_0 + s_1 c) + a_3 Z] \quad \wedge
\end{aligned}
$$

$$
\begin{aligned}
\forall X,Y,Z,Z'\,[\, a_0 + a_1(s_0 + s_1 X) + a_2(s_0 + s_1 Y) + a_3 Z \geq \\
a_0 + a_1(s_0 + s_1 X) + a_2 Y + a_3 Z'\,] \qquad\qquad \wedge
\end{aligned}
$$

$$
\begin{aligned}
\forall X,Y,Z,Z'\,[\quad & a_0^L + a_1^L(s_0 + s_1 X) + a_2^L Y + a_3^L Z' \geq \\
& a_0^R + a_1^R(s_0 + s_1 X) + a_2^R Y + a_3^R Z' \\
& \Rightarrow a_0 + a_1(s_0 + s_1 X) + a_2(s_0 + s_1 Y) + a_3 Z \geq \\
& a_0 + a_1 X + a_2 Z' + a_3 Z\,]
\end{aligned}
$$

2. There exists some dependency triple $N \in \{(2), (3), (4)\}$ with $(\succ_I, R) \models N$:

$$\forall X, Y, Z \,[\quad p_0^L + p_1^L X + p_2^L Y \geq p_0^R + p_1^R X + p_2^R Y$$
$$\Rightarrow a_0 + a_1 X + a_2 c + a_3 Z > a_0 + a_1 Y + a_2 (s_0 + s_1 c) + a_3 Z] \quad \vee$$

$$\forall X, Y, Z, Z' \,[\, a_0 + a_1(s_0 + s_1 X) + a_2(s_0 + s_1 Y) + a_3 Z >$$
$$a_0 + a_1(s_0 + s_1 X) + a_2 Y + a_3 Z'\,] \quad \vee$$

$$\forall X, Y, Z, Z' \,[\quad a_0^L + a_1^L(s_0 + s_1 X) + a_2^L Y + a_3^L Z' \geq$$
$$a_0^R + a_1^R(s_0 + s_1 X) + a_2^R Y + a_3^R Z'$$
$$\Rightarrow a_0 + a_1(s_0 + s_1 X) + a_2(s_0 + s_1 Y) + a_3 Z >$$
$$a_0 + a_1 X + a_2 Z' + a_3 Z\,]$$

3. The valid interargument condition for $p/2$:

$$\forall X \,[\, p_0^L + p_1^L(s_0 + s_1 X) + p_2^L X \geq p_0^R + p_1^R(s_0 + s_1 X) + p_2^R X\,]$$

4. The valid interargument condition for $ack/3$:

$$\forall X \,[\, a_0^L + a_1^L c + a_2^L X + a_3^L(s_0 + s_1 X) \geq a_0^R + a_1^R c + a_2^R X + a_3^R(s_0 + s_1 X)\,] \quad \wedge$$

$$\forall X, Y, Z \,[\quad p_0^L + p_1^L X + p_2^L Y \geq p_0^R + p_1^R X + p_2^R Y$$
$$\wedge \ a_0^L + a_1^L Y + a_2^L(s_0 + s_1 c) + a_3^L Z \geq$$
$$a_0^R + a_1^R Y + a_2^R(s_0 + s_1 c) + a_3^R Z$$
$$\Rightarrow a_0^L + a_1^L X + a_2^L c + a_3^L Z \geq a_0^R + a_1^R X + a_2^R c + a_3^R Z\,] \quad \wedge$$

$$\forall X, Y, Z, Z' \,[\quad a_0^L + a_1^L(s_0 + s_1 X) + a_2^L Y + a_3^L Z' \geq$$
$$a_0^R + a_1^R(s_0 + s_1 X) + a_2^R Y + a_3^R Z'$$
$$\wedge \ a_0^L + a_1^L X + a_2^L Z' + a_3^L Z \geq$$
$$a_0^R + a_1^R X + a_2^R Z' + a_3^R Z$$
$$\Rightarrow a_0^L + a_1^L(s_0 + s_1 X) + a_2^L(s_0 + s_1 Y) + a_3^L Z \geq$$
$$a_0^R + a_1^R(s_0 + s_1 X) + a_2^R(s_0 + s_1 Y) + a_3^R Z\,]$$

5. The rigidity property for $Call(P, S) = \{ack(t_1, t_2, t_3) \mid t_1 \text{ and } t_2 \text{ are ground terms}, t_3 \text{ is an arbitrary term}\} \cup \{p(t_1, t_2) \mid t_1 \text{ is a ground term}, t_2 \text{ is a variable}\}$:

$$p_2 = 0 \wedge a_3 = 0$$

All the constraints above are satisfied by the following instantiation of the symbolic variables: $c = 0$, $s_0 = s_1 = 1$, $p_0 = p_1 = p_2 = 0$, $a_0 = 0$, $a_1 = 1$, $a_2 = a_3 = 0$, $p_0^L = 0$, $p_1^L = 1$, $p_2^L = 0$, $p_0^R = p_1^R = 1$, $p_2^R = 0$ and $a_i^L = a_i^R = 0$ for all $i \in \{0, 1, 2, 3\}$. This instantiation turns the abstract polynomial interpretation of Ex. 17 into the concrete polynomial interpretation of Ex. 16 (i.e., now it corresponds to the norm and level mapping of Ex. 2). Similarly, the "abstract" interargument relations of of Ex. 17 are turned into the concrete interargument relations of Ex. 2 and Ex. 11 (i.e., $R_{p/2} = \{p(t_1, t_2) \mid t_1 \succ_I t_2\}$ and $R_{ack/3} = \{ack(t_1, t_2, t_3) \mid t_1, t_2, t_3 \in Term_P\}$).

So instead of fixing a polynomial interpretation and interargument relations *before* performing the termination proof, now we only fix the degree of the polynomials used in the polynomial interpretation (e.g., linear or quadratic ones). Then we can automatically generate symbolic constraints and try to solve them afterwards. In this way, suitable polynomial interpretations and interargument relations can be synthesized fully automatically.

5   Conclusion

We have introduced a new framework for termination analysis of LPs based on dependency triples and dependency graphs. Although the notion of dependency pairs and dependency graphs is very popular in the domain of termination analysis of TRS [1,15,16,18,19], this is the first time that it is applied for LP termination analysis directly. Our contribution is twofold: **(1)** it results in a weaker condition for verifying termination of LPs, where the decrease condition is established for the strongly connected components of the dependency graph, instead of at the clause level as it has been done before; **(2)** it introduces a modular approach in which termination conditions can be separated into different groups, each of which can be treated independently by automatically searching for different suitable well-founded orderings.

A difference between the dependency pair approach for TRSs and our approach is that instead of separating between defined symbols and constructors as for TRSs, we separate between predicate and function symbols of the LP. Another main difference is that in the dependency pair method for TRSs, one requires a weak decrease for the rules of the TRS in order to take the effect of "nested" functions in recursive arguments into account. In the LP-context, these nested functions correspond to body atoms preceding recursive calls. We store these atoms in an additional component of the dependency pair (yielding dependency triples) and take their effect into account by considering interargument relations.

The authors of this paper were involved in the implementation of two of the most powerful automated termination analysers for LPs (Polytool which follows the approach of [26,27] and AProVE [17] which transforms LPs to TRSs and then tries to prove termination of the resulting TRS [31].) AProVE was the most successful termination prover for logic programs, functional programs, and term rewrite systems in all annual *International Competitions of Termination Tools* 2004 - 2007 [24], where Polytool obtained a close second place for logic programs in the 2007 competition. As mentioned in [31], there exist many LPs where termination can currently only be proved by transformational tools like AProVE and there are also many examples where the termination proof only succeeds with direct tools like Polytool, cf. Sect. 1. Our current work intends to combine the advantages of both approaches by adapting TRS-techniques like dependency pairs to direct termination approaches for LPs. While the present paper only adapted basic concepts of the dependency pair method to the LP setting, in the future we will also try to adapt further more sophisticated "dependency pair processors" [16,18] as well.

Currently, we are working on an implementation of the results of this paper within Polytool. Here, we try to re-use algorithms from the dependency pair implementation of AProVE. As mentioned in Sect. 1, a first prototypical implementation already shows that in this way one can handle (a) examples that could up to now only be solved with direct tools such as [26, "*der*"], (b) examples that could up to now only be solved with transformational tools based on dependency pairs such as [32, "*LP/SGST06-shuffle*"], as well as (c) examples like [32, "*LP/SGST06-snake*"] that could not be solved by any tool up to now. Note that the Diophantine constraints resulting from our new approach according to Sect. 4 are usually smaller and simpler than the ones generated by the previous version of Polytool [26,27]. But already in the previous version of Polytool, solving these constraints automatically was no problem in practice. (To this end, the SAT-based constraint solver of AProVE was used [14].) Thus, this solver will also be used for the automatic generation of the required polynomial interpretations and interargument relations in our new approach.

Acknowledgement

We are grateful to the referees for many helpful suggestions. Manh Thang Nguyen is supported by *FWO/2006/09: Termination analysis: Crossing paradigm borders*. Peter Schneider-Kamp and Jürgen Giesl are supported by the *Deutsche Forschungsgemeinschaft (DFG), grant GI 274/5-1*.

References

1. Arts, T., Giesl, J.: Termination of term rewriting using dependency pairs. Theoretical Computer Science 236(1-2), 133–178 (2000)
2. Bol, R.N., Apt, K.R., Klop, J.W.: An analysis of loop checking mechanisms for logic programs. Theoretical Computer Science 86(1), 35–79 (1991)
3. Bossi, A., Cocco, N., Fabris, M.: Norms on terms and their use in proving universal termination of a logic program. Theoretical Computer Science 124(2), 297–328 (1994)
4. Bruynooghe, M., Codish, M., Gallagher, J.P., Genaim, S., Vanhoof, W.: Termination analysis of logic programs through combination of type-based norms. ACM Transactions on Programming Languages and Systems 29(2) (2007)
5. Codish, M., Taboch, C.: A semantic basis for the termination analysis of logic programs. Journal of Logic Programming 41(1), 103–123 (1999)
6. Codish, M., Genaim, S.: Proving termination one loop at a time. In: Proc. WLPE 2003 (2003)
7. Contejean, E., Marché, C., Tomás, A.P., Urbain, X.: Mechanically proving termination using polynomial interpretations. Journal of Automated Reasoning 34(4), 325–363 (2005)
8. De Schreye, D., Verschaetse, K., Bruynooghe, M.: A framework for analyzing the termination of definite logic programs with respect to call patterns. In: Proc. FGCS 1992, pp. 481–488 (1992)
9. De Schreye, D., Serebrenik, A.: Acceptability with General Orderings. In: Kakas, A.C., Sadri, F. (eds.) Computational Logic: Logic Programming and Beyond. LNCS (LNAI), vol. 2407, pp. 187–210. Springer, Heidelberg (2002)
10. Decorte, S., De Schreye, D., Vandecasteele, H.: Constraint-based automatic termination analysis of logic programs. ACM Transactions on Programming Languages and Systems 21(6), 1137–1195 (1999)
11. Dershowitz, N.: Termination of rewriting. Journal of Symbolic Computation 3(1-2), 69–116 (1987)
12. Dershowitz, N., Lindenstrauss, N., Sagiv, Y., Serebrenik, A.: A general framework for automatic termination analysis of logic programs. In: Applicable Algebra in Engineering, Communication and Computing, 12(1,2), pp. 117–156 (2001)

13. Waldmann, J., Zantema, H., Endrullis, J.: Matrix Interpretations for Proving Termination of Term Rewriting. In: Furbach, U., Shankar, N. (eds.) IJCAR 2006. LNCS (LNAI), vol. 4130, pp. 574–588. Springer, Heidelberg (2006)
14. Fuhs, C., Giesl, J., Middeldorp, A., Schneider-Kamp, P., Thiemann, R., Zankl, H.: SAT Solving for Termination Analysis with Polynomial Interpretations. In: Marques-Silva, J., Sakallah, K.A. (eds.) SAT 2007. LNCS, vol. 4501, pp. 340–354. Springer, Heidelberg (2007)
15. Giesl, J., Arts, T., Ohlebusch, E.: Modular termination proofs for rewriting using dependency pairs. Journal of Symbolic Computation 34(1), 21–58 (2002)
16. Giesl, J., Thiemann, R., Schneider-Kamp, P.: The Dependency Pair Framework: Combining Techniques for Automated Termination Proofs. In: Baader, F., Voronkov, A. (eds.) LPAR 2004. LNCS (LNAI), vol. 3452, pp. 301–331. Springer, Heidelberg (2005)
17. Giesl, J., Schneider-Kamp, P., Thiemann, R.: AProVE 1.2: Automatic termination proofs in the dependency pair framework. In: Furbach, U., Shankar, N. (eds.) IJCAR 2006. LNCS (LNAI), vol. 4130, pp. 281–286. Springer, Heidelberg (2006)
18. Giesl, J., Thiemann, R., Schneider-Kamp, P., Falke, S.: Mechanizing and improving dependency pairs. Journal of Automated Reasoning 37(3), 155–203 (2006)
19. Hirokawa, N., Middeldorp, A.: Automating the dependency pair method. Information and Computation 199(1-2), 172–199 (2005)
20. Hong, H., Jakuš, D.: Testing positiveness of polynomials. Journal of Automated Reasoning 21(1), 23–38 (1998)
21. Kusakari, K., Nakamura, M., Toyama, Y.: Argument filtering transformation. In: Nadathur, G. (ed.) PPDP 1999. LNCS, vol. 1702, pp. 48–62. Springer, Heidelberg (1999)
22. Lankford, D.S.: On proving term rewriting systems are Noetherian. Technical Report MTP-3, Louisiana Technical University, Ruston, LA, USA (1979)
23. Lee, C.S., Jones, N.D., Ben-Amram, A.M.: The size-change principle for program termination. In: Proc. POPL 2001, pp. 81–92 (2001)
24. Marché, C., Zantema, H.: The Termination Competition. In: Baader, F. (ed.) RTA 2007. LNCS, vol. 4533, pp. 303–313. Springer, Heidelberg (2007)
25. Mesnard, F., Bagnara, R.: cTI: A constraint-based termination inference tool for ISO-Prolog. In: Theory and Practice of Logic Programming, vol. 5(1, 2), pp. 243–257 (2005)
26. Nguyen, M.T., De Schreye, D.: Polynomial Interpretations as a Basis for Termination Analysis of Logic Programs. In: Gabbrielli, M., Gupta, G. (eds.) ICLP 2005. LNCS, vol. 3668, pp. 311–325. Springer, Heidelberg (2005)
27. De Schreye, D., Nguyen, M.T.: Polytool: Proving Termination Automatically Based on Polynomial Interpretations. In: Puebla, G. (ed.) LOPSTR 2006. LNCS, vol. 4407, pp. 210–218. Springer, Heidelberg (2007)
28. Plümer, L.: Termination Proofs for Logic Programs. Springer, Heidelberg (1990)
29. Podelski, A., Rybalchenko, A.: Transition invariants. In: Proc. LICS 2004, pp. 32–41 (2004)
30. Ramsey, F.P.: On a problem of formal logic. Proc. London Math. Society 30, 264–286 (1930)
31. Schneider-Kamp, P., Giesl, J., Serebrenik, A., Thiemann, R.: Automated Termination Analysis for Logic Programs by Term Rewriting. In: Puebla, G. (ed.) LOPSTR 2006. LNCS, vol. 4407, pp. 177–193. Springer, Heidelberg (2007)
32. The termination problem data base, http://www.lri.fr/~marche/tpdb.
33. Thiemann, R., Giesl, J.: The size-change principle and dependency pairs for termination of term rewriting. Applicable Algebra in Engineering, Communication and Computing 16(4), 229–270 (2005)

Type-Based Homeomorphic Embedding and Its Applications to Online Partial Evaluation

Elvira Albert[1], John Gallagher[2], Miguel Gómez-Zamalloa[1],
and Germán Puebla[3]

[1] DSIC, Complutense University of Madrid, E-28040 Madrid, Spain
[2] CBIT, Roskilde University, DK-4000 Roskilde, Denmark
[3] CLIP, Technical University of Madrid, E-28660 Boadilla del Monte, Madrid, Spain

Abstract. *Homeomorphic Embedding* (HEm) has proven to be very powerful for supervising termination of computations, provided that such computations are performed over a *finite signature*, i.e., the number of constants and function symbols involved is finite. However, there are situations, for example numeric computations, which involve an infinite (or too large) signature, in which HEm does not guarantee termination. Some extensions to HEm for the case of infinite signatures have been proposed which guarantee termination, but they either do not provide systematic means for generating such extensions or the extensions are too simplistic and do not produce the expected results in practice. We introduce *Type-based Homeomorphic Embedding* (TbHEm) as an extension of the standard, untyped HEm to deal with infinite signatures. In the paper, we show how TbHEm can be used to improve the accuracy of *online partial evaluation*. For this purpose, we propose an approach to constructing suitable types for partial evaluation automatically based on existing analysis tools for constraint logic programs. We also present useful properties of types which allow us to take full advantage of Tb-HEm in practice. Experimental results are reported which show that our work improves the state of the practice of online partial evaluation.

1 Introduction

The *homeomorphic embedding* (HEm) relation [10,11,12] has become very popular to ensure online termination of *symbolic* transformation and specialization methods and it is essential to obtain powerful optimizations, for instance, in the context of online Partial Evaluation (PE) [9]. Intuitively, HEm is a structural ordering under which an expression t_1 is greater than, i.e., it *embeds*, another expression t_2, written as $t_2 \trianglelefteq t_1$, if t_2 can be obtained from t_1 by deleting some parts, e.g., $\underline{s}(s(\underline{U} + W)\underline{\times}(\underline{U} + s(\underline{V})))$ embeds $s(U \times (U + V))$. The HEm relation can be used to guarantee termination because, provided the set of constants and functors is finite, every infinite sequence of expressions $t_1, t_2, \ldots$, contains at least a pair of elements t_i and t_j with $i < j$ s.t. $t_i \trianglelefteq t_j$. Therefore, when iteratively computing a sequence $t_1, t_2, \ldots, t_n$, finiteness of the sequence can be guaranteed by using HEm as a *whistle*. Whenever a new expression t_{n+1} is to

King, A. (Ed.): LOPSTR 2007, LNCS 4915, pp. 23–42, 2008.
© Springer-Verlag Berlin Heidelberg 2008

be added to a finite sequence $t_1, \ldots, t_n$, we first check whether t_{n+1} embeds any of the expressions already in the sequence. If that is the case, we say that HEm whistles, i.e., it has detected (potential) non-termination and the computation has to be stopped. Otherwise, t_{n+1} can be safely added to the sequence and the computation can proceed.

Two key features for the success of HEm as an approach for guaranteeing online termination are i) in the case of finite sequences, it often allows sequences to grow considerably large before the whistle blows, to the point that in a good number of cases the full sequence can be computed without the whistle blowing at all; ii) in the case of infinite sequences, it often identifies (potential) non-termination quickly, and the whistle blows without unnecessarily further expanding the sequence.

While HEm has been proved very powerful for symbolic computations, some difficulties remain in the presence of infinite signatures, such as the numbers. In the case of logic programs, infinite signatures appear as soon as certain Prolog built-ins such as `is/2`, `functor/3 name/2`, `=../2`, `atom_codes/2`, etc. are used. Some extensions to HEm over infinite signatures have been defined and used in practice (e.g. [11,2]), but they are often too ad-hoc, i.e., they only allow constants which appear explicitly in the program, regardless of which part of the program (predicate, argument position) they appear. As the approach is purely *syntactic*, it sometimes turns out to be too conservative ("whistling" too early) in practice, breaking feature i) above; while it can also be too aggressive, thus also sometimes breaking feature ii) above.

In this paper, we introduce the *type-based homeomorphic embedding* (TbHEm) relation which by taking information about the behavior of the program into account, provides more precise results in the presence of infinite signatures. In a sense, whereas [11,2] take a simple *syntactic* approach to extending the HEm relation, we propose a *semantic* approach for such extension. To achieve this, our typed relation is defined on types structured in two parts: a finite component and an infinite component. Intuitively, TbHEm allows expanding sequences as long as, whenever we compare two terms of a given type, the actual symbols which appear in such terms belong to the finite component of the type.

We illustrate the benefits of TbHEm in the context of online Partial Evaluation (PE) [9]. In particular, we use a simplified interpreter for an imperative, stack-based bytecode language written in Prolog whose specialization (if successful) allows decompiling bytecode programs to Prolog. We show how to automatically construct typings by relying on existing analysis techniques for the inference of well-typings [5]. Moreover, we present the property of a type being of *finite signature* (resp. *infinite signature*) which guarantees that all terms in the type are built out of a finite (resp. infinite) number of constant and functor symbols. We also outline how analysis of numeric bounds can be used to infer finite signature properties of types. In the case of finite signature, we can safely apply traditional HEm. We report on experimental results which compare TbHEm with previous proposals and show the benefits of our approach for the specialization of logic programs with infinite signatures.

The rest of the paper is organized as follows. Sect. 2 recalls some basic notions of PE, with special emphasis on the role of embedding. In Sect. 3, we review existing proposals in specialization of interpreters. In Sect. 4, we introduce Tb-HEm and prove its correctness. Sect. 5 proposes the use of well-typings as suitable types for the application of TbHEm in online PE and reports some experiments. Sect. 6 presents interesting properties of types to use TbHEm in practice, together with some experimental results. Finally, Sect. 7 discusses related work and concludes.

2   Basics on Embedding in Partial Evaluation

We assume familiarity with the basic concepts of logic programming and partial evaluation, as they are presented in e.g. [16,9]. We start by recalling the definition of HEm, which can be found for instance in Leuschel's work [14].

Definition 1 ($\trianglelefteq$). *Given two atoms $A = p(t_1,\ldots,t_n)$ and $B = p(s_1,\ldots,s_n)$, we say that B embeds A, written $A \trianglelefteq B$, if $t_i \trianglelefteq s_i$ for all i s.t. $1 \leq i \leq n$. The embedding relation over terms, also written $\trianglelefteq$, is defined by the following rules:*

1. *$Y \trianglelefteq X$ for all variables X, Y.*
2. *$s \trianglelefteq f(t_1,\ldots,t_n)$ if $s \trianglelefteq t_i$ for some i.*
3. *$f(s_1,\ldots,s_n) \trianglelefteq f(t_1,\ldots,t_n)$ if $s_i \trianglelefteq t_i$ for all i, $1 \leq i \leq n$.*

We now explain the role that HEm plays in online PE (see e.g. [9,12,14]), which is a semantics-based program transformation technique which specializes a program w.r.t. given input data, hence, it is often called program specialization. Essentially, partial evaluators are non-standard interpreters which evaluate goals as long as termination is guaranteed and specialization is considered profitable. Given a program P and an atom S, partial evaluation produces a new program P_S which is a specialization of P for S. In logic programming, the underlying technique is to construct (possibly) *incomplete* SLD trees for the set of atoms to be specialized. In an incomplete tree, it is possible to choose *not* to further unfold a goal. Therefore, the tree may contain three kinds of leaves: failure nodes, success nodes (which contain the empty goal), and non-empty goals which are not further unfolded. The latter are required in order to guarantee termination of the partial evaluation process, since the SLD being built may be infinite. Even if the SLD trees for fully instantiated initial atoms (as regards the *input* arguments) are finite, the SLD trees produced for partially instantiated initial atoms may be infinite. This is because the SLD for partially instantiated atoms can have (infinitely many) more branches than the actual SLD tree at run-time.

HEm *in local control.* The role of local control is to determine how to construct the (incomplete) SLD trees. In particular, the *unfolding rule* decides, for each resolvent, whether to stop unfolding or to continue unfolding it and, if so, which atom to select from the resolvent. Unfolding is continued only if termination is not endangered and specialization is considered profitable. Therefore, it is desirable to have a mechanism for guaranteeing termination which *whistles* as late as possible. State of the art local control rules based on HEm do not check for embedding against all previously selected atoms but rather only against those in its sequence of *covering ancestors* (see e.g., [18]). This increases both the efficiency of the checking and whistling later.

HEm *in global control.* Partial evaluators need to compute SLD-trees for a number of atoms in order to ensure that all atoms which appear in non-failing leaves of incomplete SLD trees are "covered" by the root of some tree (this is known as the closedness condition of partial evaluation [15]). The role of the *global control* is to ensure that we do not try to compute SLD trees for an infinite number of atoms. The usual way of achieving this is by applying an *abstraction operator* which performs "generalizations" on the atoms for which SLD trees are to be built. HEm can also be used at the global control level in order to decide when to generalize (i.e., to apply the *most specific generalization*) before proceeding to build SLD trees. Basically, for each new atom A, global control checks whether A is larger than (i.e., it embeds) any of the atoms in the set T_i (which contains the atoms in the roots of the partial trees which have already been built). If A does not embed any atom in T_i, it is added to the set; otherwise, A is generalized into $msg(A, A')$, where $A' \in T_i$ and $A' \trianglelefteq A$. At the global control level, HEm can be combined with other techniques such as *global trees, characteristic trees, trace terms*, etc. See e.g. [12] and its references.

Partial evaluation and Code Generation. As discussed above, the global control returns a set of atoms T. Finally, a partial evaluation of P w.r.t. S can then be systematically extracted from the set T. As notation, we refer to each root-to-leaf path in an SLD tree as *derivation*. The notion of *resultant* is used to generate a program rule associated with each non-failing derivation in an SLD tree. In particular, given a derivation for $P \cup \{A\}$ with $A \in T$ ending in B and θ the composition of the *mgus* in the derivation steps, then the rule $A\theta \leftarrow B$ is called the *resultant* of the derivation. A *partial evaluation* is then defined as the union of the sets of resultants associated to the SLD trees for all atoms in T.

3   Embedding with Infinite Signatures: Motivating Example

In Fig. 1 we show a fragment of a simplified imperative bytecode interpreter implemented in Prolog. If the partial evaluator is powerful enough, given a bytecode program we can obtain a decompiled version of it in Prolog (see e.g. [1] for an object-oriented stack-based interpreter). For brevity, we omit the code of some predicates like `build_init_state/2` (whose purpose is explained below) and `localVar_update/4` which simply updates the value of a local variable. We only show the definition of `step/3` for a reduced set of instructions. The bytecode to be decompiled is represented as a set of facts `bytecode(PC,Inst)` where `PC` contains a program counter and `Inst` the corresponding bytecode instruction. A state is of the form `st(PC,OStack,LocalV)` where `OStack` represents

```
main(InArgs,Top) :-                    step(const(_T,Z),st(PC,S,L),S2) :-
    build_init_state(InArgs,S0),           PCp is PC + 1,
    execute(S0,st(_,[Top|_],_)).           S2 = st(PCp,[Z|S],L).
execute(S,S):-                         step(istore(X),st(PC,[I|S],L),S2) :-
    S = st(PC,_,_),                        PCp is PC + 1,
    bytecode(PC,return).                   localVar_update(L,X,I,Lb),
execute(S1,Sf) :-                          S2 = st(PCp,S,Lb).
    S1 = st(PC,_,_),                   step(goto(O),st(PC,S,L),S2) :-
    bytecode(PC,Inst),                     PCp is PC+O,
    step(Inst,S1,S2),                      S2 = st(PCp,S,L).
    execute(S2,Sf).                    ....
```

Fig. 1. Fragment of simplified bytecode interpreter

the operand stack and LocalV the list of local variables. The predicate main/2, given the input method arguments InArgs, first builds the initial state by means of predicate build_init_state/2 and then calls predicate execute/2. In turn, execute/2 first calls predicate step/3, which produces S2, the state after executing the corresponding bytecode, and then calls predicate execute/2 recursively with S2 until we reach a return instruction.

Consider the count method which appears in the left hand side of Fig. 2, represented as a set of facts. For clarity of the presentation, on the right hand side of Fig. 2 we show a Java source program which can be compiled into the corresponding bytecode. However, it is important to note that the decompilation is performed directly from the bytecode and that the decompiler does not have access to the source. It can be seen that count receives an integer and executes a loop where a counter initialized to "0" (in bytecodes 0 and 1) is incremented by one at each iteration (bytecode 5) until the counter reaches the value of the input parameter (checking the condition comprises bytecodes 2, 3 and 4). The method returns the value of the counter in bytecodes 7 and 8. For decompiling the count method, we partially evaluate the interpreter w.r.t. the bytecode facts which appear to the left of the figure by specializing the atom: main(N,I), where N is the input parameter and I represents the return value (i.e., the top of the stack at the end of the computation).

In Figure 3, we depict (a reduced version of) one of the SLD trees that leads to an effective decompilation of our running example and that we will refer to in the next sections. For simplicity, apart from the entry atom main/2, we only show atoms for execute/2, as it is the only recursive predicate in the program. Thus, each arrow in the tree involves the application of several unfolding steps. Note that some of the statements within the body of each step operation can remain residual when they involve data which is not known at specialization time. The computation rule used in the unfolding operator is able to residualize calls which are not sufficiently instantiated and select non-leftmost atoms in a safe way [3], in particular, further calls to execute can be selected. We represent such residual calls as labels in the arrows of the tree.

```
bytecode(0,const(int,0)).
bytecode(1,istore(1)).
bytecode(2,iload(1)).
bytecode(3,iload(0)).
bytecode(4,if_icmp(geInt,3)).
bytecode(5,iinc(1,1)).
bytecode(6,goto(-4)).
bytecode(7,iload(1)).
bytecode(8,return).
```

```
static int count(int n){
  int i = 0;
  while (i < n)
    i++;
  return i;
}
```

Fig. 2. Object program for working example

$$\mathtt{main(N, I)}$$
$$\downarrow$$
$$\mathtt{execute(st(0, [], [N, 0]), S_f)}$$
$$\downarrow$$
$$\mathtt{execute(st(1, [0], [N, 0]), S_f)}$$
$$\downarrow$$
$$\boxed{\mathtt{execute(st(2, [], [N, 0]), S_f)_{(1)}}}$$
$$\downarrow$$
$$\mathtt{execute(st(4, [N, 0], [N, 0]), S_f)}$$

$$\{0 \geq N\} \swarrow \qquad \searrow \{0 < N\}$$

$$\mathtt{execute(st(8, [0], [N, 0]), S_f)} \qquad\qquad \mathtt{execute(st(6, [], [N, 1]), S_f)}$$
$$\downarrow \{I/0\} \qquad\qquad\qquad\qquad\qquad \downarrow$$
$$\mathtt{true} \qquad\qquad\qquad\qquad \boxed{\mathtt{execute(st(2, [], [N, 1]), S_f)_{(2)}}}$$
$$\downarrow (1) \unlhd_T (2), (1) \ntrianglelefteq_S^* (2)$$
$$\infty \text{ (with } \unlhd)$$

```
main(N,0) :- 0>=N.                    sp_execute(N,I,I) :- I>=N.
main(N,I) :- 0<N,                     sp_execute(N,A,I) :- A<N, A' is A+1,
          sp_execute(N,1,I).                    sp_execute(N,A',I).
```

Fig. 3. Partial unfolding SLD tree and residual code of working example

3.1   Using the Original Homeomorphic Embedding

Let us first consider an online partial evaluator (which is able to accurately handle built-in predicates and to safely perform non-leftmost and) which uses HEm to control termination both at the local and global control levels. As it can be seen in the figure, the PC value "2" corresponds to the loop entry. By applying HEm, the evaluation contains a subsequence of atoms of the form: $\mathtt{execute(st(2, [], [N, 0]), S_f)}$, $\mathtt{execute(st(2, [], [N, 1]), S_f)}$, $\mathtt{execute(st(2, []},$ $\mathtt{[N, 2]), S_f)}, \ldots$ marked within dashed frames in the figure, which correspond to consecutive iterations of the loop in which the control returns to the loop head (PC value 2 in the first position of the state) with a value for the loop counter (local variable at the second position in the resulting state) increased by one. This sequence can grow infinitely, as the HEm does not flag it as potentially dangerous, which is marked by ∞ (with $\trianglelefteq$) in the figure. This is because the interpreter uses Prolog's arithmetic (i.e., the is/2 predicate), which breaks the finite signature property featured by pure logic programs.

In order to get a quality decompilation, we need to filter out the value of the counter (local variable 1) but not that of the PC. As shown in the figure, this requires stopping the derivation when we hit the atom $\mathtt{execute(st(2, [], [N, 1]), S_f)}$ (marked as $(\mathbf{1}) \trianglelefteq_\mathbf{T} (\mathbf{2})$) and generalize it w.r.t. the above atom within a dashed frame, resulting in $\mathtt{execute(st(2, [], [N, X]), S_f)}$.

3.2 Recovering Termination: Embedding with Number Filtering

In programs which contain Prolog arithmetic but do not generate an infinite number of functors via functor/3, =../2, etc., a relatively straightforward solution in order to recover termination is to use the $\trianglelefteq_{num}$ relation, which is an adaptation of HEm which filters out numeric values, i.e., any number embeds any other number. The atom $\mathtt{execute(st(2, [], [N, 1]), S_f)}$ embeds $\mathtt{execute(st(2, [],}$ $\mathtt{[N, 0]), S_f)}$ under $\trianglelefteq_{num}$ and therefore we avoid non-termination. Unfortunately, this modification to HEm, is far too conservative, and leads to excessive precision loss. For instance, in the specialization of main(N, I), the first two atoms for execute/2 are $\mathtt{execute(st(0, [], [N, 0]), S_f)}$ and $\mathtt{execute(st(1, [0], [N, 0]), S_f)}$. By using $\trianglelefteq_{num}$, the whistle blows at this point and unfolding has to stop. Furthermore, the latter atom is generalized at the global control level into $\mathtt{execute(st(X, Y, [N, 0]), S_f)}$ before proceeding with the specialization. This turns out not to be acceptable for the specialization of our interpreter, since we lose track of which the next instruction to execute is—which prevents us from eliminating the interpretation layer—and in many cases the residual program ends up containing the whole original interpreter.

3.3 Increasing Accuracy: Static Symbols in the Program

A simple syntactic way of increasing the accuracy while preserving termination, as proposed in [11], consists in considering two sets of symbols: those which appear explicitly in the program and goal, which is obviously finite, and another infinite set which contains all other symbols. In the following, this relation is denoted as $\trianglelefteq_S^*$. When comparing two terms we keep those symbols which belong to the finite set and filter out all other ones. Under this relation, the atom $\mathtt{execute(st(1, [0],}$ $\mathtt{[N, 0]), S_f)}$ does not embed the atom $\mathtt{execute(st(0, [], [N, 0]), S_f)}$ in the figure, as the numbers 0 and 1 are different static symbols which occur in the program. Hence, we are not forced to generalize them and we can keep the PC value.

Unfortunately, the $\trianglelefteq_S^*$ relation turns out not to be optimal in our case either since $\mathtt{execute(st(2, [], [N, 1]), S_f)}$ does not embed $\mathtt{execute(st(2, [], [N, 0]), S_f)}$. This means that unfolding proceeds with a second iteration of the loop. The process is guaranteed to terminate, we will unfold at most as many iterations of the loop as distinct numbers appear in the program. However, we are not able to achieve the quality decompilation which appears at the bottom of Figure 3. For obtaining such good decompilation, we need to generalize the loop counter, i.e., the atom $\texttt{execute}(\texttt{st}(2,[],[\texttt{N},1]),\texttt{S}_\texttt{f})$ has to embed $\texttt{execute}(\texttt{st}(2,[],[\texttt{N},0]),\texttt{S}_\texttt{f})$. Intuitively, the reason why this relation does not behave optimally is because the fact that many symbols appear explicitly in the program for one argument (in our case the PC counter) should somehow not affect the set of symbols which we should consider as static for other arguments (the list of local variables).

Note that the use of characteristic trees [13] to control the degree of polyvariance does not lead to an optimal decompilation in this example either. The reason is that characteristic trees concern only global and not local control. Therefore, as already mentioned above, they do not stop the local derivation which may perform as many unrollings of the loop as different values for the loop counter there are in the program. Once the local control stops this unfolding process, the value of the counter will be generalized by the global control. However, the characteristic tree of this generalized term is clearly not equivalent to the one of the previous unrolling for the different values in the counter. Therefore, the decompilation of the loop body for the static values remains residual in the specialized code as well.

4   Type-Based Homeomorphic Embedding

In the presence of infinite signatures, a general method of defining homeomorphic embedding relations exists; an *extended homeomorphic embedding relation* is defined in [11] based on previous results by Kruskal [10] and by Dershowitz [6]. This solution defines a family of embedding relations, where a subsidiary ordering on function symbols plays an essential role. However, we argue that this does not really solve the practical problem of finding an effective embedding relation, since there is no automated mechanism for finding the "right" ordering relation on the function symbols in the signature.

In this section, we propose *typed-based homeomorphic embedding* (TbHEm for short), a relation which improves HEm by making use of additional information provided in the form of types. We outline how this approach can be seen as a way of generating instances of extended HEm as defined by Leuschel, including the possibility of taking into account the program semantics. The types required for guiding TbHEm can be provided manually or, interestingly, be automatically inferred by program analysis, as we will see in Section 5.

4.1   Types: Preliminaries and Notation

In the following, let P be a program and Σ_P be a (possibly infinite) signature including the functions and constants appearing in P and goals for P as well as in computations of P. We adopt the syntax of Mercury [20] for type definitions. *Type expressions (types)*, elements of $\mathcal{T}$, are constructed from an infinite set of type variables (parameters) $\mathcal{V}_{\mathcal{T}}$ and an alphabet of ranked type symbols $\Sigma_{\mathcal{T}}$; these are disjoint from the set of variables V and the alphabet of functors Σ_P of a given program P respectively.

Definition 2 (type definition). *A type rule for a type symbol $h/n \in \Sigma_T$ is of the form $h(\bar{T}) \longrightarrow f_1(\bar{\tau}_1); \ldots; f_k(\bar{\tau}_k); \ldots$ $(k \geq 1)$ where $\bar{T}$ is a n-tuple of distinct type variables, $f_1, \ldots, f_k, \ldots$ are distinct function symbols from Σ_P, $\bar{\tau}_i$ $(i \geq 1)$ are tuples of corresponding arity from T, and type variables in the right hand side, if any, are from $\bar{T}$ (a condition known as* transparency *[17,8]). A type definition is a finite set of type rules where no two rules contain the same type symbol on the left hand side, and there is a rule for each type symbol occurring in the type rules.*

We write $t : \tau$ to mean that term t is of type τ. As in Mercury [20], a function symbol can occur in several type rules. In the definition above we allow type rules containing an infinite number of cases. Thus, standard infinite types such as *integer* are permitted, defined by a rule with an infinite number of cases containing the numeric constants. In order to define TbHEm we introduce some extra annotation into type rules. We consider the right hand side of each type rule to consist of two disjoint components, each possibly empty. More precisely, we will structure a type rule as $h(\bar{T}) \longrightarrow F; I$, where the union $F \cup I$ are the cases in the type rule, $F \cup I$ is non-empty, F is either empty or finite and I is either empty or infinite. We say that a type $\tau \in T$ is of *infinite component* if I is non-empty in the rule defining τ. Otherwise it is said to be of *finite component*. Note that for types of infinite component there are infinitely many ways of splitting them into type rules; for example $nat \longrightarrow F; I$ where $F = \emptyset$ and $I = \mathbb{N}$, or $F = \{0, 1, 2\}$ and $I = \mathbb{N} \setminus \{0, 1, 2\}$, etc.

A *predicate signature* for an n-ary predicate p is of the form $p(\bar{\tau})$ and declares a type $\tau_i \in T$ for each argument of the predicate p/n. Programs are assumed to be *well-typed* in the usual sense, namely that every atom and term in a clause can be assigned types consistent with the type declarations such that the type assigned to each head atom is a variant of the signature for its predicate, the types of the body atoms are instances of the corresponding signatures, and multiple occurrences of the same variable in the clause are assigned the same type. Furthermore, we disallow *polymorphic recursion*; body atoms for recursive predicates are assigned a type that is a variant of the signature. The relevant consequences of well-typing for our purpose are firstly that a well-typed program and goal generate only well-typed atoms in computations and secondly that only a finite number of types arise during a computation. An infinite set of different types such as $h(T), h(h(T)), h(h(h(T))), \ldots$ cannot arise in a computation, due to the absence of polymorphic recursion.

4.2   Type-Based Homeomorphic Embedding

We now define TbHEm ($\trianglelefteq_T$). It follows closely the definition of the extended HEm relation defined in [11] on untyped terms; here we define a relation on typed terms. As in the definition in [11], two subsidiary relations $\preceq_F$ and $\preceq_S$ are needed. The first, $\preceq_F$, is a relation on function symbols paired with their associated types, and it refers to the infinite component of type rules described above.

Definition 3. *Let $\preceq_F$ be the following relation on the set of pairs $\Sigma_P \times \mathcal{T}$. $(f_1, \tau_1) \preceq_F (f_2, \tau_2)$ iff (1) the rules defining τ_i are of form $h_i(\bar{V}_i) \longrightarrow F_i; I_i$, for $i = 1, 2$ and (2) either $f_1 = f_2 \wedge \tau_1 = \tau_2$ or f_2 is in the infinite component I_2 of the rule for τ_2.*

For instance, given $\tau \longrightarrow F; I$ with $F = \{1, 2\}$ and $I = \mathbb{N} \setminus \{1, 2\}$ then $(1, \tau) \npreceq_F (2, \tau)$ and $(1, \tau) \preceq_F (5, \tau)$. The other relation, $\preceq_S$, is a relation on sequences of typed terms, and for our purposes here we can take it to be true for all pairs of sequences of typed terms. In general this relation can be defined to allow more refined treatment of associative operators, among other things; as noted in [11], whether $\wedge(a, b, c)$ is embedded in $\wedge(a, b, c, d)$ depends on the nested structure of the expressions, if $\wedge$ is taken as a binary functor. Though we do not use it here, we include the relation $\preceq_S$ in the following definition for uniformity with [11], so that our notion of typed embedding becomes an instance of the extended homeomorphic embedded defined there.

Definition 4 ($\trianglelefteq_T$). *Given two typed atoms $A = p(t_1, \ldots, t_n)$ and $B = p(s_1, \ldots, s_n)$, with predicate signature $p(\tau_1, \ldots, \tau_n)$, we say that B embeds A, written $A \trianglelefteq_T B$, if $t_i : \tau_i \trianglelefteq_T s_i : \tau_i$ for all i s.t. $1 \leq i \leq n$. The embedding relation over typed terms, also written $\trianglelefteq_T$, is defined by the following rules:*

1. *$Y : \tau_Y \trianglelefteq_T X : \tau_X$ for all variables X, Y.*
2. *$s : \tau \trianglelefteq_T f(t_1, \ldots, t_n) : \tau'$ if $s : \tau \trianglelefteq_T t_i : \tau_i'$ for some i, where $\tau_1', \ldots, \tau_n'$ are the respective types of $t_1, \ldots, t_n$.*
3. *$f(s_1, \ldots, s_n) : \tau \trianglelefteq_T g(t_1, \ldots, t_m) : \tau'$ if*
   (a) $(f, \tau) \preceq_F (g, \tau')$,
   (b) $(s_1 : \tau_1, \ldots, s_n : \tau_n) \preceq_S (t_1 : \tau_1', \ldots, t_m : \tau_m')$, and
   (c) $\exists i_1, \ldots, i_n$ such that $1 \leq i_1 < \cdots < i_n \leq m$ and $\forall j \in \{1, \ldots, n\}$, $s_j : \tau_j \trianglelefteq_T t_{i_j} : \tau_{i_j}'$,
   where $\tau_1, \ldots, \tau_n, \tau_1', \ldots, \tau_m'$ are the respective types of $s_1, \ldots s_n, t_1, \ldots, t_m$.

Rule 3 of the definition specifies that embedding can occur between terms with different function symbols, where the function symbol of the "larger" term using the $\preceq_F$ relation is from the I component of its type. However, as long as we compare distinct terms from an infinite type and remain within the finite component F of the type, no embedding (using rule 3) occurs since the condition $(f, \tau_1) \preceq_F (g, \tau_2)$ does not hold. For instance, consider the following predicate signature and type definition, $p(\tau)$ and $\tau \longrightarrow F; I$. We have that $p(1) \trianglelefteq_T p(2)$ if $F = \emptyset$ and $I = \mathbb{N}$. However, $p(1) \ntrianglelefteq_T p(2)$ if $F = \{0, 1, 2\}$ and $I = \mathbb{N} \setminus \{0, 1, 2\}$.

Proposition 1. *Given a program P that is well-typed with respect to a type definition and set of signatures, there is no infinite sequence of well-typed atoms $A_1, A_2, \ldots$ in a computation for P such that for all i, j where $i < j$, $A_i \ntrianglelefteq_T A_j$.*

Proof. First note that, by the assumption that polymorphic recursion is disallowed, only a finite number of types (up to renaming of type variables) arises in a computation. The proposition follows from the fact that is a $\trianglelefteq_T$ *well quasi order (wqo)* on typed atoms over a finite set of types. A binary relation $\leq : D \times D$ is a wqo if (i) it is reflexive and transitive, and (ii) for all infinite sequences $d_0, d_1, \ldots$ of elements of D, $\exists i < j$ such that $d_i \leq d_j$. By Theorem 4 from [11], this in turn follows if both $\preceq_F$ and $\preceq_s$ are wqos on their respective domains, which we now prove.

The proof that $\preceq_S$ is a wqo is trivial. For $\preceq_F$, it can easily be verified that the relation is reflexive and transitive. To prove the wqo property (ii) assume that there is an infinite sequence of pairs from $\Sigma_P \times T$, $(f_0, \tau_0), (f_1, \tau_1), \ldots$. First assume there is only a finite number of function symbols occurring in the sequence; in this case, since there is also a finite number of types, there must exist i and j, $i < j$, such that $f_i = f_j \wedge \tau_i = \tau_j$ and hence $(f_i, \tau_i) \preceq_F (f_j, \tau_j)$. Secondly, assume that there is an infinite set of function symbols occurring in the sequence; since the number of types is finite there must exist some $j > 0$, such that f_j is in the infinite component of the type rule for τ_j, in which case $(f_i, \tau_i) \preceq_F (f_j, \tau_j)$ for all $i < j$. Hence, $\preceq_F$ is a wqo.

Proposition 1 ensures that partial evaluation using TbHEm terminates. The idea of using a typed homeomorphic embedding generalises an idea sketched in [11] to build an extended homeomorphic embedding based on a distinction between the finite number of symbols actually occurring in the program and goal (the *static* symbols), and the rest (the *dynamic* symbols). This could be reconstructed as a TbHEm using a single type rule $term \longrightarrow F; I$ where F contains cases of the form $f(term, \ldots, term)$ where f is a static symbol, and I contains the infinite number of cases where f is not static. The predicate signatures would allocate the type $term$ to all arguments. As discussed in Section 3.3, that approach lacks control over the different contexts in which static symbols occur in the program. Sometimes a static symbol should block embedding but other times it should not.

5   Automatic Inference of Well-Typings

In this section, we outline and experimentally evaluate an approach which, given an untyped program and a goal or set of goals, automatically infers suitable types to be used in online partial evaluation in combination with TbHEm. The approach is based on existing analysis tools for constraint logic programs.

We note first that the problem does not allow a precise, computable solution. Determining the exact set of symbols that can appear at run-time at a specific program point, and in particular determining whether the set is finite, is closely related to termination detection and is thus undecidable. However, the better the derived types are, the more aggressive partial evaluation can be without risking non-termination. If the derived types have finite components that are too small, then over-generalization is likely to result; if they are too large, then specialization might be over-aggressive, producing unnecessary versions.

A procedure for constructing a monomorphic well-typing of an arbitrary logic program was described by Bruynooghe *et al.* [5][1]. The procedure scales well

---

[1] Available on-line at http://saft.ruc.dk/Tattoo/

(roughly linear in program size) and is robust, in that every program has a well-typing, and the procedure works with partial programs (modules). We first apply this procedure to illustrate the use of well-typings in the context of our running example and, then, we perform an experimental evaluation to assess the gains that we achieve in the specialization of interpreters by using well-typings in combination with TbHEm.

5.1   Well-Typings for Working Example

In the original type inference procedure, an externally defined predicate such as is/2 is treated as if defined by a clause X is Y :- true and is thus implicitly assumed not to generate any symbols not occurring elsewhere in the program. In deriving types for partial evaluation, we provide a type for such built-ins in the form of a dummy additional "fact" for is/2, namely num is num :- true. The constant num (assumed not to occur elsewhere in the program) will thus propagate during type inference into those types that unify with the types of the is predicate arguments. In the resulting inferred types, we interpret occurrences of the constant num as being an abbreviation for an infinite set of cases.

Example 1. A type is inferred for the interpreter sketched in Figure 1, together with the particular bytecode program of Fig. 2. Note that the program counter is sometimes computed in the interpreter using the predicate is/2 as an offset from the current program counter value and hence its type is in principle any number. When the extra fact num is num :- true is added to the program, the inferred type τ_{PC} for the program counter argument PC is as follows.

$\quad\tau_{PC}$ --> -4; 0; 1; 2; 3; 4; 5; 6; 7; 8; num

Type τ_{PC} can be naturally interpreted as consisting of a finite part (the named constants) and an infinite part (the numbers other than the named constants). In other words, the partition F of the rule is $\{-4, 0, 1, 2, \ldots, 8\}$ and $I = \text{num} \setminus F$. Using the rule structured in this way, TbHEm ensures that the program counter is never abstracted away during partial evaluation, so long as its value remains in the expected range (the named constants). The atom execute(st(1, [0], [N, 0]), S_f) does not embed execute(st(0, [], [N, 0]), S_f) by using the type definition above, thus, the derivation can proceed. This avoids the need for generalizing the PC what would prevent us from having a quality specialization (decompilation) as explained in Sect. 2. The derivation will either eventually end or the PC value will be repeated due to a backwards jump in the code (loops). In this case, $\unlhd_T$ will flag the relevant atom as dangerous, e.g., execute(st(2, [], [N, 0]), S_f) $\unlhd_T$ execute(st(2, [], [N, 1]), S_f), as can be seen in Fig. 3. If, however, a different value arose, perhaps due to an addressing error, the infinite part of the type rule num is encountered and embedding (followed by generalization of the program counter argument) would take place.

The decompiled program that we obtain using the inferred well-typings and combined with TbHEm is shown at the bottom of Fig. 3. We can observe that the decompilation is optimal in the sense that the interpretation layer has been completely removed and there is no superfluous residual code. Note that a more sophisticated analysis could infer that τ_{PC} becomes of finite component, i.e., $I = \emptyset$ by taking $F = \{-4, -3, -2, -1, 0, 1, 2, 3, 4, 5, 6, 7, 8, 9\}$. This can be done by computing all combinations of bytecode indeces and offsets present in the program. In fact, $F = \{0, 1, 2, 3, 4, 5, 6, 7, 8\}$ is also a correct finite component. Though this information indicates that τ_{PC} is of *finite signature* (see Section 6 below), the quality of the decompiled program does not require this extra accuracy.

5.2   Experimental Results

We have implemented the proposed TbHEm embedding relation within the partial evaluator available in CiaoPP [19] and combined it with the results obtained from the well-typing analyzer in [5]. Table 1 shows the practical benefits that we can obtain in the context of the specialization of interpreters. Each row in the table corresponds to the specialization of a bytecode interpreter w.r.t. different bytecode programs. **Counter** corresponds to the program presented in Fig. 2. We use a set of classical iterative algorithms as additional benchmarks: **Exp**, **Gcd** and **Fib** compute respectively the exponential, greatest-common-divisor and Fibonacci, and **ExpAlt** corresponds to a different implementation of the exponential. The last two benchmarks, **LinSearch** and **BinSearch**, compute respectively the classical linear and binary searches over integer arrays. Therefore, to handle them, we use an extended version of our bytecode interpreter which handles integer array manipulation. Thus, it includes a heap in the state as well as the bytecode instructions required to manipulate arrays. We have experimented as well extending the interpreter with more advanced features such as exception handling, object orientation, etc. We believe that the results obtained are generalizable to interpreters which manipulates numbers in general, and in particular to low-level language interpreters.

For each benchmark, we study the behavior of $\trianglelefteq_T$ w.r.t. $\trianglelefteq$, $\trianglelefteq_{num}$ and $\trianglelefteq_S^*$ by measuring two aspects which are crucial in the specialization of interpreters, the specialization time and the residual program size. Both aspects are directly related to the quality of the decompilation. Then, from left to right, the first two columns, **Name** and **Size**, show the name of the benchmark and the size (in KBytes) of the Prolog representation of the bytecode program. The following 9 columns show specialization times (in seconds) and residual program sizes (in KBytes) for the different strategies $\trianglelefteq$, $\trianglelefteq_{num}$, $\trianglelefteq_S^*$ and $\trianglelefteq_T$. We write "-" when the specialization does not terminate. Note that, in the group of columns corresponding to $\trianglelefteq_T$, we have an additional column T_{wt} which shows the time taken by the well-typing analysis which should be added to the specialization time in order to obtain a proper evaluation of $\trianglelefteq_T$. It should be noted also that the usage of $\trianglelefteq_S^*$ would require a preprocessing time currently not being taken into account which should be no more than the times in T_{wt}. Since we do not have an implementation of $\trianglelefteq_S^*$ the results obtained for it have been obtained using the TbHEm writing by hand the corresponding types. Finally, the last two columns show the gains (in terms of time and size) of the embedding relation $\trianglelefteq_T$ w.r.t. $\trianglelefteq_{num}$ (in column $\mathbf{T/S}_{(\trianglelefteq_{num})}$) and $\trianglelefteq_S^*$ (in column $\mathbf{T/S}_{(\trianglelefteq_S^*)}$). The gain is computed as *Old-Cost/New-Cost*. As we can observe in the table, $\trianglelefteq_T$

Table 1. Measuring the effects of $\trianglelefteq_T$ with the bytecode interpreter

Benchmark		$\trianglelefteq$		$\trianglelefteq_{num}$		$\trianglelefteq_S^*$		$\trianglelefteq_T$			Gains	
Name	Size	Tm	Size	Tm	Size	Tm	Size	T_{wt}	Tm	Size	$T/S_{(\trianglelefteq_{num})}$	$T/S_{(\trianglelefteq_S^*)}$
Counter	0.27	-	-	0.12	1.79	0.60	1.26	0.03	0.09	0.28	1.4/6.3	6.7/4.4
Exp	0.39	0.14	0.50	0.24	5.51	0.14	0.50	0.03	0.14	0.50	1.7/11.0	1.0/1.0
Gcd	0.35	0.13	0.38	0.23	4.80	0.14	0.38	0.03	0.11	0.29	2.2/16.3	1.4/1.3
ExpAlt	0.44	-	-	0.26	6.13	3.75	4.50	0.03	0.13	0.34	2.0/17.8	29.0/13.1
Fib	0.52	-	-	0.49	10.72	0.99	1.41	0.03	0.15	0.51	3.2/21.2	6.6/2.8
LinSearch	0.70	-	-	0.54	13.69	3.99	9.04	0.04	0.25	1.70	2.1/8.1	15.7/5.3
BinSearch	2.00	3.14	9.26	5.05	112.50	3.20	9.26	0.04	1.59	5.51	3.2/20.4	2.0/1.7

guarantees termination and behaves significantly better than $\trianglelefteq_{num}$ and $\trianglelefteq_S^*$ both in time and size. Furthermore, $\trianglelefteq_T$ behaves as well as $\trianglelefteq$ in the examples in which $\trianglelefteq$ terminates, even after adding the additional cost taken by the well-typing analysis. An important observation as regards the gains w.r.t. $\trianglelefteq_S^*$ is that for some benchmarks such gains are large while for others they are almost insignificant. The reason for this lack of improvement is that in the corresponding atoms, the local variables within the state are not instantiated to concrete values almost from the beginning. Therefore, the over-specialization problem of $\trianglelefteq_S^*$ pointed in Sect. 3.3 is not exposed. In fact, note that these cases correspond precisely to the cases where $\trianglelefteq$ terminates (due to the same reason).

6   Type-Based Homeomorphic Embedding in Practice

An important observation is that, in order to take full advantage of TbHEm in practice, it is not always necessary to know the actual type definitions, but only sufficient information for the relations $\preceq_F$ and $\preceq_S$ proposed in Sect. 4.2 to be well defined. In particular it suffices to know whether the infinite component of type rules is (transitively) empty or not. Moreover, it would be desirable to define a condition on types specifying that a type and all the types on which it depends are defined over a finite signature. In this case, we can safely revert to the simpler HEm applied directly to terms of such types. In the following we define such a condition.

Definition 5 (finite signature). *Given a type τ defined by a type rule $\tau \longrightarrow F;\emptyset$ we say that τ is of* finite signature, *denoted* $\mathsf{f\_sig}(\tau)$, *iff* $F = \{f_1(\tau_{11}, \ldots, \tau_{1k_1}), \ldots, f_n(\tau_{n1}, \ldots, \tau_{nk_n})\}$ *and all types* $\tau_{11}, \ldots, \tau_{nk_n}$ *are of finite signature.*

Hence, if a type τ is of *finite signature* the (possibly infinite) set of terms of type τ contains only a finite set of functors. As the following Proposition implies, we can then use $\trianglelefteq$ instead of $\trianglelefteq_T$ when comparing terms in the context of finite signatures.

Proposition 2. *Given two typed terms $t_1:\tau_1$ and $t_2:\tau_2$, if $\mathsf{f\_sig}(\tau_2)$ holds then $t_1:\tau_1 \trianglelefteq_T t_2:\tau_2 \Leftrightarrow t_1 \trianglelefteq t_2$.*

In the following, for every type τ for which $\mathsf{f\_sig}(\tau)$ holds, we simply write $\mathsf{f\_sig}$ instead of the particular type. We now propose an extension to the definition of $\trianglelefteq_T$ to consider $\mathsf{f\_sig}$ types. This is done simply by adding the following rule to Def. 4: *4.* $s\!:\!\tau_1 \trianglelefteq_T t\!:\!\mathsf{f\_sig}$ *if* $s \trianglelefteq t$.

In order to put these ideas into practice it is convenient to also have the type $\mathsf{i\_sig}$ which is assigned to an argument when we cannot guarantee it is of finite signature and we do not have further information available about its type. Note that we are assuming a scenario where infinite signatures can include functors as well as numbers.

Definition 6 ($\mathsf{i\_sig}$). *The type* $\mathsf{i\_sig}$ *is defined by the following type rule:* $\mathsf{i\_sig} \longrightarrow \emptyset; I$ *where* $I = \{f_1(\tau_{11}, \ldots, \tau_{1k_1}), \ldots, f_n(\tau_{n1}, \ldots, \tau_{nk_n}), \ldots\}$ *and* f_i *are all possible functors and all types* $\tau_{11}, \ldots, \tau_{nk_n}$ *are* $\mathsf{i\_sig}$.

Note that since every case of the type rule belongs to the infinite component then $s\!:\!\tau \trianglelefteq_T t\!:\!\mathsf{i\_sig}$ will always hold (as $\preceq_F$ holds for every s, τ and t). Hence, termination is trivially guaranteed for terms of type $\mathsf{i\_sig}$. In practice, in programs with infinite signatures, unless the user (or an automatic analysis) explicitly writes more concrete type declarations, a default *typing* will be assumed such that all predicates p/n of a program have the *predicate signature* $p(\tau_1, \ldots, \tau_n)$ with $\tau_i = \mathsf{i\_sig}$, $(0 \leq i \leq n)$. Then, more concrete declarations are allowed both by declaring particular types and signatures (always preserving the well-typing assumption, see Sect. 4) or by using the special type $\mathsf{f\_sig}$.

Example 2. Consider again the interpreter in our motivating example. Though it is natural to use integer numbers to represent program counters, the set of instructions is finite in any bytecode program. Therefore the PC can be safely declared as $\mathsf{f\_sig}$. Thus we may write the following predicate signature and type definition:

$$\mathsf{execute}(\tau_{st}, \tau_{st}).$$
$$\tau_{st} \longrightarrow \{\mathsf{st}(\mathsf{f\_sig}, \mathsf{i\_sig}, \mathsf{i\_sig})\}; \emptyset.$$

With this type declaration we are able to obtain the same results as in Sect 5.1 in a more efficient way, as we can get rid of the overhead produced by the comparisons checking that the current PC belongs to the finite part of the corresponding type. In addition, the type declaration holds for all input programs, whereas before a separate type inference was needed for each input object program.

Another interesting observation is that the relation $\trianglelefteq_S^*$ may be defined as a particular case of TbHEm by simply declaring the following particular type and assuming that every argument of every predicate is of this type: $\mathsf{s\_symb} \longrightarrow F; I$ where $F = \{f_1(\tau_{11}, \ldots, \tau_{1k_1}), \ldots, f_n(\tau_{n1}, \ldots, \tau_{nk_n})\}$ with $f_1, \ldots, f_k$ being all the functor symbols which explicitly occur in the program text plus initial goal(s) and the types $\tau_{11}, \ldots, \tau_{nk_n}, \ldots$ are $\mathsf{s\_symb}$. I contains the infinite set of all other possible functors, with auxiliary types $\mathsf{i\_sig}$ in all cases.

6.1 Automatic Inference of Finite Signature

If, in a program with builtins, we can use some static analysis which allows us to determine that the type of an argument has a finite signature, we can provide this information to the partial evaluator as an f_sig declaration, without having to specify the exact type. E.g., given a logic program processing numeric values, analyses exist that make over-approximations of the set of values that the program arguments can have. Polyhedral analyses are perhaps the most widely known of these and they have successfully been applied to constraint logic programs [4]. Let us assume for the sake of this discussion that a polyhedral analysis can return, for a given program and goal, an approximation to the set of calls to each n-ary predicate p, in the form: $p(X_1, \ldots, X_n) \leftarrow c(X_1, \ldots, X_n)$, where the expression $c(X_1, \ldots, X_n)$ is a set of linear constraints (describing a possibly not closed polyhedron). From this information it can be determined whether each argument X_i is bounded or not by projecting $c(X_1, \ldots, X_n)$ onto X_i. If it is bounded (from above and below), and it is known that the ith argument takes on integral values, then it can take only a finite set of values and thus can be declared as f_sig.

Example 3. Consider the following clauses defining a procedure for computing an exponential.

```
exp(Base,Exp,Res)      : - exp_(Base,Exp,1,Res).
exp_(_,0,Ac,Ac).
exp_(Base,Exp,Ac,Res) : - Exp > 0, Exp' is Exp-1, Ac' is Ac*Base,
                          exp_(Base,Exp',Ac',Res)
```

Type inference yields the following signature for the predicate exp_/4: exp_ (t24,t24, t24,t24) with the type t24 --> 0; 1; num. A polyhedral analysis of the same program with respect to the goal exp(Base,10,Res) yields the following approximation to the queries to exp_/4: exp_(Base,Exp,Ac,Res) :- Exp > -1, Exp =< 10. Combining this with the inferred type, and assuming that the second argument can take only integer values. the second argument (Exp) can be declared as f_sig, and hence we can revert to HEm and do not abstract away the value of the second argument of exp_/4. This allows maximum specialization to be achieved.

6.2   Experimental Results

We have incorporated the proposed predefined types f_sig and i_sig within our partial evaluator and instrumented TbHEm to properly handle them as proposed above. Table 2 shows the practical benefits that we obtain on a set of numeric programs which we make extensive use of the arithmetic builtin is/2. **exp** and **fib** correspond to the iterative implementations (using accumulators) of the exponential and Fibonacci functions respectively. **vnr** computes a combinatorial function, in this case without accumulators. **list_exp** takes a list of numbers and an exponent and computes a list in which every element is powered to the corresponding exponent (using the predicate exp/3 defined in **exp**) and also computes the length of the list by using an accumulator. Finally, **dfs** performs a depth-first search avoiding state repetitions in a two dimensional space. Predicate **path/4** computes the path and its cost (using an accumulator) given the initial and final states.

Table 2. Measuring the effects of $\trianglelefteq_T$ with numeric programs

Bench	Entry	$\mathbf{T}_{orig}$	$\mathbf{T}_{res\trianglelefteq}$	$\mathbf{T}_{res\trianglelefteq_{num}}$	PE-type	$\mathbf{T}_{res\trianglelefteq_T}$
exp	exp(11,1000,_)	19.60	14.60	19.20	exp_(i_sig,f_sig,i_sig,i_sig)	14.20
	exp(11,_,_)	19.20	-	19.20		19.00
fib	fib(1000,_)	17.20	14.20	16.00	fib_(f_sig,i_sig,i_sig,i_sig)	14.00
	fib(_,_)	16.80	-	16.00		15.60
vnr	vnr(10000,1000,_)	31.80	14.20	32.40	vnr(i_sig,f_sig,i_sig)	14.00
	vnr(10000,_,_)	30.00	-	30.00		32.20
dfs	path((1,1),(4,4),_,_)	49.79	15.60	43.39	path_(f_sig,f_sig,i_sig,i_sig,...)	15.80
	path(_,_,_,_)	43.39	-	39.79		42.19
list_exp	lel([1,...,40|_],200,_,_)	32.40	-	32.40	lel_(i_sig,i_sig,i_sig,i_sig)	14.40
	lel(_,200,_,_)	31.80	-	31.60		26.80

In this case, in order to measure the quality of the specialization we compare the execution times of the specialized programs ($\mathbf{T}_{res}$) with the execution times of the original programs ($\mathbf{T}_{orig}$) for sufficiently large inputs. From left to right, the first two columns, **Bench** and **Entry**, show respectively the name of the benchmark and the entry for which the program will be specialized. Then, for each pair benchmark-entry, we show the execution times (in seconds) of the original programs in $\mathbf{T}_{orig}$ and of the corresponding residual programs, by using the three relations $\mathbf{T}_{res\trianglelefteq}$, $\mathbf{T}_{res\trianglelefteq_{num}}$ and $\mathbf{T}_{res\trianglelefteq_T}$. We also show the particular type definition which has been used to guide $\trianglelefteq_T$. Note that in this case we do not consider $\trianglelefteq_S^*$ since it does not produce any significant improvement w.r.t. $\trianglelefteq_{num}$ (constants do not play any role in the involved terms). All times have been computed as the arithmetic means of five runs. For each run, in order to accurately compare the involved programs we run five consecutive times the call findall(_, Goal, _). The particular goals used for measuring the execution times have been chosen to match the entries proposed for each benchmark. As it can be seen, $\trianglelefteq_T$ guarantees termination and outperforms significantly $\trianglelefteq_{num}$. As expected, $\trianglelefteq$ exposes termination problems for some entries as showed in column $\mathbf{T}_{res\trianglelefteq}$. In the examples in which $\trianglelefteq$ terminates, $\trianglelefteq_T$ behaves as well as $\trianglelefteq$. In some examples, no improvements are obtained in the residual programs. This is explained by the fact that the corresponding entries do not provide static information to be used in the specialization. In these examples, it is usual to observe the (unnecessary) over-aggressive nature of $\trianglelefteq$ (even endangering termination in presence of infinite signatures) while, we can see, that the particular type declarations can prevent such undesired behavior in $\trianglelefteq_T$. An interesting observation is that, although many of the examples in this table may be handled in offline PE (by providing the corresponding annotations), there are cases, as **dfs**, where it is not possible to obtain a ranking function for the key arguments. Luckily, we may infer boundedness which is a sufficient condition to effectively use our TbHEm.

7 Discussion and Related Work

Guaranteeing termination is essential in a number of tasks which have to deal with possibly infinite computations. These tasks include PE, abstract model checking, rewriting, etc. Broadly speaking, guaranteeing termination can be tackled in an *offline* or an *online* fashion. The main difference between these two perspectives is that in offline termination we aim at statically determining termination. This means that we do not have the concrete values of arguments at each point of the computation but rather just *abstractions* of them. Traditionally, these abstractions refer to the *size* of values under some measure such as list length, term size, numeric value for natural numbers, etc. In contrast, in online termination, we aim at dynamically guaranteeing termination by supervising the computation in such a way that it is not allowed to proceed as soon as we can no longer guarantee termination. The main advantage of the offline approach is that if we can prove termination statically, there is no longer any need to supervise the computation for termination, which results in important performance gains. However, the online approach is potentially more precise, since we have the concrete values at hand. In offline PE, the problem of termination of local unfolding has been tackled by annotating arguments as "bounded static". The work of Glenstrup and Jones [7] is the main reference, though the idea of bounded static variation goes back a long way. To detect bounded static arguments it is necessary to prove some decrease in well-founded ordering (e.g. using size-change techniques). Quasi-termination is weaker than standard termination but still quite hard to prove. Recent work on this has been done by Vidal [21] and by Glenstrup and Jones [7]. On the other hand, ensuring termination in online PE is easier because we can use "dynamic" termination detection based on supervisors of the computations such as for example embeddings. This means that we do not need any well-founded orderings but only well-quasi-orderings. In effect, in our technique it is only necessary to show boundedness of an argument's values instead of decrease.

In the context of online PE, we have compared TbHEm with the extension of the embedding relation to deal with infinite signatures explained in [11], known as *extended embedding* with static symbols in Sect. 3.3, which is based on a distinction between the different static symbols which occur in the program. As we have shown in the paper, the main advantage of TbHEm is that it achieves a more refined treatment, as it allows treating different arguments in a different way depending on their particular types, which can be automatically inferred by semantic-based analysis, while previous proposals are purely syntactic. Additionally, we have shown that TbHEm can be applied to the specialization of numeric programs, by means of finite signature annotations, in which static constants do not play any role.

Acknowledgments. The authors would like to thank the anonymous referees for their useful comments. This work was funded in part by the Information Society Technologies program of the European Commission, Future and Emerging Technologies under the IST-15905 *MOBIUS* project, by the Danish Natural

Science Research Council under the FNU-272-06-0574 *SAFT* project, by the Spanish Ministry of Education under the TIN-2005-09207 *MERIT* project, and by the Madrid Regional Government under the S-0505/TIC/0407 *PROMESAS* project.

References

1. Albert, E., Gómez-Zamalloa, M., Hubert, L., Puebla, G.: Verification of Java Bytecode Using Analysis and Transformation of Logic Programs. In: Hanus, M. (ed.) PADL 2007. LNCS, vol. 4354, pp. 124–139. Springer, Heidelberg (2007)
2. Albert, E., Hanus, M., Vidal, G.: A practical partial evaluation scheme for multi-paradigm declarative languages. Journal of Functional and Logic Programming 2002(1) (2002)
3. Albert, E., Puebla, G., Gallagher, J.: Non-leftmost Unfolding in Partial Evaluation of Logic Programs with Impure Predicates. In: Hill, P.M. (ed.) LOPSTR 2005. LNCS, vol. 3901, pp. 115–132. Springer, Heidelberg (2006)
4. Benoy, F., King, A.: Inferring argument size relationships with CLP(R). In: Gallagher, J.P. (ed.) LOPSTR 1996. LNCS, vol. 1207, pp. 204–223. Springer, Heidelberg (1996)
5. Bruynooghe, M., Gallagher, J.P., Van Humbeeck, W.: Inference of Well-Typings for Logic Programs with Application to Termination Analysis. In: Hankin, C., Siveroni, I. (eds.) SAS 2005. LNCS, vol. 3672, pp. 35–51. Springer, Heidelberg (2005)
6. Dershowitz, N., Jouannaud, J.-P.: Rewrite systems. In: van Leeuwen, J. (ed.) Handbook of Theoretical Computer Science, Vol. B, pp. 243–320. Elsevier, Amsterdam (1990)
7. Glenstrup, A.J., Jones, N.D.: Termination analysis and specialization-point insertion in offline partial evaluation. ACM Trans. Program. Lang. Syst. 27(6), 1147–1215 (2005)
8. Hill, P.M., Topor, R.W.: A semantics for typed logic programs. In: Pfenning, F. (ed.) Types in Logic Programming, pp. 1–62. MIT Press, Cambridge (1992)
9. Jones, N.D., Gomard, C.K., Sestoft, P.: Partial Evaluation and Automatic Program Generation. Prentice Hall, New York (1993)
10. Kruskal, J.B.: Well-quasi-ordering, the tree theorem, and Vazsonyi's conjecture. Transactions of the American Mathematical Society 95, 210–225 (1960)
11. Leuschel, M.A.: Homeomorphic Embedding for Online Termination of Symbolic Methods. In: Mogensen, T.Æ., Schmidt, D.A., Sudborough, I.H. (eds.) The Essence of Computation. LNCS, vol. 2566, pp. 379–403. Springer, Heidelberg (2002)
12. Leuschel, M., Bruynooghe, M.: Logic program specialisation through partial deduction: Control issues. Theory and Practice of Logic Programming 2(4&5), 461–515 (2002)
13. Leuschel, M., Martens, B., De Schreye, D.: Controlling Generalisation and Polyvariance in Partial Deduction of Normal Logic Programs. ACM Transactions on Programming Languages and Systems 20(1), 208–258 (1998)
14. Leuschel, M.: On the power of homeomorphic embedding for online termination. In: Levi, G. (ed.) SAS 1998. LNCS, vol. 1503, pp. 230–245. Springer, Heidelberg (1998)
15. Lloyd, J.W., Shepherdson, J.C.: Partial evaluation in logic programming. The Journal of Logic Programming 11, 217–242 (1991)

16. Lloyd, J.W.: Foundations of Logic Programming. Springer, Heidelberg (1987) (second, extended edition)
17. Mycroft, A., O'Keefe, R.A.: A polymorphic type system for Prolog. Artif. Intell. 23(3), 295–307 (1984)
18. Puebla, G., Albert, E., Hermenegildo, M.: Efficient Local Unfolding with Ancestor Stacks for Full Prolog. In: Etalle, S. (ed.) LOPSTR 2004. LNCS, vol. 3573, pp. 149–165. Springer, Heidelberg (2005)
19. Puebla, G., Albert, E., Hermenegildo, M.: Abstract Interpretation with Specialized Definitions. In: Yi, K. (ed.) SAS 2006. LNCS, vol. 4134, pp. 107–126. Springer, Heidelberg (2006)
20. Somogyi, Z., Henderson, F., Conway, T.: The Execution Algorithm of Mercury: an Efficient Purely Declarative Logic Programming Language. JLP 3 (October 1996)
21. Vidal, G.: Quasi-Terminating Logic Programs for Ensuring the Termination of Partial Evaluation. In: Proc. of the ACM SIGPLAN 2007 Workshop on Partial Evaluation and Program Manipulation (PEPM 2007), pp. 51–60. ACM Press, New York (2007)

Towards a Normal Form for Mercury Programs

François Degrave and Wim Vanhoof

University of Namur,
Faculty of Computer Science,
Rue Grangagnage 21, B-5000 Namur, Belgium
{fde,wva}@info.fundp.ac.be

Abstract. In this work we define a program transformation that normalises a Mercury program by reordering clauses, body goals, and predicate arguments. The transformation, which preserves the well-modedness and determinism characteristics of the program, aims at reducing the complexity of performing a search for duplicated or similar code fragments between programs. In previous work, we have defined an analysis that searches for such duplicated functionality basically by pairwise comparing atoms and goals. While feasible in theory, the number of permutations to perform during the search renders it hard if not impossible to use in practice. We conjecture that the transformation to normal form, defined in this work, allows to substantially reduce the number of permutations, and hence the complexity of the search.

1 Introduction and Motivation

The problem of deciding whether two code fragments are equivalent, in the sense that they implement the same functionality, is well-known to be undecidable. Nevertheless, there seems to be an interest in developing analyses that are capable to detect such equivalence under particular circumstances and within a certain error margin [3,1,12]. Applications can be found in plagiarism detection and tools for program refactoring. Work in this area can be based on parametrised string matching, an example being the MOSS system [8], or perform a more involved analysis on a graph representation of a program [2,13]. Most of these latter works, including the more recent [11], concentrate on finding behavioral *differences* between strongly related programs and are often limited to (subsets of) imperative programs.

In recent work [10], we have studied the conditions under which two (fragments of) logic programs can be considered equivalent. The main motivation of that and the current work is to develop an analysis capable of detecting program fragments that are susceptible for refactoring, aiming in particular to the removal of duplicated code or to the generalisation of two related predicates into a new (higher-order) one. The basic idea is as follows: two code fragments (be they goals, clauses or complete predicate definitions) are equivalent if they are *isomorphic* in the sense that one can be considered to be a renaming of the other

King, A. (Ed.): LOPSTR 2007, LNCS 4915, pp. 43–58, 2008.

modulo a permutation of the body goals and the arguments of the predicate. Take for example the definitions of app1 and conc1 below:

```
app1([],Y,Y).
app1([Xe|Xs],Y,[XN|Zs]):- XN is Xe + 1, app1(Xs,Y,Zs).

conc1(A,[],A).
conc1([NB|As],[Be|Bs],C):- conc1(As,Bs,C), NB is Be + 1.
```

Both definitions basically implement the same ternary relation in which one argument is the result of concatenating both other arguments and incrementing each element by one. This can easily be deduced from the source code, since the definition of conc1 can be obtained from that of app1 by variable renaming, goal reordering and a permutation of the argument positions. Note that our notion of equivalence is limited to the syntactical equivalence of predicates. Other characteristics like computational complexity etc. are not taken into account. As a second example, let us consider two predicates that do *not* implement the same relation but that nevertheless share a common functionality.

```
rev_all([],[]).
rev_all([X|Xs],[Y|Ys]):- reverse(X,Y), rev_all(Xs,Ys).

add_and_square([],[]).
add_and_square([X|Xs],[Y|Ys]):- N=X+X, Y=N*N, add_and_square(Xs,Ys).
```

The definitions above implement two different relations: rev_all reverses all the elements of an input list, while add_and_square transforms each element x of an input list into $4x^2$. They nevertheless have a common core which consists of traversing a list and transforming each of its elements. As such, both definitions can be generalised into a single new definition (namely the map/3 predicate):

```
map([],_,[]).
map([X|Xs],P,[Y|Ys]):- P(X,Y), map(Xs,Ys).
```

and calls to rev_all and add_and_square can be replaced by calls to map with the second argument instantiated to, respectively, reverse and a lambda expression pred(X::in,Y::out) is det :- N=X+X,Y=N*N (in Mercury syntax).

In [10] we have defined an analysis that basically searches for isomorphisms between each possible pair of subgoals in a given program. As outlined above, two goals are isomorphic if they are syntactically identical modulo a renaming and a permutation of the atoms involved. While the analysis *can* be used to search for duplication within two predicate definitions, its complexity – mainly due to the fact that one needs to consider every possible permutation of the predicate's body atoms – renders it hard if not impossible to use in practice.

The work we report on in this paper is motivated by the desire to port the concepts and the analysis of [10] to the functional/logic programming language Mercury while, at the same time, rendering such an analysis more practical. The basic idea is to define a program transformation that reorders clauses, body atoms and predicate arguments in a *unique* and predefined way such that 1) the operational characteristics (well-modedness and determinism) of the program remain unchanged, but 2) the number of permutations to perform during predicate comparison is substantially reduced.

2 Mercury Preliminaries

Mercury [9] is a strongly typed and moded functional/logic programming language. Although it is an expressive and syntactically rich language, its core syntax can be defined as follows:

Definition 1 (Core Mercury syntax)

$$Atom \quad ::= Y = X \mid Y = f(\overline{X}) \mid Y = p(\overline{X}) \mid Z = Y(\overline{X}) \mid p(\overline{X}) \mid Y(\overline{X}) \mid$$
$$true \mid fail$$
$$Goal \quad ::= A \mid (G_1, \ldots, G_n) \mid (G_1; \ldots; G_n) \mid not(G) \mid if(G_1, G_2, G_3) \mid$$
$$Clause ::= p(\overline{X}) :\text{-} \ G.$$

where $A \in Atom$, G, $G_i(\forall i) \in Goal$, and X, Y, Z represent variables, $\overline{X}$ a sequence of distinct variables, and f and p respectively a functor and predicate symbol.

The syntax defined in Definition 1 is derived from the so-called superhomogeneous form, which is an intermediate form used by the Mercury compiler.[1] It defines a program as a set of predicate definitions, with each predicate definition consisting of a set of clauses. The arguments in the head of each clause and in predicate calls in the body are all distinct variables. Explicit unifications are generated for these variables in the body, and complex unifications are broken down into several simpler ones. Among these unifications we differ between term construction and matching ($X = Y$ and $X = f(\overline{Y})$) on the one hand and closure construction ($Y = p(\overline{X})$ and $Z = Y(\overline{X})$) on the other. Other goals include first-order and higher-order predicate calls ($p(\overline{X})$ and $Y(\overline{X})$ respectively), conjunction, disjunction, negation, if-then-else and the special goals *true* and *fail*.

The full Mercury language contains a number of additional constructs, such as function definitions, record syntax, state variables, DCG notation, etc. [5]. However, each of these constructions can be translated into the above syntax by introducing new predicates, adding arguments to existing predicates and introducing new unifications [5]. Note that these transformations are in principle reversible.

Example 1. Let us reconsider the example from above, this time transformed to core syntax:

```
app1(X,Y,Z):- X=[], Z=Y.
app1(X,Y,Z):- E=1, Z=[Xn|Zs], X=[Xe|Xs], Xn=(Xe + E), app1(Xs,Y,Zs).

conc1(A,B,C):- B=[], A=C.
conc1(A,B,C):- B=[Be|Bs], E=1, Bn=(Be + E), conc1(As,Bs,C), A=[Bn|As].
```

---

[1] The most important difference being that we still allow for predicates to be defined by multiple clauses rather than by a single clause.

From a programmer's point of view, the order in which the individual goals in a conjunction are written is of no importance. While this is one of the main characteristics that makes the language more declarative than other (logic) programming languages, it clearly renders the search for code isomorphisms in the sense outlined above even more dependent on the need to consider all permutations of the goals within a conjunction.

The fact that Mercury is a strongly moded language provides us with a starting point for our transformation into normal form. In Mercury, each predicate has an associated mode declaration[2] that classifies each argument as either input to the call, denoted by **in** (the argument is a ground term before and after the call) or output by the call which is denoted by **out** (the argument is a free variable that will be instantiated to a ground term at the end of the call). Given a predicate's mode declaration it is possible to derive how the instantiation of each variable changes over the execution of each individual goal in the predicate's body. In what follows we will use **in**(G) and **out**(G) to denote, for a goal G, the set of its input, respectively output variables. As such **in**(G) refers to the variables whose values are *consumed* by the goal G, whereas **out**(G) refers to the variables whose values are *produced* by G. When appropriate, we will write, for a goal G, **in**(G) and **out**(G) to denote the *sequence* of input, respectively output, variables in the order they are occurring in the goal G. For more details about modes and mode analysis in Mercury, we refer to [7].

Example 2. If we consider the `app1` predicate (see Example 1) for the mode `app1(in,in,out)` – reflecting the fact that the two first arguments are considered input whereas the third is considered output – we have:

G	in(G)	out(G)	G	in(G)	out(G)
X = []	$\{X\}$	$\emptyset$	Xn = Xe + E	$\{Xe, E\}$	$\{Xn\}$
Z = Y	$\{Y\}$	$\{Z\}$	app1(Xs,Y,Zs)	$\{Xs, Y\}$	$\{Zs\}$
X = [Xe|Xs]	$\{X\}$	$\{Xe, Xs\}$	Z = [Xn|Zs]	$\{Xn, Zs\}$	$\{Z\}$
E = 1	$\emptyset$	$\{E\}$			

In order to be accepted by the compiler, Mercury programs must be *well-moded*. Intuitively, this means that the goals in a predicate's body can be rearranged in such a way that values are produced before they are consumed when the predicate is executed by a left-to-right selection rule [6]. In case of a conjunction, the well-modedness constraint could be formalized as follows:

Definition 2. *A conjunction* $(G_1, ..., G_n)$ *verifies the well-modedness constraint if*

$$\forall 1 \leq i \leq n, \forall k > i : \mathbf{in}(G_i) \cap \mathbf{out}(G_k) = \emptyset.$$

Furthermore, we say that a conjunction is well-moded *if there exists a reordering of its goals that verifies the well-modedness constraint.*

---

[2] In general, a predicate may have more than one mode declaration, but these can easily be converted into separate predicate (or, in Mercury terminology, *procedure* definitions.

Example 3. When considering the mode `app1(in,in,out)`, the second disjunct of the `app1` definition in Example 1 does not verify the well-modedness constraint since the goal `Z=[Xn|Zs]` consumes variables `Xn` and `Zs`, which are both produced by goals further to the right in the conjunction. However, the following reordering *does*:

```
app1(X,Y,Z):- X=[Xe|Xs], E=1, Xn=(Xe + E), app1(Xs,Y,Zs), Z=[Xn|Zs].
```

It is the task of the compiler to rearrange conjunctions in a program such that they verify the well-modedness constraint, thanks to the information provided by the mode analyser.

In what follows we will limit ourselves to well-moded programs. Note however that well-modedness in itself does not suffice to obtain a *unique* reordering. In the example above one could, e.g. switch the atoms `XN=(Xe + E)` and `app1(Xs,Y,Zs)` while the conjunction would remain well-moded. Consequently, well-modedness can be used as a starting point for our normalization, but it needs to be further constrained in order to obtain a unique reordering.

3   Transformation to Normal Form

As a first step in our transformation to normal form, we will assume that programs are converted to disjunctive normal form, in which every clause body is considered to be a conjunction of literals. That is, we restrict the syntax of goals to

$$Goal \quad ::= (L_1, \ldots, L_n)$$
$$Literal := A \mid not(A)$$

where A denotes an atom $\in$ *Atom*, and $L_1, \ldots, L_n$ denote literals in *Literal*. Note that this transformation can easily be accomplished by flattening conjunctions and disjunctions, replacing if-then-else goals by disjunctions and replacing explicit disjunctions and non-atomic goals within a negation by calls to newly generated predicates.

As a second step in the transformation, we redistribute the atoms of each clause body into a sequential structure, based on a reinforcement of the well-modedness constraint.

Definition 3. *We define a* proper rearrangement *of a conjunction* $L_1, \ldots, L_n$ *to be a sequence of multisets* $\langle S_1, \ldots, S_k \rangle$ *such that*

$$\bigcup_{i \in \{1, \ldots, k\}} S_i = \{L_1, \ldots, L_n\}$$

and such that $\forall S_i$ *we have*

1. $\forall L, L' \in S_i : \mathbf{in}(L) \cap \mathbf{out}(L') = \emptyset.$
2. $\forall L \in S_i, \forall L' \in S_k$ *for* $k > i : \mathbf{in}(L) \cap \mathbf{out}(L') = \emptyset.$
3. $\forall L \in S_i, \ i > 1 : \exists L' \in S_{i-1} : \mathbf{in}(L) \cap \mathbf{out}(L') \neq \emptyset.$

Intuitively, a conjunction is properly arranged if its components can be partitioned into a sequence of sets of goals such that: (1) there are no dataflow dependencies between the goals in a single set; (2) a goal belonging to a set S_i does not consume values that are produced by a goal belonging to a set S_k that is placed *after* S_i in the sequence; and (3) each goal in a set S_i consumes at least one value that was produced by a goal placed in the previous set S_{i-1}. There are two main points of difference between our notion of a proper arrangement and that of well-modedness. First, we impose an order between *sets* of independent goals and, secondly and more importantly, consumers are pushed forward in the sequence as much as possible.

Example 4. Consider the definition of app1 of Example 1. We have that

$$\langle\{X = [], Z = Y\}\rangle$$

is a proper rearrangement of the body of the first clause, whereas

$$\langle\{X = [Xe|Xs], E = 1\}, \{XN = (Xe + E), app1(Xs, Y, Zs)\}, \{Z = [XN|Zs]\}\rangle$$

is a proper rearrangement of the body of the second clause.

Note that there always exists a proper rearrangement of a well-moded conjunction. Also note that the required partitioning into sets is unique. This observation is captured formally by the following result:

Theorem 1. *Let $p(\overline{X}) \leftarrow L_1, \ldots, L_m$ be a clause. Then there exists exactly one proper rearrangement of the conjunction $L_1, \ldots, L_m$.*

Proof. We split the proof in two parts.

1. We will first proof that there exists a proper rearrangement of the clause body $L_1, \ldots, L_m$. The proof is by construction. Let us define

$$S_1 = \{L \mid \mathbf{in}(L) \subseteq \{\overline{X}\}\}$$

and, for $j > 1$,

$$S_j = \{L \mid \mathbf{in}(L) \subseteq \{\overline{X}\} \cup \bigcup_{i=1}^{j-1} \mathbf{out}(S_i)\} \setminus \bigcup_{i=1}^{j-1} S_i.$$

These sets are well defined. Indeed:
   (a) If the clause body is not empty ($m \neq 0$), then $S_1 \neq \emptyset$. Indeed, since the clause is well-moded, we have that if the clause body is not empty, then it should contain at least one literal that either does not consume any values, or that consumes only values provided as argument to the predicate.
   (b) Furthermore, for $k > 1$, we have that if $\bigcup_{i=1}^{k-1} S_i \neq \{L_1, ..., L_m\}$, then $S_k \neq \emptyset$. Again, due to well-modedness, among the atoms that are not in $\bigcup_{i=1}^{k-1} S_i$, there is at least one that consumes only values produced before.

From (1) and (2) we can conclude that there exists a finite sequence of non-empty sets $S_1, \ldots, S_n$ (for some $n \geq 1$) such that $\bigcup_{i=1}^{n} S_i = \{L_1, \ldots, L_m\}$. Moreover, by construction we have that

(a) $\forall L, L' \in S_i : \mathbf{in}(L) \cap \mathbf{out}(L') = \emptyset$. It is obviously the case, since a set is constructed by collecting the goals consuming *only* values produced in the sets already constructed.

(b) $\forall L \in S_i, \forall L' \in S_k$ for $k > i : \mathbf{in}(L) \cap \mathbf{out}(L') = \emptyset$. This is obvious for the same reason as 1a.

(c) $\forall L \in S_j, j > 1 \; \exists L' \in S_{j-1} : \mathbf{in}(L) \cap \mathbf{out}(L') \neq \emptyset$. Indeed, if that was not the case, L would have been integrated into S_{j-1} instead of S_j

2. We will now prove uniqueness of the proper rearrangement. The proof is by contradiction. Let us assume that for a given clause, there exists two different proper rearrangements of the clause body, $PA_1 = Seq_1 = \langle S_1, \ldots, S_n \rangle$, and $PA_2 = \langle S'_1, \ldots, S'_m \rangle$. Since $PA_1 \neq PA_2$, we have that $\exists 1 \leq i \leq min\{m, n\}$, $S_i \neq S'_i$ and $S_j = S'_j$, $\forall j < i$. In other words, we take S_i to be the first subset different from S'_i.

Since $S_i \neq S'_i$, there exists $L \in S'_i$ such that $L \notin S_i$ (or the other way round, in what case the proof is similar). Since PA_1 and PA_2 are proper rearrangements of the same conjunction, the literal L must also occur in PA_1, in a set to the right of $S_i : \exists k > i$ such that $L \in S_k$.

The fact that the literal L belongs to different sets in both proper rearrangements leads to a contradiction. Since $L \in S_k$, we have that $\exists L' \in S_{k-1}$, $\mathbf{in}(L) \cap \mathbf{out}(L') \neq \emptyset$ (in other words, L consumes a value produced by L', which is the second condition for a proper rearrangement). The literal L' necessarily appears in PA_2 as well, in a set S'_k with $k \geq i$, since, again, $S_j = S'_j$, $\forall j < i$. There are two possibilities:

(a) Either $k = i$. In that case we have that $L' \in S'_i$ and $L \in S'_i$ which contradicts the fact that PA_2 is a proper rearrangement (first condition: there should be no dataflow dependencies between literals in the same set).

(b) Or $k > i$, but in that case the literal $L \in S'_i$ consumes a value produced by a literal in L' in a later set ($L' \in S'_k$ with $k > i$) which contradicts the second condition of a proper rearrangement. $\square$

The above result is important in our setting of constructing a normal form. Intuitively, the fact that a clause has a unique proper rearrangement implies that if two clauses are isomorphic (always in the sense that one being a renaming of the other modulo a permutation of its body literals), then they have the *same* proper rearrangements (modulo renaming).

Example 5. Reconsider the definition of `conc1` from Example 1. One can easily verify that

$$\langle \{B = [], A = C\} \rangle$$

is a proper rearrangement of the body of the first clause, whereas

$$\langle \{B = [Be|Bs], E = 1\}, \{Bn = (Be + E), conc1(As, Bs, C)\}, \{A = [Bn|As]\} \rangle$$

is a proper rearrangement of the body of the second clause.

When considering Examples 4 and 5, it is clear that for verifying whether two predicates implement the same relation, the search for isomorphisms can be limited to a pairwise comparison of the corresponding sets of goals in the predicate's proper rearrangements.

As such our notion of proper rearrangement seems a good starting point for a transformation that aims at rearranging predicate definitions in a unique way. All that remains, is to impose an order on the goals within the individual sets of a proper rearrangement. Since these goals share no dataflow dependencies, we can use any order without influencing well-modedness. We choose lexicographic ordering on goals in tree representation. Formally:

Definition 4. *Given a literal L, we define its tree representation, denoted $tr(L)$ as a tree over strings defined as follows:*

$$tr(not(L)) = (not, tr(L))$$
$$tr(Y = X) = (unifv, \underline{\text{in}}(Y = X)) \qquad tr(true) = (true)$$
$$tr(Y = f(\overline{X})) = (unifc, f, \underline{\text{in}}(Y = f(\overline{X}))) \qquad tr(fail) = (fail)$$
$$tr(Y = p(\overline{X})) = (closc, p, \underline{\text{in}}(Y = p(\overline{X}))) \qquad tr(p(\overline{X})) = (call, p, \underline{\text{in}}(p(\overline{X})))$$
$$tr(Z = Y(\overline{X})) = (closv, \underline{\text{in}}(Z = Y(\overline{X}))) \qquad tr(Y(\overline{X})) = (hocall, Y, \underline{\text{in}}(Y(\overline{X})))$$

Given two literals L and L', we will write $L < L'$ if and only if $tr(L) <_l tr(L')$ where $<_l$ represents the lexicographic ordering over trees of strings.

Example 6. Reconsider the `app1` predicate from Example 1 with the mode information as in Example 2. We have $tr(X = []) = (unifc, [], X)$ and $tr(Z = Y) = (unifv, Y)$. Consequently, we have $X = [] < Z = Y$. Likewise, one can easily verify that we have $X = [Xe|Xs] < E = 1$ and $app1(Xs, Y, Zs) < Xn = (Xe + E)$.

The main idea of imposing an order on the literals of a conjunction, is to be able to limit the search for isomorphisms between two conjunctions to a pairwise comparison of the corresponding literals. As such, when verifying whether two predicates implement the same relation (by verifying whether the two definitions are isomorphic), there would be no more need to consider all permutations of the body atoms since *if* the two predicate definitions are isomorphic, they should have the *same* normal form (modulo a renaming of the variables). In order to have this characteristic, the order relation $<$ defined on the literals must be total and hence it must take the variables into account. However, since the variable names used in different predicate definitions are usually unrelated, using them might make that the order we get is not the order wanted, as illustrated by the following example.

Example 7. Consider the two conjunctions:

$C_1 \equiv A = a, B = b, C = f(A), D = f(B)$
$C_2 \equiv X = b, Y = a, R = f(X), S = f(Y)$

and suppose that the associated mode information is such that the first half of C_1 produces the values for A and B that are consumed in the second half of C_1. Likewise, we assume that the values Y and X are produced in the first half of C_2 and consumed in its second half. In other words, all variables are output variables and the clauses' proper rearrangements are as follows:

$$PA_1 = \langle\{\text{A = a,B = b}\}, \{\text{C = f(A),D = f(B)}\}\rangle$$
$$PA_2 = \langle\{\text{X = b,Y = a}\}, \{\text{R = f(X),S = f(Y)}\}\rangle$$

When we use the order relation $<$ defined above to order the individual atoms in each set of the proper rearrangements, we obtain

$C_1' \equiv \text{A = a, B = b, C = f(A), D = f(B)}$
$C_2' \equiv \text{Y = a, X = b, R = f(X), S = f(Y)}$

Even-though the two clauses *are* isomorphic, there does not exist a renaming ρ such that $C_1'\rho = C_2'$. The problem is that the last two literals of C_2' are in the wrong order with respect to the order chosen for C_1' due to choice of the variable names.

The example above suggests that rather than basing the order relation on the variable names chosen by the programmer, it would be better to rename the variables in each clause in a consistent way reflecting the data flow within the clause. This is precisely what our transformation to normal form will do. Before we can define the transformation itself, we need one more concept though.

Definition 5. *Let p/n be a predicate defined in the program. An argument permutation for p/n is a bijection over $\{1, \ldots, n\}$. For an argument permutation π, we define the result of permuting by π the arguments of a call $p(X_1, \ldots, X_n)$ as the call $p(X_{\pi^{-1}(1)}, \ldots, X_{\pi^{-1}(n)})$.*

Example 8. The permutation $\pi = \{(1,3),(2,1),(3,2)\}$ is an argument permutation for conc1. The result of permuting the arguments of a call conc1(X_1, X_2, X_3) by π is conc1(X_2, X_3, X_1).

We will use the notion of an argument permutation to rearrange the arguments of each predicate in such a way that the arguments are regrouped by their mode and type. For the types, we assume an ordering $<_\tau$ that is defined on all types occurring in the program that is being normalized.

Definition 6. *Let π be an argument permutation for a predicate p/n. We call π suitable if the following conditions hold: let $p(X_{\pi_1}, \ldots, X_{\pi_n})$ denote the result of permuting by π the arguments in a call $c \equiv p(X_1, \ldots, X_n)$, then*

1. $\exists k \geq 0$ *such that* $\{X_{\pi_1}, \ldots, X_{\pi_k}\} = \mathbf{in}(c)$ *and* $\{X_{\pi_{k+1}}, \ldots, X_{\pi_n}\} = \mathbf{out}(c)$
2. *if we denote by τ_i the type of variable X_i in the call, then $\forall 1 \leq i, j \leq k$ and $\forall k + 1 \leq i, j \leq n$, if $\pi_i < \pi_j$ then $\tau_{\pi_i} <_\tau \tau_{\pi_j}$.*

In other words, an argument permutation is suitable if it places all input arguments in front of the output arguments, and if the input, respectively output, arguments are ordered according to a given ordering on their types.

It is easy to see that the following proposition holds:

Proposition 1. *Let p/n be a predicate; then there exists at least one suitable argument permutation π – as described in Definition 6 – for this predicate.*

Note that the ordering on the predicate arguments defined by a suitable argument permutation is not necessarily unique, if there are multiple arguments having the same type and mode.

Example 9. Let us consider the type and mode declarations for the predicates app1 and conc1 defined in Example 1:

```
:- pred app1(list(int),list(int),list(int)).
:- mode app1(in,in,out) is det.

:- pred conc1(list(int),list(int),list(int)).
:- mode conc1(out,in,in) is det.
```

The argument permutation π given in example 8 is a suitable argument permutation for the conc1 predicate. The argument permutation $\pi' = \{(1,3),(2,2),(3,1)\}$ is also a suitable argument permutation for conc1. The identity function and the permutation $\{(1,2),(2,1),(3,3)\}$ are suitable argument permutations for app1.

We are now in a position to define our transformation to normal form. We use the following notation: for a clause c, we use $head(c)$ and $body(c)$ to denote, respectively the head atom and body goal of the clause. If S represents a set of literals and ρ a renaming, then $S\rho$ represents the set of literals obtained by renaming every literal in S by ρ. For a renaming ρ, we represents by $codom(\rho)$ the co-domain of ρ, i.e. $\{V \mid X/V \in \rho\}$. During the transformation, we use a special kind of renaming ρ, in which $codom(\rho)$ is a set of variables of the form V_i for subsequent values of i and V a fresh variable symbol.

Definition 7 (transformation to normal form). *Let p/n be a predicate and π a suitable argument permutation for p. The normal form of p w.r.t. π is obtained by repeatedly applying the following transformation to each clause in the definition of p.*

For a clause c, let $h = p(X_{\pi_1}, \ldots, X_{\pi_n})$ denote the result of permuting $head(c)$ by π and let $\langle S_1, \ldots, S_m \rangle$ denote the proper rearrangement of $body(c)$ in which every recursive call of the form $p(Y_1, \ldots, Y_n)$ is replaced by the atom $rec(Y_{\pi_1}, \ldots, Y_{\pi_n})$.[3] The clause c is transformed into a clause

$$p(X_{\pi_1}, \ldots, X_{\pi_n}) \leftarrow C_1, \ldots, C_m$$

where (for $1 \leq i \leq m$) C_i is a conjunction of literals obtained from S_i in the following way:

$$(C_i, \rho_i) \leftarrow \textbf{reorder}(S_i, \rho_{i-1})$$

where

1. *ρ_0 is a variable renaming for the input arguments of the clause, that is if $\underline{in}(h) = \langle X_{\pi_1}, \ldots, X_{\pi_k} \rangle$ then*

$$\rho_0 = \{X_{\pi_1}/V_1, \ldots, X_{\pi_k}/V_k\}.$$

---

[3] We use rec to denote a special name, not used in the program being normalized.

2. *Given a set of literals S and a renaming ρ, the function* **reorder** *is defined as follows:*

$$\textbf{reorder}(S, \rho) = (C\sigma, \rho \cup \sigma)$$

where the conjunction C is obtained by ordering the literals in $S\rho$ by $<_l$ and if $codom(\rho) = \{V_1, \ldots, V_i\}$ then

$$\sigma = \{O_1/V_{i+1}, \ldots, O_l/V_{i+l}\}$$

for $\langle O_1, \ldots, O_l \rangle = \underline{\textbf{out}}(C)$.

Note that the transformation to normal form is such that a unique order is imposed on the body literals of each clause, first by computing the proper rearrangement of the body, and then imposing the lexicographic ordering on the literals in each set of the rearrangement. During the process, variables are systematically and consistently renamed into variables of the form V_i in which the index i represents the order in which the variable is introduced in the (reordered) clause. This renaming scheme allows to abstract from the variable names as they have been introduced by the programmer. As a result, the ordering $<$ (see Definition 4) orders identical literals (up to a variable renaming) according to the order in which their respective input arguments appear in the clause.

Example 10. Let us reconsider the two clauses C_1 and C_2 from Example 7 and their proper rearrangements

$$PA_1 = \langle \{A = a, B = b\}, \{C = f(A), D = f(B)\}\rangle$$
$$PA_2 = \langle \{X = b, Y = a\}, \{R = f(X), S = f(Y)\}\rangle$$

It can easily be verified that the transformation as defined above transforms PA_1 into

$$C_1' \equiv \text{V1 = a, V2 = b, V3 = f(V1), V4 = f(V2)}$$

The transformation of PA_2 proceeds as follows. The set $\{X = b, Y = a\}$ is transformed into the conjunction V1 = a, V2 = b as such creating the renaming $\rho_1 = \{Y/V1, X/V2\}$. This renaming is applied to the second set of literals: $\{R = f(X), S = f(Y)\}$, giving $\{R = f(V2), S = f(V1)\}$ which is subsequently reordered into the conjunction S = f(V1), R = f(V2) and, finally, renamed into V3 = f(V1), V4 = f(V2). As a result, both clauses have an identical normal form.

Also note that recursive calls are replaced by a call to a special (predicate) symbol **rec** and that the arguments are permuted according to π. The use of the symbol **rec** for *each* recursive call, regardless the predicate, makes sure that recursive calls are ordered in a consistent way, regardless the predicate being normalized.

As a final note, observe that the normal form of a predicate is unique *for a given suitable permutation*. Indeed, the choice of another permutation induces another ordering on the renamed variables and, thus, another normal form, as is illustrated by the following examples.

Example 11. The `app1` predicate of Example 1 has two normal forms, the first one with respect to the identity argument permutation, the second with respect to the permutation $\{1, 2), (2, 1), (3, 3)\}$.

```
app1(V1, V2, V3) :- V3 = V2, V1 = [].
app1(V1, V2, V8) :- V3 = 1, V1 = [|](V4, V5), V6 = +(V4, V3),
                    rec(V2, V5, V7), V8 = [|](V6, V7).

app1(V1, V2, V3) :- V3 = V1, V2 = [].
app1(V1, V2, V8) :- V3 = 1, V2 = [|](V4, V5), V6 = +(V4, V3),
                    rec(V1, V5, V7), V8 = [|](V6, V7).
```

Likewise, the `conc1` predicate of Example 1 has two normal forms, the first one with respect to the argument permutation $\{(1, 3), (2, 2), (3, 1)\}$, the second one with respect to the permutation $\{(1, 3), (2, 1), (3, 2)\}$.

```
conc1(V1, V2, V3) :- V3 = V1, V2 = [].
conc1(V1, V2, V8) :- V3 = 1, V2 = [|](V4, V5), V6 = +(V4, V3),
                     rec(V1, V5, V7), V8 = [|](V6, V7).

conc1(V1, V2, V3) :- V3 = V2, V1 = [].
conc1(V1, V2, V8) :- V3 = 1, V1 = [|](V4, V5), V6 = +(V4, V3),
                     rec(V2, V5, V7), V8 = [|](V6, V7).
```

The examples above illustrate that the transformation to normal form offers a substantial help for detecting duplicated functionality. Indeed, the transformation makes the existence of isomorphisms explicit in the code, by reordering and renaming corresponding clause bodies in exactly the same way. In other words, detecting duplication between predicates in normal form does not require to consider permutations of the conjunctions (nor of the predicate arguments), thereby removing a layer of complexity.

4   Detecting Duplicated Functionality and Experimental Results

The described transformation to normal form was implemented in Mercury. In order to perform some experiments and to provide us with a proof of concept, we have also implemented a number of algorithms for searching for duplicated functionality:

1. **Naïve search.** Basically an implementation of the analysis described in [10]. The predicates are *not* transformed to normal form, and search is performed by computing all possible permutations of the clauses body atoms.
2. **Identical search.** Predicate definitions are transformed to normal form, possibly resulting in different versions if multiple suitable argument permutations exist. In a next step, each such version of a predicate is compared with each version of the other predicates. Given that the predicates are in normal form, the comparison is a simple check for identity. Consequently, this algorithm is able to detect *duplication* between relations (such as app1

and conc1), but it has no means to detect *similarity* between relations (such as reverse_all and add_and_square.

3. **Similar search.** Predicate definitions are transformed to normal form as in the **identical search** algorithm. However, in a next step the normal forms are compared using a more involved algorithm that checks whether the corresponding clauses of two predicate definitions in normal form are identical *modulo* 1) variable renaming, and 2) a set of adjacent body atoms (a so-called *gap*). The **similar search** algorithm is capable of detecting duplication between relations (in what case there are *no* gaps) *and* certain forms of similarity.

Table 1 provides timings for some basic examples. All times are in milliseconds, and experiments were performed on a Pentium 4 running at 3.06GHz with 1GB of memory. Three examples were tested:

1. The app1 and conc1 predicates from Example 1.
2. The rev_all and add_and_square predicates from the introduction.
3. Two different implementations of the member predicates, one using an if-then-else, the other using disjunction and negation.

The column labeled **Normal form** represents the time needed for the normal form transformation, the other columns represent the times needed for executing the mentioned algorithms (naïve, identical or similar search). Since only individual predicate definitions are compared, each algorithm was repeatedly executed 500 times in order to obtain a measurable timing.

Table 1. Execution time for identical and similar predicates detection

Program (500 executions)	Naïve search	Normal form	Identical search	Similar search
app1 and conc1	590	180	10	140
rev_all and add_and_sqr	4250	340	80	420
member	809	170	10	140

In the case of the rev_all, add_and_sqr and member examples, the execution times given for the naïve and identical search algorithms represent the times needed to conclude that the given examples do *not* implement duplicated relations, since these algorithms are unable to detect only similarities. The similar search algorithm is able to detect that these predicates are identical modulo a *gap*.

Table 1 shows that even for these small examples, the transformation to normal form followed by either the identical search or similar search algorithm easily outperforms the analysis of [10]. This justifies the viability of our current approach.

In what follows, we compare the performance of our algorithm for detecting duplication with that of the naïve search algorithm when dealing with programs containing several predicate definitions. Note that even if not much duplication is present, all definitions must be pairwise compared in order to drop to conclusions. Table 2 contains the execution times of all the algorithms on programs with a different number of predicate definitions. All predicates have 1 or 2 clauses, and each of these clauses has between 3 and 6 atoms. The given execution times represent the total time needed for 100 repeated executions of each algorithm. In this table, the column labeled **Total** represent the time needed for the normalization followed by the identical search algorithm. The column labeled **Speedup** represents the speedup of identical search (with normalization) with respect to the naïve algorithm.

Table 2. Comparison of the algorithms for identical predicates detection

Program (100 executions)	Naïve search	Normal form	Identical search	Total	Speedup
2 predicates	890	95	10	105	8.5
5 predicates	3769	120	10	130	29.0
10 predicates	10,970	160	60	320	34.3
20 predicates	54,860	310	150	460	119.3
40 predicates	243,520	580	910	1,490	163.4

As shown in this table, the transformation of a program into its normal form enables an important speedup when searching for identical predicates across a program. Moreover, this speedup increases strongly when the size of the program to explore increases, showing a reduction in complexity due to dealing with programs in normal form.

Table 3 compares the performance of the identical search and similar search algorithms when used on programs containing several predicate definitions. The table shows that the similar search algorithm is substantially slower (about a factor 10). This is as one would expect, given that this algorithm needs to consider renamings and still needs to perform a number of permutations in order to find the smallest *gaps* in two predicate definitions such that their code (these gaps aside) is duplicated.

Table 3. Comparison of the algorithms for identical and similar predicates detection.

Program (100 executions)	Identical search	Similar search
2 predicates	10	115
5 predicates	10	240
10 predicates	60	520
20 predicates	150	2090
40 predicates	910	9780

5   Discussion and Further Work

In this work we have defined a program transformation that normalizes a Mercury program by reordering body goals and predicate arguments. The transformation, which preserves the well-modedness and determinism characteristics of the program, aims at reducing the complexity of performing a search for duplicated or similar code fragments between programs. The defined normal form is unique (with respect to a suitable argument permutation). The transformation is implemented and some basic algorithms for the detection of duplicated and similar code have been implemented and evaluated. The evaluation is limited and should be seen as a proof of concept showing that the use of a normal form is viable rather than as a thorough evaluation of the search algorithms.

Topics of further work include the development of more involved algorithms for the detection of similarities between predicate definitions, based on our normal form. The similar search algorithm that was used to evaluation is a first step in this direction. It is able to detect the similarity between the `reverse_all` and `add_and_square` predicates (showing they can be generalised into `map`) but a more involved algorithm is needed if more interesting cases of similar code have to be detected.

The normal form as we have defined it is meant to be an *internal* representation that is not shown to the programmer. If the normal form is to be used as a basis for developing tools for program refactoring, it must be investigated if and how the proposed transformation to normal form can be reversed, such that the results of the analysis (indications of what code fragments are identical) can be displayed on the *original* source code rather than the normalized code.

As a last topic for further research, we mention the normalization of type definitions. It needs to be investigated whether such normalization is possible, and in what cases it might be interesting to detect similarities between type definitions, and possibly generalise them into a single more general type definition.

Acknowledgments

We thank the LOPSTR participants and the anonymous referees for their constructive comments and feedback.

References

1. Chen, X., Francia, B., Li, M., McKinnon, B., Seker, A.: Shared information and program plagiarism detection. IEEE Transactions on Information Theory 50(7), 1545–1551 (2004)
2. Horwitz, S.: Identifying the semantic and textual differences between two versions of a program. ACM SIGPLAN Notices 25(6), 234–245 (1990)
3. Kontogiannis, K.A., Demori, R., Merlo, E., Galler, M., Bernstein, M.: Pattern matching for clone and concept detection. In: Reverse engineering, pp. 77–108 (1996)

4. Mycroft, A., O'Keefe, R.A.: A polymorphic type system for Prolog. Artificial Intelligence 23, 295–307 (1984)
5. Univ. of Melbourne. Mercury language reference manual (2006)
6. Overton, D., Somogyi, Z., Stuckey, P.: Constraint-based mode analysis of Mercury. In: Proceedings of the 4th ACM SIGPLAN international conference on Principles and practice of declarative programming, New York, USA, 2002, pp. 109–120. ACM Press, New York (2002)
7. Overton, D., Somogyi, Z., Stuckey, P.J.: Constraint-based mode analysis of Mercury. In: Kirchner, C. (ed.) Proceedings of the Fourth International Conference on Principles and Practice of Declarative Programming, pp. 109–120. ACM Press, New York (2002)
8. Schleimer, S., Wilkerson, D.S., Aiken, A.: Winnowing: Local algorithms for document fingerprinting. In: Proceedings of the 2003 ACM SIGMOD international conference on Management of Data, San Diego, CA (2003)
9. Somogyi, Z., Henderson, H., Conway, T.: The execution algorithm of Mercury, an efficient purely declarative logic programming language. Journal of Logic Programming 29(1) (1996)
10. Vanhoof, W.: Searching Semantically Equivalent Code Fragments in Logic Programs. In: Etalle, S. (ed.) LOPSTR 2004. LNCS, vol. 3573, pp. 1–18. Springer, Heidelberg (2005)
11. Winstead, J., Evans, D.: Towards differential program analysis. In: Proceedings of the 2003 Workshop on Dynamic Analysis (2003)
12. Wise. YAP3: Improved detection of similarities in computer program and other texts. SIGCSEB: SIGCSE Bulletin (ACM Special Interest Group on Computer Science Education), 28 (1996)
13. Yang, W.: Identifying syntactic differences between two programs. Software Practice and Experience 21(7), 739–755 (1991)
14. W. Yang, S. Horwitz, T. Reps. Detecting program components with equivalent behaviors. Technical Report CS-TR-1989-840, University of Wisconsin, Madison (1989)

Aggregates for CHR through Program Transformation

Peter Van Weert*, Jon Sneyers**, and Bart Demoen

Department of Computer Science, K.U.Leuven, Belgium
FirstName.LastName@cs.kuleuven.be

Abstract. We propose an extension of Constraint Handling Rules (CHR) with aggregates such as sum, count, findall, and min. This new feature significantly improves the conciseness and expressiveness of the language. In this paper, we describe an implementation based on source-to-source transformations to CHR (extended with some low-level compiler directives). We allow user-defined aggregates and nested aggregate expressions over arbitrary guarded conjunctions of constraints. Both an on-demand and an incremental aggregate computation strategy are supported.

1 Introduction

Constraint Handling Rules (CHR) [1,4] is a powerful, elegant committed-choice CLP language, based on multi-headed, guarded multiset rewrite rules. Originally designed for the implementation of constraint solvers, CHR has matured towards a general purpose language, used in a wide range of application domains, including natural language processing, multi-agent systems, and type system design.

In [8,9] we proposed an extension of CHR with *aggregates*. This declarative language feature allows the aggregation of information from an unbounded number of constraints to be captured concisely in a single expression in the head of a CHR rule. Example aggregates are sum, count, findall, and min. Without language support for aggregates, these common programming idioms require cumbersome, low-level auxiliary constructs, cross-cutting the entire program. Case studies show aggregates reduce program size by up to 50%. The resulting programs are also significantly more understandable, maintainable, and robust.

This paper presents how existing CHR systems can be extended with a general, extensible aggregate framework using source-to-source transformations to lower-level CHR. Only a small number of easily implemented low-level compiler directives have to be added to the CHR system itself. The transformation takes care of introducing auxiliary and cross-cutting code, not unlike an aspect weaver in Aspect-Oriented Programming [5].

The source-to-source transformation schemes presented in this paper support user-defined, application-tailored aggregates, nested aggregate expressions, and

---

* Research Assistant of the Research Foundation – Flanders (FWO-Vlaanderen).
** Research funded by a Ph.D. grant of the Institute for the Promotion of Innovation through Science and Technology in Flanders (IWT-Vlaanderen).

King, A. (Ed.): LOPSTR 2007, LNCS 4915, pp. 59–73, 2008.

efficient aggregate computation using either on-demand or incremental aggregate computation. The design of these non-trivial transformation schemes is discussed in detail, the different issues identified and addressed one by one.

Overview. Section 2 briefly recalls the syntax and operational semantics of CHR. More information can be found in [3,4]. Section 3 motivates and introduces the extension of CHR with aggregates. Next, two different source-to-source schemes are presented in Section 4. The implementation approach is evaluated in Section 5. Finally, Section 6 provides conclusions and directions of future work.

2   Preliminaries: Constraint Handling Rules

2.1   Syntax of CHR

A constraint $c(x_1, \ldots, x_n)$ is an atom of predicate c/n, with all x_i values of a host language data type. Two types of constraints exist: *built-in constraints*, solved by an underlying solver, and *CHR constraints*, solved by the CHR program.

A CHR program consists of a sequence of CHR rules of the form:

$$name \ @ \ \ H_k \setminus H_r \Longleftrightarrow G \mid B$$

The *name* is optional and unique; rules without a name get one implicitly. The *head* consists of two conjunctions of CHR constraints, H_k and H_r. Their conjuncts are called *occurrences* (*kept* and *removed occurrences* resp.). The *guard* G is a conjunction of built-in constraints. If "$G \mid$" is omitted, it is considered to be "*true* $\mid$". The *body* B is a conjunction of CHR and built-in constraints.

There are three types of rules. If H_k is empty, the rule is a *simplification* rule. If H_r is empty, the rule is a *propagation* rule and the symbol "$\Longrightarrow$" is used instead of "$\Longleftrightarrow$". If both parts are non-empty, the rule is a *simpagation* rule. At least one of H_r and H_k must be non-empty.

Logically, a simplification rule corresponds to an equivalence: $G \to (H_r \leftrightarrow B)$, while a propagation rule corresponds to an implication: $G \to (H_k \to B)$.

2.2   Operaional Semantics of CHR

Informally, the operational semantics of a CHR rule is as follows: if for each occurrence in the head a matching constraint is found in the *constraint store*, and the guard is satisfied, then the rule *fires*: the constraints that matched the removed occurrences (H_r) are deleted from the store and the body is executed.

Formally, the execution of a CHR program follows the *theoretical* or *high-level* operational semantics, denoted as ω_t. For brevity, we do not present the formal transition rules of ω_t here; we refer to [3,4] instead. A version of ω_t extended with aggregates is presented in Section 3.3.

The *theoretical* operational semantics is highly nondeterministic. Only programs that do not depend on the order of rule application have guaranteed behavior under ω_t. Such programs are called *confluent* (cf. [4]). However, writing confluent programs is often overly difficult. Many programs are non-confluent under ω_t as CHR programmers exploit the execution strategy implemented by most CHR systems to obtain the desired behavior. The *refined operational semantics*, denoted with ω_r, instantiates ω_t to capture the behavior of most current systems. A complete exposition, including a formal description, is found in [3].

A central concept in the refined semantics is the *active constraint*. Each time a constraint becomes active, all CHR rules are tried in a *top-down textual order*, until all applicable rules that match the active constraint have been executed, or the active constraint is removed. If a rule fires, the constraints in its body are processed one at a time, in a *left-to-right textual order*. If a CHR constraint is processed, it is added to the constraint store and immediately becomes the new active constraint. Processing a built-in constraint entails solving it, and reactivating all CHR constraints whose arguments are affected, one at a time. The order in which CHR constraints are reactivated is undetermined. The activation and reactivation of a CHR constraint is treated as a *procedure call*: only when its execution is finished, the execution returns to the previous active constraint.

3 Extending CHR with Aggregates

As CHR is already Turing complete [7], aggregates do not add to the computational power of CHR. Section 3.1 shows they are nevertheless invaluable when it comes to expressiveness, maintainability and conciseness. The extension of CHR with aggregates is introduced in Section 3.2, and given a formal operational semantics in Section 3.3. A more thorough introduction to the proposed extension, more examples and case studies can be found in [8,9].

3.1 Motivation and Running Example

As the head of each CHR rule only considers a fixed number of constraints, any form of aggregation over unbounded parts of the constraint store necessarily requires explicit encoding, using auxiliary constraints and rules. The following example clearly shows the inadequacy of such ad hoc approaches. It is also used as a running example throughout the paper.

Example 1. Suppose the constraints `account(AccountId,ClientId,Balance)` and `client(ClientId)` constitute a simplified representation of the accounts and clients of a bank. At some point, the bank decides to add the business rule:

"A client whose accumulated sum of account balances is \$25,000 or more is a *platinum client*"

As a client can have any number of accounts, this seemingly simple rule cannot be expressed straightforwardly in CHR. CHR practitioners therefore commonly introduce a constraint such as `accumulated_balance/2`. This allows the logic of platinum clients to be captured concisely in a single rule as follows:

```
client(C), accumulated_balance(C,Sum) ==> Sum ≥ 25000 | platinum(C).
```

This approach, however, also necessitates the explicit maintenance of the accumulated balance. This inherently cross-cutting concern requires invasive modifications to all rules that alter the balance of an account. The bank e.g. has to add at least the following underlined code:

```
deposit(A,X), account(A,C,B), accumulated_balance(C,Acc) <=>
  account(A,C,B+X), accumulated_balance(C,Acc+X).
...

withdraw(A,X), account(A,C,B), accumulated_balance(C,Acc) <=>
  B > X, account(A,C,B-X), accumulated_balance(C,Acc-X).
```

Many variations to the above maintenance scheme can be concocted, but they all require similar modifications scattered throughout the entire program. Similar auxiliary code has to be written for *every* aggregate; a very tedious and repetitive task. Clearly, this approach displays poor compliance with common software quality criteria: it is highly error-prone, and it impairs the readability and maintainability of the program, as the logic of many rules becomes tangled with obfuscating auxiliary code. In other words, many practical advantages of declarative programming – understandability, maintainability, robustness, and shortened development time – are severely handicapped.

3.2   An Extensible Framework for Aggregates in CHR

This section introduces an extension of CHR with aggregates, designed to overcome the expressivity problems outlined in the previous section. It allows rule heads to contain *aggregates*. These expressions accumulate information over possibly unbounded parts of the constraint store. Aggregates can be written in both the kept and the removed part of the head; there is no semantical difference.

This section provides a short summary on the proposed, extensible aggregate framework. More information can be found in [8,9].

Predefined aggregates. Our framework provides a wide range of predefined aggregates, including all aggregates commonly found in related paradigms such as database query languages [10] (i.e. min, max, sum, count and avg) and production rule systems (i.e. not, exists and forall). A complete list of predefined aggregates, together with a number of example uses, can be found in [8,9].

Example 2. Using the sum aggregate (in italics), the platinum client business rule of Example 1 is again declaratively expressed in a single rule:

```
client(C), sum(B,account(_,C,B),Sum) ==> Sum ≥ 25000 | platinum(C).
```

However, no further changes to the program are required, as the aggregate's semantics already guarantees the correct behavior implicitly: it accumulates the sum of the balances B of all matching account/3 constraints, and ensures that the rule fires as soon as this sum, Sum, reaches 25,000.

Contrasting the above example with the approach outlined in Example 1 in the previous section clearly shows that aggregates render CHR programs more declarative, readable and maintainable. Relieved from the cumbersome and repetitive task of implementing aggregates, the programmer can focus exclusively on the application domain. So, productivity is improved considerably as well.

User-defined aggregates. Often information has to be aggregated in application-specific ways. Therefore, we designed a general high-level mechanism that enables CHR end-users to create *user-defined aggregates*:

```
aggregate(Start, Inc, Dec, Final, Template, Goal, Result)
```

The `aggregate/7` construct is expressive enough to effectively specify any aggregate. In fact, all predefined aggregates are also implemented by it.

Example 3. The predefined `sum(T,G,R)` aggregate for instance is specified as `aggregate(=(0),plus,minus,=,T,G,R)`, where '=(0)' indicates unification with zero, and `plus/3` and `minus/3` are two straightforward Prolog predicates computing the sum, respectively the difference of the first two arguments.

The first four arguments of `aggregate/7` specify the host language procedures or CHR constraints that determine how the aggregate is computed. First, an intermediate working value is *initialized* using `Start`. Then, for each matching found for `Goal`, a corresponding instance of `Template` is passed to `Inc` to *increment* the current working value. After all increments required are made, the working value is *finalized* using `Final`, to obtain the aggregate's result `Result`. The function of `Dec` is explained in Section 4.3.

These seven arguments thus completely determine an aggregate's semantics, as also reflected in the formal operational semantics presented in the next section.

Complex aggregate goals. Example 2 showed an aggregate over a simple `Goal`, i.e., consisting of a single CHR constraint. The *aggregate goal* `Goal` however can be an arbitrary conjunction of CHR constraints and guards: for example `count((platinum(C),account(_,C,_)), N)` counts the number of accounts owned by platinum clients. We further allow *nested aggregates*, that is, aggregate expressions inside the goal of another aggregate: for instance, `max(S, (client(C), sum(B,account(_,C,B),S)), M)` returns the largest total balance `M` of any individual client.

3.3   Formal Operational Semantics

We extend the theoretical operational semantics ω_t [3,4] to deal with the general `aggregate/7` expressions introduced in the previous section (recall that this also covers all predefined aggregates). The extended semantics is denoted ω_a. We extend ω_t because of brevity, and because it allows more implementation freedom then extending a more deterministic instance such as e.g. ω_r (cf. Section 2.2).

The ω_a semantics is formulated as a state transition system. Transition rules define the relation between an execution state and its subsequent execution state.

Definition 1 (Identified constraints). *To differentiate amongst otherwise identical copies of constraints, CHR constraints are assigned unique identifiers.*

An identified *CHR constraint with* constraint identifier i *is denoted $c\#i$. We further introduce the functions $chr(c\#i) = c$ and $id(c\#i) = i$, and extend them to sequences and sets of identified CHR constraints in the obvious manner.*

Definition 2 (Execution state). *An* execution state σ *is a tuple $\langle \mathbb{G}, \mathbb{S}, \mathbb{B}, \mathbb{T} \rangle_n$. The goal $\mathbb{G}$ is a multiset of constraints. The CHR constraint store $\mathbb{S}$ is a set of identified CHR constraints (while $\mathbb{S}$ is a set, $chr(\mathbb{S})$ is a multiset). The built-in constraint store $\mathbb{B}$ is the conjunction of all built-in constraints passed to the underlying solver. The propagation history $\mathbb{T}$, necessary to prevent trivial non-termination, is a set of tuples, each recording the name of a rule and a sequence of identities of the CHR constraints that fired that rule. Finally, the counter $n \in \mathbb{N}$ represents the next unique constraint identifier.*

The semantics of the built-in constraints is determined by a constraint theory $\mathcal{D}_\mathcal{B}$. Let $vars(A)$ be the variables occurring freely in A, then $\bar{\exists}_A F$ denotes $\exists x_1, \ldots, \exists x_n F$, with $\{x_1, \ldots, x_n\} = vars(F) \backslash vars(A)$.

Because aggregates can be nested, we use two mutually recursive definitions:

Definition 3 (Matching substitutions). *Let* matchings$(A \wedge H \wedge G, S_h, \mathbb{S}, \mathbb{B})$

$$= \left\{ \theta \mid H = \theta(S_h) \wedge \mathcal{D}_\mathcal{B} \models \mathbb{B} \rightarrow \bar{\exists}_\mathbb{B}(\theta \wedge G \wedge \mathsf{agg\_cond}(A, S_h \cup \mathbb{S}, \mathbb{B})) \right\}$$

where H and S_h are conjunctions of CHR constraints, G and $\mathbb{B}$ conjunctions of built-in constraints, A is a conjunction of aggregates, and $\mathbb{S}$ is a set of identified CHR constraints (a CHR store).

Definition 4 (Aggregate Condition). *For an aggregate A of the form* aggregate(s, i, d, f, T, G, R), *a CHR store $\mathbb{S}$ and a built-in store $\mathbb{B}$:*

$$\mathsf{agg\_cond}(A, \mathbb{S}, \mathbb{B}) = \quad s(V_0) \wedge \bigwedge_{k=1}^{n} i(V_{k-1}, \theta_k(T), V_k) \wedge f(V_n, R)$$

where $V_0, \ldots, V_n$ are new variables and $\{\theta_1, \ldots, \theta_n\} = \bigcup_{H \subseteq \mathbb{S}} \mathsf{matchings}'(G, H, \mathbb{S}, \mathbb{B})$. The condition is extended to conjunctions of aggregates in the obvious manner.

In its generic syntactic form (cf. Section 2.1), the head of a rule is prepended with a conjunction of aggregates A (recall that an aggregate's location in the head has no semantic meaning):

Definition 5 (Transition rules). *Given a CHR program $\mathcal{P}$, execution proceeds by exhaustively applying the following transition rules, starting from an initial state of the form $\langle \mathbb{G}, \emptyset, true, \emptyset \rangle_1$:*

   *1. **Solve.*** $\langle \{c\} \uplus \mathbb{G}, \mathbb{S}, \mathbb{B}, \mathbb{T} \rangle_n \rightarrowtail_\mathcal{P} \langle \mathbb{G}, \mathbb{S}, c \wedge \mathbb{B}, \mathbb{T} \rangle_n$
                where c is a built-in constraint and $\mathcal{D}_\mathcal{B} \models \bar{\exists}_\emptyset \mathbb{B}$.
   2. **Introduce.** $\langle \{c\} \uplus \mathbb{G}, \mathbb{S}, \mathbb{B}, \mathbb{T} \rangle_n \rightarrowtail_\mathcal{P} \langle \mathbb{G}, \{c\#n\} \cup \mathbb{S}, \mathbb{B}, \mathbb{T} \rangle_{n+1}$
                where c is a CHR constraint and $\mathcal{D}_\mathcal{B} \models \bar{\exists}_\emptyset \mathbb{B}$.

3. Apply. $\langle \mathbb{G}, H_1 \cup H_2 \cup \mathbb{S}, \mathbb{B}, \mathbb{T} \rangle_n \rightarrowtail_{\mathcal{P}} \langle B \uplus \mathbb{G}, H_1 \cup \mathbb{S}, \theta \wedge \mathbb{B}, \mathbb{T} \cup \{h\} \rangle_n$
where $\mathcal{D}_{\mathcal{B}} \models \bar{\exists}_\theta \mathbb{B}$ and $\mathcal{P}$ contains a rule r @ $A, H_1' \backslash H_2' \iff G \mid B$ and
$\theta \in \mathsf{matchings}((A, H_1', H_2', G), H_1 \cup H_2, \mathbb{S}, \mathbb{B})$ and $h = (r, id(H_1, H_2)) \notin \mathbb{T}$

The propagation history does not record an aggregate in any way, so a rule is never fired more then once with the same combination of constraints, even if the aggregate's value changes. We call this *fire-once semantics*. More information regarding this choice can be found in [9].

4   Implementation through Program Transformation

The transformation schemes presented here improve earlier schemes described in [9]. Two different aggregate computation strategies are supported: *on-demand* (Section 4.2), and *incremental* (Section 4.3). The source-to-source transformations are implemented in the K.U.Leuven CHR system [6] in SWI-Prolog [12], but the approach is equally applicable to other systems implementing the refined operational semantics. The implementation is based on high-level *meta CHR rules*. Their basic syntax and semantics is outlined first in Section 4.1.

4.1   Meta CHR Rules

Meta CHR rules allow concise specification of CHR source-to-source transformations. They somewhat resemble ordinary CHR rules, both syntactically and semantically. Only, instead of rewriting constraint multisets, they rewrite the CHR rules of another CHR program, called the *object program*.

A meta rule is applicable if its head can be matched with occurrences in a single *object rule*. When a meta rule fires, the occurrences that matched its removed meta occurrences, are removed from the object rule. In a meta rule's body, the '+' prefix operator adds kept occurrences to the object rule, '−' adds removed occurrences, and '?' adds extra conjuncts to the object rule's guard. Writing a CHR rule in the body of a meta rule adds this rule to the object program. The `remaining_head/1` operation returns those occurrences of the object rule not matched by the meta rule, and `guard/1` returns the object rule's guard.

4.2   On-Demand Aggregate Computation

This section gradually introduces and explains a transformation scheme for *on-demand aggregate computation*. The scheme, depicted in Figure 1, outputs code in which aggregates are computed from scratch each time they are required.

Lines 1 to 4. The simplification rule removes each occurrence of `aggregate/7`, and replaces it with a guard (line 4). This guard calls an auxiliary CHR constraint[1], $\mathsf{agg}_i/2$, that computes the aggregate's result A. The `shared_vars/3`

---

[1] Even though not actually allowed by the CHR language (cf. Section 2), several CHR implementations do support CHR constraints in guards this way, a feature often exploited by expert users. To properly support such guards though, a number of changes were required to the K.U.Leuven CHR compiler ([9] provides an overview).

```
1   aggregate(Start,Inc,_,Final,T,G,A) <=>
2     new_unique_identifier(i),
3     remaining_head(Head), shared_vars(Head, (T-G), V),
4     ?agg_i(V,A),
5     +G#on_active, +G#on_removal,
6     ( agg_i(V,A) <=> Start(I), result_i(I), match_i(V), get_i(R), Final(R,A) ),
7     ( match_i(V), G ==> incr_i(T) ),
8     ( incr_i(T), result_i(R_1) <=> Inc(R_1, T, R_2), result_i(R_2) ),
9     ( result_i(R), match_i(_), get_i(Q) <=> Q = R ).
```

Fig. 1. The core of a transformation scheme using on-demand aggregate computation. For compactness, pseudo code is used. The function of each line is explained below.

predicate returns the variables shared by its first two arguments. It is used to compute V, the list of all variables required to compute the aggregate (line 3–4). The implementation of the aggregate computation (lines 6–9) is discussed below. The identifier i (line 2) ensures all auxiliary functors, such as $agg_i/2$, are unique.

Line 5 (on_active and on_removal heads). Under the refined operational semantics, by default, the guard added on line 4 is called each time a matching is found for the remaining occurrences. In general, this does not suffice: the aggregate also has to be (re)computed when its outcome changes. To indicate such extra conditions under which a rule, and thus its guard, have to be (re)considered, we introduced two special types of heads: on_active heads and on_removal heads. An *on_active head* indicates an additional trigger to fire the rule: when constraints matching the on_active head are *activated* (i.e. newly added or reactivated, cf. Section 2.2), the rule is tried. Similarly, an *on_removal head* indicates that the rule additionally has to be tried when constraints matching the on_removal head are *removed* from the constraint store. Neither of these types of heads is considered when an occurrence in the regular head is active. Both new types of heads are implemented with a straightforward source-to-source transformation. More information can be found in [9].

Line 5 adds the aggregate's goal G to the original object rule, both as an on_active and as a on_removal head. This ensures the guard computing the aggregate is called, not only when the remainder of the original head is matched, but also when constraints matching G are added, reactivated, or removed.

Example 4. The rule from Example 2 (Section 3.2) becomes:

```
account(_,C,_)#on_active, account(_,C,_)#on_removal,
  client(C) ==> agg_0(C,Sum), Sum ≥ 25000 | platinum(C).
```

A client's accumulated balance is thus also (re)computed when the accumulated balance changes, i.e. each time an account/3 constraint is added or removed.

Issue 1: *Updates.* Recall the following rule from Example 1 (Section 3.1):

```
deposit(A,X), account(A,C,B) <=> account(A,C,B+X).
```

The above rule is an instance of a common CHR programming pattern, called an *update*: a constraint is removed and immediately replaced with a similar, updated version. In the context of aggregates however, the removal of the former may cause aggregates to be recomputed prior to the insertion of the updated version[2]. This behavior is not always desired. For instance, in the intermediate state right after the above rule removes 'account(A,C,B)', the accumulated balance in Example 4 would clearly be incorrect.

As a solution, we introduce pragma passive_removal. If a constraint annotated with passive_removal is removed, no on_removal heads are activated:

```
deposit(A,X), account(A,C,B) # passive_removal <=> account(A,C,B+X).
```

Consequently, the aggregate is only recomputed when the new, updated account is added. This allows the CHR programmer to easily specify the desired behavior.

Lines 6–9. The rules performing the actual aggregate computation are added to the object program by lines 6 to 9. Line 6 implements the $agg_i/2$ operation. First, the intermediate aggregate result is initialized using the aggregate's Start operation. This intermediate result is stored as a $result_i/1$ constraint. Then the $match_i/1$ constraint is called, causing the intermediate result to be incremented for each matching aggregate goal G (lines 7–8). To perform the matching with the aggregate goal G (line 7), the variables V it shares with the remaining head of the original object rule are needed (line 3).

Example 5. For the sum/3 aggregate in Example 2 the following code is generated (recall from Example 3 that $sum(T,G,A) \equiv aggregate(=(0),plus,minus,=,T,G,A)$):

```
agg0(C,Sum) <=> 0=I, result0(I), match0(C), get0(R), R=A.
match0(C), account(_,C,B) ==> incr0(B).
incr0(B), result0(R1) <=> plus(R1, B, R2), result0(R2).
result0(R), match0(_), get0(Q) <=> Q = R.
```

If the sum aggregate (the accumulated balance) has to be computed, the result is initialized to zero, stored as a constraint, and then incremented with the balance B of each matching account/3 constraint. To perform this match, the variable C (the client's identifier) is indeed required.

The intermediate result $result_i/1$ is incremented through the auxiliary constraint $incr_i/1$ (line 8). This way, the propagation history of the rule on line 7 ensures that each matching goal G contributes only once. The argument passed to $incr_i/1$ (line 7), and subsequently to Inc (line 8), is the aggregate's template T. The refined operational semantics (cf. Section 2.2) ensures that the call to $match_i/1$ only returns to the rule body on line 6 after all matchings and increments are performed. A last auxiliary constraint, $get_i/1$, is then used to retrieve and remove the computed result (line 8). Finally, this result is finalized using Final to obtain the aggregate result A (line 6).

---

[2] Similar issues were outlined in [11] in the context of negation as absence.

4.3   Incremental Aggregate Computation

The performance of on-demand aggregate computation, described in the previous section, is not always adequate. Aggregates ranging over large portions of the constraint store may be recomputed from scratch many times. In such cases, it is obviously more efficient to maintain the aggregate value incrementally.

```
1    aggregate(Start,Inc,Dec,Final,T,G,A) <=>
2      new_unique_identifier(i),
3      guard(Guard), remaining_head(Head), shared_vars(Head, (T-G), V),
4      +match_i(V,I), +result_i(I,R), ?Final(R,A),
5      ( Head ==> Guard | init_i(V) ),
6      ( match_i(V,_) \ init_i(V) <=> true ),
7      ( init_i(V) <=> Start(R), match_i(V,I), result_i(I,R) ),
8      ( match_i(V,I), G ==> incr_i(I,T) ),
9      ( incr_i(I,T), result_i(I,R_1) <=> Inc(R_1, T, R_2), result_i(I,R_2) ),
10     ( match_i(V,I)#passive, G#on_removal ==> decr_i(I,T) pragma no_history),
11     ( decr_i(I,T), result_i(I,R_1) <=> Dec(R_1, T, R_2), result_i(I,R_2) ).
```

Fig. 2. Transformation scheme for maintained aggregates (a basic, first attempt)

The meta rule in Figure 2 illustrates a basic transformation scheme for incrementally maintained aggregates. The scheme is not yet fully correct with respect to the ω_a operational semantics (cf. Section 3.3) though. Subsequent subsections will refine it to deal with certain semantical issues, and more complex aggregates such as nested and non-ground aggregates.

Basic scheme. Similar to the transformation scheme of Section 4.2, aggregate results are stored in $result_i/2$ constraints, and $match_i/2$ constraints are used to find matches with the aggregate's goal G (lines 8 and 10). The need for the extra argument, an aggregate identifier, is explained below.

Line 4. The aggregate is no longer replaced by a guard that computes the aggregate result, but instead with a $match_i/2$ and a $result_i/2$ occurrence in the object rule's head. Both new occurrences are kept because the computed aggregate result may be needed more than once. Line 4 also adds a guard to finalizes the aggregate result.

Incremental maintenance (lines 8–11). The $result_i/2$ and $match_i/2$ constraints remain in the store, and the rules added by lines 8–11 ensure these results remain consistent. Maintained results are incremented each time a new matching is found for G (lines 8–9), and decremented each time such a matching is removed (lines 10–11). For the latter, the Dec argument of aggregate/7 is used. This argument indicates the inverse operation of Inc.

Line 10. The different pragmas and annotations in the rule on line 10 warrant extra clarification. The rule must not fire when a $match_i/2$ is active, only when constraints matching G are removed. Therefore, the $match_i/2$ occurrence is made passive (pass is short for passive, a common CHR pragma). Reacting to constraint removals is done, as in Section 4.2, using an on_removal head. Finally, pragma no_history is added, indicating no propagation history has to be kept for this rule. Otherwise, the rule would only fire once per $match_i/2$ constraint, as the on_removal head is not included in propagation history tuples.

Aggregate identifiers. More than one result may have to be maintained at the same time. To ensure the right result is updated after a match is found (lines 8 and 10), we let corresponding $match_i/2$ and $result_i/2$ constraints share a unique identifier, and pass this to the $incr_i/2$ or $decr_i/2$ constraint. Other than that, the pattern used to increment and decrement the maintained results is the same as the pattern used in Section 4.2.

Initialization (lines 5–7). Eagerly maintaining all possible aggregate results would be overly expensive. Aggregate maintenance is instead only started once a matching is found for the remainder of the head, as realized by the rule added on line 5. The head and guard of this rule are copied from the original object rule (without copying the aggregate head itself), and its body calls an $init_i/2$ auxiliary constraint. This constraint is removed by the rule on line 6 if the same aggregate result is already being maintained; in the other case, the rule on line 7 initializes a new result, stores it as a $result_i/2$, and adds a $matching_i/2$ constraint.

Issue 1: *Multiple Removals.* The basic scheme does not fully implement the ω_a semantics defined in Section 3.3. This subsection addresses a first issue:

Example 6. Consider the following artificial example:

```
a, count(c, Cs) <=> Cs \== 2 | writeln(Cs).
b \ c, c <=> true.
```

where the "count(c, Cs)" aggregate counts the number of c/0 constraints. Now consider the query "c, c, a, b". First two c constraints are added, then a is called. The latter causes the count/2 aggregate to be computed. As the result is equal to two, the first rule does not fire. After adding b, the second rule fires and removes both c constraints. Suppose the count is maintained incrementally. The removal of the first c constraint causes the maintained result to be decremented. The count becomes equal to one, causing the first rule to fire with Cs equal to *one*, even though there are *no c constraints left*. This is clearly not correct. The reason is that, whilst both c constraints are removed simultaneously, the updates to the maintained aggregate are performed, and visible, one by one.

Our solution is based on splitting the activation of on_removal heads into two phases: on_removal1 and on_removal2. When a rule fires, the removed constraints are first matched against on_removal1 heads. Only after this is done for *all* removed constraints, the same is repeated for the on_removal2 heads.

Lines 10–11 of Figure 2 are replaced with those in Figure 3. The rules added on lines 10*–11* ensure that first, in the on_removal1 phase, all affected aggregates are made consistent. The updated results are not yet used immediately as in Example 6. Instead, the $result_i/2$ constraint is added *passively* to the

```
     ...
10*  ( match_i(V,I)#passive, G#on_removal1 ==> decr_i(I,T) pragma no_history),
11*  ( decr_i(I,T), result_i(I,R_1) <=> Dec(R_1,T,R_2), result_i(I,R_2)#passive)
12*  ( match_i(V,I)#passive, G#on_removal2,
13*                    result_i(I,_)#Id ==> chr_reactivate_i(Id) pragma no_history).
```

Fig. 3. Code to replace lines 10–11 of the transformation scheme of Figure 2 to correctly deal with multiple constraint removals. Several new lower-level CHR constructs are used. Their semantics is explained in the accompanying text.

constraint store, that is, without searching for matching occurrences. Hence the '#passive' annotation in the body of the rule on line 11*. The results only become active once *all* results are guaranteed consistent again, that is, in the on_removal2 phase (line 12*). Activating a constraint is done using the low-level chr_reactivate/1 primitive (line 13*).

Issue 2: *Updates.* The update pattern causes similar issues in the context of incrementally computed aggregates as described before in Section 4.2, Issue 1. The solution is analogous as well, only with a slightly refined semantics of pragma passive_removal: if a constraint annotated with passive_removal is removed, no on_removal2 heads are activated, only on_removal1 heads (cf. previous issue). As such, the maintained result is passively decremented, but the aggregate only becomes active when the new, updated account is added.

Issue 3: *Nested Aggregates.* A second semantical problem with the basic transformation scheme occurs when applying it to nested aggregates. The maintained value of a nested aggregate is incremented and decremented using the update pattern. The outer aggregate consequently observes the intermediate state in which the result/2 constraint holding the old maintained value of the nested aggregate is removed and the new, updated version is not yet added. The solution consists of slightly adjusting lines 9 and 11 in Figure 2, and line 11* in Figure 3, to use pragma passive_removal for updates to result/2 constraints.

Issue 4: *Propagation Histories.* The transformation scheme adds two extra heads per aggregate. However, according to the ω_a semantics these are not allowed to be part of the propagation history. Pragma history/2, introduced in [9], can be used to explicitly specify which occurrence identifiers have to be included in the history tuples. Thus the issue is solved by adding the following code after line 3 of Figure 2 ($hist_i$ is a unique identifier):

```
..., identifiers(Head, Ids), pragma( history(hist_i, Ids) ), ...
```

Issue 5: *Non-ground Aggregates.* Two final issues occur when aggregating over goals containing non-ground variables:

– A single built-in constraint (e.g. unification) may cause *multiple goals* to match. The problem is analogous to Issue 1 on *multiple removals*. It has to

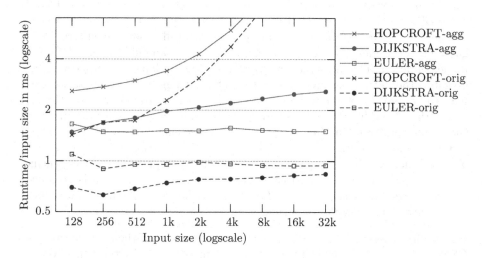

Fig. 4. Runtimes for three programs, with and without aggregates

be ensured that *first* all aggregates are updated, i.e. incremented in this case, *before* the aggregate results are activated.

- A unification can cause two or more `match/2` constraints to coincide. To preserve correctness, we would have to add the following rule to Figure 2:

    ..., (match$_i$(V,_) \ match$_i$(V,I), result(I,_) <=> true), ...

Unfortunately, the refined operational semantics (which is used to execute the result of the transformation), does not determine the order in which constraints are reactivated (cf. Section 2.2). This implies their is no clear-cut way to ensure all aggregates are made consistent, or duplicate maintained results are removed, *before* other CHR constraints are reactivated and use the incorrect aggregate values. This lack of control is a general problem of current CHR systems, that warrants further research outside the scope of this paper (see also [2] and Section 5). Fortunately, most aggregates range over ground data. For aggregates ranging over non-ground data, only the on-demand transformation is correct.

5   Discussion and Evaluation

Performance Evaluation. In [8,9] we revised a number of existing CHR programs to use aggregates. Because our transformation schemes have to deal with all possible use patterns of aggregates, and the original programs are manually specialized, we expect the programs using aggregates to be slower than the original programs. Our prototype implementation however shows the runtime complexity can be maintained, with an acceptable constant overhead. Figure 4 plots benchmark results for the different versions of the DIJKSTRA, EULER, and HOPCROFT programs (cf. [8,9]). The DIJKSTRA-agg program is about three times slower than the manually specialized DIJKSTRA-orig. For EULER and HOPCROFT, the version with aggregates is only about 1.5 times slower.

The DIJKSTRA-agg program uses an incrementally maintained min aggregate. The implementation of this aggregate relies on an efficient priority queue implementation. This illustrates another advantage of language support for aggregates: the data structures required for efficient aggregate computation only have to be implemented once; end users no longer have to worry about this.

For the above figures, a transformation scheme presented in [9] is used for the incrementally maintained aggregates. This scheme is an extended version of the scheme of Section 4.3, in which aggregates are still replaced by guards. The incremental scheme of Section 4.3 considerably improves the latter scheme: it permits efficient indexing on aggregate results, and failing guards no longer backtrack over result maintenance. For the above benchmarks though, we expect no significant difference in performance.

Discussion. Section 4 indicated several issues that occur when transforming to CHR code. A common thread is the lack of control offered by the refined operational semantics, a problem also perceived outside the context of aggregates (cf. [2]). Whilst the low-level constructs we introduced in this paper are acceptable for generated code or expert use, more high-level, declarative control structures are required for the CHR programmer. A first step are the *user-definable rule priorities* introduced by [2].

Related Work. Constructs related to aggregates are found in many languages. For SQL [10], which unlike CHR [7] is not Turing-complete, aggregates do add computational power. The original SQL standard only supports five aggregates: min, max, count, sum, and avg. Many recent database systems also include the possibility to extend the database query language with user-defined aggregates.

Recently, several production rule systems introduced a general accumulate construct, similar to our aggregate/7. As far as we know, current versions lack support for nested aggregates, complex goals, and incremental maintenance.

In logic programming, the best-known practical implementation of aggregates are the *all solutions* predicates findall/3, bagof/3 and setof/3. Other aggregates can be implemented in terms of these all solutions predicates.

In [11] we introduced CHR⁻, an extension of CHR with negation as absence. CHR with aggregates is a far more expressive generalization of CHR⁻ as negation as absence can easily be expressed using the count/2 aggregate.

6   Conclusion and Future Work

In this paper we presented an implementation approach for aggregates, a new declarative language feature for CHR that considerably increases its expressiveness. The approach is based on source-to-source transformation to regular CHR (extended with some low-level constructs). As a side-effect of our work, we created a practical, high-level source-to-source framework based on meta CHR rules. We outlined the design of non-trivial transformation schemes for on-demand and incremental aggregate computation, and clearly showed the effectiveness of CHR-to-CHR transformations. The source-to-source implementation approach allows for flexible and rapid implementations, easily portable to existing CHR systems. The current generation of optimizing CHR compilers ensure the desired runtime complexity is achieved, with an acceptable constant overhead. We clearly identified the issues that occur when transforming to CHR, and showed how they can be addressed using newly introduced low-level constructs. Several of these constructs have already proven useful outside the context of aggregates (e.g. [2]).

In future work, various ways can be investigated to improve the efficiency of our aggregates implementation. In particular, both specializations on the source level and dedicated support in the CHR compiler can be considered. Even though source-to-source transformation remains effective for aggregates in their full generality, specific cases can e.g. be distinguised where incremental maintenance of aggregates can be embedded directly in the constraint store insertion and removal operations. Also, static and dynamic analyses can be developed to automatically select the aggregate computation strategy (on-demand, incremental, or maybe hybrid strategies).

References

1. The CHR Home Page. http://www.cs.kuleuven.be/~dtai/projects/CHR/.
2. De Koninck, L., Schrijvers, T., Demoen, B.: User-definable rule priorities for CHR. In: 9th International ACM SIGPLAN Symposium on Principles and Practice of Declarative Programming, Wrocław, Poland, July 2007, pp. 25–36 (2007)
3. Duck, G.J., Stuckey, P.J., de la Banda, M.G., Holzbaur, C.: The Refined Operational Semantics of Constraint Handling Rules. In: Demoen, B., Lifschitz, V. (eds.) ICLP 2004. LNCS, vol. 3132, pp. 90–104. Springer, Heidelberg (2004)
4. Frühwirth, T.: Theory and practice of Constraint Handling Rules. Journal of Logic Programming 37(1–3), 95–138 (1998)
5. Kiczales, G., Lamping, J., Mendhekar, A., Meda, C., Lopes, C., Loingtier, J.-M., Irwing, J.: Aspect-Oriented Programming. In: Aksit, M., Matsuoka, S. (eds.) ECOOP 1997. LNCS, vol. 1241, pp. 220–242. Springer, Heidelberg (1997)
6. Schrijvers, T., Demoen, B.: The K.U.Leuven CHR system: Implementation and application. In: Selected Contributions, First Workshop on Constraint Handling Rules, (May 2004), http://www.cs.kuleuven.be/~toms/CHR/
7. Sneyers, J., Schrijvers, T., Demoen, B.: The computational power and complexity of Constraint Handling Rules. In: Second Workshop on Constraint Handling Rules, October 2005, pp. 3–17. Sitges, Spain (2005)
8. Sneyers, J., Van Weert, P., Schrijvers, T., Demoen, B.: Aggregates in CHR. In: Fourth Workshop on Constraint Handling Rules (2007) (to appear)
9. Sneyers, J., Van Weert, P., Schrijvers, T., Demoen, B.: Aggregates in CHR. Technical Report CW481, Dept. Computer Science, K.U.Leuven (2007)
10. ISO/IEC 9075:2003: Information technology – Database languages – SQL
11. Van Weert, P., Sneyers, J., Schrijvers, T., Demoen, B.: Extending CHR with negation as absence. In: Third Workshop on Constraint Handling Rules, Venice, Italy, pp. 125–139 (2006)
12. Wielemaker, J.: An overview of the SWI-Prolog programming environment. In: 13th Intl. Workshop on Logic Programming Environments, pp. 1–16. Heverlee, Belgium (2003), http://www.swi-prolog.org

Preserving Sharing in the Partial Evaluation of Lazy Functional Programs*

Sebastian Fischer[1], Josep Silva[2], Salvador Tamarit[2], and Germán Vidal[2]

[1] University of Kiel, Olshausenstr. 40, D-24098 Kiel, Germany
sebf@informatik.uni-kiel.de
[2] Technical University of Valencia, Camino de Vera S/N, E-46022 Valencia, Spain
{jsilva,stamarit,gvidal}@dsic.upv.es

Abstract. The goal of partial evaluation is the specialization of programs w.r.t. part of their input data. Although this technique is already well-known in the context of functional languages, current approaches are either overly restrictive or destroy sharing through the specialization process, which is unacceptable from a performance point of view. In this work, we present the basis of a new partial evaluation scheme for first-order lazy functional programs that preserves sharing through the specialization process and still allows the unfolding of arbitrary function calls.

1 Introduction

Partial evaluation [12] is an automatic technique for the specialization of programs. Currently, one can find partial evaluation techniques for a variety of programming languages, like C [5], Curry [17], Prolog [14], Scheme [8], etc.

In this work, we focus on solving a problem associated with the partial evaluation of *lazy* functional languages. In these languages (e.g., Haskell [15]), it is essential to *share* program variables in order to avoid losing efficiency due to the repeated evaluation of the same expression. Consider, e.g., the following program excerpt (we use [ ] and ":" as constructors of lists):

$$\text{sumList}([\,]) \quad = 0 \qquad\qquad \text{incList}(n, [\,]) \quad = [\,]$$
$$\text{sumList}(x : xs) = x + \text{sumList}(xs) \quad \text{incList}(n, x : xs) = (x+n) : \text{incList}(n, xs)$$

where function sumList sums the elements of a list and incList increments the elements of a list by a given number. Let us now consider different alternatives for the partial evaluation of the following expression:

$$\text{sumList}(\text{incList}(\boxed{e}, [a, b]))$$

where $\boxed{e}$ is a closed expression (i.e., without free variables) whose evaluation is expensive, a, b are natural numbers, and $[a, b]$ is a shorthand for $a : b : [\,]$.

* This work has been partially supported by the EU (FEDER) and the Spanish MEC under grants TIN2005-09207-C03-02 and *Acción Integrada* HA2006-0008.

First Try: Downgrading Program Efficiency. A naive partial evaluator may reduce the previous expression as follows:

$$\texttt{sumList}(\texttt{incList}(\boxed{e}, [\texttt{a}, \texttt{b}]))$$
$$\Rightarrow \texttt{sumList}(\texttt{a} + \boxed{e}) : \texttt{incList}(\boxed{e}, [\texttt{b}]))$$
$$\Rightarrow \texttt{sumList}(\texttt{a} + (\boxed{e1} + 42)) : \texttt{incList}(\boxed{e}, [\texttt{b}]))$$

where we assume that $\boxed{e}$ is unfolded to $\boxed{e1} + 42$ in one reduction step. Now, we would build the following residual rule—called *resultant*—associated to the above partial computation:

$$\texttt{new\_function} = \texttt{sumList}(\texttt{a} + (\boxed{e1} + 42)) : \texttt{incList}(\boxed{e}, [\texttt{b}]))$$

Then, if we evaluate `new_function` using the above rule, the original expression $\boxed{e}$ will be eventually evaluated twice since $\boxed{e}$ and $\boxed{e1}$ are not shared anymore. Actually, since their degree of evaluation is different (i.e., $\boxed{e1}$ comes from a one-step reduction of $\boxed{e}$), the identification of common subexpressions by means of some post-processing analysis is not generally feasible.

Clearly, the duplicate evaluation of $\boxed{e}$ is unacceptable from a performance point of view. Note that, in the original program, the expression $\boxed{e}$ is only evaluated once since the two occurrences of the variable n in the second rule of function `incList` are shared.

Second Try: Conservative Partial Evaluation. In order to avoid downgrading performance, partial evaluators of lazy languages usually include a restriction so that the unfolding of functions which are not *right-linear* (i.e., whose right-hand side contains multiple occurrences of the same variable) is forbidden.

In this case, the partial evaluation of $\texttt{sumList}(\texttt{incList}(\boxed{e}, [\texttt{a}, \texttt{b}]))$ would mainly return the original program unchanged since the function `incList` is not right-linear and, thus, cannot be unfolded. Unfortunately, this strategy is often overly restrictive since it may happen that $\boxed{e}$ can be completely evaluated at partial evaluation time, thus allowing the subsequent reduction of `sumList`.

Our Proposal: Sharing-Based Partial Evaluation. Current partial evaluation techniques for lazy functional (logic) languages have mostly ignored the issue of sharing,[1] generally implementing the conservative approach.

In this work, we present an alternative to such trivial, overly restrictive treatment of sharing during partial evaluation. Basically, we allow the unfolding of arbitrary function calls but still ensure that sharing is never destroyed. For this purpose, our partial evaluation scheme is based on a lazy semantics that models sharing by means of an updatable heap. For instance, given the above expression, we could produce a partial computation of the form

$$[\,] \ \& \ \texttt{sumList}(\texttt{incList}(\boxed{e}, [\texttt{a}, \texttt{b}]))$$
$$\Rightarrow [\texttt{n} \mapsto \boxed{e}, \texttt{x} \mapsto \texttt{a}, \texttt{xs} \mapsto [\texttt{b}]] \ \& \ \texttt{sumList}(\texttt{x} + \texttt{n} : \texttt{incList}(\texttt{n}, \texttt{xs}))$$
$$\Rightarrow [\texttt{n} \mapsto \boxed{e1} + 42, \texttt{x} \mapsto \texttt{a}, \texttt{xs} \mapsto [\texttt{b}]] \ \& \ \texttt{sumList}(\texttt{x} + \texttt{n} : \texttt{incList}(\texttt{n}, \texttt{xs}))$$

---

[1] We note that this is a critical issue that has been considered in the context of *inlining* (see, e.g., [16]), which could be seen like a rather simple form of partial evaluation.

$$P ::= D_1 \dots D_m \qquad \text{(program)}$$
$$D ::= f(x_1, \dots, x_n) = e \qquad \text{(function definition)}$$
$$e ::= x \qquad \text{(variable)}$$
$$\mid c(x_1, \dots, x_n) \qquad \text{(constructor call)}$$
$$\mid f(x_1, \dots, x_n) \qquad \text{(function call)}$$
$$\mid let \; \{\overline{x_k = e_k}\} \; in \; e \qquad \text{(let binding)}$$
$$\mid case \; x \; of \; \{\overline{p_k \to e_k}\} \qquad \text{(case expression)}$$
$$p ::= c(x_1, \dots, x_n) \qquad \text{(pattern)}$$

Domains

$P_1, P_2, \dots \in Prog$ (Programs)
$x, y, z, \dots \in Var$ (Variables)
$a, b, c, \dots \in \mathcal{C}$ (Constructors)
$f, g, h, \dots \in \mathcal{F}$ (Functions)
$p_1, p_2, p_3, \dots \in Pat$ (Patterns)

Fig. 1. Syntax for normalized flat programs

where *states* are informally denoted by a pair *heap & expression* and $[\,]$ denotes the empty heap. Observe that there is a single binding for all occurrences of variable n and, thus, duplicated computations are not possible. Here, we would produce the following associated residual rule:

new_function $= \; $ let n $= \boxed{e1} + 42$ in sumList(a $+$ n : incList(n, [b]))

where the bindings for variables x and xs are inlined since they only occur once in the expression, and the binding for n that appears twice is kept in a let expression so that sharing is preserved.

In summary, our new approach is based on the definition of an unfolding strategy that extends a lazy semantics [1] (which models variable sharing by means of an updatable heap) in order to perform symbolic computations, i.e., in order to deal with free variables in expressions denoting missing information at partial evaluation time. Then, we introduce how residual rules should be extracted from these partial computations. For simplicity, we will not introduce the details of a complete partial evaluation scheme (but it would be similar to that of [2] by replacing the underlying partial evaluation semantics and the construction of residual rules from partial computations, i.e., control issues would remain basically unaltered).

2   Preliminaries

We consider in this work a simple, first-order lazy functional language. The syntax is shown in Fig. 1, where we write $\overline{o_n}$ for the *sequence of objects* $o_1, \dots, o_n$. A program consists of a sequence of function definitions such that the left-hand side has pairwise different variable arguments. The right-hand side is an expression composed by variables, data constructors, function calls, let bindings (where the local variables $\overline{x_k}$ are only visible in $\overline{e_k}$ and e), and case expressions of the form *case* x *of* $\{c_1(\overline{x_{n_1}}) \to e_1; \dots; c_k(\overline{x_{n_k}}) \to e_k\}$, where x is a variable, $c_1, \dots, c_k$ are different constructors, and $e_1, \dots, e_k$ are expressions. The *pattern variables* $\overline{x_{n_i}}$ are introduced locally and bind the corresponding variables of e_i. We say that an expression is *closed* if it contains no occurrences of free variables (i.e., variables which are not bound by let bindings).

Observe that, according to Fig. 1, the arguments of function and constructor calls are variables. As in [13], this is essential to express sharing without the use of graph structures. This is not a serious restriction since source programs can be *normalized* so that they follow the syntax of Fig. 1 (see, e.g., [13,1]).

Laziness of computations will show up in the description of the behavior of function calls and case expressions. In a function call, parameters are not evaluated but directly passed to the body of the function. In a case expression, the outermost symbol of the case argument is required. Therefore, the case argument should be evaluated to *head normal form* [7] (i.e., a variable or an expression with a constructor at the outermost position).

3 Partial Evaluation of Lazy Functional Programs

The main ingredients of our new proposal for preserving sharing through the specialization process are the following: i) partial computations are performed with a lazy semantics that models sharing by means of an updatable heap (cf. Sect. 3.1); ii) this semantics is then extended in order to perform symbolic computations during partial evaluation (cf. Sect. 3.2); iii) finally, we introduce a method to extract residual rules from partial computations (cf. Sect. 3.3).

3.1 The Standard Semantics

First, we present a lazy evaluation semantics for our first-order functional programs that models sharing. The rules of the small-step semantics are shown in Fig. 2 (they are a simplification of the calculus in [1], which in turn originates from an adaptation of Launchbury's natural semantics [13]). It follows these naming conventions:

$$\Gamma, \Delta, \Theta \in \mathit{Heap} \ = \ \mathit{Var} \to \mathit{Exp} \qquad v \in \mathit{Value} \ ::= \ x \mid c(\overline{x_n})$$

A *heap* is a partial mapping from variables to expressions (the *empty heap* is denoted by $[\,]$). The value associated to variable x in heap Γ is denoted by $\Gamma[x]$. $\Gamma[x \mapsto e]$ denotes a heap with $\Gamma[x] = e$, i.e., we use this notation either as a condition on a heap Γ or as a modification of Γ. A *value* is a constructor-rooted term (i.e., a term whose outermost function symbol is a constructor symbol).

A *state* of the small-step semantics is a triple $\langle \Gamma, e, S \rangle$, where Γ is the current heap, e is the expression to be evaluated (often called the *control* of the small-step semantics), and S is the stack which represents the current context. We briefly describe the transition rules:

In rule var, the evaluation of a variable x that is bound to an expression e proceeds by evaluating e and adding to the stack the reference to variable x. If a value v is eventually computed and there is a variable x on top of the stack, rule val updates the heap with $x \mapsto v$. This rule achieves the effect of sharing since the next time the value of variable x is demanded, the value v will be immediately returned thus avoiding the repeated evaluation of e.

$$\text{var}$$
$$\langle \Gamma[x \mapsto e], x, S \rangle \Rightarrow \langle \Gamma[x \mapsto e], e, x : S \rangle$$

$$\text{val}$$
$$\langle \Gamma, v, x : S \rangle \Rightarrow \langle \Gamma[x \mapsto v], v, S \rangle \qquad \text{where } v \text{ is a value}$$

$$\text{fun}$$
$$\langle \Gamma, f(\overline{x_n}), S \rangle \Rightarrow \langle \Gamma, \rho(e), S \rangle \qquad \text{where } f(\overline{y_n}) = e \in P \text{ and } \rho = \{\overline{y_n \mapsto x_n}\}$$

$$\text{let}$$
$$\langle \Gamma, let \ \{\overline{x_k = e_k}\} \ in \ e, S \rangle \Rightarrow \langle \Gamma[\overline{y_k \mapsto \rho(e_k)}], \rho(e), S \rangle \quad \begin{array}{l} \text{where } \rho = \{\overline{x_k \mapsto y_k}\} \\ \text{and } \overline{y_n} \text{ are fresh variables} \end{array}$$

$$\text{case}$$
$$\langle \Gamma, case \ e \ of \ \{\overline{p_k \to e_k}\}, S \rangle \Rightarrow \langle \Gamma, e, \{\overline{p_k \to e_k}\} : S \rangle$$

$$\text{select}$$
$$\langle \Gamma, c(\overline{x_n}), \{\overline{p_k \to e_k}\} : S \rangle \Rightarrow \langle \Gamma, \rho(e_i), S \rangle \quad \begin{array}{l} \text{where } p_i = c(\overline{y_n}) \text{ and } \rho = \{\overline{y_n \mapsto x_n}\}, \\ \text{with } i \in \{1, \ldots, k\} \end{array}$$

Fig. 2. Small-step semantics for (sharing-based) lazy functional programs

Rule fun implements a simple function unfolding. Here, $\rho : Var \to Var$ denotes a variable *substitution*. We assume that the considered program P is a global parameter of the calculus.

In order to reduce a let construct, rule let adds the bindings to the heap and proceeds with the evaluation of the main argument of *let*. Note that the variables introduced by the let construct are renamed with fresh names in order to avoid variable name clashes. For this purpose, we use *variable renamings*, a particular case of substitutions which are bijections on the domain of variables Var.

Rule case initiates the evaluation of a case expression by evaluating the case argument and pushing the alternatives $\{\overline{p_k \to e_k}\}$ on top of the stack. If a value is eventually reached, then rule select is used to select the appropriate branch and continue with the evaluation of this branch.

In order to evaluate an expression e, we construct an *initial state* of the form $\langle [\ ], e, [\ ] \rangle$ and apply the rules of Fig. 2. We denote by $\Rightarrow^*$ the reflexive and transitive closure of $\Rightarrow$. A derivation $\langle [\ ], e, [\ ] \rangle \Rightarrow^* \langle \Gamma, e', S \rangle$ is *complete* if e' is a value and S is the empty stack.[2]

Example 1. Consider the following simple functions:

$$\text{double}(x) = \text{add}(x, x)$$
$$\text{add}(n, m) = \text{case n of } \{Z \to m; \ S(u) \to let \ \{v = \text{add}(u, m)\} \ in \ S(v)\}$$

where natural numbers are built from Z and S. In order to evaluate the expression $\text{double}(\text{add}(Z, Z))$, we proceed as follows. First, we normalize it, i.e.,

$$exp \equiv let \ \{x_1 = Z, \ x_2 = Z\} \ in \ (let \ \{y = \text{add}(x_1, x_2)\} \ in \ \text{double}(y))$$

Then, we construct the initial state $\langle [\ ], exp, [\ ] \rangle$ and apply the rules of the standard semantics. The complete derivation is shown in Fig. 3 (where variables x_1, x_2, y are renamed as w_1, w_2, v, respectively).

---

[2] We ignore failing derivations (e.g., a case expression with no matching branch) in this work in order to keep the presentation simple.

$$\langle [\,], exp, [\,]\rangle \Rightarrow_{\mathsf{let}} \quad \langle \Gamma_1 \equiv [\mathtt{w}_1 \mapsto \mathtt{Z}, \mathtt{w}_2 \mapsto \mathtt{Z}], \ \mathtt{let}\ \{\mathtt{v} = \mathtt{add}(\mathtt{w}_1, \mathtt{w}_2)\}\ \mathtt{in}\ \mathtt{double}(\mathtt{v}), [\,]\rangle$$

$$\Rightarrow_{\mathsf{let}} \quad \langle \Gamma_2 \equiv \Gamma_1[\mathtt{v} \mapsto \mathtt{add}(\mathtt{w}_1, \mathtt{w}_2)], \ \mathtt{double}(\mathtt{v}), [\,]\rangle$$

$$\Rightarrow_{\mathsf{fun}} \quad \langle \Gamma_2, \mathtt{add}(\mathtt{v}, \mathtt{v}), [\,]\rangle$$

$$\Rightarrow_{\mathsf{fun}} \quad \langle \Gamma_2, \mathtt{case\ v\ of}\ \{\mathtt{Z} \to \mathtt{v};\ \mathtt{S}(\mathtt{u}) \to \mathtt{let}\ \{\mathtt{v} = \mathtt{add}(\mathtt{u}, \mathtt{v})\}\ \mathtt{in}\ \mathtt{S}(\mathtt{v})\}, [\,]\rangle$$

$$\Rightarrow_{\mathsf{case}} \quad \langle \Gamma_2, \mathtt{v}, S_1 \equiv [\{\mathtt{Z} \to \mathtt{v};\ \mathtt{S}(\mathtt{u}) \to \mathtt{let}\ \{\mathtt{v} = \mathtt{add}(\mathtt{u}, \mathtt{v})\}\ \mathtt{in}\ \mathtt{S}(\mathtt{v})\}]\rangle$$

$$\Rightarrow_{\mathsf{var}} \quad \langle \Gamma_2, \mathtt{add}(\mathtt{w}_1, \mathtt{w}_2), S_2 \equiv \mathtt{v} : S_1\rangle$$

$$\Rightarrow_{\mathsf{fun}} \quad \langle \Gamma_2, \mathtt{case\ w}_1\ \mathtt{of}\ \{\mathtt{Z} \to \mathtt{w}_2;\ \mathtt{S}(\mathtt{u}) \to \mathtt{let}\ \{\mathtt{v} = \mathtt{add}(\mathtt{u}, \mathtt{w}_2)\}\ \mathtt{in}\ \mathtt{S}(\mathtt{v})\}, S_2\rangle$$

$$\Rightarrow_{\mathsf{case}} \quad \langle \Gamma_2, \mathtt{w}_1, S_3 \equiv \{\mathtt{Z} \to \mathtt{w}_2;\ \mathtt{S}(\mathtt{u}) \to \mathtt{let}\ \{\mathtt{v} = \mathtt{add}(\mathtt{u}, \mathtt{w}_2)\}\ \mathtt{in}\ \mathtt{S}(\mathtt{v})\} : S_2\rangle$$

$$\Rightarrow_{\mathsf{var}} \quad \langle \Gamma_2, \mathtt{Z}, \mathtt{w}_1 : S_3\rangle$$

$$\Rightarrow_{\mathsf{val}} \quad \langle \Gamma_2, \mathtt{Z}, S_3\rangle$$

$$\Rightarrow_{\mathsf{select}} \quad \langle \Gamma_2, \mathtt{w}_2, S_2\rangle$$

$$\Rightarrow_{\mathsf{var}} \quad \langle \Gamma_2, \mathtt{Z}, \mathtt{w}_2 : S_2\rangle$$

$$\Rightarrow_{\mathsf{val}} \quad \langle \Gamma_2, \mathtt{Z}, S_2\rangle$$

$$\Rightarrow_{\mathsf{val}} \quad \langle \Gamma_3 \equiv [\mathtt{w}_1 \mapsto \mathtt{Z}, \mathtt{w}_2 \mapsto \mathtt{Z}, \mathtt{v} \mapsto \mathtt{Z}], \mathtt{Z}, S_1\rangle$$

$$\Rightarrow_{\mathsf{select}} \quad \langle \Gamma_3, \mathtt{v}, [\,]\rangle$$

$$\Rightarrow_{\mathsf{var}} \quad \langle \Gamma_3, \mathtt{Z}, [\mathtt{v}]\rangle$$

$$\Rightarrow_{\mathsf{val}} \quad \langle \Gamma_3, \mathtt{Z}, [\,]\rangle$$

Fig. 3. Complete derivation for $\mathtt{double}(\mathtt{add}(\mathtt{Z}, \mathtt{Z}))$

Observe that the expression $\mathtt{add}(\mathtt{Z}, \mathtt{Z})$ is only evaluated once: look at the 6th state in the derivation, where its evaluation is first demanded (since variable v is bound to this expression in the heap), and at the 16th state, where it is demanded again and the computed value is just returned from the heap.

3.2   The Partial Evaluation Semantics

While expressions to be evaluated at run time should be *closed* (i.e., without free variables), expressions to be partially evaluated are usually *incomplete* so that missing information is denoted by means of free variables. The standard semantics of Fig. 2 is not appropriate to perform computations at partial evaluation time since there is no rule for evaluating variables that are not bound in the associated heap.

In this work, we follow the approach of [3] and introduce a *residualizing* version of the standard semantics.[3] Essentially, the resulting partial evaluation semantics has the following features:

- A free variable x is represented in a heap Γ by a circular binding $x \mapsto x$ such that $\Gamma[x] = x$. Furthermore, such free variables are now considered as *values* in rule val.
- Sharing is preserved thanks to the use of an unfolding strategy based on a (residualizing) semantics that models sharing, together with an appropriate procedure for extracting residual rules from partial computations (see

---

[3] Note, however, that [3] does not consider a sharing-based standard semantics and, thus, the residualizing extensions are rather different.

fun_stop
$$\langle \Gamma, \underline{f(\overline{x_n})}, x : \{\overline{p_k \to e_k}\} : S \rangle \;\Rightarrow\; \langle \Gamma[x \mapsto \underline{f(\overline{x_n})}], \underline{case}\ x\ of\ \{\overline{p_k \to e_k}\}, S \rangle$$

case_stop
$$\langle \Gamma, \underline{case}\ y\ of\ \{\overline{p'_q \to e'_q}\}, x : \{\overline{p_k \to e_k}\} : S \rangle$$
$$\Rightarrow\; \langle \Gamma[x \mapsto \underline{case}\ y\ of\ \{\overline{p'_q \to e'_q}\}], \underline{case}\ x\ of\ \{\overline{p_k \to e_k}\}, S \rangle$$

guess
$$\langle \Gamma[x \mapsto x], x, \{\overline{p_k \to e_k}\} : S \rangle \;\Rightarrow\; \langle \Gamma[x \mapsto x], \underline{case}\ x\ of\ \{\overline{p_k \to e_k}\}, S \rangle$$

case_of_case
$$\langle \Gamma[x \mapsto x], \underline{case}\ x\ of\ \{\overline{p'_m \to e'_m}\}, \{\overline{p_k \to e_k}\} : S \rangle$$
$$\Rightarrow\; \langle \Gamma[x \mapsto x], \underline{case}\ x\ of\ \{\overline{p'_m \to case\ e'_m\ of\ \{\overline{p_k \to e_k}\}}\}, S \rangle$$

residualize
$$\langle \Gamma[x \mapsto x], \underline{case}\ x\ of\ \{\overline{p_k \to e_k}\}, [\,] \rangle \;\Rightarrow\; case\ x\ of\ \{\overline{p'_k \to \langle \Gamma[x \mapsto p'_k, \overline{y_{nk} \mapsto y_{nk}}], e'_k, [\,] \rangle}\}$$
$$\text{where } p_i = c(\overline{x_{ni}}),\ \rho_i = \{\overline{x_{ni} \mapsto y_{ni}}\},\ \overline{y_{ni}}\ \text{are fresh,}$$
$$\text{with } p'_i = \rho_i(p_i),\ \text{and } e'_i = \rho_i(e_i),\ \text{for all } i = 1,\ldots,k$$

Fig. 4. Partial evaluation rules

Sect. 3.3). This is orthogonal to control issues and, thus, our approach can be integrated in both online or offline partial evaluation schemes (see, e.g., [10] for a gentle introduction to online and offline partial evaluation). For simplicity, though, we consider in the following an *offline* scheme for partial evaluation and assume that the program contains some function *annotations* that can be used to ensure the termination of partial computations.

To be precise, we denote annotated function calls by underlining the function name and annotated case expressions by underlining the word *case*. Basically, annotated function calls or case expressions *should not be reduced* in order to have a finite computation.[4]

Underlined function calls and case expressions are no longer evaluable and, thus, they are also treated as values in rule val.

Because of the introduction of the new "values" (free variables and annotated functions and cases), rule select does not suffice anymore to evaluate a case expression whose argument reduces to a value. Therefore, we introduce the rules shown in Fig. 4, which we now briefly describe.

Rule fun_stop applies when the argument of a case expression evaluates to an annotated function call $\underline{f(\overline{x_n})}$. Here, the form of the current stack is $x : \{\overline{p_k \to e_k}\} : S$, which means that the original case expression had the form $case\ x\ of\ \{\overline{p_k \to e_k}\}$ and x was eventually reduced to $\underline{f(\overline{x_n})}$. In this case, we annotate the original case expression (since it is not reducible because $\underline{f(\overline{x_n})}$ is not reducible), update the binding for x, and return the annotated case expression. Intuitively speaking, once an annotated function call suspends the computation, we should go *backwards* and reconstruct the case expression whose branches were stored in the stack: $\underline{case}\ \underline{f(\overline{x_n})}\ of\ \{\overline{p_k \to e_k}\}$.

---

[4] We do not deal with termination issues and the computation of program annotations in this paper but refer the interested reader to, e.g., [9,11,12,17,6] (within the functional and functional logic paradigms).

Rule case_stop proceeds in a similar way, the only difference being that the computed value is now an annotated case expression.

Rule guess applies when the argument of a case expression reduces to a free variable. Similarly to the previous rules, an annotated case expression is returned. Observe, however, that it does not mean that the computation is suspended; rather, the annotated case expression can still be further evaluated by rules case_of_case and residualize (see below).

Rule case_of_case, originally introduced in the context of deforestation [18], is used to reduce a case expression whose argument is another case with a free variable as argument. It moves the outer case to the branches of the inner case, e.g., it transforms an expression like

$$\text{case } (\text{case x of } \{p_1 \mapsto e_1; p_2 \mapsto e_2\}) \text{ of } \{q_1 \mapsto t_1; q_2 \mapsto t_2\}$$

into case x of { $p_1 \mapsto$ case e_1 of $\{q_1 \mapsto t_1; q_2 \mapsto t_2\}$;
$\qquad\qquad\quad p_2 \mapsto$ case e_2 of $\{q_1 \mapsto t_1; q_2 \mapsto t_2\}$ } .

It is often the case that the transformed expression has more opportunities for further reduction (look at the inner cases, where possibly known arguments e_1 and e_2 may allow the application of rule select). Basically, we use this rule to *lift* case expressions with a free variable to the topmost position so that rule residualize applies.

Finally, rule residualize *residualizes* a case expression (i.e., it is already considered part of the residual code) but allows us to continue evaluating the states in the branches of the residualized case expression. Observe that, because of this rule, the type of the semantics is no longer $State \rightarrow State$, where $State$ is the domain of possible states, but $State^{Exp} \rightarrow State^{Exp}$, where $State^{Exp}$ is defined as follows: $State^{Exp} ::= State \mid case\ x\ of\ \{p_k \rightarrow State^{Exp}\}$. Note that bindings of the form $x \mapsto p'_i$, $i = 1, \ldots, k$, are applied to the different branches so that information is propagated forward in the computation. As in rule let, we rename the variables of the case patterns to avoid variable name clashes, so that p'_i and e'_i denote the renaming of p_i and e_i, respectively. Moreover, since the pattern variables of p'_i are not bound in e'_i, we add them to the heap as free variables, i.e., as circular bindings of the form $\overline{y_{ni} \mapsto y_{ni}}$.

Now, our *partial evaluation semantics* includes the rules of Fig. 2 (standard component) and Fig. 4 (residualizing component). We note that rule val overlaps with rules fun_stop and case_stop since annotated expressions are considered values. This overlapping is not intended and can easily be avoided by adding an additional side condition for rule val:

(val redefined)

$$\langle \Gamma, v, x : S \rangle \Rightarrow \langle \Gamma[x \mapsto v], v, S \rangle \text{ if rules fun\_stop \& case\_stop are not applicable}$$
$$\text{where } v \text{ is a value}$$

Also, we note that an additional condition should be added in rule var in order to avoid undesired loops due to the evaluation of free variables:

(var redefined)

$$\langle \Gamma[x \mapsto e], x, S \rangle \Rightarrow \langle \Gamma[x \mapsto e], e, x : S \rangle \quad \text{where } e \neq x$$

In our partial evaluation semantics, we should always construct *complete* computations, i.e., we should apply the rules of the partial evaluation semantics as much as possible. Note that it does not mean that every function is unfolded, since one can still stop the unfolding process by means of annotations (so that termination is guaranteed). Then, we have the following trivial property:

Lemma 1. *Let $s_0, s_n \in State^{Exp}$ be states such that there exists a complete derivation $s_0 \Rightarrow^* s_n$ using the rules of the partial evaluation semantics (Figures 2 and 4). Then, every state $s \in State$ occurring in s_n has an empty stack.*

This result is an easy consequence of the fact that every function and case expression is either reduced, annotated or residualized, so that an empty stack is eventually obtained.

Another trivial but important property relates the standard and the partial evaluation semantics as follows:

Lemma 2. *Let $\mathcal{P}$ be a program without annotations and $s_0 = \langle [\,], e, [\,] \rangle$ be an initial state where e is closed. Then, $s_0 \Rightarrow^* s_n$ holds in the standard semantics iff $s_0 \Rightarrow^* s_n$ holds in the partial evaluation semantics.*

Intuitively speaking, the above lemma says that, as long as no annotated function call occurs, both calculi have exactly the same behavior.

The following simple example illustrates the way our partial evaluation semantics deals with sharing in a partial computation.

Example 2. Consider again functions `double` and `add` from Example 1 and the initial expression `double(double(x))`. By normalizing this expression, we build the following initial state:

$$\langle [\,], \texttt{let } \{\texttt{x} = \texttt{x}, \texttt{w} = \underline{\texttt{double}}(\texttt{x})\} \texttt{ in double(w)}, [\,] \rangle$$

The associated complete computation with the partial evaluation semantics is shown in Fig. 5 (variables `x` and `w` are renamed as `n` and `m`, respectively). Note that, thanks to the use of the partial evaluation semantics, we can evaluate the considered expression as much as needed but we still keep track of shared expressions in the associated heap.

3.3   Extracting Residual Rules

Now, we consider how residual rules are extracted from the computations performed with the semantics of Figures 2 and 4.

Definition 1 (resultant). *Let P be an annotated program and e be an expression. Let $\langle [\,], e, [\,] \rangle \Rightarrow^* e'$ be a complete derivation with the rules of Figures 2 and 4 (i.e., e' is irreducible). The associated resultant is given by the following rule:*

$$f(\overline{x_n}) = [\![del(e')]\!]$$

$$\Rightarrow_{\text{let}} \quad \begin{array}{lll} \langle[\,], & \text{let } \{x = x, w = \underline{\text{double}}(x)\} \text{ in double}(w), & [\,]\rangle \\ \langle[n \mapsto n, & \text{double}(m), & [\,]\rangle \\ \quad m \mapsto \underline{\text{double}}(n)], & & \end{array}$$

$$\Rightarrow_{\text{fun}} \quad \begin{array}{lll} \langle[n \mapsto n, & \text{add}(m, m), & [\,]\rangle \\ \quad m \mapsto \underline{\text{double}}(n)], & & \end{array}$$

$$\Rightarrow_{\text{fun}} \quad \begin{array}{lll} \langle[n \mapsto n, & \text{case } m \text{ of} & [\,]\rangle \\ \quad m \mapsto \underline{\text{double}}(n)], & \{Z \to m; \ S(u) \to \text{let } \{v = \text{add}(u, m)\} \text{ in } S(v)\} & \end{array}$$

$$\Rightarrow_{\text{case}} \quad \begin{array}{lll} \langle[n \mapsto n, & m, & [\{\ldots\}]\rangle \\ \quad m \mapsto \underline{\text{double}}(n)], & & \end{array}$$

$$\Rightarrow_{\text{var}} \quad \begin{array}{lll} \langle[n \mapsto n, & \underline{\text{double}}(n), & [m, \{\ldots\}]\rangle \\ \quad m \mapsto \underline{\text{double}}(n)], & & \end{array}$$

$$\Rightarrow_{\text{fun\_stop}} \quad \begin{array}{lll} \langle[n \mapsto n, & \underline{\text{case } m \text{ of}} & [\,]\rangle \\ \quad m \mapsto \underline{\text{double}}(n)], & \{Z \to m; \ S(u) \to \text{let } \{v = \text{add}(u, m)\} \text{ in } S(v)\} & \end{array}$$

Fig. 5. Derivation with the partial evaluation semantics

where f is a fresh function symbol,[5] $\overline{x_n}$ are the free variables of e (appropriately renamed as in the considered computation), function del removes the annotations (if any), and function $[\![\,]\!]$ is defined as follows:

$$[\![e]\!] = \begin{cases} \textit{case } x \textit{ of } \{\overline{p_k \to [\![e_k]\!]}\} & \textit{if } e = \textit{case } x \textit{ of } \{\overline{p_k \to e_k}\} \\ \textit{let } \overline{\Gamma} \textit{ in } e' & \textit{if } e = \langle \Gamma, e', [\,]\rangle \end{cases}$$

Here, $\overline{\Gamma}$ represents the set of bindings stored in Γ except those for $\overline{x_n}$ (which are now the parameters of the new function).

Let us illustrate the extraction of a residual rule with an example.

Example 3. Consider the computation of Example 2 shown in Fig. 5. The associated resultant is as follows:

$$\mathtt{f}(n) = [\![\langle [n \mapsto n, \quad \text{case } m \text{ of}$$
$$m \mapsto \text{double}(n)], \ \{Z \to m; \ S(u) \to \text{let } \{v = \text{add}(u, m)\} \text{ in } S(v)\}, [\,]\rangle]\!]$$

which is reduced to

$$\mathtt{f}(n) = \text{let } \{m \mapsto \text{double}(n)\} \text{ in}$$
$$\text{case } m \text{ of } \{Z \to m; \ S(u) \to \text{let } \{v = \text{add}(u, m)\} \text{ in } S(v)\}$$

Observe that sharing is preserved despite the unfolding of a function which is not right-linear (i.e., the outer call to function double). Note also that inlining the let expression (i.e., replacing all occurrences of m by double(n)) would destroy this property since double would be evaluated twice, once as an argument of the case expression and once when selecting the corresponding case branch.

---

[5] Consequently, some calls in the right-hand side should also be renamed. We do not deal with renaming of function calls in this paper; nevertheless, standard techniques for functional (logic) languages like those in [4] would be applicable.

3.4   Correctness

The correctness of our approach to the partial evaluation of first-order lazy functional programs relies on two results. On the one hand, one should prove that the partial evaluation semantics is somehow equivalent to the standard one. Regarding the extraction of resultants from computations with the partial evaluation semantics, its correctness can easily be proved by exploiting the clear operational equivalence between a state of the form $\langle \Gamma, e, [\,] \rangle$ and an expression like $let\ \overline{\Gamma}\ in\ e$ (i.e., we have that $\langle [\,], let\ \overline{\Gamma}\ in\ e, [\,] \rangle$ reduces to $\langle \Gamma, e, [\,] \rangle$ in one reduction step by applying rule let).

Let us first consider the equivalence between the standard and the partial evaluation semantics for closed expressions. In the following, we say that two states $\langle \Gamma, e, S \rangle$ and $\langle \Gamma', e', S' \rangle$ are *equivalent under annotations*, in symbols $\langle \Gamma, e, S \rangle \approx \langle \Gamma', e', S' \rangle$, iff Γ and Γ' become equal when removing bindings with annotated expressions, $e = e'$, and $S = S'$. By abuse, we say that a derivation is complete when no more rules are applicable, even if this is due to an annotated function call (which is irreducible in the standard semantics since it does not deal with annotations).

Theorem 1. *Let $\mathcal{P}$ be an annotated program and s be an initial state. If $s \Rightarrow^* s'$ is a complete derivation in $\mathcal{P}$ with the standard semantics then, for any derivation $s \Rightarrow^* s' \Rightarrow^* \langle \Gamma, e, [\,] \rangle$ in $\mathcal{P}$ with the partial evaluation semantics, we have $\langle \Gamma, e, [\,] \rangle \Rightarrow^* s''$ with the standard semantics and $s' \approx s''$.*

Intuitively, the above result can be depicted graphically as follows (SS and PES stand for Standard Semantics and Partial Evaluation Semantics, respectively):

Proof. Let $s \Rightarrow^* s'$ in $\mathcal{P}$ with the standard semantics, where $s' = \langle \Gamma_s, e_s, S_s \rangle$. Now, we distinguish two possibilities. If e_s is a value (and, thus, $S_s = [\,]$) then the proof is trivial by Lemma 2, with $\langle \Gamma, e, [\,] \rangle = \langle \Gamma_s, e_s, S_s \rangle$.

Otherwise, $e_s \equiv \underline{f(\overline{x_n})}$ for some function symbol f. By Lemma 2, we have $s \Rightarrow^* s'$ with the partial evaluation semantics. Trivially, since e was closed, only rules fun_stop and case_stop from the partial evaluation semantics can be applied to s'. Let $s' \Rightarrow^* \langle \Gamma, e, [\,] \rangle$ be a derivation with the partial evaluation semantics where rules fun_stop and case_stop are applied as much as possible. Then, we can also construct a sort of inverse computation using rules case and var from the standard semantics; namely, every application of rule fun_stop or case_stop can be undone by applying rules case and var in this order. Hence, we have $\langle \Gamma, e, [\,] \rangle \Rightarrow^* \langle \Gamma'', e'', S'' \rangle \equiv s''$ by applying rules case and var as much as possible. Finally, it is clear that $s' \approx s''$ since Γ'' adds only bindings with annotated expressions to Γ_s, $e'' = e_s$, and $S'' = S_s$.

Now, we focus on expressions which are not closed. Since this is orthogonal to program annotations, we now consider programs without annotations.

In the following, we introduce the following reduction rules over the expressions produced by the partial evaluation semantics:

$$case\ c(\overline{v_n})\ of\ \{\overline{p_k \to e_k}\} \hookrightarrow \sigma_i(e_i)\quad if\ p_i = c(\overline{y_n})\ and\ \sigma_i = \{\overline{y_n \mapsto v_n}\}$$
$$s \hookrightarrow s'\qquad\qquad if\ s \Rightarrow s'\ with\ the\ standard\ semantics$$

These rules are used to evaluate expressions from $State^{Exp}$ (as returned by rule residualize). Our next result is then stated as follows:

Theorem 2. *Let $\mathcal{P}$ be a program and e be a (not necessarily closed) expression. Let σ be a substitution mapping the free variables of e to values. If there exists a complete derivation $\langle [\,], \sigma(e), [\,] \rangle \Rightarrow^* \langle \Gamma, v, [\,] \rangle$ with the standard semantics, then for all derivations $\langle [\,], e, [\,] \rangle \Rightarrow^* s$ with the partial evaluation semantics we have $\sigma(s) \hookrightarrow^* s'$ and $s' \approx \langle \Gamma, v, [\,] \rangle$.*

Intuitively speaking, this result ensures that computations with the partial evaluation semantics and some incomplete expression including free variables appropriately capture every possible computation with the standard semantics and a closed instance of the incomplete expression.

Proof. For simplicity, we consider that e contains a single free variable x and that $\sigma = \{x \mapsto c\}$ maps x to a constructor constant c. Assume that the derivation with the standard semantics has the form

$$
\begin{aligned}
\langle [\,], \sigma(e), [\,] \rangle \Rightarrow^* \quad & \langle \Gamma_x[x \mapsto c], x, [\{\overline{p_k \to e_k}\}] \rangle \\
\Rightarrow_{var} \quad & \langle \Gamma_x[x \mapsto c], c, x : \{\overline{p_k \to e_k}\} \rangle \\
\Rightarrow_{val} \quad & \langle \Gamma_x[x \mapsto c], c, [\{\overline{p_k \to e_k}\}] \rangle \\
\Rightarrow_{select} \quad & \langle \Gamma_x[x \mapsto c], e_i, [\,] \rangle \qquad\qquad (with\ p_i = c,\ i \in \{1, \ldots, k\}) \\
\Rightarrow^* \quad & \langle \Gamma, v, [\,] \rangle
\end{aligned}
$$

Observe that we considered a stack with the branches of a single case expression. A generalization to consider nested case expressions is not difficult and only require some additional applications of rule case_of_case.

Trivially, we have $\langle [\,], e, [\,] \rangle \Rightarrow^* \langle \Gamma_x, x, [\{\overline{p_k \to e_k}\}] \rangle$ with the standard semantics. Therefore, $\langle [\,], e, [\,] \rangle \Rightarrow^* \langle \Gamma_x, x, [\{\overline{p_k \to e_k}\}] \rangle$ is also a derivation with the partial evaluation semantics by Lemma 2.

We now consider two possibilities for the partial evaluation semantics. If the derivation is stopped before applying rule guess, the claim follows trivially by the definition of $\hookrightarrow$. Otherwise, we have a derivation of the form

$$
\begin{aligned}
\langle [\,], e, [\,] \rangle \Rightarrow^* \quad & \langle \Gamma_x[x \mapsto x], x, [\{\overline{p_k \to e_k}\}] \rangle \\
\Rightarrow_{guess} \quad & \langle \Gamma_x[x \mapsto x], \underline{case\ x\ of\ \{\overline{p_k \to e_k}\}}, [\,] \rangle \\
\Rightarrow_{residualize} \quad & case\ x\ of\ \{p_k \to \langle \Gamma_x[x \mapsto \rho_k(p_k), \overline{y_{nk} \mapsto y_{nk}}], \rho_k(e_k), [\,] \rangle\} \\
\Rightarrow^* \quad & \ldots
\end{aligned}
$$

Now, the claim follows since

$$case\ \sigma(x)\ of\ \{p_k \to \langle \Gamma_x[x \mapsto \rho_k(p_k), \overline{y_{nk} \mapsto y_{nk}}], \rho_k(e_k), [\,] \rangle\} \hookrightarrow \langle \Gamma_x[x \mapsto c], e_i, [\,] \rangle$$

and the fact that there are no more free variables (and, thus, computations in the standard and the partial evaluation semantics coincide from this point on).

4   Partial Evaluation in Practice

We have already developed an offline partial evaluator for functional and functional logic programs following the basic technique of [17] (later improved with a stronger termination analysis in [6]). The implementation is publicly available from http://www.dsic.upv.es/~gvidal/german/offpeval/.

Now, we have added the new unfolding strategy presented so far (i.e., the rules of Figures 2 and 4), together with the procedure for the extraction of resultants of Sect. 3.3. In order to check the usefulness of the new approach, we have considered three different unfolding strategies:

(aggressive) This strategy does not take into account the linearity of functions, i.e., a function call is annotated (classified as "not unfoldable") only if there is a risk of nontermination (according to the already implemented termination analysis [6]). Furthermore, unfolding is performed with a semantics that does not model sharing.

(conservative) This strategy annotates a function call if either there is a risk of nontermination or the associated function definition is not right-linear. Again, unfolding is performed with a semantics that does not model sharing.

(sharing-based) This is the new strategy described in this paper, where function calls are annotated only if there is a risk of nontermination but a sharing-based unfolding is used.

The first two strategies could easily be adopted by the old partial evaluator, but the third one required the implementation of the sharing-based partial evaluation semantics.

We have tested the implemented system on a number of examples, and the sharing-based strategy generally produces residual programs which are as good as the best of the other two strategies.

Let us illustrate this point with some examples. Consider the program (in Haskell-like notation) shown in Fig. 6. The annotations are given by the termination analysis of our partial evaluator when considering the expression

dapp (incList (S^{100} Z) x)

to be partially evaluated, where (S^{100} Z) is a shorthand for the natural number S (S (... Z)) with 100 nested applications of S.

Now, the three strategies mentioned above proceed as follows:

(aggressive) Here, we get the following residual program:

new [] = []
new (y : ys) = (S^{100} y) : append (incList100 ys) (incList100 (y : ys))

incList100 [] = []
incList100 (x : xs) = (S^{100} x) : (incList100 xs)

together with the original definition of append. The following function renamings were considered:

dapp (incList (S^{100} Z) x) $\mapsto$ new x
incList (S^{100} Z) x $\mapsto$ incList100 x

append $[\,]$ x = x   dapp x = append x x
append (x : xs) ys = x : <u>append xs ys</u>

incList n $[\,] = [\,]$ add Z m = m
incList n (x : xs) = (add n x) : (<u>incList</u> n xs)   add (S n) m = S (add n m)

Fig. 6. Double-append program

Observe that function **new** has repeated calls to function incList100, which will cause a slower execution of the residual program.

(conservative) This strategy basically returns the original program unchanged because the call to **dapp** is also annotated in order to avoid the unfolding of a function which is not right-linear. In this case, no slowdown is produced in the residual program, but its run time is essentially the same as that of the original program.

(sharing-based) By using our new partial evaluation semantics, we get the following residual program:

new $[\,] = [\,]$
new (y : ys) = let w = incList100 (y : ys) in append w w
incList100 $[\,] = [\,]$
incList100 (x : xs) = $(S^{100}$ x) : (incList100 xs)

together with the original definition of **append**. Here, we use the same renamings of the **aggressive** strategy.

In this case, the performance of the residual program is comparable to the outcome of the **conservative** approach, i.e., we avoid producing a slower residual program but no significant improvement is achieved.

Now, consider the following expression to be partially evaluated:

dapp (decList x $[Z, Z, Z]$)

where function decList is defined as follows:

decList n $[\,] = [\,]$
decList n (x : xs) = (minus n x) : (decList n xs)

minus n Z = n
minus (S n) (S m) = minus n m

The difference with the previous example is that the inner call to decList can be fully unfolded. Now, the three strategies mentioned above proceed as follows:

(aggressive) It returns a residual program of the form

new x = $[x, x, x, x, x, x]$

where (dapp (decList x $[Z, Z, Z]$)) is renamed as (new x).

(conservative) This strategy basically returns the original program unchanged because the call to **dapp** is not unfolded.

(sharing-based) We get the same residual program as in the **aggressive** case. No let expression is necessary in the residual rule since the argument of **dapp** is fully evaluated and thus repeated values are not problematic (note that the residual function **new** can only be called with a *value*, see Theorem 2).

To summarize, our preliminary experiments are encouraging and show that the new sharing-based approach could be able to get the best of previous approaches.

5   Discussion

Despite the extensive literature on partial evaluation, we are not aware of any approach to the specialization of lazy functional languages where sharing is preserved through the specialization process in a non-trivial way. For instance, [2,3] presents a partial evaluation scheme for a lazy language but sharing is not preserved since the underlying semantics does not model variable sharing.

In this paper, we have presented a novel approach by first extending a standard lazy semantics (where sharing is modeled by using an updatable heap) and, then, defining a method to properly extract the associated residual rules. Our approach is not overly restrictive since every function can be unfolded (even if it is not right-linear) and still preserves sharing, thus avoiding the introduction of redundant computations in the residual program.

Acknowledgements

We gratefully acknowledge the anonymous referees as well as the participants of LOPSTR 2007 for many useful comments and suggestions.

References

1. Albert, E., Hanus, M., Huch, F., Oliver, J., Vidal, G.: Operational Semantics for Declarative Multi-Paradigm Languages. Journal of Symbolic Computation 40(1), 795–829 (2005)
2. Albert, E., Hanus, M., Vidal, G.: A Practical Partial Evaluation Scheme for Multi-Paradigm Declarative Languages. Journal of Functional and Logic Programming 2002(1) (2002)
3. Albert, E., Hanus, M., Vidal, G.: A Residualizing Semantics for the Partial Evaluation of Functional Logic Programs. Information Processing Letters 85(1), 19–25 (2003)
4. Alpuente, M., Falaschi, M., Julián, P., Vidal, G.: Specialization of Lazy Functional Logic Programs. In: Proc. of the ACM SIGPLAN Conf. on Partial Evaluation and Semantics-Based Program Manipulation, PEPM 1997, vol. 32, pp. 151–162. ACM Press, New York (1997)
5. Andersen, L.O.: Program Analysis and Specialization for the C Programming Language. PhD thesis, DIKU, University of Copenhagen (1994)

6. Arroyo, G., Ramos, J.G., Silva, J., Vidal, G.: Improving Offline Narrowing-Driven Partial Evaluation using Size-Change Graphs. In: Puebla, G. (ed.) LOPSTR 2006. LNCS, vol. 4407, pp. 60–76. Springer, Heidelberg (2007)

7. Barendregt, H.P.: The Lambda Calculus—Its Syntax and Semantics. Elsevier, Amsterdam (1984)

8. Bondorf, A.: Similix 5.0 Manual (1993)

9. Bondorf, A., Jørgensen, J.: Efficient Analyses for Realistic Off-Line Partial Evaluation. Journal of Functional Programming 3(3), 315–346 (1993)

10. Consel, C., Danvy, O.: Tutorial notes on Partial Evaluation. In: Proc. of the ACM Symp. on Principles of Programming Languages, pp. 493–501. ACM, New York (1993)

11. Glenstrup, A.J., Jones, N.D.: Termination analysis and specialization-point insertion in offline partial evaluation. ACM TOPLAS 27(6), 1147–1215 (2005)

12. Jones, N.D., Gomard, C.K., Sestoft, P.: Partial Evaluation and Automatic Program Generation. Prentice-Hall, Englewood Cliffs, NJ (1993)

13. Launchbury, J.: A Natural Semantics for Lazy Evaluation. In: Proc. of the ACM Symp. on Principles of Programming Languages (POPL 1993), pp. 144–154. ACM Press, New York (1993)

14. Leuschel, M., Elphick, D., Varea, M., Craig, S., Fontaine, M.: The Ecce and Logen Partial Evaluators and Their Web Interfaces. In: Proc. of PEPM 2006, pp. 88–94. IBM Press (2006)

15. Peyton-Jones, S. (ed.): Haskell 98 Language and Libraries—The Revised Report. Cambridge University Press, Cambridge (2003)

16. Peyton Jones, S.L., Marlow, S.: Secrets of the Glasgow Haskell Compiler Inliner. Journal of Functional Programming 12(4&5), 393–433 (2002)

17. Ramos, J.G., Silva, J., Vidal, G.: Fast Narrowing-Driven Partial Evaluation for Inductively Sequential Systems. In: Proc. of the 10th ACM SIGPLAN Int'l Conf. on Functional Programming (ICFP 2005), pp. 228–239. ACM Press, New York (2005)

18. Wadler, P.L.: Deforestation: Transforming programs to eliminate trees. Theoretical Computer Science 73, 231–248 (1990)

Denotation by Transformation[*]
Towards Obtaining a Denotational Semantics by Transformation to Point-Free Style

Bernd Braßel and Jan Christiansen

Institute of Computer Science
University of Kiel, 24098 Kiel, Germany
{bbr,jac}@informatik.uni-kiel.de

Abstract. It has often been observed that a *point-free style* of programming provides a more abstract view on programs. We aim to use the gain in abstraction to obtain a denotational semantics for *functional logic languages* in a straightforward way. Here we propose a set of basic operations based on which arbitrary functional logic programs can be transformed to point-free programs. The semantics of the resulting programs are strict but, nevertheless, the semantics of the original program is preserved.

There is a one-to-one mapping from the primitives introduced by the transformation to operations in relation algebra. This mapping can be extended to obtain a relation algebraic model for the whole program. This yields a denotational semantics which is on one hand closely related to point-free functional logic programs and on the other hand connects to the well-developed field of algebraic logic including automatic proving.

1 Introduction

The importance of a *point-free* view on *programming* has been emphasized particularly in the applications of category theory to semantics of programming languages. The concrete advantage of point-free style is the possibility to treat programs adhering to it in an *algebraic way*. The goals of an algebraic approach are mainly: a) elegance of the provided formalism which in practice directly results in what we call "proof economy" and b) the possibility to employ automatic proof procedures. Both goals have received a serious damper in the recent development of the field [7, 8]. There we find the disillusioning summary that the state of the art "contradicts the general assumption that calculations in this [point-free] style are more amenable to mechanization" [7, Chapter 8]. In our opinion the situation can be improved by two means: 1.) develop transformations to point-free style which keep much more structure of the original programs and 2.) connect to a well-developed theory with an existing approach to automated proving. The first point is important to enable the formulation of the lemmas needed in any substantial proof and even more important to understand

---

[*] This work has been partially supported by the DFG under grant Ha 2457/1-2.

King, A. (Ed.): LOPSTR 2007, LNCS 4915, pp. 90–105 , 2008.
© Springer-Verlag Berlin Heidelberg 2008

the resulting proof or a counter example, respectively. The interested reader is referred to [5] for an example comparing the readability of our approach to two others, [16] and [8]. The second point is realized by providing a semantics for the point-free programs within the framework of relation algebra. The semantics of the whole program is directly obtained by interpreting the primitive operations, which were introduced by the transformation, as relation algebraic operations. Relation algebra is a well-developed field of algebraic logic [19] for which approaches to proof automation have been developed, cf, e.g., [15]. In this paper we describe the transformation to point free style (Section 2) and prove its correctness (Section 3). The relation algebraic model we developed for our programs is described in [4].

1.1 Functional Logic Programming Languages

We consider a functional logic program as a constructor-based rewriting system, allowing extra variables on the right hand side. This section establishes some of the involved notation, which is mostly following [10, 12]. For our examples we adopt the syntax of Curry [14] although the transformation we develop is compatible with other functional logic languages like Toy [17].

Σ_P is the signature of a program P partitioned into two sets, the set of *constructors* C_P and the set of defined *operations* O_P. We denote n-ary constructor (operation) symbols by c^n (f^n, g^n) omitting the arity where it is apparent. For a set of variables $\mathcal{X}$, the sets of *terms* and *constructor terms* are denoted by $\mathcal{T}(\Sigma_P, \mathcal{X})$ and $\mathcal{T}(C_P, \mathcal{X})$, respectively. The function $var(t)$ yields the set of variables occurring in term t. A term is *linear* if every variable occurs at most once. A linear constructor term is called a *pattern*. Constructors are introduced by a data declaration, as shown in Example (1). The "a" in the third declaration denotes that [a] is a polymorphic type. Operations are defined by *rewrite rules* of the

```
data Success = Success
data Bool = True | False  (1)
data [a] = [] | a : [a]
```

form "$f\ p_1\ \ldots\ p_n = e$" where $f^n \in O_P$ and $p_1, \ldots, p_n$ are *patterns*. The right hand side e may contain *extra variables*, i.e., variables which do not occur in the patterns of the left hand side. To cope with extra variables rewriting is extended to *narrowing* [9]. In our context this means that a *narrowing step* is a rewrite step that includes the replacement of extra variables by constructor terms. We call such a replacement a *constructor substitution* and denote it by σ or by θ. The set of all constructor substitutions is denoted by *CSubst*.

```
app []      ys = ys
app (x:xs) ys = x : (app xs ys)  (2)
```

A possible narrowing step for Example 2 is app x [True] $\rightarrow \{x \mapsto$ []$\}$ [True], where x is an extra variable.

In addition to defining rules, *type signatures* are used to declare the sorts of an operation. For example, app :: [a] -> [a] -> [a] declares that app maps two (polymorphic) lists to a list. These lists have elements of the same type.

As in Example (2) there might be more than one possible narrowing step. Functional logic languages provide *non-deterministic search* to obtain values in this situation. Non-determinism does not only stem from narrowing but

```
coin :: Bool        also from operator definitions with overlapping left hand
coin = True   (3)   sides. For Example (3), there are two derivations coin →
coin = False        True and coin → False or, for short, coin → True | False.
```

2 Transformation to Point-Free Style By Example

The term *point-free* originates from topology where you have points in a space and functions that operate on these points. In functional programming spaces are types, functions are functions and points are the arguments of a function. In *point-free* style you do not explicitly access the points, that is, the arguments of a function. The idea of the *point-free* programming paradigm is to build functions by combining simpler ones. The term was introduced by John Backus in his Turing Award Lecture in 1977 [2]. The counterpart of *point-free* is *point-wise*, that is, functions that explicitly access their arguments. In this section we define a small set of *point-wise* operations which allow the definition of arbitrary functional logic operations in a point-free style. We present only the idea of the transformation here and give a formal definition in the next section.

Composition of Operations. The first "primitive" is *sequential composition*, occasionally simply referred to as "composition".

$$(*) :: (a \to b) \to (b \to c) \to a \to c \qquad (4)$$
$$(f * g)\ x = g\ (f\ x)$$

The primitive (*) is a flipped version of (.). Whereas (f . g) reads as "f after g", (f * g) is more like "f before g". This is more convenient with regard to our aim of a relation-algebraic treatment of programming semantics. Furthermore, the left-to-right reading provides a very descriptive graphical representation. The composition is visualised by connecting two operations with a line, indicating that the output of one is the input of the other. Simple definitions can be made point-free using sequential composition (5).

```
involution x = not (not x)   (5)
involution = not * not
```

Operations with several arguments are composed by *parallel composition*.

$$(/) :: (a \to c) \to (b \to d) \to (a,b) \to (c,d) \qquad (6)$$
$$(f\ /\ g)\ (x,y) = (f\ x, g\ y)$$

Example (7) shows the use of parallel composition. All primitives are right associative. Instead of using precedences we use parenthesises to increase readability.

```
nor :: Bool -> Bool -> Bool
nor x y = not x && not y
                              (7)
nor :: (Bool,Bool) -> Bool
nor = (not / not) * and
```

We have effectively changed the type of nor to a so called "uncurried" version. That is, instead of taking a pair of arguments it takes only a single argument. Multiple arguments are combined by using tuples. We use curried operations only when higher order is employed, as discussed in Paragraph "Higher Order".

Interface Adaption. So far, we can express only right linear rules. Sharing arguments is the first of the primitives deal-

```
fork :: a -> (a,a)
fork x = (x,x)
```
(8)

ing with what we call "interface adaption". Interface adaption means that the connectives of two operations have to be copied or reordered in some way. An uncurried and point-free version of "if and only if" (9) can be formulated using fork.

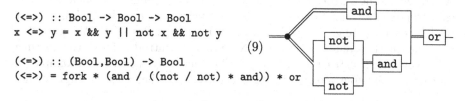

```
(<=>) :: Bool -> Bool -> Bool
x <=> y = x && y || not x && not y

(<=>) :: (Bool,Bool) -> Bool
(<=>) = fork * (and / ((not / not) * and)) * or
```
(9)

There are four more primitives for interface adaption. The operator unit to "discard a value", the identity id to "pass a value on" and fst and snd to "select a value". All these primitives are exemplified in the following sections.

```
unit :: a -> ()
unit x = ()
```
(10)

```
id :: a -> a
id x = x
```
(11)

```
fst :: (a,b) -> a
fst (x,y) = x
```
(12)

```
snd :: (a,b) -> b
snd (x,y) = y
```
(13)

Data Structures and Pattern Matching. We do not wish to abstract from concrete domains in order to make the resulting programs more readable. We re-

```
data List a = Nil  ()
            | Cons (a,List a)
data Bool   = True ()
            | False ()
```
(14)

place constructor definitions by their uncurried versions. For instance, instead of the declarations for [a] and Bool from Example (1) we obtain the declarations shown in Example (14).

Note that for uniformity also the constants True, False, and Nil are extended with an argument. This simplifies the definitions of destructors in the following.

To express pattern matching we introduce a *destructor* for every constructor. This operation inverts the constructor, i.e., it peels off the outermost constructor and yields its arguments. Example (15) presents the destructors corresponding to the constructors from Example (14).

```
invNil :: List a -> ()              invTrue, invFalse :: Bool -> ()
invNil (Nil x)  = x                 invTrue  (True x)  = x
invCons :: List a -> (a,List a)     invFalse (False x) = x
invCons (Cons x) = x
```
(15)

Now it becomes apparent why constant constructors are extended with an argument: to make them invertible. Note also that the definition of the destructors follows a very simple pattern. Using the destructor `invCons` and `fst` and `snd` the standard functions `head` and `tail` can easily be expressed.

$$\begin{array}{ll}
\texttt{head :: List a -> a} & \texttt{tail :: List a -> List a} \\
\texttt{head = invCons * fst} & \texttt{tail = invCons * snd}
\end{array} \quad (16)$$

To combine several rules we employ an additional feature of functional *logic* programming, i.e., non-determinism. The operator (`?`) allows a very elegant way of expressing pattern matching in a point-free style.

$$\begin{array}{l}
\texttt{(?) :: (a -> b) -> (a -> b) -> a -> b} \\
\texttt{(f ? g) x = f x} \\
\texttt{(f ? g) x = g x}
\end{array} \quad (17) \qquad
\begin{array}{l}
\texttt{coin :: () -> Bool} \\
\texttt{coin = True ? False}
\end{array} \quad (18)$$

As stated in the introduction, overlapping rules in functional logic languages lead to non-deterministic search [13]. In principle, all non-determinism can be introduced by a single operation with overlapping rules (17). We use (`?`) to combine the rules of a function (18). Note that the introduction of the argument `()` for constant constructors extends to all definitions of constants. Example (19) shows the point-free version of `null` which tests whether a list is empty or not.

$$\texttt{null = (invNil * True) ? (invCons * unit * False)} \quad (19)$$

The astute reader might wonder why we introduce non-determinism for a perfectly deterministic operation like the pattern matching of `null`. The reason for this is twofold. 1) From a semantic point of view the non-deterministic branching does not matter. If the matching was indeed deterministic, for a given deterministic value all but one branch will finitely (even immediately) fail. 2) In a functional logic language patterns are *not* always deterministic nor treated in a sequential way (like in Haskell). Overlapping patterns induce non-determinism which is eas-

```
member :: [a] -> a
member (x:xs) = x
member (x:xs) = member xs
```
(20)

ily captured by our approach. For example, the operation `member` defined in (20) non-deterministically relates a list with each of its elements. Without further additions this behaviour is captured by the transformation. The following definition shows a point-free version of `member`. It also illustrates that recursive functions simply stay recursive. There is no need for changes, e.g., a special recursion operator.

$$\texttt{member = (invCons * fst) ? (invCons * snd * member)} \quad (21)$$

```
unknown :: () -> a
unknown () = x
  where x free
```
(22)

There is one more feature that is specific to functional logic languages: free variables. To introduce free variables we employ the primitive `unknown` (22). The keyword `free` is used to define extra variables.

Higher Order. In order to introduce higher-order operations we need to adapt the well-known pair `apply` and `curry` to our setting.

$$\begin{array}{l}
\texttt{apply :: (a -> b,a) -> b} \\
\texttt{apply (f,x) = f x}
\end{array} \quad (23) \qquad
\begin{array}{l}
\texttt{curry :: ((a,b) -> c) -> a -> b -> c} \\
\texttt{curry f x y = apply (f,(x,y))}
\end{array} \quad (24)$$

The operations `apply` and `curry` are very similar to the original operations. In the point-free world `apply` takes a tuple of arguments and `curry` uses this apply operation instead of the predefined application. We illustrate the use of `apply` by a standard example of a higher-order operation in Example (25). We assume `adapt` to map the tuple structure `(f,(x,xs))` to `((f,x),(f,xs))` and omit

```
map :: (a -> b) -> [a] -> [b]
map f []     = []                    (25)
map f (x:xs) = f x : map f xs
```

its concrete definition by means of (`/`), `fst`, `snd` and `fork`.

```
map :: (a -> b,[a]) -> [b]
map = ((id / invNil) * unit * Nil)                           (26)
    ? ((id / invCons) * adapt * (apply / map) * Cons)
```

We map the operation `not` on the list `Cons (False (),Cons (True (),Nil ()))`. We have to consider that values of type `a` in the original program correspond to operations of type

```
val :: a -> () -> a
val f () = f          (27)
```

`() -> a` in the point-free program. For example, the point-free version of `coin :: Bool` is `coin :: () -> Bool`. Because higher-order operations should be first class objects we need to translate them in the same way. An operation of type `(a -> b)` must become an object of type `() -> (a -> b)`. Therefore we introduce the primitive `val` which takes a higher order object and yields a value.[1] By using `val` in the definition of `mapNot` we get a higher order value representing the operation `not`. We do not need to use `curry` because `not` takes only one argument and is therefore uncurried. The application `(mapNot ())` evaluates to `Cons (False (),Cons (True (),Nil ()))` as intended.

```
not = (invTrue * False) ? (invFalse * True)
listFalseTrue = fork * (False / (fork * (True / Nil) * Cons)) * Cons    (28)
mapNot = fork * (val not / listFalseTrue) * map
```

We have illustrated all the point-wise primitives necessary to translate arbitrary functional logic programs: (`*`) (4), (`/`) (6), `fork` (8), `unit` (10), `id` (11), (`?`) (17), `fst` (12), `snd` (13), `unknown` (22), `apply` (23) and `curry` (24).

3   Obtaining Point-Free Style in General

In this section we give a formal definition of the transformation that was motivated in Section 2. There is a necessary preliminary step to the transformation described so far. This step is quite interesting in itself, as it transforms a lazy functional logic program to a strict functional logic program nevertheless preserving its denotational semantics. The main idea is to replace laziness by the non-deterministic choice of whether to evaluate a given function application or not. Whereas such a transformation might be a bad idea from an operational point of view, it is very convenient for semantic purposes. As we will see, it is straightforward to prove the main properties of the transformation to strict programs with respect to existing semantics of functional logic languages.

---

[1] Incidentally, the type of `val` is more general and does not only work for higher order types. In an extended setting with base types we also use it to wrap, e.g., integers.

Next is an introductory section for the framework which is used to prove the soundness of the transformations, Section 3.1. We define the transformation to strict programs and show its soundness in Section 3.2. Section 3.3 contains the definition of and the proof for the transformation to point-free style.

3.1 The Core Language and the Reference Semantics

Modern functional logic languages provide syntactic sugar to formulate very concise and readable code. We consider the following core language:

$$
\begin{array}{lll}
P ::= \{R\} & & \{\text{program}\} \\
R ::= f^n\ p_1\ \ldots\ p_n = e & f \in O_P & \{\text{rule}\} \\
p ::= x & x \in \mathcal{X} & \{\text{pattern variable}\} \\
\quad |\ (c^n\ p_1\ \ldots\ p_n) & c \in C_P, p_i\ \text{linear} & \{\text{complex pattern}\} \\
e ::= x & x \in \mathcal{X} & \{\text{variable}\} \\
\quad |\ s^n & s \in \Sigma_P & \{\text{symbol}\} \\
\quad |\ (e_1\ e_2) & & \{\text{application}\}
\end{array}
$$

For our programs, we assume type correctness. In the following we abbreviate application of the form $(\ldots (e_1\ e_2) \ldots e_n)$ by $(e_1\ e_2\ \ldots\ e_n)$. In correspondence to applications we abbreviate tuples as if constructed by a left associative binary operator, i.e., $(x_1, x_2, \ldots, x_n)$ is short for $(\ldots (x_1, x_2), \ldots, x_n)$. Along the same line of conventions, we also assume the binary operator / to be left associative.

We formulate the proofs in the so called CRWL setting for functional logic programming languages [10]. This setting has been successfully used and expanded in several publications. We take a selection of these extensions by a) employing higher order in accordance with [11] b) preferring the variance called $CRWL^+$ allowing the replacement of function applications with $\perp$ only [6, Section 4.1] and c) choosing the simple and suggestive notation introduced in [18, Figure 4]. To understand the proofs, the reader does not have to be familiar with any of these papers. The complete semantics is given by the two rules of Figure 1. The rules make use of *context notation*. A context $\mathcal{C}$ (with a hole) is either a hole [] or one of the complex alternatives $(\mathcal{C}'\ e)$ or $(e\ \mathcal{C}')$ where e is an expression and $\mathcal{C}'$ a context. A context defines a mapping from expressions to expressions, written as $\mathcal{C}[e]$ which is inductively defined by

$$
[][e] = e \qquad (\mathcal{C}\ e')[e] = (\mathcal{C}[e]\ e') \qquad (e'\ \mathcal{C})[e] = (e'\ \mathcal{C}[e])
$$

The set of all contexts is denoted by *Cntxt*.

(B) $\mathcal{C}[(f\ e_1\ \ldots\ e_n)] \rightarrowtail \mathcal{C}[\perp]$ $\mathcal{C} \in \textit{Cntxt}, f^n \in O_P \vee f = \perp,$
                                              $e_1, \ldots, e_n \in \mathcal{T}(\Sigma_P \cup \{\perp\}, \mathcal{X})$

(OR) $\mathcal{C}[(f\ t_1\theta\ \ldots\ t_n\theta)] \rightarrowtail \mathcal{C}[r\theta]$ $\mathcal{C} \in \textit{Cntxt}, f\ t_1\ \ldots\ t_n = e \in P, \theta \in \textit{CSubst}$

Fig. 1. Rules of $HOCRWL^+$ in Context Notation

Whenever the program is not apparent, we write $\rightarrowtail_P$ for a step with respect to program P. By $\rightarrowtail^*$ we denote the reflexive transitive closure of $\rightarrowtail$. By $[\![e]\!]^\perp$ we denote the set $\{t \mid e \rightarrowtail^* t, t \in \mathcal{T}(C_P \cup \{\perp\}, \mathcal{X})\}$ and we call each t in this set a normal form. Note that by definition normal forms are constructor terms.

Rule **B** is used to model laziness. It allows the replacement of unneeded expressions by $\perp$.

3.2   Transformation to Strict Programs

We define a transformation $str(\cdot)$ of arbitrary lazy programs into strict programs preserving its semantics. We achieve this by adding the possibility to abort the evaluation of any function application non-deterministically. We get a strict program by replacing each application $(e_1\ e_2)$ by a call to the higher order function $(\text{app}\ e_1\ e_2)$. Function **app** takes two expressions and evaluates both to head normal form before applying the first to the second, see the rules of **app** below. As *all* applications, including constructor applications, are replaced by **app**, the resulting program is strict. The non-deterministic abortion of evaluation is achieved by adding an additional rule to each operation definition. The right hand side of this rule contains only the new constructor symbol U^0 (short for unevaluated). The point is that unevaluated expressions can be non-deterministically replaced by the new constructor U. In this sense, non-determinism is more general than laziness. This fact can be used to obtain simple semantic approaches to functional logic languages. The following transformation yields a strict functional logic programs.

$$str(P) = \{l = str(r) \mid l = r \in P\} \cup \{f\ x_1\ \ldots\ x_n = \text{U} \mid f^n \in O_P\}$$
$$\cup\ \{\text{app}\ (s\ x_1\ \ldots\ x_n)\ (c\ y_1\ \ldots\ y_m) = (s\ x_1\ \ldots\ x_n)\ (c\ y_1\ \ldots\ y_m)$$
$$\mid s^i \in \Sigma_P, i > n, c^m \in C_P \cup \{\text{U}\}\}$$
$$\cup\ \{\text{app}\ \text{U}\ (c\ x_1\ \ldots\ x_n) = \text{U} \mid c^n \in C_P \cup \{\text{U}\},\}$$

$$str(x) = x, x \in \mathcal{X} \qquad str(s) = s, s \in \Sigma_P \qquad str(e_1\ e_2) = \text{app}\ str(e_1)\ str(e_2)$$

Transformation $str(\cdot)$ preserve semantics in the sense that programs resulting from it yield the newly introduced constructor U instead of $\perp$. All other values are identical. Indeed, the way transformed programs work is very similar to the behavior of the semantics of Figure 1. We prove this by stating three simple observations which then allow us to formulate a very tight correspondence between the original program with lazy semantics and the transformed program with strict semantics.

The first observation formalizes our claim that the resulting programs are indeed strict. Recall that rule **B** of Figure 1 is responsible for modelling laziness. Therefore strictness means the following: if rule **B** was used in a derivation $str(e) \rightarrowtail^*_{str(P)} t$ of an expression e to a normal form t then $t = \perp$. Equivalently if there is a derivation $str(e) \rightarrowtail^*_{str(P)} t$ with $t \neq \perp$ then rule **B** is not used in this derivation. By $\rightarrowtail_{\mathcal{L}}$ we denote a derivation without rule **B**, i.e., with rule **OR** only and by $[\![e]\!]$ we denote the set $\{t \mid e \rightarrowtail^*_{\mathcal{L}} t, t \in \mathcal{T}(C_P, \mathcal{X})\}$.

Proposition 1. $[\![str(e)]\!]^{\perp}_{str(P)} \setminus \{\perp\} = [\![str(e)]\!]_{str(P)}$

Proof (Idea). Structural induction on $\mathcal{C}$ shows that $str(\mathcal{C}[e']) \rightarrowtail str(\mathcal{C}[\perp]) \rightarrowtail^* t$ implies $t = \perp$.

We have seen that rule **B** is useless to derive any value but $\perp$. On the other hand it is worth noting that if we do not use that rule, strict application (app e_1 e_2) is identical to standard application (e_1 e_2).

Proposition 2. $(e_1\ e_2) \rightarrowtail^*_{\not{\,}} v$ iff (app e_1 e_2) $\rightarrowtail^*_{\not{\,}} v$

Proof (Idea). For all $e_1, e_2 \neq \perp$ app e_1 e_2 is defined as (e_1 e_2)

We alter rule **B** slightly and replace it by the following rule **B'**. By $\twoheadrightarrow$ we denote the rewrite relation where all applications of **B** are replaced by proofs for **B'**.

$$(\mathbf{B'})\ \mathcal{C}[(f\ t_1\ \ldots\ t_n)] \twoheadrightarrow \mathcal{C}[\perp] \quad \mathcal{C} \in Cntxt, f^n \in O_P \vee (n = 1 \wedge f = \perp),$$
$$t_1, \ldots, t_n \in \mathcal{T}(C_P \cup \{\perp\}, \mathcal{X})$$

The difference between the two rules is that applications can only be discarded if its arguments are constructor terms (with $\perp$) and that applications of $\perp$ to such terms have to be replaced by $\perp$ one by one. It is easy to prove that the relations defined by $\rightarrowtail$ and $\twoheadrightarrow$ are identical.

Proposition 3. $e \rightarrowtail^* t$ iff $e \twoheadrightarrow^* t$

Proof (Idea). Before discarding the whole expression discard all sub terms.

The notation $\rightarrowtail_{\not{\,}}$ introduced above also excludes the use of variant **B'**. We are now ready to prove the strong correspondence between the original program P and the transformed program $str(P)$.

Lemma 1. *For all programs P and all expressions $e \in Expr_P$ holds $e \rightarrowtail^*_P t$ iff $str(e^{\not{\,}}) \rightarrowtail^*_{str(P)} t^{\not{\,}}$ where $\not{\,}$ replaces all occurences of $\perp$ by $\cup$.*

Proof. By Proposition 1 we may consider the derivation $str(e^{\not{\,}}) \rightarrowtail^*_{\not{\,}\ str(P)} t^{\not{\,}}$ instead of $str(e^{\not{\,}}) \rightarrowtail^*_{str(P)} t^{\not{\,}}$. By Proposition 2 we may treat the appearances of (app e_1 e_2) in the $\rightarrowtail^*_{\not{\,}}$-derivation as ($e_1$ e_2). This means essentially that $str(e^{\not{\,}}) \rightarrowtail^*_{\not{\,}\ str(P)} t^{\not{\,}}$ iff $e^{\not{\,}} \rightarrowtail^*_{\not{\,}\ P'} t^{\not{\,}}$ where $P' := P \cup \{f\ x_1\ \ldots\ x_n = \cup \mid f^n \in O_P\}$. Adding Proposition 3 this means we only need to show that $e \twoheadrightarrow^*_P t$ iff $e^{\not{\,}} \rightarrowtail^*_{\not{\,}\ P'} t^{\not{\,}}$. Between these derivations there is such a close correspondence that there is a one-to-one mapping between them. We show this by induction on the length n of both derivations.

The base case $n = 0$ holds trivially. For the induction we distinguish two cases:
Case 1: Rule **B'** corresponds to one of the new rules.
$$\mathcal{C}[f\ t_1, \ldots, t_n] \twoheadrightarrow_P \mathcal{C}[\perp] \qquad \text{iff}$$
$$\mathcal{C}[f\ t_1, \ldots, t_n]^{\not{\,}} = \mathcal{C}[f\ t_1^{\not{\,}}, \ldots, t_n^{\not{\,}}]^{\not{\,}} \rightarrowtail_{\not{\,}\ P'} \mathcal{C}[\cup]^{\not{\,}} = \mathcal{C}[\perp]^{\not{\,}}$$
Case 2: Applications of the original rules are unchanged.
$$\mathcal{C}[f\ t_1\theta, \ldots, t_n\theta] \twoheadrightarrow_P \mathcal{C}[r\theta] \qquad \text{iff}$$
$$\mathcal{C}[f\ t_1, \ldots, t_n]^{\not{\,}} = \mathcal{C}[f\ t_1\theta^{\not{\,}}, \ldots, t_n\theta^{\not{\,}}]^{\not{\,}} \rightarrowtail_{\not{\,}\ P'} \mathcal{C}[r\theta^{\not{\,}}]^{\not{\,}} = \mathcal{C}[r\theta]^{\not{\,}}$$
Since with θ being a constructor substitution, also $(\cdot^{\not{\,}}) \circ \theta$ is in *CSubst*.

3.3   Transformation to Point-Free Style

We use an intermediate transformation which yields programs that contain only function definitions in first order style with the single exception of curry f x y = apply (f,(x,y)), cf. the paragraph "Higher Order" in Section 2. We have stated in the introduction that after transforming a program the only source of non-determinism is the operation (?). Likewise, in uncurried programs all higher order functions stem from curry. There is a simple transformation to map functions defined with n patterns $p_1 \ldots p_n$ to functions with one argument which is a tuple $(p_1, \ldots, p_n)$ employing the function pair curry and apply to preserve higher order semantics. We have formalized such a transformation but feel that the procedure is well known such that we present that transformation in the technical report [5] only. Uncurried programs allow us to abstract from the arity of all functions but the primitives we introduce.

In this section we present the general transformation of programs into point-free style. First we introduce the notion of an interface of an expression. The *interface* of an expression is an abstraction from its actual structure. An interface is a tree with the same branching structure as the expression and this tree contains the variables that occur in the expression. The mapping from expressions to interfaces is defined as follows, where s ranges over symbols in Σ_P:

$$int(s) = () \quad int(x) = x \quad int(s\ (e_1, \ldots, e_n)) = (int(e_1), \ldots, int(e_n))$$

This mapping is frequently used throughout the definition of the transformation. We denote complex interfaces, i.e, those not in $\mathcal{X} \cup \{()\}$ by $i, i_1, i_2 \ldots$ and by $var(i)$ the set of all variables occurring in i. For example, the interface of the right hand side of the original definition of (<=>) in Example (9) is $((x,y),(x,y))$. The first use of interfaces is *variable selection* defined as follows:

$$sel(x,x) \quad = \mathtt{id}$$
$$sel(x,(i,i')) = \begin{cases} \mathtt{fst} * sel(x,i) & \text{, if } x \in var(i) \wedge x \notin var(i') \\ \mathtt{snd} * sel(x,i') & \text{, if } x \notin var(i) \wedge x \in var(i') \end{cases}$$

Each occurrence of the selected variable is passed on by id, while all other variables are discarded by fst and snd. Note that this definition requires that variable x actually occurs in interface i. To get an intuition about what variable selection is used for reconsider Example (16). The definition of head has been derived from head (x:xs) = x whose uncurried version is head (Cons (x,xs)) = x. To finally yield x we select x from the interface of Cons (x,xs) which simply is (x,xs). The result is fst * id which can be simplified to fst.

The next lemma states in general that $sel(x,i)$ selects the correct sub-term of any substitution of interface i.

Lemma 2. *For all interfaces i, $\theta \in CSubst$ and $C \in Cntxt$ $x \in var(i)$ implies $C[sel(x,i)\ i\theta] \rightarrowtail^* C[x\theta]$.*

Proof (Idea). Structural induction on i.

On the basis of $sel(x, i)$ we define the general approach to "Interface Adaption", cf. the paragraph of the same name in Section 2 as follows:

$$adapt(i, i') = \begin{cases} \text{id} & \text{, if } i = i' \\ adapt'(i, i') & \text{otherwise} \end{cases}$$

$$\begin{aligned} adapt'(i, ()) &= \text{unit} \\ adapt'(i, x) &= sel(x, i) \\ adapt'(i, (i_1, i_2)) &= \text{fork} * (adapt(i, i_1)/adapt(i, i_2)) \end{aligned}$$

The effect of mapping $adapt(\cdot, \cdot)$ is twofold. First, an application of the mapping $sel(\cdot, \cdot)$ is introduced for every leaf of the interface adapted to. Second, the incoming argument is copied as often as needed by employing the primitive fork. For instance, for the definition of (<=>) in Example 9 the interface (x, y) is adapted to $((x, y), (x, y))$ and the result is fork $*$ (id/id). This expression can be shown to be equivalent to fork which is what one would expect for this example.

The next lemma states that mapping $adapt(i, i')$ indeed yields an interface adaption from interface i to i'. More concretely, if $adapt(i, i')$ is applied to a tuple of the form i the result is a tuple of form i'. Note that Lemma 3 requires that the variables of the target interface are a subset of the variables of the argument interface.

Lemma 3. *For all interfaces i, i' with $var(i') \subseteq var(i)$, all $\theta \in CSubst$ and all contexts C: $C[adapt(i, i') \ i\theta] \rightarrowtail^* C[i'\theta]$.*

Proof. By structural induction on i'.
Case 1 $i = i'$:
$\quad C[adapt(i, i') \ i\theta]$ {def $adapt(\cdot, \cdot)$}$= C[\text{id} \ i\theta]$ {def id}$\rightarrowtail C[i\theta] = C[i'\theta]$
Case 2 $i \neq i'$:
$\quad C[adapt(i, i') \ i\theta]$ {def $adapt(\cdot, \cdot)$}$= C[adapt'(i, i') \ i\theta]$
$i' = ()$:
$\quad C[adapt'(i, ()) \ i\theta]$ {def $adapt'(\cdot, \cdot)$}$= C[\text{unit} \ i\theta]$ {def unit}$\rightarrowtail C[()] = C[i'\theta]$
$i' = x$:
$\quad C[adapt'(i, i') \ i\theta]$ {def $adapt'(\cdot, \cdot)$}$= C[sel(x, i) \ i\theta]$ {Lemma 2}$\rightarrowtail^* C[x\theta]$
$i' = (i_1, i_2)$:

$$\qquad\qquad\qquad C[adapt'(i, i') \ i\theta]$$
$\{ \text{def } adapt'(\cdot, \cdot) \} \quad = C[(\text{fork} * (adapt(i, i_1)/adapt(i, i_2))) \ i\theta]$
$\{ \text{def } * \} \qquad\qquad \rightarrowtail C[(adapt(i, i_1)/adapt(i, i_2)) \ (\text{fork } i\theta)]$
$\{ \text{def fork} \} \qquad\quad \rightarrowtail C[(adapt(i, i_1)/adapt(i, i_2)) \ (i\theta, i\theta)]$
$\{ \text{def } / \} \qquad\qquad \rightarrowtail C[(adapt(i, i_1) \ i\theta, adapt(i, i_2) \ i\theta)]$
$\{ \text{ind. hypothesis} \} \rightarrowtail^* C[(i_1\theta, i_2\theta)] = C[i\theta]$

The last missing step of interface adaption is to introduce extra variables by function unknown, cf. the last paragraph of Section 2. We assume $\times$ to be a left associative operator symbol. The required applications of unknown are introduced by the mapping $addfree(\cdot, \cdot)$, defined as follows:

$$addfree(i_1, i_2) = \underbrace{(\textit{free} \times \ldots \times \textit{free}}_{n} \times \text{id}) * adapt(i_1', i_2)$$

$$
\begin{aligned}
\text{where} \quad \textit{free} \quad &= (\text{unit} * \text{unknown}) \\
i_1' \quad &= (x_1, \ldots, x_n, i_1) \\
\{x_1, \ldots, x_n\} &= var(i_2) \setminus var(i_1) \\
e \times e' \quad &= \text{fork} * (e/e')
\end{aligned}
$$

Proposition 4. *For all interfaces* i: $\mathcal{C}[((\underbrace{\textit{free} \times \ldots \times \textit{free}}_{n}) \, i)] \rightarrowtail^* \mathcal{C}[(x_1, \ldots, x_n)]$
where $x_k, x_j \notin var(\mathcal{C}[i])$ *and* $x_k \neq x_j$ *for all* $k \in \{1, \ldots, n\}$.

Proof (Idea). Induction on n using the definitions of $(/)$, unit and unknown.

The following lemma extends Lemma 3 by the introduction of extra variables.

Lemma 4. *For all interfaces* i_1, i_2, *all substitutions* θ *and all contexts* $\mathcal{C}$:
$\mathcal{C}[addfree(i_1, i_2) \, i_1 \theta] \rightarrowtail^* \mathcal{C}[i_2 \theta]$.

Proof (Idea). The proof connects Proposition 4 and Lemma 3.

The next step in the transformation to point-free programs is the transformation of expressions. Applications are replaced by the operator $(*)$ and the arguments are combined by $(/)$. Higher order functions, i.e., single symbols (s) are made values by using val. Expressions are translated as follows:

$$
\begin{aligned}
exp(s \, ()) \quad &= s \\
exp(s \, (e_1, \ldots, e_{n>0})) &= (exp(e_1)/ \ldots /exp(e_n)) * s \\
exp(s) \quad &= \text{val}(s) \\
exp(x) \quad &= \text{id}
\end{aligned}
$$

The next lemma states that an application of $exp(e)$ to the interface of e can be reduced to the original expression.

Lemma 5. *For all expressions* e, $\theta \in CSubst$ *and contexts* $\mathcal{C}$:
$\mathcal{C}[exp(e) \, int(e)\theta] \rightarrowtail^* \mathcal{C}[e\theta]$.

Proof (Idea). Structural Induction on e.

Next we define the transformation of pattern matching to point-free style. The mapping $invert(\cdot)$ is very similar to $exp(\cdot)$. All occurrences of constructors c are replaced by the corresponding destructors $invC$.

$$
\begin{aligned}
invert(c \, ()) \quad &= invC \\
invert(c \, (e_1, \ldots, e_{n>0})) &= invC * (invert(e_1)/ \ldots /invert(e_n)) \\
invert(x) \quad &= \text{id}
\end{aligned}
$$

Furthermore the destructors $invC$ are applied *before* the resulting arguments are processed. The next lemma states that the application of $invert(p)$ yields the argument of a constructor if it matches the pattern and fails otherwise.

Lemma 6. *Let p be a linear pattern, e a term and C a context.*
If there exists a $\theta \in CSubst$ with $e = p\theta$ then $C[invert(p) \; e] \rightarrowtail^* C[int(p)\theta]$ and otherwise $[\![C[invert(p) \; e]]\!] = \emptyset$.

Proof. By induction on the structure of p.

$p = x : C[invert(x) \; e] = C[\text{id } e] \rightarrowtail C[e] = C[x\{x \mapsto e\}] = C[int(x)\{x \mapsto e\}]$

$p = c(p_1, \ldots, p_n) : \; C[invert(c(p_1, \ldots, p_n)) \; e]$

$\{\text{ def } invert(\cdot) \} \quad = C[(invC * (invert(p_1)/\ldots/invert(p_n))) \; e]$

$\{\text{ def } * \} \qquad\quad \rightarrowtail C[(invert(p_1)/\ldots/invert(p_n)) \; (invC \; e)]$

case 1 $e = c(e_1, \ldots, e_n)$

$\{\text{ def } invC \} \qquad \rightarrowtail C[((invert(p_1)/\ldots/invert(p_n)) \; (e_1, \ldots, e_n))]$

$\{\text{ def } / \} \qquad\quad \rightarrowtail^* C[(invert(p_1) \; e_1, \ldots, invert(p_n) \; e_n)]$

case 1.1 there exists a θ with $e = p\theta$ which implies $e_1 = p_1\theta \wedge \ldots \wedge e_n = p_n\theta$

$\{\text{ ind. hypothesis } \} \rightarrowtail^* C[(int(p_1)\theta, \ldots, int(p_n)\theta)]$

$\{\theta \in CSubst \} \qquad \rightarrowtail C[(int(p_1), \ldots, int(p_n))\theta]$

$\{\text{ def } int(\cdot) \} \qquad = C[int(p)\theta]$

case 1.2 e_i and p_i not unifiable for an $i \in \{1, \ldots n\}$

By induction hypothesis $(invert(p_i) \; e_i)$ is not reducible to a constructor normal form. As all applications are strict this implies

$\qquad [\![C[(invert(p_1)/\ldots/invert(p_n)) \; (invC \; e)]]\!] = \emptyset$

case 2 $e \neq c(e_1, \ldots, e_n)$

By definition $(invC \; e)$ does not have a constructor normal form. As all applications are strict this implies $[\![C[(invert(p_1)/\ldots/invert(p_n)) \; (invC \; e)]]\!] = \emptyset$

The general technique of the transformation of rules is: invert the pattern then apply interface adaption and finally transform the body of the rule. The rules of an operation are transformed as follows:

$$rule(f \; (p_1, \ldots, p_n) = e) = (invert(p_1)/\ldots/invert(p_n)) * adp * exp(e)$$
$$\text{where } adp = addfree(int((p_1, \ldots, p_n)), int(e))$$

The following lemma extents the pattern matching Lemma 6 to rules.

Lemma 7. *Let $p = (p_1, \ldots, p_n)$ and $f \; p = r$ be a rule in P. Let $e_1, \ldots, e_n$ be terms, $e = (e_1, \ldots, e_n)$ and $a = C[rule(f \; p = r) \; e]$.*
If there exists $\theta \in CSubst$ with $e = p\theta$, then $a \rightarrowtail^* C[r\theta]$ and otherwise $[\![a]\!] = \emptyset$.

Proof (Idea). Unfold definition of $rule(\cdot)$ until Lemma 6 is applicable.

We can finally define how a whole program is transformed. The signature of the resulting program P' is an extension of the original one. For every constructor symbol c we introduce a new unary symbol $invC$, the corresponding destructor.

$$O_{P'} = O_P \cup \{invC^1 \mid c^1 \in C_P\} \cup Prim$$
$$C_{P'} = C_P$$
$$Prim = \{(*)^3, (/)^3, (?)^3, \text{fork}^1, \text{id}^1, \text{unit}^1, \text{fst}^1, \text{snd}^1, \text{val}^2 \; \text{curry}^2, \text{apply}^1\}$$

In the following definition *prims* are the operation definitions of $(*)$ (4), $(/)$ (6), fork (8), unit (10), id (11), unknown (22), fst (12), snd (13), and $(?)$ (17).

$$op(f) \quad = f = rule(r_1) \; ? \; \ldots \; ? \; rule(r_n) \text{ where } \{r_1, \ldots, r_n\} = \{f \; p = r \in P\}$$
$$prog(P) = prims \; \cup \{op(f) \mid f \in O_P\} \cup \{invC \; (c \; \mathbf{x}) = \mathbf{x} \mid c \in C_P\}.$$

Finally, we can put together the insights about the transformation.

Theorem 1. *Let P be a program. Then $[\![P]\!]^{\perp \not\perp} = [\![prog(str(P))]\!]$.*

Proof. By Lemma 1 we have that the semantics of $str(P)$ is equivalent to the semantics of P when replacing $\perp$ with the special constructor $\mathtt{U}$, i.e., $[\![str(P)]\!]^{\perp \not\perp} = [\![P]\!]^{\perp \not\perp}$. Also by Lemma 1 strict and lazy semantics for $str(P)$ are equivalent, i.e., $[\![str(P)]\!]^{\perp \not\perp} = [\![str(P)]\!]$. We now prove that there is a derivation $e \rightarrowtail^* t$ to a normal form t in the program $str(P)$ iff there is a derivation $(exp \; (e) \; int(e)) \rightarrowtail^* t$ in the transformed program $prog(str(P))$.

($\Rightarrow$): By induction on the length n of the derivation $e \rightarrowtail^* t$.

$n = 0$: By Lemma 5 we have $(exp \; (t) \; int(t)) \rightarrowtail^* t$.

$n+1$: The derivation is of the form $C[f(p_1, \ldots, p_n)\theta] \rightarrowtail C[r\theta] \rightarrowtail^* t$. By Lemma 7 the existence of θ yields $C[rule(f(p_1, \ldots, p_n) = r) \; (p_1, \ldots, p_n)\theta] \rightarrowtail^* C[r\theta]$. Therefore the induction hypothesis ensures the claim.

($\Leftarrow$): By induction on the number n of applications of functions $f \in O_P$ (i.e., excluding the applications of primitives introduced by the transformation).

$n = 0$: By definition $exp(e)$ contains exactly as many applications of functions $f \in O_P$ as e. Naturally, the primitive functions do not apply functions of the original program P. As the semantics is strict such that all functions in e will actually be applied, $n = 0$ implies that e is a constructor term. Lemma 5 yields therefore $e = t$ and the derivation $e \rightarrowtail^* e$ in P exists trivially.

$n + 1$: By definition of the transformation $prog$ all functions of the resulting program but (?) have only a single rule. Therefore their application is the only source of non-determinism. Moreover, (?) is only introduced to combine the transformed rules of a function of the original program. Because of this and by Lemma 7 derivations in the transformed program are always of the form

$$C[f \; p\theta] \rightarrowtail C[(r_1 \; ? \; \ldots \; ? \; r_m) \; p\theta] \rightarrowtail C[r_i \; p\theta]$$

where $f^n \in O_P$, $p = (x_1, \ldots, x_n)$, $i \in \{1, \ldots, m\}$ and $r_i = rule(f(p_1, \ldots, p_n) = e_i)$.

By Lemma 7 the existence of a derivation to a normal form t implies that there exists a constructor substitution σ with $p\theta = (p_1, \ldots, p_n)\sigma$ and that the derivation above can be continued as:

$$C[r_i \; (p_1, \ldots, p_n)\sigma] \rightarrowtail^* C[e_i\sigma] \rightarrowtail^* t$$

By induction hypothesis we may assume that there exists a derivation D corresponding to $C[e_i\sigma] \rightarrowtail^* t$. And, all in all, we can construct the following corresponding derivation in the original program:

$$C[f(p_1, \ldots, p_n)\sigma] \rightarrowtail \underbrace{C[e_i\sigma] \rightarrowtail^* t}_{D}$$

4   Related and Future Work

Cunha, Pinto and Proença [8, 7] present a framework for transformations of functional programs into point-free style. They implemented a library for point-free programming in Haskell and transform Haskell programs into point-free programs which are based on this library. Conceptually, their approach first transforms a subset of Haskell to a simply-typed λ-calculus, and back to a Haskell program. Because of the intermediate transformation to λ-calculus, the resulting programs bear only a remote resemblance to the original. In contrast, one of our aims is to keep the resulting programs close to the original. For example, we preserve the recursive structure of the program instead of expressing it by primitive recursion operators and we keep the data types and definitions of the original program instead of transforming them into generic sum and product types.

There is a lot of work to employ category theory in order to enable the algebraic manipulation of *functional programs* from which we only mention [3]. We have the intuition that the framework of functional *logic* languages is an even more natural and promising field for this style of reasoning about programs. The elementary difference is the existence of non-determinism. Whereas in [3] and similar works every inversion and every non-deterministic definition resulting from inversion *must* be eliminated, the framework of functional logic languages allows much less restricted use of algebraic methods.

As mentioned in the introduction we aim at using automatic proving like presented in [15] to prove for example the correctness of transformations. Furthermore we hope that the well-known area of relation algebra provides new insights into functional logic programming.

[20] presents a semantics for a functional language employing relation algebra. We want to investigate the relation with our approach as future work.

One of our future goals is to extent the presented approach to cover *function patterns* [1] for the first time. Function patterns allow operator definitions with arbitrary first order patterns. There seems to be a close correlation between function patterns and the inversion operator of relation algebra. The use of function patterns allows to generate even simpler point-free programs than presented here. Function patterns can be used to express arbitrary pattern matching by inverting the corresponding expression. Furthermore by employing function patterns we could decrease the number of primitives introduced by the transformation. For example, we could define unknown as the inversion of unit.

References

1. Antoy, S., Hanus, M.: Declarative programming with function patterns. In: Hill, P.M. (ed.) LOPSTR 2005. LNCS, vol. 3901, pp. 6–22. Springer, Heidelberg (2006)
2. Backus, J.: Can programming be liberated from the von Neumann style? A functional style and its algebra of programs. Com. ACM 21(8), 613–641 (1978)
3. Bird, R., de Moor, O.: Algebra of programming. Prentice-Hall, Inc., Upper Saddle River, NJ, USA (1997)
4. Braßel, B., Christiansen, J.: A Relation Algebraic Semantics for a Lazy Functional Logic Language. In: Submitted to the 10th International Conference on Relational Methods in Computer Science (RelMiCS 10),
   http://www.informatik.uni-kiel.de/prog/mitarbeiter/bernd-brassel/publications/

5. Braßel, B., Christiansen, J.: Denotation by transformation - towards obtaining a denotational semantics by transformation to point-free style. Technical report no. 0711, Christian-Albrechts-University of Kiel (2007)
6. Cleva, J.M., Leach, J., López-Fraguas, F.J.: A logic programming approach to the verification of functional-logic programs. In: Moggi, E., Warren, D.S. (eds.) PPDP, pp. 9–19. ACM Press, New York (2004)
7. Cunha, A.: Point-free program calculation. PhD thesis, Universidade do Minho, Departamento de Informática (2005)
8. Cunha, A., Sousa Pinto, J., Proença, J.: A Framework for Point-Free Program Transformation. In: Butterfield, A., Grelck, C., Huch, F. (eds.) IFL 2005. LNCS, vol. 4015, pp. 1–18. Springer, Heidelberg (2006)
9. Fay, M.J.: First-order unification in an equational theory. In: Proc. 4th Workshop on Automated Deduction, Austin (Texas), pp. 161–167. Academic Press, London (1979)
10. González-Moreno, J.C., Hortalá-González, M.T., López-Fraguas, F.J., Rodríguez-Artalejo, M.: An approach to declarative programming based on a rewriting logic. Journal of Logic Programming 40, 47–87 (1999)
11. González-Moreno, J.C., Hortalá-González, M.T., Rodríguez-Artalejo, M.: A higher order rewriting logic for functional logic programming. In: Proc. of the Fourteenth International Conference on Logic Programming (ICLP 1997), pp. 153–167. MIT Press, Cambridge (1997)
12. Hanus, M.: The integration of functions into logic programming: From theory to practice. Journal of Logic Programming 19&20, 583–628 (1994)
13. Hanus, M.: A unified computation model for functional and logic programming. In: Proc. of the 24th ACM Symposium on Principles of Programming Languages (Paris), pp. 80–93 (1997)
14. Hanus, M. (ed.): Curry: An integrated functional logic language (vers. 0.8.2) (2006), http://www.informatik.uni-kiel.de/~curry
15. Höfner, P., Struth, G.: Automated reasoning in kleene algebra. In: Pfenning, F. (ed.) CADE 2007. LNCS (LNAI), vol. 4603, pp. 279–294. Springer, Heidelberg (2007)
16. Hu, Z., Iwasaki, H., Takeichi, M.: Deriving structural hylomorphisms from recursive definitions. In: ICFP, pp. 73–82 (1996)
17. López-Fraguas, F., Sánchez-Hernández, J.: TOY: A multiparadigm declarative system. In: Narendran, P., Rusinowitch, M. (eds.) RTA 1999. LNCS, vol. 1631, pp. 244–247. Springer, Heidelberg (1999)
18. López-Fraguas, F.J., Rodríguez-Hortalá, J., Sánchez-Hernández, J.: A simple rewrite notion for call-time choice semantics. In: Proceedings of the 9th ACM SIGPLAN International Conference on Principles and Practice of Declarative Programming (PPDP 2007), pp. 197–208. ACM Press, New York (2007)
19. Schmidt, G., Ströhlein, T.: Relations and Graphs - Discrete Mathematics for Computer Scientists. In: EATCS Monographs on Theoretical Computer Science, Springer, Heidelberg (1993)
20. Zierer, H.: Programmierung mit Funktionsobjekten: Konstruktive Erzeugung semantischer Bereiche und Anwendung auf die partielle Auswertung. PhD thesis, Technische Universität München, Fakultät für Informatik (1988)

Generation of Rule-Based Constraint Solvers: Combined Approach

Slim Abdennadher and Ingi Sobhi

Computer Science Department, German University in Cairo
{slim.abdennadher,ingi.sobhi}@guc.edu.eg
http://www.cs.guc.edu.eg

Abstract. *Inductive Constraint Solving* is a subfield of inductive machine learning concerned with the automatic generation of rule-based constraint solvers. In this paper, we propose an approach to generate constraint solvers given the definition of the constraints that combines the advantages of generation by construction with generation by testing. In our proposed approach, semantically valid rules are constructed symbolically, then the constructed rules are used to prune the search tree of a generate and test method. The combined approach leads in general to more expressive and efficient constraint solvers. The generated rules are implemented in the language Constraint Handling Rules.

1 Introduction

In rule-based constraint solving, the execution of constraints consists of a repeated application of rules. In general, we distinguish between two types of rules:

- Simplification rules that rewrite constraints to simpler constraints while preserving logical equivalence (e.g. $min(A, A, C) \Leftrightarrow C{=}A$).
- Propagation rules that add new constraints, which are logically redundant but may cause further simplification (e.g. $min(A, B, C) \Rightarrow C{\leq}A \wedge C{\leq}B$).

Writing rule-based constraint solvers is a hard task as the programmer has to determine the propagation algorithms. Several methods have been proposed in the field of inductive constraint solving to automate the generation of constraint solvers for constraints defined extensionally over finite domains by means of a truth table [5,9,2] or intentionally over infinite domains by means of a constraint logic program (CLP) [3,4]. In general, the algorithms follow a generate and test approach. Rule candidates are enumerated and subjected to a validity test against the definition of the constraint.

In this paper, we present a joined approach that combines the generate and test method presented in [3] with a symbolic construction method [10]. Each method has its advantages and drawbacks. The construction method is an orthogonal approach to the general direction of the work done in the field. While it is able to generate recursive rules that cannot be generated by the generate

King, A. (Ed.): LOPSTR 2007, LNCS 4915, pp. 106–120, 2008.

and test method, it is likely to cover a narrower spectrum of rules. The generate and test method on the other hand generates a more exhaustive set of rules, however this does come at a cost. Our aim is to combine the advantages of the two approaches, while minimizing the drawbacks.

In our combined approach, we first construct semantically valid rules symbolically. Then, we use the constructed rules to prune the search tree of the generate and test method. This will generally lead to more powerful and expressive constraint solvers at a reduced cost.

In the following, we will illustrate the combined approach by an example.

Example 1. Given the following CLP program defining $min(A, B, C)$ that holds if C is the minimum of A and B.

$$min(A, B, C) \leftarrow A{\leq}B \ \wedge \ C{=}A.$$
$$min(A, B, C) \leftarrow A{>}B \ \wedge \ C{=}B.$$

The combined approach will construct rules symbolically.

Symbolic Construction. The basic idea of the symbolic construction method stems from the observation that in general, the execution of one clause in a CLP program excludes the execution of all other clauses. Thus, to construct a simplification rule that replaces the head of a clause by the body of the clause while preserving the semantics of the CLP program, the construction algorithm adds to the head of the rule the negation of the bodies of all the other clauses. The negation of the bodies of clauses may result in a disjunction of constraints, thus for each clause a set of rules might be generated. Note that constraints that are added to the head of the rule are also added to its body to ensure that constraints removed unnecessarily are added again.

The construction algorithm generates the following simplification rules:

$$min(A, B, C) \ \wedge \ A{\leq}B \ \Leftrightarrow \ A{\leq}B \ \wedge \ C{=}A.$$
$$min(A, B, C) \ \wedge \ C{\neq}B \ \Leftrightarrow \ A{\leq}B \ \wedge \ C{=}A \ \wedge \ C{\neq}B.$$
$$min(A, B, C) \ \wedge \ A{>}B \ \Leftrightarrow \ A{>}B \ \wedge \ C{=}B.$$
$$min(A, B, C) \ \wedge \ C{\neq}A \ \Leftrightarrow \ A{>}B \ \wedge \ C{=}B \ \wedge \ C{\neq}A.$$

To generate a simplification rule that replaces the head of the first clause with the body of the clause, the construction algorithm negates the bodies of all other clauses (i.e. second clause) to add to the head of the rule. The negation of the body of the second clause gives $A{\leq}B \ \vee \ C{\neq}B$, a disjunction of constraints. This results in two separate rules (first and second rule), one for each disjunct. Similarly, the last two rules are generated from the second clause.

Then the combined approach will eliminate the above constructed rules from the search tree of the generate and test algorithm. The generate and test algorithm used is the one proposed in [4].

Generate and Test. All possible candidate constraints for the left hand side C of the rule and right hand side D of the rule are generated and tested based on the observation that a rule of the form $C \Rightarrow D$ is valid if the execution of the goal $C \wedge \neg(D)$ finitely fails with respect to the definition.

The generate and test algorithm will add the following rules to the constraint solver:

$$min(A, B, C) \Rightarrow C{\leq}A \wedge C{\leq}B.$$
$$min(A, B, C) \wedge B{\leq}A \Leftrightarrow B{\leq}A \wedge C{=}B.$$

The propagation rule (first rule) is generated by calling the CLP system to execute the goal $min(A, B, C) \wedge C{>}A \wedge C{>}B$ that fails.

The generated solvers are implemented in the language Constraint Handling Rules (CHR) [8].

The paper is organized as follows. The generate and test algorithm of [4] is summarized in Section 2. In Section 3, we present the construction algorithm. Then in Section 4, we present the combined approach. Finally, we conclude in Section 5 with a summary and future work.

2   Generate and Test Method

In this section, we summarize the generate and test algorithm that we use for the combined approach and which is given in [4]. The algorithm requires as input a CLP program defining the user-defined constraint for which the solver is needed.

Definition 1. *A CLP program is a finite set of CLP clauses. A CLP clause is a rule of the form $H \leftarrow B_1 \wedge \ldots \wedge B_n \wedge C_1 \wedge \ldots \wedge C_m$ where $H, B_1, \ldots, B_n$ are atoms and $C_1, \ldots, C_m$ are built-in constraints. H is called the* head *of the clause and $B_1 \wedge \ldots \wedge B_n \wedge C_1 \wedge \ldots \wedge C_m$ is called the* body *of the clause. A user-defined constraint is defined in a CLP program if it occurs in the head of the clause.*

The algorithm also requires the following sets which specify the syntactic form of the generated rules of the solver:

- A set of built-in and user-defined constraints denoted by $Base_{lhs}$. These constraints are the common part that must appear in the left hand side (lhs) of all rules.
- A set of built-in and user-defined constraints denoted by $Cand_{lhs}$. These are the candidate constraints to be used in conjunction with the $Base_{lhs}$ to form the lhs of a rule.
- A set containing built-in constraints denoted by $Cand_{rhs}$. These are the candidate constraints that may appear in the right hand side (rhs) of a rule. This set can be expanded to contain user-defined constraints.

Example 2. To generate a constraint solver for min constraint of Example 1, the algorithm takes as input the CLP program defining the constraint, as well as, the following sets:

$$Base_{lhs} = \{min(A, B, C)\}$$
$$Cand_{lhs} = \{A{=}B, A{=}C, B{=}C, A{\neq}B, A{\neq}C, B{\neq}C,$$
$$A{\leq}B, A{\leq}C, B{\leq}A, B{\leq}C, C{\leq}A, C{\leq}B\}$$
$$Cand_{rhs} = Cand_{lhs}$$

Example 3. To generate a constraint solver for $append(A, B, C)$ that holds if list C is the concatenation of lists A and B, the algorithm takes as input the following CLP program:

$$append(A, B, C) \leftarrow A{=}[] \wedge C{=}B.$$
$$append(A, B, C) \leftarrow A{=}[D|E] \wedge C{=}[F|G] \wedge D{=}F \wedge append(E, B, G).$$

As well as, the following sets:

$$Base_{lhs} = \{append(A, B, C)\}$$
$$Cand_{lhs} = \{A{=}[], B{=}[], C{=}[], A{=}B, A{=}C, B{=}C, A{\neq}B, A{\neq}C, B{\neq}C,$$
$$A{\neq}[], B{\neq}[], C{\neq}[]\}$$
$$Cand_{rhs} = Cand_{lhs}$$

Given the specified input parameters, candidate propagation rules are generated of the form $C \Rightarrow D$, where C the lhs of the rule is a subset of $Base_{lhs} \cup Cand_{lhs}$, and D the rhs of the rule is a subset of $Cand_{rhs}$. The candidate rules are then subjected to a validity test as follows:

- For *primitive* propagation rules (i.e. rules with rhs consisting of only built-in constraints), the validity test is based on the observation that a rule of the form $C \Rightarrow D$ is valid if the execution of the goal $C \wedge \neg(D)$ finitely fails with respect to the given CLP program and the predefined solver for the built-in constraints.
- For *general* propagation rules (i.e. rules with rhs consisting of both built-in and user-defined constraints) to avoid the problems relating to the negation of user-defined constraints, a different validity test is proposed where the negation is performed on the set of answers to a goal (set of constraints) rather than on the constraints themselves.

For the execution of the goals, a bounded depth tabled resolution [6,7] for CLP is used to avoid non-termination. The intuitive basic principle of tabled resolution is the following: each new subgoal S is compared to the previous intermediate subgoals (not necessarily in the same branch of the resolution tree). If there is a previous subgoal I which is equivalent to S or more general than S, then no more unfolding is performed on S and answers for S are selected among the answers of I. This process is repeated for all subsequent computed answers that correspond to the subgoal I.

Example 4. Consider the following primitive propagation rule which is generated by the algorithm for the *append* constraint:

$$append(A, B, C) \wedge B{=}[] \Rightarrow A{=}C.$$

The validity test for the rule is determined from the execution of the goal $append(A, B, C) \wedge B=[] \wedge A{\neq}C$. Using a classical CLP resolution scheme, the goal will lead to an infinite derivation tree, whereas in the case of a tabled resolution, the execution of the goal will fail as shown by the derivation tree below:

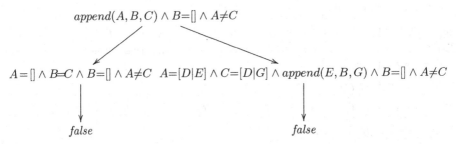

The initial goal $G_1 = (append(A, B, C) \wedge B=[] \wedge A{\neq}C)$ is more general than the subgoal $G_2 = (A=[D|E] \wedge C=[D|G] \wedge append(E, B, G) \wedge B=[] \wedge A{\neq}C)$, in the sense that $(append(X, Y, Z) \wedge U=[W|X] \wedge V=[W|Z] \wedge Y=[] \wedge U{\neq}V)$ entails $(append(X, Y, Z) \wedge Y=[] \wedge X{\neq}Z)$. So no unfolding is made on G_2, and the process waits for answers of G_1 to compute answers of G_2. Since G_1 has no further possibility of having answers, then G_2 fails and thus G_1 also fails.

Since a propagation rule does not remove constraints but adds new ones, the constraint store may contain superfluous information. To improve the time and space behavior of constraint solving, propagation rules should be transformed into equivalent simplification rules. For some of the automatically generated propagation rules a transformation to simplification rules is possible. For a valid propagation rule of the form $C \Rightarrow D$, if a proper subset E of C can be found such that $D \cup E \Rightarrow C$ is valid too then the propagation rule can be transformed to a simplification rule of the form $C \Leftrightarrow D \cup E$.

Example 5. For the *min* constraint of Example 1, the generate and test algorithm generates the following valid rules:

$$min(A, B, C) \Rightarrow C{\leq}A \wedge C{\leq}B. \tag{1}$$
$$min(A, B, C) \wedge C{\neq}A \Leftrightarrow C=B \wedge C{\neq}A. \tag{2}$$
$$min(A, B, C) \wedge C{\neq}B \Leftrightarrow C=A \wedge C{\neq}B. \tag{3}$$
$$min(A, B, C) \wedge A{\leq}B \Leftrightarrow C=A \wedge A{\leq}B. \tag{4}$$
$$min(A, B, C) \wedge B{\leq}A \Leftrightarrow C=B \wedge B{\leq}A. \tag{5}$$

The set of generated rules is complete, i.e. it propagates all built-in constraints (equalities and inequalities) that logically follow from the *min* constraint definition and some given equalities or inequalities.

Example 6. For the *append* constraint of Example 3, the generate and test algorithm generates among others the following valid rules:

$$append(A, B, C) \wedge A=[] \Leftrightarrow A=[] \wedge B=C.$$
$$append(A, B, C) \wedge B=[] \Leftrightarrow A=C \wedge B=[].$$
$$append(A, B, C) \wedge C=[] \Leftrightarrow A=[] \wedge B=[] \wedge C=[].$$

$append(A, B, C) \wedge A{=}C \Leftrightarrow B{=}[] \wedge A{=}C.$
$append(A, B, C) \wedge A{\neq}[] \Rightarrow C{\neq}[].$
$append(A, B, C) \wedge B{\neq}[] \Rightarrow A{\neq}C \wedge C{\neq}[].$

The rules handle only special cases, where equality or inequality constraints are checked between the arguments of the constraint and the empty list. The solver is incomplete due to the absence of recursive rules that are able to handle more general cases.

3   Symbolic Construction Method

In this section, we present an algorithm that constructs simplification rules symbolically for a constraint H defined by a CLP program, as follows:

$$H \leftarrow C_1, H \leftarrow C_2, \ldots, H \leftarrow C_n.$$

where C_i is a conjunction of constraints, n is the total number of clauses and the clauses are non-overlapping (i.e. in a computation at most one clause can be chosen for a goal). Note that any overlapping CLP program can be transformed into an equivalent non-overlapping one.

The algorithm is presented in Figure 1. The basic idea of the algorithm stems from the observation that in general, the execution of one clause in a CLP program excludes the execution of all other clauses. Thus, to construct a valid simplification rule that simplifies the constraint H to C_i (the body of the *ith* clause), the negation of the bodies of all other clauses is added to the head of the rule to ensure that the rule will only be *applicable* if the bodies of all the other clauses are not. This is needed to preserve the semantics of the CLP program defining the constraint.

The algorithm works as follows. For each clause $H \leftarrow C_i$ in the CLP program, it constructs the simplification rule(s) by:

- Setting the head of the rule to H.
- Setting the body of the rule to C_i.
- Adding to the head of the rule G_i^j; a disjunct from G_i, the expression resulting from negating the bodies of all the CLP clauses excluding C_i.
- Adding to the body of the rule G_i^j. This is done to ensure that constraints removed unnecessarily from the constraint store are added again.

The constructed simplification rules are of the form:

$$H \wedge G_i^j \Leftrightarrow C_i \wedge G_i^j \quad 1{\leq}j{\leq}m_i, \ 1{\leq}i{\leq}n$$

where G_i^j is a conjunction of built-in constraints from G_i and m_i is the number of disjuncts G_i^j in G_i.

Determination of G_i. Given a clause $H \leftarrow C_i$, the expression G_i is formally determined as follows:

begin
　　　H: the head of the clauses.
　　　B: the set of clause bodies.
　　　R: the set of resultant simplification rules initialized to $[]$.

　　　while B is not empty **do**
　　　　　Remove from B its first element denoted C_i.
　　　　　$Other_B$: the set of all clause bodies except C_i.
　　　　　G_i: the set resulting from negating $Other_B$.
　　　　　while G_i is not empty **do**
　　　　　　　Remove from G_i its first element denoted G_i^j.
　　　　　　　Add rule $(H \wedge G_i^j \Leftrightarrow C_i \wedge G_i^j)$ to R.
　　　　　end while
　　　end while
end

Fig. 1. The Symbolic Construction Algorithm

- Negate the bodies of all clauses of the CLP program except the body C_i:

$$\neg\, (C_1 \vee \ldots \vee C_{i-1} \vee C_{i+1} \vee \ldots \vee C_n)$$

- Distribute the negation:

$$\neg C_1 \wedge \ldots \wedge \neg C_{i-1} \wedge \neg C_{i+1} \wedge \ldots \wedge \neg C_n$$

Since C_i is a conjunction of constraints, this expands to:

$$\neg \left(c_1^1 \wedge \ldots \wedge c_1^{k_1} \right) \wedge \ldots \wedge \neg \left(c_{(i-1)}^1 \wedge \ldots \wedge c_{(i-1)}^{k_{(i-1)}} \right) \wedge$$

$$\neg \left(c_{(i+1)}^1 \wedge \ldots \wedge c_{(i+1)}^{k_{(i+1)}} \right) \wedge \ldots \wedge \neg \left(c_n^1 \wedge \ldots \wedge c_n^{k_n} \right)$$

where k_i denotes the number of constraints in a body C_i.
- Push the negation into the conjunctions. This transforms the conjunctions of constraints to disjunctions of negated constraints:

$$\left(\neg c_1^1 \vee \ldots \vee \neg c_1^{k_1} \right) \wedge \ldots \wedge \left(\neg c_{(i-1)}^1 \vee \ldots \vee \neg c_{(i-1)}^{k_{(i-1)}} \right) \wedge$$

$$\left(\neg c_{(i+1)}^1 \vee \ldots \vee \neg c_{(i+1)}^{k_{(i+1)}} \right) \wedge \ldots \wedge \left(\neg c_n^1 \vee \ldots \vee \neg c_n^{k_n} \right)$$

- Replace each negated constraint $\neg c_q^d$ by a corresponding simplified positive constraint. The algorithm distinguishes between two cases:
  - If c_q^d is a built-in constraint, the algorithm replaces $\neg c_q^d$ by its corresponding positive constraint after simplification. The set of built-in constraints is assumed to be closed under negation. For obtained constraints that consist of local variables (i.e. variables that do not occur in H), the algorithm adds the built-in constraints (in their positive form) from the body C_q that define the local variables.

- Otherwise, c_q^d is a user-defined constraint and since the negation of user-defined constraints is still not well-defined, the algorithm discards $\neg c_q^d$ (i.e. no rules will be constructed for this case).

This results in a formula of the form:

$$\left(P_1^1 \vee \ldots \vee P_1^{l_1}\right) \wedge \ldots \wedge \left(P_{(i-1)}^1 \vee \ldots \vee P_{(i-1)}^{l_{(i-1)}}\right) \wedge$$

$$\left(P_{(i+1)}^1 \vee \ldots \vee P_{(i+1)}^{l_{(i+1)}}\right) \wedge \ldots \wedge \left(P_n^1 \vee \ldots \vee P_n^{l_n}\right)$$

where P_i^e is a built-in constraint or a conjunction of built-in constraints and l_i denotes the number of built-in constraints in a disjunct C_i.
- Distribute the conjunction over the disjunction:

$$\left(P_1^1 \wedge \ldots \wedge P_{(i-1)}^1 \wedge P_{(i+1)}^1 \wedge \ldots \wedge P_n^1\right) \vee \ldots \vee$$

$$\left(P_1^{l_1} \wedge \ldots \wedge P_{(i-1)}^{l_{(i-1)}} \wedge P_{(i+1)}^{l_{(i+1)}} \wedge \ldots \wedge P_n^{l_n}\right)$$

This results in G_i, which is a formula in disjunctive normal form $G_i^1 \vee \ldots \vee G_i^{m_i}$, where G_i^j is a conjunction of built-in constraints.

Example 7. Given the CLP program for the *append* of Example 3:

$append(A, B, C) \leftarrow A=[] \wedge C=B.$
$append(A, B, C) \leftarrow A=[D|E] \wedge C=[F|G] \wedge D=F \wedge append(E, B, G).$

The symbolic construction algorithm will construct rules for the first clause by setting the head of the rules to $append(A, B, C)$ and the body of the rules to the body of the clause, $A=[] \wedge C=B$. It then determines G_1, the expression resulting from negating the bodies of all other clauses as follows:

- Negate the body of the second clause:

$$\neg(A=[D|E] \wedge C=[F|G] \wedge D=F \wedge append(E, B, G))$$

- Distribute the negation:

$$\neg(A=[D|E]) \vee \neg(C=[F|G]) \vee \neg(D=F) \vee \neg(append(E, B, G))$$

- Given that the equality constraint is a built-in constraint defined by a constraint theory and for which a solver is available, the algorithm performs the following operations:
  - It replaces $\neg(A=[D|E])$ and $\neg(C=[F|G])$ by $A \neq [D|E]$ and $C \neq [F|G]$ which will be simplified by the built-in solver to $A=[]$ and $C=[]$, respectively.
  - It replaces $\neg(D=F)$ by $D \neq F$. Since D and F are local variables, the built-in constraints $A=[D|E]$ and $C=[F|G]$ that define the local variables to be the first elements of the lists A and C are added.
- Negated user-defined constraint $\neg(append(E, B, G))$ is discarded.

This results in

$$A=[] \lor C=[] \lor (D{\neq}F \land A=[D|E] \land C=[F|G])$$

and the following three simplification rules are constructed:

$append(A, B, C) \land A=[] \Leftrightarrow A=[] \land C=B.$

$append(A, B, C) \land C=[] \Leftrightarrow A=[] \land C=B \land C=[].$

$append(A, B, C) \land D{\neq}F \land A=[D|E] \land C=[F|G] \Leftrightarrow A=[] \land C=B \land$
$$D{\neq}F \land A=[D|E] \land C=[F|G].$$

Similarly, the following simplification rules are constructed for the second clause:

$append(A, B, C) \land A{\neq}[] \Leftrightarrow A=[D|E] \land C=[F|G] \land D=F \land$
$$append(E, B, G) \land A{\neq}[].$$

$append(A, B, C) \land C{\neq}B \Leftrightarrow A=[D|E] \land C=[F|G] \land D=F \land$
$$append(E, B, G) \land C{\neq}B.$$

The rules are recursive. The power of the symbolic construction algorithm is in the generation of such recursive rules given a recursive constraint definition.

Simplification. In general, the simplification rules constructed are not in the simplest form. To simplify the constructed rules, the head and body of the rules are executed against the solvers for the built-in constraints.

Example 8. Consider the following constructed rule for *append*:

$append(A, B, C) \land D{\neq}F \land A=[D|E] \land C=[F|G] \Leftrightarrow \underline{A=[]} \land C=B \land$
$$D{\neq}F \land \underline{A=[D|E]} \land C=[F|G].$$

Since the existence of the constraints $A=[]$ and $A = [D|E]$ leads to a contradiction, the rule will be simplified to :

$append(A, B, C) \land D{\neq}F \land A=[D|E] \land C=[F|G] \Leftrightarrow false.$

Redundancy. In general, the generated rules may contain redundant rules. To remove redundant rules, the same algorithm is used as the one summarized in the redundancy pruning in Section 4, which basically states that a rule is redundant and should be removed if its operation is covered by the remaining rules of the solver.

Example 9. Consider the following two rules of the constructed solver for *append*:

$append(A, B, C) \land D{\neq}F \land A=[D|E] \land C=[F|G] \Leftrightarrow false.$

$append(A, B, C) \land A{\neq}[] \Leftrightarrow A=[D|E] \land C=[F|G] \land D=F \land$
$$append(E, B, G).$$

The first rule is redundant and can be removed since removing it and executing the goal $append(A, B, C) \land D{\neq}F \land A=[D|E] \land C=[F|G]$ on the remaining rules, the second rule will be fired and leads to a contradiction.

Example 10. For the *append* of Example 3, the simplification rules reduce to the following set:

$append(A, B, C) \land A=[] \Leftrightarrow C=B \land A=[].$

$append(A, B, C) \land C=[] \Leftrightarrow C=B \land A=[] \land C=[].$

$append(A, B, C) \land A{\neq}[] \Leftrightarrow A=[D|E] \land C=[F|G] \land D=F \land$
$$append(E, B, G).$$

$append(A, B, C) \land C{\neq}B \Leftrightarrow A=[D|E] \land C=[F|G] \land D=F \land$
$$append(E, B, G) \land C{\neq}B.$$

The rules cover some of the cases, where list A is empty (first and second rules), as well as, when it consists of at least one element (third and fourth rules). In the latter case, the simplification rule is called recursively on each of the elements of list A. However, it should be noted that the solver is not propagation complete, i.e. it does not produce all built-in constraints that logically follows from the constraint definition such as that the list B is empty if it is known that the lists A and C are equal.

Recursive Rules. The power of the symbolic construction approach is its ability to generate recursive rules which cannot be generated by other approaches.

Example 11. Consider the following CLP program that defines the constraint $replace(A, B, C, D)$ that holds if list D is the result of replacing all occurrences of A in list C by B.

$replace(A, B, C, D) \leftarrow C=[] \land D=[].$

$replace(A, B, C, D) \leftarrow C=[E|F] \land D=[G|H] \land E=A \land G=B \land$
$$replace(A, B, F, H).$$

$replace(A, B, C, D) \leftarrow C=[E|F] \land D=[G|H] \land E{\neq}A \land G=E \land$
$$replace(A, B, F, H).$$

The symbolic construction algorithm will generate the following simplification rules:

$replace(A, B, C, D) \wedge C=[] \Leftrightarrow C=[] \wedge D=[].$

$replace(A, B, C, D) \wedge D=[] \Leftrightarrow C=[] \wedge D=[].$

$replace(A, B, C, D) \wedge C=[E|F] \wedge E=A \Leftrightarrow C=[E|F] \wedge D=[G|H] \wedge$
$\qquad E=A \wedge G=B \wedge replace(A, B, F, H).$

$replace(A, B, C, D) \wedge C=[E|F] \wedge E{\neq}A \Leftrightarrow C=[E|F] \wedge D=[G|H] \wedge$
$\qquad G=E \wedge E{\neq}A \wedge replace(A, B, F, H).$

$replace(A, B, C, D) \wedge D=[G|H] \wedge G{\neq}B \Leftrightarrow C=[E|F] \wedge D=[G|H] \wedge$
$\qquad G=E \wedge E{\neq}A \wedge G{\neq}B \wedge replace(A, B, F, H).$

$replace(A, B, C, D) \wedge C=[E|F] \wedge D=[G|H] \wedge G{\neq}E \Leftrightarrow C=[E|F] \wedge$
$\qquad D=[G|H] \wedge E=A \wedge G=B \wedge G{\neq}E \wedge replace(A, B, F, H).$

The symbolic construction algorithm constructs the rules by direct derivation from the definition. The first two rules apply when the lists are empty. The last four rules apply when information is known about either of the leading list elements E or G or when the relationship between them is sufficiently known. The rules do not cover all possibilities, however they represent a good basis for a constraint solver for $replace(A, B, C, D)$.

4   Combined Approach

Both the symbolic construction method and the generate and test method have advantages and disadvantages. The symbolic construction method is able to generate recursive rules where all other approaches based on generation and testing failed. However, the generate and test, in general, generates a more exhaustive set of rules.

In this section, we will present a combination of the symbolic construction method and the generate and test method that will lead to more powerful and expressive constraint solvers at a reduced cost of generation.

We will first construct semantically valid rules using the symbolic construction method then we will use the generated rules to prune the search tree of the generate and test method using the closure pruning technique. However, even with this pruning technique, the combined approach generates redundant rules that should be removed. This will be done using the second pruning technique.

1. *Closure Pruning:* If a rule of the form $C \Leftrightarrow D$ is generated using the symbolic construction algorithm then in the generate and test method there is no need to consider rules where the lhs constraint is C. Thus, during the enumeration of all possible rule lhs, unnecessary lhs candidates are removed from this list. For efficiency reasons, the concrete implementation is not based on a list but on a tree containing lhs candidates on its nodes.

2. *Redundancy Pruning:* To suppress the generation of redundant rules, we use the algorithm proposed in [1]. The idea of the algorithm is based on operational equivalence of programs. The operational equivalence test for redundancy removal is to check if the computation step due to the candidate rule that is tested for redundancy can be performed by the remainder of the program. This is done by executing the prefix of the candidate rule in both programs and comparing the results. If the results are identical, then the rule is obviously redundant and can be removed.
A redundant rule is defined formally as follows:

Definition 2. *A rule R is redundant in a program P if and only if for all states S: If $S \mapsto_P^* S_1$ then $S \mapsto_{P \setminus \{R\}}^* S_2$, where S_1 and S_2 are final states and are identical upto renaming of variables and logical equivalence of built-in constraints. $\mapsto_P^*$ denotes the reflexive and transitive closure of $\mapsto_P$.*

The redundancy pruning technique is non-deterministic since the resulting solver may vary depending on the order in which rules are tried and removed.

Example 12. For the *min* constraint of Example 1, the symbolic construction method generates the following rules:

$$min(A, B, C) \wedge A \leq B \Leftrightarrow A \leq B \wedge C = A. \tag{6}$$

$$min(A, B, C) \wedge C \neq B \Leftrightarrow A \leq B \wedge C = A \wedge C \neq B. \tag{7}$$

$$min(A, B, C) \wedge A > B \Leftrightarrow A > B \wedge C = B. \tag{8}$$

$$min(A, B, C) \wedge C \neq A \Leftrightarrow A > B \wedge C = B \wedge C \neq A. \tag{9}$$

The generate and test algorithm will first generate the propagation rule (Rule 1). Using the closure pruning technique, Rules 2, 3, and 4 are not checked. Rule 5 will be generated since there is no rule that checks for $B \leq A$. Combining both sets of rules, Rule 8 will be eliminated using the redundancy pruning technique since it is covered by Rule 5. The combined approach generates the same rules as the ones generated using the generate and test method however less candidate rules are checked.

In general, the set of rules generated using the combined approach is more expressive and powerful than the ones generated either using the generate and test method or using the symbolic construction method as illustrated in the following example.

Example 13. For the *append* constraint, the combined approach generates the following rules using the symbolic construction method:

$$append(A, B, C) \wedge A = [] \Leftrightarrow C = B \wedge A = [].$$

$$append(A, B, C) \wedge C = [] \Leftrightarrow C = B \wedge A = [] \wedge C = [].$$

$$append(A, B, C) \wedge A \neq [] \Leftrightarrow A = [D|E] \wedge C = [F|G] \wedge D = F \wedge$$

$$append(E, B, G).$$

$$append(A, B, C) \ \wedge \ C{\neq}B \Leftrightarrow A{=}[D|E] \ \wedge \ C{=}[F|G] \ \wedge \ D{=}F \ \wedge$$

$$append(E, B, G) \ \wedge \ C{\neq}B.$$

Then the following rules (among others) will be added from the generate and test method:

$$append(A, B, C) \ \wedge \ B{=}[] \ \Leftrightarrow A{=}C \ \wedge \ B{=}[]. \tag{10}$$
$$append(A, B, C) \ \wedge \ A{=}C \ \Leftrightarrow B{=}[] \ \wedge \ A{=}C. \tag{11}$$
$$append(A, B, C) \ \wedge \ B{\neq}[] \ \Rightarrow A{\neq}C. \tag{12}$$

Adding these rules improves the efficiency of the solver. For example, with Rule 10 the recursion over the list A is replaced by a simple unification $A = C$ if list B is empty.

Implementation in CHR. The head of the generated rules may contain constraints that are built-in constraints for the CHR system. To have a running CHR solver, these constraints should be removed from the head. This is done in two steps:

- Equality constraints appearing in the head of a rule are propagated all over the constraints in the head and body of the rule. Then the resulting constraints are simplified. This can be performed as follows. In turn, each equality constraint appearing in the head is removed and transformed in a substitution that is applied to the head and body.
- For other built-in constraints, the transformation leads to guarded CHR rules [8].

Example 14. The following simplification rule for *min*:

$$min(A, B, C) \ \wedge \ B{\leq}A \Leftrightarrow B{\leq}A \ \wedge \ C{=}B.$$

will be transformed to the following guarded CHR simplification rule:

$$min(A, B, C) \Leftrightarrow B{\leq}A \mid C{=}B.$$

Equivalent Definitions – Same Solvers. The generate and test method is based on enumerating rule candidates and checking their validity against the intentional definition. Thus, having two equivalent definitions the generate and test will generate always the same set of rules.

However, using the symbolic construction method, the set of generated rules for a constraint may differ for different but equivalent definitions of the constraint. The following example will show that the more compact the set of clauses is, the more expressive the constructed solver is. This is intuitively clear since the construction method generates rules for a clause by negating the bodies of all other clauses which are added to the head and the body of the rule. In general, negating more than a clause will lead to adding more than one constraint to the head of the rule making it more restrictive.

Example 15. The constraint *min* of Example 1 can be defined by an equivalent CLP program consisting of three clauses instead of two as follows:

$min(A, B, C) \leftarrow A<B \land C=A.$

$min(A, B, C) \leftarrow A>B \land C=B.$

$min(A, B, C) \leftarrow A=B \land C=A.$

The symbolic construction algorithm generates the following set of simplification rules:

$$min(A, B, C) \land A<B \Leftrightarrow C=A \land A<B. \tag{13}$$

$$min(A, B, C) \land A>B \Leftrightarrow C=B \land A>B. \tag{14}$$

$$min(A, B, C) \land A=B \Leftrightarrow C=A \land C=B \land A=B. \tag{15}$$

$$min(A, B, C) \land C\neq A \Leftrightarrow C=B \land A>B \land C\neq A. \tag{16}$$

$$min(A, B, C) \land C\neq B \land A\neq B \Leftrightarrow C=A \land A<B \land C\neq B. \tag{17}$$

$$min(A, B, C) \land C\neq B \land A\geq B \Leftrightarrow false. \tag{18}$$

Although the number of generated rules has increased compared to the set of rules presented in Example 1, these rules are less expressive since:

– Rule 6 subsumes the two rules 13 and 15. Whereas Rule 6 will be applied for the goal $min(A, B, C) \land A\leq B$, no rule is applicable using the rules above.
– Rule 7 of the first solver is more general than its counterparts, Rule 17 and Rule 18.

Using the combined approach, all rules of the generate and test method will be added except Rule 16 which will not be checked or generated. Using the redundancy pruning technique, all rules of the construction method will be removed except Rule 16. The resulting solver of the combined approach is identical to the solver generated for the *min* constraint defined using two clauses. However, it should be noted that the solver obtained by construction using only two clauses pruned the search tree better.

5   Conclusion

In this paper, we have extended the work done in the field of *Inductive Constraint Solving* by providing a method that combines the advantages of the generate and test approach with a symbolic construction method based on rewriting of CLP programs.

In the combined approach, we first generate rules using the symbolic construction method then we use them to prune the search tree of the generate and test method. In general, the combined approach leads to more expressive and efficient constraint solvers at a reduced cost. Some rules, like recursive rules that cannot be generated using the generate and test method are generated using the symbolic construction method.

One interesting direction for future work is to investigate the completeness of the solvers generated. It is clear that in general this property cannot be guaranteed, but in some cases it should be possible to check it, or at least to characterize the kind of consistency the solver can ensure.

References

1. Abdennadher, S., Frühwirth, T.: Integration and Optimization of Rule-based Constraint Solvers. In: International Symposium on Logic-based Program Synthesis and Transformation, LOPSTR 2003. LNCS, Springer, Heidelberg (2004)
2. Abdennadher, S., Rigotti, C.: Automatic Generation of Propagation Rules for Finite Domains. In: Dechter, R. (ed.) CP 2000. LNCS, vol. 1894, Springer, Heidelberg (2000)
3. Abdennadher, S., Rigotti, C.: Towards Inductive Constraint Solving. In: Walsh, T. (ed.) CP 2001. LNCS, vol. 2239, pp. 31–45. Springer, Heidelberg (2001)
4. Abdennadher, S., Rigotti, C.: Automatic Generation of CHR Constraint Solvers. Journal of Theory and Practice of Logic Programming (TPLP) 5(2) (2005)
5. Apt, K., Monfroy, E.: Automatic Generation of Constraint Propagation Algorithms for Small Finite Domains. In: Jaffar, J. (ed.) CP 1999. LNCS, vol. 1713, pp. 58–72. Springer, Heidelberg (1999)
6. Codognet, P.: A Tabulation Method for Constraint Logic Programs. In: 8th Symposuim and Exibition on Industrial Applications of Prolog (1995)
7. Warren, D.S., Cui, B.: A System for Tabled Constraint Logic Programming. In: Palamidessi, C., Moniz Pereira, L., Lloyd, J.W., Dahl, V., Furbach, U., Kerber, M., Lau, K.-K., Sagiv, Y., Stuckey, P.J. (eds.) CL 2000. LNCS (LNAI), vol. 1861, Springer, Heidelberg (2000)
8. Frühwirth, T.: Theory and Practice of Constraint Handling Rules, Special Issue on Constraint Logic Programming. Journal of Logic Programming 37(1–3), 95–138 (1998)
9. Monfroy, E., Ringeissen, C.: Generating Propagation Rules for Finite Domains: A Mixed Approach. In: Apt, K.R., Kakas, A.C., Monfroy, E., Rossi, F. (eds.) Compulog Net WS 1999. LNCS (LNAI), vol. 1865, Springer, Heidelberg (2000)
10. Sobhi, I.: Constructive generation of rule-based constraint solvers. Master's thesis, German University in Cairo (2007)

A Scalable Inclusion Constraint Solver Using Unification

Ye Zhang and Flemming Nielson

Informatics and Mathematical Modelling, Technical University of Denmark
{yez,nielson}@imm.dtu.dk

Abstract. We describe a parameterized framework with which users can take advantage of unification over analysis variables to implement efficient or precise analyses, or even both. To be illustrative we instantiate the framework with reaching definition analysis and conduct a systematic evaluation of performance and precision of the analysis. We compare our result with that of a state-of-the-art solver, the Succinct Solver and show our solver is at least 10-times faster than the Succinct Solver. On some benchmarks linearity is reached by the use of unification. Although the result of unification is often imprecise, a heuristic study is conducted to detect where the loss of precision may happen. We apply the heuristics on benchmarks and achieve not only efficient but also precise analysis.

1 Introduction

Program analyses are often expressed as a collection of constraints and then implemented by an existing solver. This strategy separates analysis specification from implementation and thus enables program analysis designers to share the insights and efforts in solver technology. The challenge remains to develop an analysis which is efficient and precise at the same time. For instance, in order to speed up its computation the Succinct Solver [19] adopts former insights of state-of-the-art solvers [15,9,8], including the use of recursion, continuations, prefix tree and memorization. On the other hand, the solver consumes a large amount of memory to maintain its complex data structures. This becomes a problem for large programs and can significantly decrease efficiency as observed in [25].

In this paper we aim to achieve the two aspects simultaneously by introducing unification of equality constraints over analysis variables. This is based on two insights. First, the analysis result of unification is always sound with respect to that of set-inclusion. Second, unification can be solved in almost linear time and reduces memory consumption as explained later. Actually our experimental results show that our solver significantly outperforms the Succinct Solver: it is at least 10-times faster and in some cases even 200-times faster than the Succinct Solver. A substantially lower asymptotic complexity is also observed in some benchmarks when using unification. Although using equality constraints may lead to a loss in precision, a heuristic study shows that equivalence relation between analysis variables widely exists in programs and can be taken advantage

King, A. (Ed.): LOPSTR 2007, LNCS 4915, pp. 121–137, 2008.
© Springer-Verlag Berlin Heidelberg 2008

of by our solver to make both fast and precise analysis. Indeed the same approach can be naturally applied on other analyses, like live variables analysis, very busy expression analysis, etc.

Section 2 gives an introduction to related works. In section 3 we present a constraint language and a framework for its solutions under which users can tune the systems to achieve the best balance between performance and precision by switching between equality constraints and inclusion constraints. We give two versions of semantic explanation to the constraint language: the first one (Section 3) is standard and represents the users' view of the language; the second (Section 4) makes clearer how the equality benefits us in time and space. Furthermore it sheds light on the algorithm design. We study the properties of both versions and show the connections between them. In Section 5 we consider the systematic design of a fixpoint engine whose complexity is between cubic and almost linear. To make our ideas concrete, in Section 6 we implement a classical data flow analysis, reaching definitions analysis, and demonstrate unification can improve performance considerably while still achieving a high degree of precision.

2   Related Works

In this paper we shall look at analysis problems over a finite universe and compute complete solutions. The Succinct Solver is a constraint solver which works over the same universe as ours. It is built on previous insights on adopting functional programming for implementing solvers [15,9,8] and uses the alternation-free fragment of *Least Fixpoint Logic* (ALFP) as the specification logic. Because of the expressiveness of this logic, the solver has been used for the implementation of a variety of analyses [20,10,3]. The result of [4] shows that reordering constraints can improve performance considerably. The further study in [21] shows that the performance of the Succinct Solver is at most a small constant factor worse than XSB Prolog but in optimum cases the solver outperforms XSB Prolog significantly. In order to generate efficiently solvable constraints, however, one needs to understand how clauses are solved in the Succinct Solver. We here attempt to optimize the performance of our solver from the user's point of view by simply adjusting the use of set-inclusion and equality. Therefore users do not have to know any technical details inside a solver but are still able to tune a system to fit their specific needs. While all of our constraints can be expressed in ALFP, we gain much in terms of efficiency by having equality constraints explicitly.

Unification has been used to yield efficient implementation and concise results in program analyses, such as type inference system [17,13,22] and control flow analyses [12]. The work of [7] further presents a parameterized framework for a type system that allows expression of constraint-based analyses in varying levels of efficiency and precision with mixed-terms [1,14]. While our approach is close in spirit to this framework, we include equality constraints over analysis variables and confine ourselves to the flat universe as in most Datalog solvers.

Heintze and Jaffar [11] investigate definite set constraints and show that all satisfiable constraints in the class have a least model. Charatonik and Podelski [5] further showed that solving definite set constraints has DEXPTIME complexity. Although the set minus operation, which contains negative set expression, i.e. $\alpha \setminus c \equiv \alpha \cap \neg c$, makes our constraints fall out of the scope of definite set constraints, we show that the Moore family result still holds for the constraints of interest. Melski and Reps [16] proved a subclass of definite set constraints can be solved in cubic time in studying a simple data-flow reachability problem. While their constraints use only projection and terms, we include the operations set minus and intersection on a flat universe and show that the constraint solving has the same complexity. With unification, however, the complexity can be reduced to almost linear time. The question, then, is what is the tradeoff from doing this. Our experimental results show that many equivalent analysis variables arise and the level of efficiency and precision achieved are also quite encouraging. We are optimistic about finding more places of using unification for more analyses of process calculi or real imperative languages, e.g. C.

3   Inclusion Constraint Language

We present an inclusion constraint language over sets of tuples of atomic values. In terms of set constraints, an atomic value is a term of arity 0. We describe a parameterized framework in having both set-inclusion and equality over analysis variables. The ability to switch between the two relations gives users the flexibility of tuning the performance and precision of analyses. The constraint language is different from the set constraints studied by Melski and Reps [16] in having both set minus and intersection. It also deviates from definite set constraints [11] in including set minus. We will show, however, that any satisfiable constraints of the class can be solved in cubic time and still have a least model. Specifically a constraint clause $\mathbf{P}$ is defined by

$$\varphi ::= c \subseteq \alpha \mid \beta \subseteq^s \alpha \mid \beta \subseteq^e \alpha \mid \alpha \setminus c \subseteq \beta \mid \alpha \setminus (D) \subseteq \beta \mid \alpha \cap \beta \subseteq \gamma \mid \varphi_1 \wedge \varphi_2$$
$$D ::= ? \mid ?, D \mid m \mid m, D$$

where α, β and $\gamma \in \mathbf{AVar}$ are analysis variables over constants $c \in \widehat{\mathbf{Const}}$, i.e. a set of tuples consisting of a list of abstract elements $m \in \mathbf{E}$ separated by ','. The two new operators $\subseteq^s$ and $\subseteq^e$ are considered as subset-inclusion and equality respectively. The superscript functions as a pointer marking where a set-inclusion might be changed to equality and vise versa. It is possible to express the constraints $\alpha \cup \beta \subseteq^s \gamma$ and $\alpha \subseteq^s \beta \cap \gamma$ in terms of more primitive operations, e.g. $\alpha \cup \beta \subseteq^s \gamma$ is equivalent to $\alpha \subseteq^s \gamma \wedge \beta \subseteq^s \gamma$; thus they are not included among the primitive operations. We dispense with the union on the right hand side $\alpha \subseteq^s \beta \cup \gamma$ since it would destroy the Moore family property. For set minus constraint, besides standard set minus operation over constants, we introduce a new syntax category D to represent a set of tuples: the values of some positions of all these tuples are fixed and the rest can be any elements (represented

Table 1. Standard Semantics

1. $\hat{\psi} \models c \subseteq \alpha$	iff $c \subseteq \hat{\psi}(\alpha)$		4.2 $\hat{\psi} \models \alpha \setminus (D) \subseteq \beta$ iff $\hat{\psi}(\alpha) \setminus (D) \subseteq \hat{\psi}(\beta)$	
2. $\hat{\psi} \models \beta \subseteq^s \alpha$	iff $\hat{\psi}(\beta) \subseteq \hat{\psi}(\alpha)$		5. $\hat{\psi} \models \alpha \cap \beta \subseteq \gamma$ iff $\hat{\psi}(\alpha) \cap \hat{\psi}(\beta) \subseteq \psi(\hat{\gamma})$	
3. $\hat{\psi} \models \beta \subseteq^e \alpha$	iff $\hat{\psi}(\beta) = \hat{\psi}(\alpha)$		6. $\hat{\psi} \models \varphi_1 \wedge \varphi_2$ iff $\hat{\psi} \models \varphi_1$ and $\hat{\psi} \models \varphi_2$	
4.1 $\hat{\psi} \models \alpha \setminus c \subseteq \beta$ iff $\hat{\psi}(\alpha) \setminus c \subseteq \hat{\psi}(\beta)$				

by '?'). The overloaded set minus operation removes all tuples matching (D) from a set S, formally

$$S \setminus (m_1, \cdots, m_{i_1-1}, ?, m_{i_1+1}, \cdots, m_{i_k-1}, ?, m_{i_k+1}, \cdots, m_n) =$$
$$S \setminus \{(m_1, \cdots, m_{i_1-1}, \ell_1, m_{i_1+1}, \cdots, m_{i_k-1}, \ell_k, m_{i_k+1}, \cdots, m_n) \mid \ell_1, \cdots, \ell_k \in \mathbf{E}\}$$

This syntax category not only generates a succinct coding but also reduces sharply the number of constraints generated as further demonstrated in Section 6.

Standard Interpretation. Given an interpretation $\hat{\psi} \in \widehat{\mathbf{Env}}$, which maps analysis variables to constants, for a clause φ the satisfaction relation $\hat{\psi} \models \varphi$ is specified as in Table 1. Consider, for instance, a constraint

$$\{(a,b)\} \subseteq \alpha \wedge \alpha \subseteq^s \beta \wedge \{(c,d)\} \subseteq \beta \tag{Ex.1}$$

It is easy to verify that $\hat{\psi}$ given by $\hat{\psi}(\alpha) = \{(a,b)\}$ and $\hat{\psi}(\beta) = \{(a,b),(c,d)\}$ is a solution. Actually it is also the least one: any estimate $\hat{\psi}'$ such that $\hat{\psi} \sqsubseteq \hat{\psi}'$ satisfies **Ex.1** (where we use the standard partial order $\sqsubseteq$ on the mappings of $\widehat{\mathbf{Env}}$, formally, for $\hat{\psi}, \hat{\psi}' \in \widehat{\mathbf{Env}} : \hat{\psi} \sqsubseteq \hat{\psi}'$ iff $\forall x \in \mathbf{AVar} : \hat{\psi}(\alpha) \subseteq \hat{\psi}'(\alpha)$.) Since in general we are interested in a least solution, the following theorem then guarantees that a unique least solution does exist for any solvable constraints.

Theorem 1. *For each clause φ, the set $\{\hat{\psi} \mid \hat{\psi} \models \varphi\}$ is a Moore family.*

First observe that $(\widehat{\mathbf{Env}}, \subseteq)$ is a complete lattice. The proof is then a straightforward structural induction on φ.

Intuitively, using equality instead of set-inclusion is safe since equality is more strict than set-inclusion. To formalize this observation, we define a relation $\leq$ over clauses: For all $\varphi_1, \varphi_2 \in \mathbf{P}$, $\varphi_1 \leq \varphi_2$ if and only if φ_2 can be obtained by substituting operator $\subseteq^e$ for some or all operators $\subseteq^s$ of φ_1. We shall also say that φ_1 can be *lifted* to φ_2 if $\varphi_1 \leq \varphi_2$. Prop. 1 and 2 state that any acceptable solution to a lifted clause is also valid to its original one and so is the least solution.

Proposition 1. *For all $\varphi_1, \varphi_2 \in \mathbf{P}$, if $\hat{\psi} \models \varphi_2$ and $\varphi_1 \leq \varphi_2$, then $\hat{\psi} \models \varphi_1$.*

The proof is conducted by an induction on φ_1 based on the observation that $\hat{\psi}(\alpha) = \hat{\psi}(\beta) \Rightarrow \hat{\psi}(\alpha) \subseteq \hat{\psi}(\beta)$. Finally from Prop. 1 and Thm. 1, we have that

Proposition 2. *For all $\varphi_1, \varphi_2 \in \mathbf{P}$, if $\varphi_1 \leq \varphi_2$, then $\sqcap\{\hat{\psi} \mid \hat{\psi} \models \varphi_1\} \sqsubseteq \sqcap\{\hat{\psi} \mid \hat{\psi} \models \varphi_2\}$.*

On the other hand, equality constraints do not necessarily lead to a loss in precision. For example, consider the clause

$$\{(a,b),(c,d)\} \subseteq \alpha \wedge \{(c,d)\} \subseteq \beta \wedge \alpha \subseteq^s \beta \wedge \beta \setminus \{(a,b)\} \subseteq \gamma \qquad \textbf{(Ex.2)}$$

Here a least model β has no more data than α. In fact switching s to e in the constraint would preserve precision.

As we show in Section 5, general constraints can be solved in cubic time while unification on equality constraints is nearly linear. Under the framework we present, a general strategy of tuning systems is to try set-inclusion first since normally we would always prefer a precise solution if performance is acceptable. If the efficiency of the computation is unsatisfactory, we can syntactically adjust the superscript symbols of clauses and repeat the procedure until we reach a good balance between performance and precision.

4   Interpretation Using Type Variables

The standard semantics is user-friendly but unclear in specifying how unification benefits our computation. We would like to make it explicit in the semantic specification so that the interesting properties of the new interpretation can be addressed separately from the algorithm of constraint solving. We present a double-layer interpretation using a new category, type variables $i \in \textbf{TV}$, and enforce that equivalent analysis variables map onto the same type variable explicitly in semantics and hence the corresponding constants are collapsed into one constant. One challenge of adopting the type-variable solution is that now the least solution is not unique and may even potentially be infinite. We study the relation between the least solutions and present the principle of *designated solution* to remove the non-determinism of the choice of type variables. We show further the correctness of the second semantics with respect to the first. Therefore our user only need to understand the first semantics and the strategy of tuning systems, and he may leave the technical details of solving constraints to us.

A type-variable solution has two components: the type environment $\hat{\psi}_1 \in \textbf{Env}_\textbf{T}$, which maps analysis variables to type variables, and the type-binding environment $\hat{\psi}_2 \in \widehat{\textbf{Env}_\textbf{TB}}$, which maps type variables to constants. The rules are given in Table 2. If we assume that $\psi = \hat{\psi}_2 \circ \hat{\psi}_1$ then the rules are the same as before except for the third one, which enforces that two equivalent analysis variables must be unified onto the same type variable, i.e. $\hat{\psi}_1(\beta) = \hat{\psi}_1(\alpha)$. In this way unification is required explicitly. To further illustrate the difference, consider the two estimates of the lifted version of the example **Ex.1**,

(a) $\hat{\psi}_1(\alpha) = 1$ $\hat{\psi}_2(1) = \{(a,b),(c,d)\}$ (b) $\hat{\psi}_1(\alpha) = 1$ $\hat{\psi}_2(1) = \{(a,b),(c,d)\}$
 $\hat{\psi}_1(\beta) = 1$ $\hat{\psi}_1(\beta) = 2$ $\hat{\psi}_2(2) = \{(a,b),(c,d)\}$
 $\hat{\psi}_1(\gamma) = 2$ $\hat{\psi}_2(2) = \{(a,b)\}$ $\hat{\psi}_1(\gamma) = 3$ $\hat{\psi}_2(3) = \{(a,b)\}$

Ex.3

Table 2. Semantics Using Type Variables

1. $(\hat\psi_1, \hat\psi_2) \models_T c \subseteq \alpha$	iff $c \subseteq \hat\psi_2(\hat\psi_1(\alpha))$
2. $(\hat\psi_1, \hat\psi_2) \models_T \beta \subseteq^s \alpha$	iff $\hat\psi_2(\hat\psi_1(\beta)) \subseteq \hat\psi_2(\hat\psi_1(\alpha))$
3. $(\hat\psi_1, \hat\psi_2) \models_T \beta \subseteq^e \alpha$	iff $\hat\psi_1(\beta) = \hat\psi_1(\alpha)$
4.1 $(\hat\psi_1, \hat\psi_2) \models_T \alpha \setminus c \subseteq \beta$	iff $\hat\psi_2(\hat\psi_1(\alpha)) \setminus c \subseteq \hat\psi_2(\hat\psi_1(\beta))$
4.2 $(\hat\psi_1, \hat\psi_2) \models_T \alpha \setminus (D) \subseteq \beta$ iff $\hat\psi_2(\hat\psi_1(\alpha)) \setminus (D) \subseteq \hat\psi_2(\hat\psi_1(\beta))$	
5. $(\hat\psi_1, \hat\psi_2) \models_T \alpha \cap \beta \subseteq \gamma$	iff $\hat\psi_2(\hat\psi_1(\alpha)) \cap \hat\psi_2(\hat\psi_1(\beta)) \subseteq \hat\psi_2(\hat\psi_1(\gamma))$
6. $(\hat\psi_1, \hat\psi_2) \models_T \varphi_1 \wedge \varphi_2$	iff $(\hat\psi_1, \hat\psi_2) \models_T \varphi_1$ and $(\hat\psi_1, \hat\psi_2) \models_T \varphi_2$

Both of them are acceptable for the first semantics whereas only **(a)** is valid this time since $\hat\psi_1(\alpha) \neq \hat\psi_1(\beta)$. Notice also that the unification coalesces the analysis variables onto one type variable and hence avoids storing redundant information in the environment $\widehat{\mathbf{Env_{TB}}}$. However since the choice of type variables is nondeterministic, the ordering on the set of solutions is not a partial-order but a pre-order, i.e. reflexive, transitive but not antisymmetric.

Definition 1. *For* $(\hat\psi_1, \hat\psi_2), (\hat\psi_1', \hat\psi_2') \in \mathbf{Env_T} \times \widehat{\mathbf{Env_{TB}}}$, *define*

$$(\hat\psi_1, \hat\psi_2) \preceq (\hat\psi_1', \hat\psi_2') \Longleftrightarrow \exists \pi : \mathbf{TV} \to \mathbf{TV} : \hat\psi_1' = \pi \circ \hat\psi_1 \quad \wedge \quad \hat\psi_2 \sqsubseteq \hat\psi_2' \circ \pi$$

where π *is a total function and* $\hat\psi_2 \sqsubseteq \hat\psi_2' \circ \pi \Leftrightarrow \forall i \in \mathbf{TV} : \hat\psi_2(\alpha) \subseteq \hat\psi_2'(\pi(i)).$

Apparently, for the set of solutions of a clause, a unique least model is not assured any more. However we can show that given a constraint, if a pair is acceptable then so are all its equivalences.

Proposition 3. *If* $(\hat\psi_1, \hat\psi_2) \models_T \varphi \wedge (\hat\psi_1, \hat\psi_2) \equiv (\hat\psi_1', \hat\psi_2')$, *then* $(\hat\psi_1', \hat\psi_2') \models_T \varphi.$

where $\equiv$ is the induced equivalence, i.e. $\equiv$ is $\preceq \wedge \succeq$. In preparation for the proof we first show two lemmata as follows.

Lemma 1. $(\hat\psi_1, \hat\psi_2) \preceq (\hat\psi_1', \hat\psi_2')$ *if and only if*

$$\forall x, y \in \mathbf{AVar} : \hat\psi_1(x) = \hat\psi_1(y) \Rightarrow \hat\psi_1'(x) = \hat\psi_2'(y) \wedge \tag{1}$$
$$\forall z \in \mathbf{AVar} : \hat\psi_2(\hat\psi_1(z)) \subseteq \hat\psi_2'(\hat\psi_1'(z)) \tag{2}$$

Following from the Def. 1 the lemma is proved by the observation that every equivalence analysis variable should bind to the same type variable and the functional compositions of the two pairs have the relation $\hat\psi_2 \circ \hat\psi_1 \sqsubseteq \hat\psi_2' \circ \hat\psi_1'$. Lemma 1 provides a more constructive way of verifying the relation $\preceq$ than Def. 1. We further extend the lemma over the equivalence relation straightforwardly.

Lemma 2. $(\hat{\psi}_1, \hat{\psi}_2) \equiv (\hat{\psi}'_1, \hat{\psi}'_2)$ *iff*

$$\forall x, y \in \mathbf{AVar} : \hat{\psi}_1(x) = \hat{\psi}_1(y) \Leftrightarrow \hat{\psi}'_1(x) = \hat{\psi}'_2(y) \ \wedge \tag{3}$$

$$\forall z \in \mathbf{AVar} : \hat{\psi}_2(\hat{\psi}_1(z)) = \hat{\psi}'_2(\hat{\psi}'_1(z)) \tag{4}$$

This shows that the equivalence of two pairs amounts to checking the conjuncts (3) and (4).

Proof. We now prove Prop. 3 by induction on φ. For the case $c \subseteq \alpha$ assume that $(\hat{\psi}_1, \hat{\psi}_2) \models_{\mathcal{T}} c \subseteq \alpha$ and $(\hat{\psi}_1, \hat{\psi}_2) \equiv (\hat{\psi}'_1, \hat{\psi}'_2)$ From rule 1 in Table 2 we have $c \subseteq \hat{\psi}_2(\hat{\psi}_1(\alpha))$ and by Lemma 2 we have $\hat{\psi}_2(\hat{\psi}_1(x)) = \hat{\psi}'_2(\hat{\psi}'_1(x))$ and hence $c \subseteq \hat{\psi}'_2(\hat{\psi}'_1(x))$ because of the transitivity of inclusion relation. Finally the first rule in Table 2 allows us to conclude that $(\hat{\psi}'_1, \hat{\psi}'_2) \models_{\mathcal{T}} c \subseteq x$ as desired. Other cases can be proved similarly.

It is straightforward to verify that least upper bounds of a pre-ordered set (if there are any) are equivalent to each other as stated below.

Fact 1. *If x and y are two least upper bounds (greatest lower bounds) of a set $S \subseteq P$ then $x \equiv y$.*

To prove the existence of least solution(s) we introduce the concepts of the designated greatest lower bound (least upper bound) of a subset S of a pre-ordered set P denoted by $\hat{\sqcap} S$ ($\hat{\sqcup} S$). We shall assume that there is a choice function which, given a set of elements, returns a designated one. Accordingly we present the concepts of complete prelattice and Moore family in complete prelattice in order to show that the least models exist for any satisfiable clauses.

Definition 2 (Complete Prelattice). *A complete prelattice $P = (P, \preceq, \hat{\sqcup}, \hat{\sqcap}, \hat{\perp}, \hat{\top})$ is a preordered set such that all its subsets have least upper bounds (with $\hat{\sqcup} S$ a designated least upper bound for S) and greatest lower bounds (with $\hat{\sqcap} S$ a designated greatest lower bound for S). Furthermore, $\hat{\perp} = \hat{\sqcup} \emptyset = \hat{\sqcap} P$ is a designated least element and $\hat{\top} = \hat{\sqcap} \emptyset = \hat{\sqcup} P$ is a designated greatest element.*

Lemma 3. *For a preordered set $(P, \preceq)$ the following statements are equivalent:*
(1) $(P, \preceq)$ can be extended to a complete prelattice $(P, \preceq, \hat{\sqcup}, \hat{\sqcap}, \hat{\perp}, \hat{\top})$;
(2) Every subset of P has a least upper bound;
(3) Every subset of P has a greatest lower bound.

Following from the above definition and lemma, we have

Fact 2. $(\mathbf{Env_T} \times \widehat{\mathbf{Env_{TB}}}, \preceq)$ *is a complete prelattice.*

The definition and lemma above are quite similar to their counterparts in the partially ordered world. This is because the designated bound allows us to work around the randomness of choosing type variables. However, sticking to the designated solutions may be too strict in defining a Moore family for complete prelattices. For instance, consider a subset S of a pre-ordered set R. A rather restrictive definition of Moore family could be: $\forall S' \subseteq S : \hat{\sqcap} S' \in S$, i.e. S is closed under the designated greatest lower bound. However since the Moore family property is really concerned with the existence of the greatest lower bound, we prefer a more flexible definition that retains the original meaning of Moore family: Instead of enforcing $\sqcap S' \in S$ we want to express that $\exists u : u \equiv \sqcap S' \wedge u \in S$. This idea is further formalized by a compositional operator $\equiv\in$ (read as "is represented in").

Definition 3 (Relation $\equiv\in$). *For an element e and a set P, we say that $e \equiv\in P$ if and only if there exists an element e' such that $e \equiv e'$ and $e' \in P$.*

Definition 4 (Moore Family for A Complete Prelattice). *A Moore family for a complete prelattice is a subset M of a complete prelattice $P = (P, \preceq)$ such that it is closed under greatest lower bounds, formally $\forall M' \subseteq M : \sqcap M' \equiv\in M$. Similar to Moore families for partially ordered sets, a Moore family for a complete prelattice always contains at least one least element and one greatest element, formally $\sqcap \emptyset \equiv\in M$ and $\sqcap M \equiv\in M$. Thus it is never empty.*

Applying the above definition, we have that the least solution is guaranteed for the set of pairs $(\hat{\psi}_1, \hat{\psi}_2)$ such that $(\hat{\psi}_1, \hat{\psi}_2) \models_T \varphi$, formally:

Theorem 2. *A set of solutions given by $\{(\hat{\psi}_1, \hat{\psi}_2) | (\hat{\psi}_1, \hat{\psi}_2) \models_T \varphi\}$ is a Moore family for a complete prelattice.*

The proof is by a structural induction on φ based on two observations. First note that $(\mathbf{Env_T} \times \widehat{\mathbf{Env_{TB}}}, \preceq, \hat{\sqcap}_T)$ is a complete prelattice. Second, let $\hat{\sqcap}(\hat{\psi}_1^i, \hat{\psi}_2^i) = (\hat{\psi}_1^\sqcap, \hat{\psi}_2^\sqcap)$ then for any analysis variables α, β and γ, we have that $\hat{\psi}_1^i(\alpha) = \hat{\psi}_1^i(\beta) \Leftrightarrow \hat{\psi}_1^i(\alpha) = \hat{\psi}_1^i(\beta)$ and $\hat{\psi}_2^\sqcap(\hat{\psi}_1^\sqcap(\gamma)) = \sqcap_i \hat{\psi}_2^i(\hat{\psi}_1(\gamma))$. Accordingly we can show $(\hat{\psi}_1^\sqcap, \hat{\psi}_2^\sqcap)$ is also satisfiable for each case.

Finally we relate the results of the type variable interpretation back to those of the standard one by showing (1) the second semantics complies with the lifting strategy (in Prop. 4) and (2) the least solution using type variable is as precise as that of the standard one (in Prop. 4).

Proposition 4. *If $\varphi_1 \leq \varphi_2$ and $(\hat{\psi}_1, \hat{\psi}_2) \models_T \varphi_2$ then $(\hat{\psi}_1, \hat{\psi}_2) \models_T \varphi_1$.*

Proof. The proof is a straightforward induction on the clause φ_1.

Proposition 5. *Let $(\hat{\psi}_1^\sqcap, \hat{\psi}_2^\sqcap) = \hat{\sqcap}\{(\hat{\psi}_1, \hat{\psi}_2) | (\hat{\psi}_1, \hat{\psi}_2) \models_T \varphi\}$ for some $\varphi \in$ Term, and $\hat{\psi}^\sqcap = \sqcap\{\hat{\psi} | \hat{\psi} \models \varphi\}$, then $\hat{\psi}_2^\sqcap \circ \hat{\psi}_1^\sqcap = \hat{\psi}^\sqcap$.*

Before proving the proposition, we first observe that

Lemma 4. *If $(\hat{\psi}_1, \hat{\psi}_2) \models_T \varphi$, then $\hat{\psi}_2 \circ \hat{\psi}_1 \models \varphi$.*

and the proof is a straightforward induction on φ.

Finally to prove Prop. 5 we further observe that under a least model the map from analysis variable to data fields for two semantics is exactly same: type variables have no effect on it.

5   Constraint Solving

We refer to the approach of [18] and present a graph formulation of constraints for computing a least solution for a program. A graph has nodes $i \in \mathbf{TV}$ and the two maps $\mathsf{D}_1 : \mathbf{AVar} \rightarrow \mathbf{TV}$ and $\mathsf{D}_2 : \mathbf{TV} \rightarrow \widehat{\mathbf{Const}}$ are used to associate nodes with analysis variables and constants with nodes respectively. A directed edge connecting nodes is decorated with the construct that gives rise to it: the constraints $\alpha \subseteq^s \beta$, $\alpha \setminus c \subseteq \beta$ and $\alpha \setminus (D) \subseteq \beta$ give rise to an edge from $\mathsf{D}_1[\alpha]$ to $\mathsf{D}_1[\beta]$; similarly the constraint $\alpha \cap \beta \subseteq \gamma$ contributes two edges at the same time, i.e. from $\mathsf{D}_1[\alpha]$ to $\mathsf{D}_1[\gamma]$, and $\mathsf{D}_1[\beta]$ to $\mathsf{D}_1[\gamma]$.

An equality relation never generates any edge. Thus when lifting is applied fewer edges are generated and thus the generated graph is smaller. In contrast it helps to remove redundant edges. For example, assume that $\alpha \subseteq^e \gamma$, then the edge from α to γ is not needed for any of the constraints $\alpha \subseteq^s \gamma, \alpha \setminus c \subseteq \gamma$ or $\alpha \setminus (D) \subseteq \gamma$ and $\alpha \cap \beta \subseteq \gamma$.

To be more specific consider the algorithm of Table 3. It takes as input a pair of constraint lists (U, N), where U contains all equality constraints and N all the others. Given a conjunction of constraints it is straightforward to generate the pair. Finally the algorithm outputs a solution $(\mathsf{D}_1, \mathsf{D}_2) \in \mathbf{Env_T} \times \mathbf{Env_{TB}}$. We restrict ourselves to entities occurring in the constraints of interest: Let $\mathbf{AVar}_\star \subseteq \mathbf{AVar}$ and $\mathbf{TV}_\star \subseteq \mathbf{TV}$ be the finite sets of interest respectively. The data structure W is a list of analysis variables, whilst given a type variable i, the data structure E returns a list of decorations of edges starting from i.

Step 1 is to initialize the data structures used through the algorithm and Step 2 implements the fast union/find data structure [23] to coalesce equivalent analysis variables onto the designated type variables according to the given equality constraints. Next the graph is built and the initial assignments to D_2 are executed in Step 3. This is conducted by the procedure $\mathsf{add}(\alpha, c)$ that incorporates d into $\mathsf{D}_2[\mathsf{D}_1[\alpha]]$ and adds α to the worklist if c was not contained in $\mathsf{D}_2[\mathsf{D}_1[\alpha]]$. Here equality constraints are dispensed with since they can never be part of N. The iteration in the fourth step then continues propagating contributions along edges until the worklist is empty. We use the worklist strategy LIFO and consider the benefit of using unification remains for other worklist strategies since simplifying the constraint graph by using unification always benefits iterative computation.

Concerning algorithm complexity, observe that for a clause of size n there are $O(n)$ nodes and $O(n)$ constructs. Thus Steps 1 and 3 are $O(n)$. Step 2 takes time $O(m \cdot \alpha(m, n))$ where m is the number of equality constraints that is bounded by $O(n)$, n is the number of analysis variables and α is the inverse Ackermann's function that grows very slowly. Finally $O(n)$ operations are needed to re-associate equivalence analysis variables with a designated type variable.

Before analyzing the complexity of Step 4, we need first to clarify what the complexity of the operations upon constants (set of tuples) actually is. In our implementation, each tuple is encoded as a bit and the number of tuples is $O(n)$; thus the set operations are over bit-vectors of the length n and take linear time. Next observe two facts: (1) there are $O(n)$ edges generated from a clause of size n

Table 3. Worklist Algorithm

INPUT : (U, N)
OUTPUT : (D_1, D_2)
Step 1 : $W := \text{nil};$
            for α_i in $AVar_*$ do $D_1[\alpha_i] := i$; $D_2[i] = \emptyset$; $E[i] = \text{nil};$
Step 2 :   unify(U)   (* Function implementing fast union/find data structure *)
Step 3 :   for cc in N do
              case cc of
                $c \subseteq \alpha$:   add$(\alpha, c);$
                $\alpha \subseteq^s \beta$:   if $D_1[\alpha] \neq D_1[\beta]$ then $E[D_1[\alpha]] := \text{cons}(cc, E[D_1[\alpha]]);$
                $\alpha \backslash c \subseteq \beta$:   if $D_1[\alpha] \neq D_1[\beta]$ then $E[D_1[\alpha]] := \text{cons}(cc, E[D_1[\alpha]]);$
                $\alpha \backslash (D) \subseteq \beta$: if $D_1[\alpha] \neq D_1[\beta]$ then $E[D_1[\alpha]] := \text{cons}(cc, E[D_1[\alpha]]);$
                $\alpha \cap \beta \subseteq \gamma$:   if $D_1[\alpha] \neq D_1[\gamma]$ then $E[D_1[\alpha]] := \text{cons}(cc, E[D_1[\alpha]]);$
                              if $D_1[\beta] \neq D_1[z]$ then $E[D_1[\beta]] := \text{cons}(cc, E[D_1[\beta]]);$

Step 4 :   While $W \neq \text{nil}$ do
              $\gamma := \text{head}(W); W := \text{tail}(W);$
              $t_e := E[D_1[\gamma]];$
              for cc in t_e do
                case cc of
                  $\alpha \subseteq^s \beta$: add$(\beta, D_2[D_1[\alpha]]);$
                  $\alpha \backslash c \subseteq \beta$: add$(\beta, D_2[D_1[\alpha]] \backslash c);$ (* standard set minus   *)
                  $\alpha \backslash (D) \subseteq \beta$: add$(\beta, D_2[D_1[\alpha]] \backslash (D));$ (* overloaded set minus *)
                  $\alpha \cap \beta \subseteq \gamma$: add$(\gamma, D_2[D_1[\alpha]] \cap D_2[D_1[\beta]]);$

---

procedure add(α, c) is
  if $\neg(c \subseteq D_2[D_1[\alpha]])$ then $D_2[D_1[\alpha]] := D_2[D_1[\alpha]] \cup c;$
                      $W := \text{cons}(\alpha, W);$

---

and (2) each edge can be traversed at most $O(n)$ times as there are $O(n)$ nodes. Therefore letting n_i be the number of edges bound to the node i, we have that the time of iteration is $O(\Sigma_{i \in \mathbf{TV}_*}(n \cdot n_i \cdot n)) = O(n^3)$ where the first n is the number of traversals on each edge and the second is the time of set operations. Therefore the overall complexity of our algorithm is $O(n^3)$.

Finally we prove the correctness of the algorithm:

Theorem 3. *Given a clause φ the output of the algorithm of Table 3 satisfies*

$$(D_1, D_2) \equiv \widehat{\cap}\{(\psi_1', \psi_2') | (\psi_1', \psi_2') \models_T \varphi\}$$

i.e., (D_1, D_2) is a least solution to φ.

The proof is based on two observations. First we can show that $(D_1, D_2) \models_T \varphi$ by inspecting the calculation of the algorithm for each construct. Second observe that for all $(\hat{\psi}_1, \hat{\psi}_2)$ such that $(\hat{\psi}_1, \hat{\psi}_2) \models_T \varphi$ we have two invariants: (1) $\forall \alpha, \beta \in$ **AVar** : $D_1(\alpha) = D_1(\beta) \Rightarrow \hat{\psi}_1(\alpha) = \hat{\psi}_1(\beta)$ and (2) $\forall \gamma : D_2(D_1(\gamma)) \subseteq \hat{\psi}_2(\hat{\psi}_1(\gamma))$, thereby proving (D_1, D_2) is a least model.

Table 4. Reaching Definitions Analysis: Set Inclusion

[ass]	$(RD_\circ, RD_\bullet) \models [x := e]^l$ iff $RD_\circ(l) \setminus (x, ?) \subseteq RD_\bullet(l)$	
	$\{(x, l)\} \subseteq RD_\bullet(l) \wedge$	
[skip]	$(RD_\circ, RD_\bullet) \models [skip]^l$ iff $RD_\circ(l) \subseteq^s RD_\bullet(l)$	(i)
[exp]	$(RD_\circ, RD_\bullet) \models [exp]^l$ iff $RD_\circ(l) \subseteq^s RD_\bullet(l)$	(ii)
[comp]	$(RD_\circ, RD_\bullet) \models S_1; S_2$ iff $(RD_\circ, RD_\bullet) \models S_1 \wedge$	
	$(RD_\circ, RD_\bullet) \models S_2 \wedge$	
	$\wedge_{\forall l \in \text{final}(S_1)} RD_\bullet(l) \subseteq^s RD_\circ(\text{init}(S_2))$	(iii)
[if]	$(RD_\circ, RD_\bullet) \models$ if $[b]^l$ then S_1 else S_2	
	iff $(RD_\circ, RD_\bullet) \models S_1 \wedge$	
	$(RD_\circ, RD_\bullet) \models S_2 \wedge$	
	$(RD_\circ, RD_\bullet) \models b \wedge$	
	$RD_\bullet(l) \subseteq^s RD_\circ(\text{init}(S_1)) \wedge$	(iv)
	$RD_\bullet(l) \subseteq^s RD_\circ(\text{init}(S_2))$	(v)
[wh]	$(RD_\circ, RD_\bullet) \models$ while $[b]^l$ do S	
	iff $(RD_\circ, RD_\bullet) \models S \wedge$	
	$(RD_\circ, RD_\bullet) \models b \wedge$	
	$RD_\bullet(l) \subseteq^s RD_\circ(\text{init}(S)) \wedge$	(vi)
	$\wedge_{\forall l' \in \text{final}(S)} RD_\bullet(l') \subseteq^s RD_\circ(l)$	(vii)

6   Case Study: Reaching Definitions Analysis

In this section we study the effect of applying unification on an intraprocedural reaching definitions analysis for a subset of the C language. We demonstrate that a significant improvement in performance can be achieved by using unification. The analysis is also implemented with the Succinct Solver for comparison.

The syntax of the C-like language is given by

$$S ::= [x := a]^\ell \mid [\text{skip}]^\ell \mid [\text{exp}]^\ell \mid S_1; S_2 \mid \text{if } [b]^\ell \text{ then } S_1 \text{ else } S_2 \mid \text{while } [b]^\ell \text{ do } S$$

and we shall assume each elementary block is assigned a *unique* label $\ell \in \mathbf{Lab}$. The analysis specification using only set-inclusion is specified in Table 4 and the liftable constraints are numbered. Two caches are used for recording the analysis results of program points, i.e. the entry and exit of elementary statements, $RD_\circ, RD_\bullet : Lab \times \mathcal{P}(\mathbf{Var} \times \mathbf{Lab})$. The judgement of the analysis has the form $(RD_\circ, RD_\bullet) \models S$ and it is true if and only if the analysis result $(RD_\circ, RD_\bullet)$ correctly describes S. The two auxiliary functions initial and final are standard and return the initial label and the set of final labels of a statement respectively; for the while loop the initial label is l and the set of final labels is $\{l\}$. Note that we use the extended version of set minus to generate constraints of constant size, which could otherwise be linear.

In order to control the level of imprecision we conduct a heuristic study of when and how imprecision may occur with respect to set-inclusion. Initially we would try lifting all the constraints from (i) to (vi), while retaining the flexibility of changing back to set-inclusion for the constraints of the last four cases when necessary. Lifting the constraint (vii), however, is very likely to decrease precision and is therefore not recommended. We explain our choices in the following.

Lifting the constraints (i) and (ii) does not lead to imprecision because intuitively the labels are unique and no data is changed between the entry and exit of the statements. The cases [comp], [if] and [wh] are more complex and we study [wh] first. To be illustrative, we visualize the flow of data by the graphs below where ∘ and • denote the entry and exit point(s) respectively and the square represents statements.

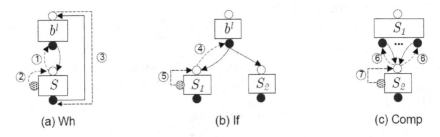

(a) Wh   (b) If   (c) Comp

For the moment ignore the dashed lines in (a) and the remaining part basically shows that the information goes through the test $[b]^l$, flows to S where the information may be updated and finally goes back to the entry of the test. Now consider lifting the constraint of (vi) which may be represented by adding the dashed line labeled 1. Checking if the change preserves precision then amounts to verifying if the entry of S has no more data than the exit of $[b]^l$. This is the case if the first basic statement, say S_t, of S is not a while-loop following the same argument of the cases [skip] and [exp] above. Otherwise as shown by the dashed line labeled 2, some updated RD information would flow back to the entry of S from the exit of S_t, denoted by a dotted circle on the side of a square. (We here differentiate the two exit points in order to make the presentation clear but note that they could be the same.) Finally the new RD information reaches the exit and entry of $[b]^l$ assuming lifting is applied on (vi). Now there are two possibilities: (1) if this information is not further updated by any assignment in the rest of S, using equality at (vi) would give no more data to the exit of $[b]^l$ than before considering the circle of data given by the loop and accordingly no imprecision occurs. (2) Otherwise some analysis variable assigned in S_t must be re-assigned later in S and instead of removing the former RD information both of them are kept at the entry and exit of $[b]^l$ and hence imprecision happens.

For the same reason as the case (2), replacing set-inclusion with equality in (vii) is very likely to decrease precision. To be concrete, suppose some variable x is assigned at some block labeled as l' before $[b]^l$ and re-assigned in S so that the pair (x, l') should be removed at the exit of S. Using equality, however, will re-add the deleted information to the exit of S as denoted by the line labeled 3.

Similarly we have that lifting the constraint (iv) and (v) of [if] maintains precision if S_1 does not start with a while-loop and otherwise may decrease

Table 5. Execution time of the Inclusion Solver and the Succinct Solver

Program	LOC	$T_{\subseteq^s}$	$T_{\subseteq^e}$	T_{SS}	$\triangle T_1$	$\triangle T_2$	$\triangle T_3$
fibonacci	15	0.24	0.11	1.47	53	84	92
isPrime	18	0.24	0.13	1.20	48	80	90
lcm	23	0.25	0.20	3.80	21	93	95
ext_gcd	22	0.23	0.16	2.54	32	91	94
nwtIter	14	0.16	0.07	1.09	56	85	93
wlfIter	20	0.38	0.20	1.87	48	80	89
sum	16	0.17	0.13	1.15	25	85	89
calculator	258	6.04	4.30	25.36	29	76	83
Improvement on Avarage					32	79	86

where:
$$\triangle T_1 = 1 - T_{\subseteq^e}/T_{\subseteq^s}$$
$$\triangle T_2 = 1 - T_{\subseteq^s}/T_{\subseteq^{ss}}$$
$$\triangle T_3 = 1 - T_{\subseteq^e}/T_{\subseteq^{ss}}$$

precision at the exit $RD_\bullet(l)$. For the case [comp] observe that S_1 may have several exits and thus lifting all constraints of (iii) results in unifying the data of these exits and hence decreases precision. On the other hand, if S_2 starts with a loop, we may also have more data as argued in the cases [if] and [wh]. This completes our discussion.

6.1 Benchmarks: Representative Programs

We evaluate the performance of our solver on a set of representative programs ranging in lines of code from 14 to 258. All experiments were run on a PC with 2.0 GHz CPU and 1.5 GB RAM and each experiment was repeated 5 times, and average numbers have been used. All the time T is in millisecond (ms.) and the improvement $\triangle T$ is in percent %. The results in terms of time performance are presented in Table 5. The first column is the program name of which the first 7 programs implement a series of mathematical algorithms respectively while 'calculator' is a simple application. The columns $T_{\subseteq^s}$ and $T_{\subseteq^e}$ give the time to perform the analysis before and after lifting respectively. The column T_{SS} reports the time to run the analysis on the Succinct Solver. Using unification results in a significant reduction in execution time - on average 39% ($\triangle T_1$). Considering the Succinct Solver, we observe that our solver is considerably faster - on average 84% faster using inclusion constraints and 91% faster using equality constraints[1]. This may be explained by the fact that our solver employs much simpler data structure than the Succinct Solver and thus has lower space usage.

We apply the heuristics to quickly detect all equality constraints that may introduce extra false-positives and switch them back to inclusion constraints. The adjusted constraints have exactly the same solution as the pure inclusion one, i.e. $S_{\subseteq^s} = S_{\subseteq^e}^{\text{impr}}$. But the remaining equivalences still enables our solver to solve the constraints much faster. In fact the precision-improved version has almost the same execution time as before. This demonstrates that many equivalent analysis variables do exist and can be used to speed up the calculation significantly.

---

[1] Note that the inclusion solution will be as precise as that of the Succinct Solver.

Table 6. Performance of programs with improved precision

Program	$\dfrac{S_{\subseteq^s} = S_{\subseteq^e}^{impr}}{T_{\subseteq^s}}$	$T_{\subseteq^e}^{impr}$	$\Delta T_1'$
fibonacci	0.24	0.12	52
isPrime	0.24	0.15	39
lcm	0.25	0.21	18
extended_gcd	0.23	0.16	32
newtonIter	0.16	0.09	43
wolfframIter	0.38	0.21	46
sum	0.17	0.13	25
calculator	6.04	4.45	26
Improvement on Avarage			29

where:

$$\Delta T_1' = 1 - T_{\subseteq^e}^{impr} / T_{\subseteq^s}$$

Last but not least adopting a bit imprecise solution may still have its own value if this does not prevent its client analysis from conducting any key optimization, as described by Das et al.[6], or scalability is much more important than precision in analyzing a huge system. If this is the case, we would expect to gain more efficiency by lifting more inclusion constraints.

6.2   Benchmarks: Scalable Programs

The real programs allow us to measure the effect of using equality constraints on time performance and precision. These programs, however, cannot easily be extended to the required size. In order to evaluate scalability we design a series of scalable programs with the desired size potential. Especially with well-designed scalable programs we are able to measure asymptotic complexity of benchmarks and further analyze the impact of using unification on complexity. Two families of scalable programs are selected for detailed presentation in the following.

$Wh_{(1,n)}$: while $x_0 < 2$ do $(x_1 := x_2;$

$\qquad \vdots$

$\qquad x_{n-1} := x_n;$
$\qquad x_n := 1)$

$If_{(n,1)}$: if $x_1 < 0$ then skip

$\qquad$ else $\quad \vdots$

$\qquad\qquad$ if $x_n < 0$ then skip
$\qquad\qquad$ else $x_0 := 1$

Here the first number of the subscript denotes the nesting depth of conditions, and the second yields the number of all assignments. The constraints generated for $Wh_{(1,n)}$ and $If_{(n,1)}$ are both of size $O(n)$. Indeed it can be shown using an amortization technique that both of the graphs have $O(n)$ edges. We then measure time performance of the two programs along with the increase of the number n and the results are summarized in Figure 1.

The first figure shows that using equality and inclusion mixed constraints is on average 25% faster than using pure inclusion constraints, which is at least 30-times and up to 200-times faster than the Succinct Solver. We observe that the larger a program is the faster our solver is compared to the Succinct Solver. Our solver also scales to much larger programs than the Succinct Solver. In fact

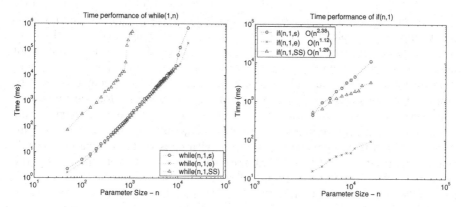

Fig. 1. Experimental results: $\text{Wh}_{(1,n)}$ and $\text{If}_{(n,1)}$

the Succinct Solver does not scale to programs of size $n \geq 1300$. We observe that both of the solvers suffer a sharp performance decline for large values of n: $n \geq 750$ in the case of the Succinct Solver, and $n \geq 9000$ and $n \geq 11000$ in the case of our solver. We hypothesize that this is because the large memory consumption requires much extra effort in memory management. For our solver especially, the computation time is so small when n is less than 250 that the initialization time becomes a large constant factor impacting the asymptotic complexity. To get the asymptotic growth rate of the solvers, we select the data before performance deterioration happens and after the constant factor is no longer dominating. By a least square fit technique on the model $t = c_1 \cdot m^c + c_0$, we estimate that the time complexity of the Succinct Solver, and our solver without and with unification are $O(n^{2.21}), O(n^{2.02})$ and $O(n^{2.01})$ respectively.

A significant improvement is observed in the program family $\text{If}_{(1,n)}$ (the second graph of Fig. 1). As shown, our solver remains 30-times faster than the Succinct Solver when using unification. Since no performance deterioration is observed, the estimated complexities are printed out directly. Furthermore unification results in almost linear time complexity while set-inclusion takes more than quadratic time and the Succinct Solver takes time $O(n^{1.3})$.

The very different effects observed are because the constraints generated for n assignments of $\text{Wh}_{(1,n)}$ remain $O(n)$ by the rule [ass]. But applying unification to $\text{If}_{(n,1)}$ means we only keep set-inclusion in the constraints for a constant number of assignments and therefore the resulting graph has only a constant number of edges.

7   Conclusion

We have presented a framework with which users can take advantage of unification to implement efficient or precise analyses, or even both. We instantiate the framework with our worked example and from the experimental results we conclude that (1) our constraint solver is a large constant factor faster than the Succinct Solver for all the well designed benchmarks; using unification may lower the asymptotic complexity even down to almost linear time; (3) unification need not give rise to imprecision: a careful study of the conditions where imprecision may or may not be incurred pays off in gaining the expected level of precision.

In future work, we would like to apply the framework to implementing control flow analyses of process calculi like Klaim [2] and analyses for the imperative languages, e.g. Java or C in order to better understand the extent to which unification can help achieve much more efficient implementation. This may require some extension to the constraint language with constructs, for example, conditional constraints, etc. Whaley et al. recently use BDDs to get efficient Datalog implementation for pointer analysis [24]. It would also be interesting for us to see how unification can be integrated with BDDs in achieving better performance.

References

1. Aiken, A.: Introduction to set constraint-based program analysis. Sci. Comput. Program. 35(2), 79–111 (1999)
2. Bettini, L., Bono, V., Nicola, R.D., Ferrari, G.L., Gorla, D., Loreti, M., Moggi, E., Pugliese, R., Tuosto, E., Venneri, B.: The Klaim Project: Theory and Practice. In: Priami, C. (ed.) GC 2003. LNCS, vol. 2874, pp. 88–150. Springer, Heidelberg (2003)
3. Bodei, C., Buchholtz, M., Degano, P., Nielson, F., Nielson, H.R.: Static validation of security protocols. Journal of Computer Security 13(3), 347–390 (2005)
4. Buchholtz, M., Nielson, H.R., Nielson, F.: Experiments with succinct solvers. Technical report, Informatics and Mathematical Modelling, Richard Petersens Plads, Building 321, DK-2800 Kgs. Lyngby, Denmark (February 2002)
5. Charatonik, W., Podelski, A.: Set constraints with intersection. Inf. Comput. 179(2), 213–229 (2002)
6. Das, M., Liblit, B., Fähndrich, M., Rehof, J.: Estimating the Impact of Scalable Pointer Analysis on Optimization. In: Cousot, P. (ed.) SAS 2001. LNCS, vol. 2126, Springer, Heidelberg (2001)
7. Fähndrich, M., Aiken, A.: Program analysis using mixed term and set constraints. In: Van Hentenryck, P. (ed.) SAS 1997. LNCS, vol. 1302, pp. 114–126. Springer, Heidelberg (1997)
8. Fecht, C., Seidl, H.: Propagating differences: An efficient new fixpoint algorithm for distributive constraint systems. Nord. J. Comput. 5(4), 304–329 (1998)
9. Fecht, C., Seidl, H.: A faster solver for general systems of equations. Sci. Comput. Program. 35(2), 137–161 (1999)
10. Gao, H.: Using the Succinct Solver to implement flow logic specifications of classical data flow analysis. Master's thesis, Technical University of Denmark (2004)
11. Heintze, N., Jaffar, J.: A decision procedure for a class of set constraints (extended abstract). In: LICS, pp. 42–51. IEEE Computer Society, Los Alamitos (1990)
12. Heintze, N., McAllester, D.A.: Linear-time subtransitive control flow analysis. In: SIGPLAN Conference on Programming Language Design and Implementation, pp. 261–272 (1997)
13. Henglein, F.: Global tagging optimization by type inference. In: LISP and Functional Programming, pp. 205–215 (1992)

14. Kodumal, J., Aiken, A.: Banshee: A scalable constraint-based analysis toolkit. In: Hankin, C., Siveroni, I. (eds.) SAS 2005. LNCS, vol. 3672, pp. 218–234. Springer, Heidelberg (2005)
15. Le Charlier, B., Van Hentenryck, P.: A universal top-down fixpoint algorithm. Technical Report CS-92-25, Brown University (1992)
16. Melski, D., Reps, T.W.: Interconveritibility of set constraints and context-free language reachability. In: PEPM, pp. 74–89 (1997)
17. Milner, R.: A theory of type polymorphism in programming. J. Comput. Syst. Sci. 17(3), 348–375 (1978)
18. Nielson, F., Nielson, H.R., Hankin, C.L.: Principles of Program Analysis. Springer, Heidelberg (1999)
19. Nielson, F., Seidl, H., Nielson, H.R.: A succinct solver for ALFP. Nord. J. Comput. 9(4), 335–372 (2002)
20. Nielson, H.R., Nielson, F., Buchholtz, M.: Security for mobility. In: Focardi, R., Gorrieri, R. (eds.) FOSAD 2001. LNCS, vol. 2946, pp. 207–265. Springer, Heidelberg (2004)
21. Pilegaard, H.: A feasibility study: The Succinct Solver v2.0, XSB prolog v2.6, and flow-logic based program analysis for carmel. Technical Report SECSAFE-IMM-008-1.0, Technical University of Denmark (2003)
22. Steensgaard, B.: Points-to analysis in almost linear time. In: POPL, pp. 32–41 (1996)
23. Tarjan, R.E.: Data Structures and Network Algorithms, volume CMBS44 of Regional Conference Series in Applied Mathematics. SIAM (1983)
24. Whaley, J., Avots, D., Carbin, M., Lam, M.S.: Using datalog with binary decision diagrams for program analysis. In: Yi, K. (ed.) APLAS 2005. LNCS, vol. 3780, pp. 97–118. Springer, Heidelberg (2005)
25. Zhang, Y.: Static analysis for protocol validation in hierarchical networks. Master's thesis, Technical University of Denmark (2005)

Annotation Algorithms for Unrestricted Independent And-Parallelism in Logic Programs

Amadeo Casas[1], Manuel Carro[2], and Manuel V. Hermenegildo[1,2]

[1] Depts. of Comp. Science and Electr. and Comp. Eng., Univ. of New Mexico, USA
{amadeo,herme}@cs.unm.edu
[2] School of Computer Science, Universidad Politécnica de Madrid, Spain
{mcarro,herme}@fi.upm.es

Abstract. We present two new algorithms which perform automatic parallelization via source-to-source transformations. The objective is to exploit goal-level, *unrestricted* independent and-parallelism. The proposed algorithms use as targets new parallel execution primitives which are simpler and more flexible than the well-known &/2 parallel operator. This makes it possible to generate better parallel expressions by exposing more potential parallelism among the literals of a clause than is possible with &/2. The difference between the two algorithms stems from whether the order of the solutions obtained is preserved or not. We also report on a preliminary evaluation of an implementation of our approach. We compare the performance obtained to that of previous annotation algorithms and show that relevant improvements can be obtained.

Keywords: Logic Programming, Automatic Parallelization, And-Parallelism, Program Transformation.

1 Introduction

Parallelism capabilities are becoming ubiquitous thanks to the widespread use of multi-core processors. Indeed, most laptops on the market contain two cores (capable of running up to four threads simultaneously) and single-chip, 8-core servers are now in widespread use. Furthermore, the trend is that the number of on-chip cores will double with each processor generation. In this context, being able to exploit such parallel execution capabilities in programs as easily as possible becomes more and more a necessity. However, it is well-known [17] that parallelizing programs is a hard challenge. This has renewed interest in language-related designs and tools which can simplify the task of producing parallel programs.

The comparatively higher level of abstraction of declarative languages and, among them, logic programming languages, allows writing programs which are closer to the specification of the solution. Besides, there is often more freedom in the implementation of different operational semantics which respect the declarative semantics. In particular, the notion of control in declarative languages frequently allows for more flexibility to arrange the evaluation order of some

King, A. (Ed.): LOPSTR 2007, LNCS 4915, pp. 138–153, 2008.

operations, including executing them in parallel if deemed convenient, without affecting the semantics of the original program. Additionally, the cleaner declarative semantics makes it possible to automatically detect more accurately any lack of dependencies among operations and hence to exploit opportunities for parallelism more easily than in imperative languages. At the same time, in most other respects in the case of logic programs the presence of dynamic data structures with "declarative pointers" (logical variables), irregular computations, or complex control makes the parallelization of logic programs a particularly interesting case that allows tackling the more complex parallelization-related challenges in a formally simple and well-understood context [11].

Because of this potential, automatic parallelization has received significant attention in logic programming [10], where two main forms of parallelism have been studied. *Or-parallelism* is exploited when the alternatives created by non-deterministic goals are explored simultaneously. Some relevant or-parallelism systems are Aurora [20] and MUSE [1]. *And-parallelism* aims at executing simultaneously (conjunctive) goals in clauses or in the resolvent. Examples of systems that have exploited and-parallelism are DDAS [25] and &-Prolog [12]. Additionally, some systems such as ACE [9], AKL [16], and Andorra [24] exploit certain combinations of both and- and or-parallelism. While or-parallelism can only obtain speedups when there is search involved, and-parallelism can be used in more algorithmic schemes, with divide-and-conquer and map-style algorithms being classic representatives. In this paper, we concentrate on and-parallelism.

A correct parallelization has been defined as one that preserves during and-parallel execution some key properties, typically correctness and no-slowdown [14]. The preservation of these properties is ensured by executing in parallel goals which meet some notion of *independence*, meaning that the goals to be executed in parallel do not interfere with each other in some particular sense. This can include for example absence of competition for binding variables plus other considerations such as, e.g., absence of side effects. For simplicity, in the rest of the paper we will assume that we are only dealing with side-effect free program sections. Note however that this does not affect the generality of our presentation, as we deal with dependencies in a generic way.

One of the best understood sufficient conditions for ensuring that goals meet the efficiency and correctness criteria for parallelization is *strict independence* [14], which entails the absence of shared variables at runtime between any two goals being parallelized. It should be noted that some proposals exploit and-parallelism between goals which do not meet this condition, but on which other restrictions are imposed which also ensure no-slowdown and correctness. Examples of such restrictions are determinism and non-failure [14] (determinism is exploited for example in [24]) and absence of conflicts due to the binding of shared variables (as in *non-strict* independent and-parallelism [14]). Another interesting issue is at what level of granularity the notion of independence is applied: at the goal level, at the binding level, etc. Our work in this paper will focus on *goal-level* (strict and non-strict) independent and-parallelism.

One particularly successful approach to automatically parallelizing a logic program uses three different stages [15,2,10]. The first one detects data (and control) dependencies between pairs of literals in the original program. A dependency graph (see Figure 1 as an example) is built to capture this information. Nodes in the graph correspond to literals in the body of the clause and edges represent dependencies between them. Edges are labeled with the associated dependency conditions (which may be trivially *true* or *false* —we will not represent those edges labeled with *true*). The second stage performs (global) analysis [3] to gather information regarding, e.g., variable aliasing, groundness, side effects, etc. in order to remove edges from the dependency graph or to simplify the conditions labeling these edges, if they cannot be evaluated statically to completion. Labeled edges will result in run-time checks if conditional parallel expressions are allowed. Alternatively, unresolved dependencies can be assumed to always hold, and parallel execution will be allowed only between literals which have been statically determined to be independent. This approach saves run-time checks at the expense of losing some parallelism. Finally, the third stage transforms the original program into a parallel version by *annotating* it with parallel execution operators using the information gathered by the analyzers [22]. This annotation should respect the dependencies found in the original program while, at the same time, exploiting as much parallelism as possible.

This annotation process is the focus of this paper. We will present and evaluate new annotation algorithms which target and-parallelism primitives which can express richer dependency graphs than those which can be encoded with the *nested fork-join* approaches which have been previously proposed (e.g., [22]). Our hope is that since the transformed programs will contain in some cases more parallelism, we will be able to obtain better speedups for such cases.

2   Background and Motivation

We will introduce, with the help of an example, the well-known &/2 operator for parallelism and its limitations, and we will show how better annotations for parallelism are possible when other, simpler primitives, are used.

2.1   *Fork-Join*-Style Parallelization

We will use as running example the following clause:

$$p(X,Y,Z) :- a(X,Z), b(X), c(Y), d(Y,Z).$$

and will assume that the dependencies detected between the literals in the predicate are defined by the graph $G = (V, E)$, shown in Figure 1. The vertices V correspond to the literals of the clause and there exists an edge between two literals L_i and L_j in E if $ind(L_i, L_j) \neq true$ (i.e., the literals

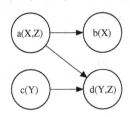

Fig. 1. Dependency graph for p/3

```
p(X, Y, Z):-                          p(X, Y, Z):-
    (a(X, Z), b(X)) & c(Y),               a(X, Z) & c(Y),
    d(Y, Z).                              b(X) & d(Y, Z).
```

(a) *fj1*: Order-preserving   (b) *fj2*: Non-order-preserving

Fig. 2. *Fork-Join* annotations for p/3 (Section 2)

L_i and L_j are dependent and thus the literal L_i has to be completed before the literal L_j), where *ind* is the notion of independence. As mentioned before, this information is obtained in our case from global data-flow analysis [3].

We will assume in the rest of the paper that all the dependencies are unconditional —i.e., conditional dependencies are assumed to be always false. This brings simplicity and avoids potentially costly run-time checks in the parallelized code at the expense of having fewer opportunities for parallelism. However, it has been experimentally found to be a good compromise [22,3].

Conjunctive parallel execution has traditionally been denoted using the &/2 operator instead of the sequential comma (','). The former binds more tightly than the latter. Thus, the expression "a, b & c, d" means that literals b and c can be safely executed in parallel after the execution of literal a finishes. When both b and c have successfully finished, execution continues with d.

While this single operator is enough to parallelize many programs, the class of dependencies it can express directly (i.e., dependency graphs with a nested fork-join structure) is a subset of that which can possibly appear in a program [22]. This makes parallelism opportunities to be inevitably lost in cases with a complex enough structure (e.g., that in Figure 1). Likewise, inter-procedural parallelism (i.e., parallel conjunctions which span literals in different predicates) cannot be exploited without program transformation.

In general, several annotations are possible for a given clause. As an example, Figure 2 shows two annotations for our running example.[1] Some goals appear switched w.r.t. their order in the sequential clause. This respects the dependencies in Figure 1, which reflects a valid notion of parallelism (i.e., if solution order is not important). If additional ordering requirements are needed (due to, e.g., side effects or impurity), these should appear as additional edges in the graph.

Note that none of the annotations in Figure 2 fully exploits all parallelism available in Figure 1: Figure 2(a) misses the parallelism between b(X) and d(Y, Z), and Figure 2(b) misses the parallelism between b(X) and c(Y).

One relevant question is which of these two parallelizations is better. Arguably, a meaningful measure of their quality is how long each of them takes to execute. We will term those times T_{fj1} and T_{fj2} for Figures 2(a) and 2(b), respectively. This length depends on the execution times of the goals involved (i.e., T_a, T_b, T_c, T_d), which we assume to be non-zero. T_{fj1} and T_{fj2} are:

$$T_{fj1} = \max(T_a + T_b, \ T_c) + T_d \qquad (1)$$

---

[1] The parallelization p :- a(X, Z), b(X) & c(Y), d(Y, Z) has been left out of Figure 2. It would not add anything to the discussion as it would not change the comparison we make in Section 2.2.

$$T_{fj2} = \max(T_a, T_c) + \max(T_b, T_d) \tag{2}$$

Comparing the quality of the annotations in Figure 2(a) and Figure 2(b) boils down to finding out whether it is possible to show that $T_{fj1} < T_{fj2}$ or the other way around. It turns out that they are non-comparable. In fact:

- $T_{fj1} < T_{fj2}$ holds if, for example, $T_a + T_b < T_c$, $T_d < T_b$, and then $T_{fj2} = T_b + T_c$, $T_{fj1} = T_d + T_c$, and
- $T_{fj2} < T_{fj1}$ holds if, for example, $T_c \leq T_a$, $T_d \leq T_b$, and then $T_{fj1} = T_a + T_b + T_d$, $T_{fj2} = T_a + T_b$.

Several annotation algorithms have been proposed so far [22,4] which use the &/2 operator as the basic construction to express parallelism between goals. These annotators produce clauses that are parallelized differently, such as those in Figure 2. It is in principle possible to statically decide (or, at least, approximate) whether some annotation is better than some other, for example by using the number of goals annotated for parallelism in a clause or, more interestingly, by using information regarding the expected runtime of goals (see, e.g., [21,19] and its references). However, finding an optimal solution is a computationally expensive combinatorial problem [22] and, in practice, annotators use heuristics which may be more or less appropriate in concrete cases.

2.2   Parallelization with Finer Goal-Level Operators

It has been observed [4,5] that more basic constructions can be used to represent and-parallelism by using two operators, &>/2 and <&/1, defined as follows:

Definition 1. G &> H *schedules goal* G *for parallel execution and continues executing the code after* G &> H. H *is a* handler *which contains (or points to) the state of goal* G.

Definition 2. H <& *waits for the goal associated with* H *to finish. After that point any bindings made by* G *are available to the executing thread.*

With the previous definitions, the &/2 operator can be written as
A & B :- A &> H, call(B), H <&. This indicates that any parallelization performed using &/2 can be made using &>/2 and <&/1 without loss of parallelism. We will term these operators *dep-operators* henceforth.

Two motivations justify the use of these operators instead of &/2. Firstly, their implementation is (in our experience) actually easier to devise and maintain than the monolithic &/2 [8], and, secondly, the dep-operators allow more freedom to the annotator (and to the programmer, if parallel code is written by hand) to

```
p(X, Y, Z) :-
    c(Y) &> Hc,
    a(X, Z),
    b(X) &> Hb,
    Hc <&,
    d(Y, Z),
    Hb <&.
```

Fig. 3. dep-operator-annotated clause

express data dependencies and, therefore, to extract more potential parallelism. We will now illustrate this last point (the former is out of our current scope).

Figure 3 shows an annotation of our running example using dep-operators. Note that this code allows executing in parallel a/2 with c/1, b/2 with c/1, and b/1 with d/2. The execution time of p/3, based on that of the individual goals, is:

$$T_{dep} = \max(T_a + T_b, \; T_d + \max(T_a, \; T_c)) \tag{3}$$

If we compare expression (3) with expressions (1) and (2), it turns out that:

- It is possible that $T_{dep} < T_{fj1}$, $T_{dep} < T_{fj2}$, $T_{dep} = T_{fj1}$, and $T_{dep} = T_{fj2}$ (possibly with different lengths for every goal in each case).
- It is **not** possible that $T_{dep} > T_{fj1}$ or that $T_{dep} > T_{fj2}$.

This means that the annotation in Figure 3 cannot be worse than those in Figure 2, and can perform better in some cases. It is, therefore, a better option than any of the others, assuming no preparation / startup time for the parallel goals in either case.

In addition to these basic operators, other specialized versions can be defined and implemented in order to increase performance by adapting better to some particular cases. In particular, it appears interesting to introduce variants for the very relevant and frequent case of deterministic goals. For this purpose we propose additionally two new operators: &!>/2 and <&!/1. These specialized versions do not perform backtracking and do not prepare the execution data structures to cope with that possibility, which has previously been shown to result in a significant efficiency increase in the underlying machinery [23].

3   The **UOUDG** and **UUDG** Algorithms

In this section we will present two concrete algorithms which generate code annotated for unrestricted independent and-parallelism (as in Figure 3), starting from sequential code. The proposed algorithms process one clause at a time by working on a directed acyclic dependency graph $G = (V, E)$, such as that in Figure 1, where nodes are associated with body literals (or, as we will see, sequences thereof) and which represent units of sequential work which cannot be split. We require that literals which are lexically identical give rise to different nodes, by, e.g., attaching a unique identifier to them. This is necessary in order not to lose information when building sets of nodes.

The idea behind the annotation algorithms is to publish goals for parallel execution as soon as possible and to delay issuing joins as much as possible — but always respecting the dependencies in the graph (as in Figure 1). Intuitively, this should maximize the number of goals available for parallel execution. In the following, both algorithms will use the following auxiliary definitions. $G|_U$ will denote the subgraph $(U, E|_U)$ of G in which there are only edges connecting those nodes in U. The relation $(u \leadsto v)$ holds whenever a path from u to v exists. The auxiliary definition incoming(v, E) = $\{u \mid (u, v) \in E\}$ denotes the set of nodes which are connected to some particular node v. Finally, set difference is, as usual, defined as $A \setminus B = \{x \mid x \in A,\ x \notin B\}$.

Note that, as mentioned in Section 2.1, we will consider in this paper only unconditional parallelism. However, the algorithms that we describe can be adapted to deal with conditional parallelism without too much effort.

3.1   Collapsing Mutually Dependent Goals

In order to ensure the correctness of the algorithms in Sections 3.2 and 3.3, every sequence of mutually dependent goals has to be grouped into a unique node of the dependency graph before each iteration. Since no parallelism can be exploited between mutually dependent goals, no parallelism is lost by this transformation. We will not describe this *grouping* process here in detail —we will only sketch the conditions the resulting nodes have to fulfill. We will assume that an adequate processing is performed at the beginning of each iteration. The reader is referred to [7] for more precise details.

Let Gr be a sequence $v_1, \ldots, v_n$ of literals. They are said to be mutually dependent if the following condition holds:

$$(\forall v_i, v_j \in Gr,\ (v_i \rightsquigarrow v_j) \ \vee \ (v_j \rightsquigarrow v_i)) \ \wedge$$
$$(\forall (v_i, v_j) \in E,\ v_i \notin Gr \Rightarrow v_j \notin Gr)$$

In addition, in the case of the UOUDG algorithm, those goals must be consecutive in the original clause in order to preserve the order of the solutions.

Example 1. Suppose the following clause:

```
p:- a(X), b(X), c(X), d(Y), e(Y), f(X, Y).
```

The sequences $\langle$a/1, b/1, c/1$\rangle$ and $\langle$d/1,e/1$\rangle$ contain mutually dependent literals in the clause which have a single outgoing dependency on f/2, and therefore they can be grouped to form a graph of three nodes. Every one of these sequences of literals can, for efficiency reasons, be folded into a unique predicate in order to avoid meta-interpretation of sequential conjunctions.

3.2   Order-Preserving Annotation: The UOUDG Algorithm

Algorithm 1 parallelizes a clause while preserving the order of the solutions by respecting the relative order of literals in the original clause. In order to keep track of that order, we assume that there is a relation $\prec$ on the literals L_i of the body of every clause $H :- L_1, L_2, \ldots, L_{k-1}, L_k$ such that $L_i \prec L_j$ iff $i < j$. Additionally, we assume that there is a partial function $pred$ defined as $pred(L_{i+1}) = L_i$, i.e., the literal at the left of some other literal in a clause. We assume $\prec$ and $pred$ are suitably extended to the nodes of the graph.[2]

---

[2] Note, also, that the graph edges must respect the $\prec$ relation: $(u, v) \in E \Rightarrow u \prec v$. The graph would have been incorrectly generated otherwise.

Algorithm: UOUDG(G, *Pub*)

Input   : **(1)** A directed acyclic graph $G = (V, E)$.
    (2) A set of already forked goals.

Output: A clause parallelized in *unrestricted and* fashion in which the order of
    the solutions in the original clause is preserved.

begin
 if $V = \emptyset$ **then return** (**true**)
 else
   $Indep \leftarrow \{v \mid v \in V, \texttt{incoming}(v, E) = \emptyset\};$
   $Dep \leftarrow \{(v, I_v) \mid v \in V, I_v = \texttt{incoming}(v, E), I_v \neq \emptyset, I_v \subseteq Indep\};$
   if $Dep = \emptyset$ **then**
    $(pvt, Join) \leftarrow (u, V)$ s.t. $\forall(w \in (V \setminus \{u\}))\, .\, w \prec u;$
   else
    $(pvt, Join) \leftarrow$
     (u, S) s.t. $(u, S) \in Dep \wedge \forall((w, D) \in (Dep \setminus \{(u, S)\}))\, .\, u \prec w;$
   end
   $Seq \leftarrow \{v \mid v \in (Indep \setminus Pub), (v, pvt) \in E, v = pred(pvt)\};$
   $Fork \leftarrow \{v \mid v \in (Indep \setminus Pub), v \prec pvt\} \setminus Seq;$
   $Join \leftarrow Join \setminus Seq;$
   $Pub \leftarrow Pub \cup Fork \cup Seq;$
   $G \leftarrow G|_{(V \setminus Join) \setminus Seq};$
   return (**gen_body**($Fork$, Seq, $Join$, $\emptyset$), UOUDG(G, Pub));
 end
end

Algorithm 1. UOUDG annotation algorithm

At every recursion step, new nodes (i.e., literals) in the graph are selected to be published, joined, and executed sequentially. Subsequent iterations proceed with a simplified graph in which the literals which have been joined and executed sequentially, together with their outgoing edges, have been removed. The set of goals which have already been published is kept in a separate argument to schedule goals for parallel execution only once.

Two sets are key in each iteration: *Indep*, which contains the *sources* (i.e., all vertices without incoming edges in the current graph, which can therefore be published), and *Dep*, which contains tuples (v, I_v) where, for each non-source vertex v which can be reached from source vertices only, I_v is the set of source vertices ($I_v \subseteq Indep$) on which v depends. I.e., I_v is the set of vertices to be joined before v can start.

Also, *pvt* is the *pivot* vertex which will be used to decide which nodes are to be joined, taking into account that we do not want to change the order of solutions. If there are no *Dep* nodes, then all the remaining literals are already independent and we can join up to the rightmost literal in the clause. Otherwise, we select the leftmost node among those which have dependencies which can be fulfilled in one step. These dependencies are readily available in *Dep*. Note that as we select the leftmost node among those which can be joined, we are delaying as much as possible joining nodes —or, alternatively, we are performing in every step only the joins which are needed to continue one more step. This is aimed at maximizing the number of goals being executed in parallel at any moment.

It is possible for a literal to be scheduled to be forked and then immediately joined. In order to detect these situations, which in practice would cause unnecessary overhead, we select (in *Seq*) the literal (only one) to which this applies, and it is not taken into account for the set of *Forked* literals and removed from the set of the *Joined* literals.

The algorithm then continues outputting a parallelized expression (returned by gen_body, Algorithm 3) composed with the parallelization of a simplified graph, generated by a recursive call. Algorithm 3 is able to use determinism information, if available, to reorder goals. Since Algorithm 1 preserves the order of solutions, we do not use this capability at the moment. Therefore an empty set is passed as determinism data and we define the function $det(Lit, DetInfo)$ (used by Algorithm 3) to return *false* if $DetInfo = \emptyset$, thus safely assuming non-determinism.

Termination can be proved based on the following observation: G is a finite graph and it is simplified in each iteration provided *Join* or *Seq* are non-empty. But *Join* is always non-empty because it is either V (which is non-empty) when $Dep = \emptyset$ or else it is the second component of a tuple in Dep when $Dep \neq \emptyset$, and this component is by definition non-empty. Note that we are not using acyclicity to prove termination. However, all input graphs will be acyclic by definition.

3.3 Non Order-Preserving Annotation: The UUDG Algorithm

Algorithm 2 follows the same idea underlying Algorithm 1: publish early and join late. However, it has more freedom to publish goals, since the order of solutions does not need to be preserved. This is implemented by selecting, among the sets of goals which can be joined at every moment, the one with the lowest cardinality —i.e., we join as few goals as possible, thus postponing the rest of the joins as much as possible, in order to exploit more parallelism. This is taken care of by min_card(S) = $\min(\{|s| \mid s \in S\}$, which returns the size of the smallest set in S.

Note that a random selection from a set is done at two points. Data regarding, e.g., the relative run time of goals would allow us to take a more informed decision and therefore precompute a perhaps better scheduling. Since we are not using this information here, we just pick any available goal to join / execute sequentially.

Algorithm 2 uses Algorithm 3 again to output a parallelized clause. In this case Algorithm 3 makes use of determinism information as follows:

- Since we already have the possibility of switching goals around, we try to minimize relaunching goals which are likely to be executed in parallel by forking deterministic goals first.
- Additionally, when a goal is known to have exactly one solution, we can use specialized versions of the dep-operators [8] which do not need to perform bookkeeping for backtracking (always complex in parallel implementations), and are thus more efficient.

This program information can often be automatically inferred by the abstract interpretation-based determinism analyzer in CiaoPP [18], and is provided as

Algorithm: UUDG(G, *Pub*, I_D)

Input : (1) A directed acyclic graph $G = (V, E)$. (2) A set of goals already forked. (3) Determinacy information.

Output: An unrestricted parallelized clause in which the order of the solutions in the original clause needs not be preserved.

begin
    if $V = \emptyset$ **then return** (**true**);
    else
        $Indep \leftarrow \{v \mid v \in V, \text{ incoming}(v, E) = \emptyset\}$;
        $Dep \leftarrow \{I_v \mid v \in V, I_v = \text{incoming}(v, E), I_v \neq \emptyset, I_v \subseteq Indep\}$;
        if $Dep = \emptyset$ **then**
            $SS \leftarrow \emptyset$;
            $Join \leftarrow V$;
        else
            $SS \leftarrow \{I \mid I \in Dep, |I| = \text{min\_card}(Dep)\}$;
            $Join \leftarrow s$ s.t. $s \in SS$;   /* s any element from SS */
        end
        if $(Join \cap (Indep \setminus Pub)) = \emptyset$ **then**
            $Seq \leftarrow \emptyset$;
        else
            $Seq \leftarrow \{v\}$ s.t. $v \in (Join \cap (Indep \setminus Pub))$;   /* v any element */
        end
        $Fork \leftarrow Indep \setminus (Pub \cup Seq)$;
        $Join \leftarrow Join \setminus Seq$;
        $Pub \leftarrow Pub \cup Fork \cup Seq$;
        $G \leftarrow G|_{(V \setminus Join) \setminus Seq}$;
        return (**gen_body**($Fork$, Seq, $Join$, I_D), UUDG(G, Pub, I_D));
    end
end

Algorithm 2. UUDG annotation algorithm

input to the proposed annotators. Alternatively, this information can be stated by the programmer via assertions [13].

Example 2 (UUDG Annotation). In order to illustrate how the UUDG algorithm works, Table 1 shows the results obtained at each of the iterations of the parallelization process for the p/3 predicate introduced in Section 2.1. Columns are labeled with the first character of each of the variables they represent. Note that in the first algorithm step, both a and c are candidates for parallel execution (they are in *Indep*). However, as a has to be joined too (it is necessary to continue executing either b or d) it is selected to be sequentially executed.

Further examples and the total correctness proofs of both the UUDG and UOUDG algorithms can be found in [7].

4   Performance Evaluation

Our annotation algorithms have been integrated in the Ciao/CiaoPP system [13]. Information gathered by the analyzers on variable sharing, groundness, and

Algorithm: gen_body(*Fork, Seq, Join, I_D*)

Input : **(1)** A set of vertices to be forked. **(2)** A set of vertices to be sequentialized. **(3)** A set of vertices to be joined. **(4)** Determinacy information.

Output: A parallelized sequence of literals *Exp*.

begin

    Exp ← (**true**);

    ForkDet ← $\{g \mid g \in Fork, det(g, I_D)\}$;

    ForkNonDet ← $\{g \mid g \in Fork, \neg det(g, I_D)\}$;

    JoinDet ← $\{g \mid g \in Join, det(g, I_D)\}$;

    JoinNonDet ← $\{g \mid g \in Join, \neg det(g, I_D)\}$;

    forall $v_i \in ForkDet$ **do** *Exp* ← (*Exp*, v_i &!> H_{v_i});

    forall $v_i \in ForkNonDet$ **do** *Exp* ← (*Exp*, v_i &> H_{v_i});

    if $Seq = \{v\}$ **then** *Exp* ← (*Exp*, *v*);

    forall $v_i \in JoinDet$ **do** *Exp* ← (*Exp*, H_{v_i} <&!);

    forall $v_i \in JoinNonDet$ **do** *Exp* ← (*Exp*, H_{v_i} <&);

    return *Exp*;

end

Algorithm 3. Determinism-aware generation of a parallel body

Table 1. Iterations of the UUDG algorithm when parallelizing p/3

G=(V,E)	I	D	J	S	F	J\S	P	Parallel Code
$(\{a,b,c,d\},\{(a,b),(a,d),(c,d)\})$							∅	p(X,Y,Z) :-
$(\{a,b,c,d\},\{(a,b),(a,d),(c,d)\})$	$\{a,c\}$	$\{b,d\}$	$\{a\}$	$\{a\}$	$\{c\}$	∅	$\{a,c\}$	c(Y) &> Hc, a(X,Z),
$(\{b,c,d\},\{(c,d)\})$	$\{b,c\}$	$\{d\}$	$\{c\}$	∅	$\{b\}$	$\{c\}$	$\{a,b,c\}$	b(X) &> Hb, Hc <&,
$(\{b,d\},∅)$	$\{b,d\}$	∅	$\{b,d\}$	$\{d\}$	∅	$\{b\}$	$\{a,b,c,d\}$	d(Y,Z), Hb <&.
$(∅,∅)$								

freeness is used to determine goal independence, using the libraries available in CiaoPP. Determinism is used in the annotators as described previously.

As execution platform we have used a high level implementation of the proposed parallelism primitives [8], which we have developed as an extension of the Ciao system. This implementation is an evolution and simplification of [12] which is based on raising the level of certain components to the level of the source language and keeping only some selected operations (related to thread handling, locking, etc.) at a lower level. This approach does not eliminate altogether modifications to the abstract machine, but it greatly simplifies them. It should be noted however that the dep-operators do not assume any particular architecture: while our current implementation and all the performance results were obtained on a multicore machine, the techniques presented can be also applied in distributed memory machines —and in fact, the first prototype implementation of the dep-operators [5,4] was actually made with a distributed environment in mind.

We have evaluated the impact of the different annotations on the execution time by running a series of benchmarks (briefly described in Table 2) in parallel. Table 3 shows the speedups obtained *with respect to the sequential execution*, i.e., they are *actual* speedups,[3] when using from 1 to 8 threads. The machine we

---

[3] This is the reason why some speedups start below 1 for, e.g., one thread.

Table 2. Benchmark programs

AIAKL	An abstract interpreter for the AKL language.
FFT	An implementation of the Fast Fourier transform.
FibFun	A version of **Fib** written in functional notation.
Hamming	A program to compute the first N Hamming numbers.
Hanoi	A program to compute movements to solve the well-known puzzle.
Takeuchi	Computes the Takeuchi function.
WMS2	A scheduler assigning a number of workers to a series of jobs.

Table 3. Speedups for several benchmarks and annotators

Benchmark	Annotator	Number of threads							
		1	2	3	4	5	6	7	8
AIAKL	UMEL	0.97	0.97	0.98	0.98	0.98	0.98	0.98	0.98
	UOUDG	0.97	1.55	1.48	1.49	1.49	1.49	1.49	1.49
	UDG	0.97	1.77	1.66	1.67	1.67	1.67	1.67	1.67
	UUDG	0.97	1.77	1.66	1.67	1.67	1.67	1.67	1.67
FFT	UMEL	0.98	1.76	2.14	2.71	2.82	2.99	3.08	3.37
	UOUDG	0.98	1.76	2.14	2.71	2.82	2.99	3.08	3.37
	UDG	0.98	1.76	2.14	2.71	2.82	2.99	3.08	3.37
	UUDG	0.98	1.82	2.31	3.01	3.12	3.26	3.39	3.63
FibFun	UMEL	1.00	1.00	1.00	1.00	1.00	1.00	1.00	1.00
	UOUDG	0.99	1.95	2.89	3.84	4.78	5.71	6.63	7.57
	UDG	1.00	1.00	1.00	1.00	1.00	1.00	1.00	1.00
	UUDG	0.99	1.95	2.89	3.84	4.78	5.71	6.63	7.57
Hamming	UMEL	0.93	1.13	1.52	1.52	1.52	1.52	1.52	1.52
	UOUDG	0.93	1.15	1.64	1.64	1.64	1.64	1.64	1.64
	UDG	0.93	1.13	1.52	1.52	1.52	1.52	1.52	1.52
	UUDG	0.93	1.15	1.64	1.64	1.64	1.64	1.64	1.64
Hanoi	UMEL	0.89	0.98	0.98	0.97	0.97	0.98	0.98	0.99
	UOUDG	0.89	1.70	2.39	2.81	3.20	3.69	4.00	4.19
	UDG	0.89	1.72	2.43	3.32	3.77	4.17	4.41	4.67
	UUDG	0.89	1.72	2.43	3.32	3.77	4.17	4.41	4.67
Takeuchi	UMEL	0.88	1.61	2.16	2.62	2.63	2.63	2.63	2.63
	UOUDG	0.88	1.62	2.17	2.64	2.67	2.67	2.67	2.67
	UDG	0.88	1.61	2.16	2.62	2.63	2.63	2.63	2.63
	UUDG	0.88	1.62	2.39	3.33	4.04	4.47	5.19	5.72
WMS2	UMEL	0.85	0.81	0.81	0.81	0.81	0.81	0.81	0.81
	UOUDG	0.99	1.09	1.09	1.09	1.09	1.09	1.09	1.09
	UDG	0.99	1.01	1.01	1.01	1.01	1.01	1.01	1.01
	UUDG	0.99	1.10	1.10	1.10	1.10	1.10	1.10	1.10

used is a Sun UltraSparc T2000 (a *Niagara*) with 8 4-thread cores.[4] The *fork-join* annotators we chose to compare with are MEL [22] (which preserves goal order

---

[4] We did not use more than 8 threads (1 in each core) since otherwise, and due to access conflicts to shared units, speedups can be significantly sublinear even for completely independent tasks.

and tries to maximize the length of the parallel expressions) and UDG [4] (which can reorder goals). MEL can add runtime checks to decide dynamically whether to execute or not in parallel. In order to make the annotation unconditional (as the rest of the annotators we are dealing with), we simply removed the conditional parallelism in the places where it was not being exploited. This is why it appears in Table 3 under the name *UMEL*.

All the benchmarks executed were parallelized automatically by CiaoPP, starting from their sequential code. Since UOUDG and UUDG can improve the results of fork-join annotators only when the code to parallelize has at least a certain level of complexity, not all benchmarks with (independent) parallelism can benefit from using the dep-operators. Additionally, comparing speedups obtained with programs parallelized using order-preserving and non-order-preserving annotators is not completely meaningful.

Note that in this paper we are not focusing on the speedups themselves. Although of utmost practical interest, raw speed is very connected with the implementation of the underlying parallel abstract machine, and improvements on it can be expected to uniformly affect all parallelized programs. Rather, our main focus of attention is in the *comparison* among the speedups obtained using different annotators.

A first examination of the experimental results in Table 3 allows inferring that in no case is UUDG worse than any other annotator, and in no case is UOUDG worse than (U)MEL. They should therefore be the *annotators of choice* if available. Besides, there are cases where UOUDG is better than UDG, and the other way around, which is in accordance with the non-comparable nature of these two algorithms.

Among the cases in which a better speedup is obtained by some of the U(O)UDG annotators, improvements range between "no improvement" (because no benefit is obtained for some particular cases and combinations of annotators) to an increase of 757% in speedup, with several other stages in between. Also, it is worth pointing out that the speedup does not stabilize in any benchmark (at least in a sizable amount) as the number of threads increases; moreover, in some cases the difference in speedup between the restricted and the unrestricted versions grows substantially with the number of threads. This can (clearly) be seen in, e.g., Figure 4(b).

Finally, we would like to comment specially on three benchmarks. **FibFun** is the result of parallelizing a definition of the Fibonacci numbers written using the functional notation capabilities of Ciao [6]. Because of the order in which code is generated in the (automatic) translation into Prolog, the result is only parallelizable by UOUDG and UUDG, hence the speedup obtained in this case. The case of **Hanoi** is also interesting, as it is the first example in [22]: in the arena of order-preserving parallelizers, UOUDG can extract more parallelism than MEL for this benchmark. Lastly, the **Takeuchi** benchmark has a relatively small loop which only allows parallelizing with a simple &/2. However, by unrolling one iteration the resulting body has dependencies which are complex enough to take advantage of the increased flexibility of the dep-operator annotators.

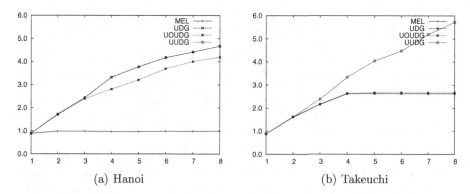

(a) Hanoi   (b) Takeuchi

Fig. 4. Speedups with different annotations for Hanoi and Takeuchi

5 Conclusions

We have proposed two annotation algorithms which perform a source-to-source transformation of a logic program into an unrestricted independent and-parallel version of itself. Both algorithms rely on the use of more basic high-level primitives than the fork-join operator, and differ on whether the order of the solutions in the original program must be preserved or not. We have implemented the proposed algorithms in the CiaoPP system, which infers automatically groundness, sharing, and determinacy information, used to simplify the initial dependency graph. The results of the experiments performed show that, although the parallelization provided by the new annotation algorithms is the same in quite a few of the traditional parallel benchmarks, it is never worse and in some cases it is significantly better. This supports the observations made based on the expected performance of the annotations. We have also noticed that the benefits are larger for programs with high numbers of goals in their clauses, since more complex graphs make the ability to exploit unrestricted parallelism more relevant.

Acknowledgments. This work was funded in part by Ministry of Education and Science (MEC) project TIN2005-09207-C03 *MERIT-COMVERS*, by Ministry of Industry (MIN) PROFIT project FIT-350400-2006-44 *GGCC*, by Madrid Regional Government (CM) project S-0505/TIC/0407 *PROMESAS*, and by IST program of the European Commission FP6 FET project IST-15905 *MOBIUS*. Manuel Hermenegildo and Amadeo Casas were also funded in part by the Prince of Asturias Chair in Information Science and Technology at UNM.

References

1. Ali, K.A.M., Karlsson, R.: The Muse Or-Parallel Prolog Model and its Performance. In: 1990 North American Conference on Logic Programming, pp. 757–776. MIT Press, Cambridge (1990)
2. Bueno, F., de la Banda, M.G., Hermenegildo, M.: Effectiveness of Abstract Interpretation in Automatic Parallelization: A Case Study in Logic Programming. ACM Transactions on Programming Languages and Systems 21(2), 189–238 (1999)

3. Bueno, F., de la Banda, M.G., Hermenegildo, M.: Effectiveness of Abstract Interpretation in Automatic Parallelization: A Case Study in Logic Programming. ACM TOPLAS 21(2), 189–238 (1999)
4. Cabeza, D.: An Extensible, Global Analysis Friendly Logic Programming System. PhD thesis, Universidad Politécnica de Madrid (UPM), Facultad Informatica UPM, 28660-Boadilla del Monte, Madrid-Spain (August 2004)
5. Cabeza, D., Hermenegildo, M.: Implementing Distributed Concurrent Constraint Execution in the CIAO System. In: Proc. of the AGP 1996 Joint conference on Declarative Programming, San Sebastian, Spain, U. of the Basque country, pp. 67–78 (July 1996), http://www.cliplab.org/
6. Casas, A., Cabeza, D., Hermenegildo, M.: A Syntactic Approach to Combining Functional Notation, Lazy Evaluation and Higher-Order in LP Systems. In: Hagiya, M., Wadler, P. (eds.) FLOPS 2006. LNCS, vol. 3945, pp. 146–162. Springer, Heidelberg (2006)
7. Casas, A., Carro, M., Hermenegildo, M.: Automatic Unrestricted Independent And-Parallelism in Logic Programs. Technical Report CLIP11/2007.0, Technical University of Madrid (UPM), School of Computer Science, UPM (December 2007)
8. Casas, A., Carro, M., Hermenegildo, M.: Towards a High-Level Implementation of Execution Primitives for Non-restricted, Independent And-parallelism. In: Warren, D.S., Hudak, P. (eds.) 10th International Symposium on Practical Aspects of Declarative Languages (PADL 2008). LNCS, vol. 4902, Springer, Heidelberg (2008)
9. Gupta, G., Hermenegildo, M., Pontelli, E., Santos-Costa, V.: ACE: And/Or-parallel Copying-based Execution of Logic Programs. In: International Conference on Logic Programming, pp. 93–110. MIT Press, Cambridge (1994)
10. Gupta, G., Pontelli, E., Ali, K., Carlsson, M., Hermenegildo, M.: Parallel Execution of Prolog Programs: A Survey. ACM TOPLAS 23(4), 472–602 (2001)
11. Hermenegildo, M.: Parallelizing Irregular and Pointer-Based Computations Automatically: Perspectives from Logic and Constraint Programming. Parallel Computing 26(13–14), 1685–1708 (2000)
12. Hermenegildo, M., Greene, K.: The &-Prolog System: Exploiting Independent And-Parallelism. New Generation Computing 9(3,4), 233–257 (1991)
13. Hermenegildo, M., Puebla, G., Bueno, F., López García, P.: Integrated Program Debugging, Verification, and Optimization Using Abstract Interpretation (and The Ciao System Preprocessor). Science of Computer Programming 58(1–2), 115–140 (2005)
14. Hermenegildo, M., Rossi, F.: Strict and Non-Strict Independent And-Parallelism in Logic Programs: Correctness, Efficiency, and Compile-Time Conditions. Journal of Logic Programming 22(1), 1–45 (1995)
15. Hermenegildo, M., Warren, R.: Designing a High-Performance Parallel Logic Programming System. Computer Architecture News, Special Issue on Parallel Symbolic Programming 15(1), 43–53 (1987)
16. Janson, S.: AKL. A Multiparadigm Programming Language. PhD thesis, Uppsala University (1994)
17. Karp, A.H., Babb, R.C.: A Comparison of 12 Parallel Fortran Dialects. In: IEEE Software (September 1988)
18. López-García, P., Bueno, F., Hermenegildo, M.: Determinacy Analysis for Logic Programs Using Mode and Type Information. In: Etalle, S. (ed.) LOPSTR 2004. LNCS, vol. 3573, pp. 19–35. Springer, Heidelberg (2005)
19. López-García, P., Hermenegildo, M., Debray, S.K.: A Methodology for Granularity Based Control of Parallelism in Logic Programs. Journal of Symbolic Computation, Special Issue on Parallel Symbolic Computation 21(4–6), 715–734 (1996)

20. Lusk, E., et al.: The Aurora Or-Parallel Prolog System. New Generation Computing 7(2,3) (1990)
21. Mera, E., López-García, P., Puebla, G., Carro, M., Hermenegildo, M.: Combining Static Analysis and Profiling for Estimating Execution Times. In: Hanus, M. (ed.) PADL 2007. LNCS, vol. 4354, pp. 140–154. Springer, Heidelberg (2006)
22. Muthukumar, K., Bueno, F., de la Banda, M.G., Hermenegildo, M.: Automatic Compile-time Parallelization of Logic Programs for Restricted, Goal-level, Independent And-parallelism. Journal of Logic Programming 38(2), 165–218 (1999)
23. Pontelli, E., Gupta, G., Tang, D., Carro, M., Hermenegildo, M.: Improving the Efficiency of Nondeterministic And–parallel Systems. The Computer Languages Journal 22(2/3), 115–142 (1996)
24. Santos-Costa, V., Warren, D.H.D., Yang, R.: Andorra-I: A Parallel Prolog System that Transparently Exploits both And- and Or-parallelism. In: Proceedings of the 3rd. ACM SIGPLAN Symposium on Principles and Practice of Parallel Programming, pp. 83–93. ACM, New York (April1991) (SIGPLAN Notices, vol. 26(7), July 1991)
25. Shen, K.: Overview of DASWAM: Exploitation of Dependent And-parallelism. Journal of Logic Programming 29(1–3), 245–293 (1996)

A Flexible, (C)LP-Based Approach to the Analysis of Object-Oriented Programs*

Mario Méndez-Lojo[1], Jorge Navas[1], and Manuel V. Hermenegildo[1,2]

[1] University of New Mexico, USA
[2] Technical University of Madrid, Spain

Abstract. Static analyses of object-oriented programs usually rely on intermediate representations that respect the original semantics while having a more uniform and basic syntax. Most of the work involving object-oriented languages and abstract interpretation usually omits the description of that language or just refers to the Control Flow Graph (CFG) it represents. However, this lack of formalization on one hand results in an absence of assurances regarding the correctness of the transformation and on the other it typically strongly couples the analysis to the source language. In this work we present a framework for analysis of object-oriented languages in which in a first phase we transform the input program into a representation based on Horn clauses. This facilitates on one hand proving the correctness of the transformation attending to a simple condition and on the other allows applying existing analyzers for (constraint) logic programming to automatically derive a safe approximation of the semantics of the original program. The approach is flexible in the sense that the first phase decouples the analyzer from most language-dependent features, and correct because the set of Horn clauses returned by the transformation phase safely approximates the standard semantics of the input program. The resulting analysis is also reasonably scalable due to the use of mature, modular (C)LP-based analyzers. This allows us to report good results for medium-sized programs.

1 Introduction

Analysis of object-oriented languages using abstract interpretation [9] is currently the subject of significant research (see, e.g., [21] and its references). The abstract interpretation approach brings an interesting and useful combination of characteristics: it is automatic and practical, producing useful results for a good number of applications, while at the same time being rigorous and semantics-based. The gap between programs and semantics is greater in the case of object-oriented languages than in, for example, declarative languages. For this reason,

---

* This work was supported in part by the Prince of Asturias Chair in Information Science and Technology at UNM, the Information Society Technologies program of the European Commission, Future and Emerging Technologies under the IST-15905 *MOBIUS* project, the Spanish Ministry of Education under the TIN-2005-09207 *MERIT* project, and the Madrid Regional Government under the S-0505/TIC/0407 *PROMESAS* program.

King, A. (Ed.): LOPSTR 2007, LNCS 4915, pp. 154–168, 2008.

static analyses of object-oriented programs usually rely on intermediate languages that respect the original semantics while having a more uniform and basic syntax (e.g., block-based representations) and a more declarative semantics (e.g., static single assignment transformations). Some significant concrete examples which have been proposed of such intermediate representations for object-oriented programs are Jimple [32] for Java or BoogiePL [10] for .NET.

In this paper we propose the use of a Horn clause-based representation as an intermediate language. Our objective is twofold. On one hand we would like to take advantage of existing analyzers for (constraint) logic programs. On the other, we want to be able to offer assurances that the output of the process of transformation into the intermediate representation safely approximates the standard semantics of the input program. Performing the analysis using logic programming tools offers a number of advantages, such as the relative maturity and sophistication of the solutions available, like abstract interpreters (which offer parametric, efficient, and modular fixpoint algorithms) and verifiers (see, e.g., [15,12] and their references). A second strength of our transformational approach is that the framework can be easily adapted to the analysis of other languages without having to redefine the fixpoint algorithm [24]. In fact, using the intermediate representation that we propose, from the analyzer point of view an object-oriented program is indistinguishable from, e.g., a Prolog one (although of course different abstract domains and definitions of pseudo-builtins are used). This brings in the additional advantage of being able to analyze multiple languages within the same framework.

We start by describing our methodology (Section 2) and our approach to ensuring correctness using some fundamental parts of the transformation of Java programs into our representation as examples (Section 3). Section 4 shows how analysis of specific aspects of Java can be optimized using metainformation. We then illustrate the application of our approach to other languages, such as C# (Section 5). We also report on an implementation of the ideas presented in this paper using the abstract interpretation-based CiaoPP framework [15]. It can be configured for many different analyses by simply plugging the corresponding abstract domain. The examples try to detect null pointer dereferences (nullity analysis) and eliminate dynamic dispatch (class analysis) in Java programs. The experiments in Section 6 show that the technique scales well in non trivial scenarios, and results in smaller analysis times than similar previous work. Related abstract interpretation-based frameworks, and how they differ from ours, are discussed in Section 7, and Section 8 presents our conclusions.

2   Methodology: The Transformational Approach

Our framework is composed of a front-end preprocessor and a back-end analyzer, as shown in Figure 1. The preprocessor transforms an input in Java source format into a set of Horn clauses that represent a safe approximation of its standard semantics (Sect 3). Sometimes the source code is not available, so we also accept Java bytecode as a valid input format. In this case the (de)compilation from

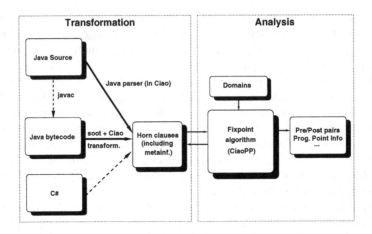

Fig. 1. Transformation and analysis pipeline

bytecode to Horn clauses is based on a postprocessing of the Jimple representation returned by the Soot [32] tool. It is beyond the scope of this paper to provide a detailed description of this particular transformation; the reader is referred to [24] (which presents our transformation and a specific fixpoint algorithm for analysis) for details. In both cases the same subset of the language is covered by the framework. Our ultimate objective is to support the full Java language but the current implementation has some limitations: it does not support dynamic loading of classes, threads, or runtime exceptions. Also, analysis of the JDK libraries is done under worst-case assumptions.

The resulting Horn-clause intermediate representation is then analyzed using the CiaoPP framework [15] and benefits from its advanced features: efficient computation of fixpoints using memoization, context-sensitivity, modularity, etc. The programmer needs only to implement (in Ciao [6], or in plain Prolog) the particular abstract domain of interest, which includes also defining the abstract meaning of a set of "built-in" predicates that represent the language-dependent semantics of the basic operations of the source language. On the other hand, our approach does liberate the designer of an analysis from the burden of coding a fast, reliable, and efficient abstract interpretation platform. Analysis results are given in the standard form (p, σ), where p uniquely identifies a program point and σ is an abstract state which safely approximates all the possible states at that program point during runtime. Metainformation computed during the transformation process allows relating those line numbers with the ones of the original bytecode or source program, making it possible to reflect back the results on the original program text (as JML-like assertions [18]), pinpoint errors in the original program, or implement compiler optimizations.

Other languages can be incorporated into the framework (i.e., analyzed) by providing a correct transformation for them. For example, support for other object-oriented languages like C#, that share many syntactic and semantics features with Java, is easily achievable as illustrated in Section 5. In addition, programs written in Ciao, which CiaoPP deals with natively, are obviously also accepted by the system as input.

3 Overview of the Semantic Basis and Correctness of the Transformation Phase

Our Horn clause representation of a Java program is basically an unfolded, three-address version of the source where the operational semantics of some instructions is made explicit. The transformed code is denoted by the c subindex: for example, the result of transforming a virtual invocation $v.\texttt{m}(v_1, \ldots, v_n)$ is $v_c.\texttt{m}_c(v_{1_c}, \ldots, v_{n_c}) = v.\texttt{m}_c(v_1, \ldots, v_n)$, since variable expressions are not transformed $(v_c = v)$.

Correctness of the transformation requires that the original program $prog$ be emulated by $prog_c$ thus $\mathcal{C}[\![prog]\!] = \mathcal{C}[\![prog_c]\!]$, where the semantics operator $\mathcal{C}[\![]\!] : com \mapsto (\mathcal{D} \mapsto \mathcal{D})$ takes as input a command com and a concrete state, and returns the output state. The operator has been defined in [14] and (from a denotational point of view) in [2,29]. Correctness of preprocessing and analysis requires that if the Horn clause program is safely approximated (using a given abstract domain) by the analysis, so is the original: $\mathcal{C}^*[\![prog]\!] = \mathcal{C}^*[\![prog_c]\!]$. The $\mathcal{C}^*[\![]\!] : com \mapsto (\mathcal{D}^* \mapsto \mathcal{D}^*)$ operator is the abstract counterpart of $\mathcal{C}[\![]\!]$.

We will take a slightly different approach by interpreting Java semantics as a particular case of SLD [17] resolution, in which the *computation* rule in use is left-to-right (commands are executed in the order they appear in the program) and the *search* rule used to determine the target method in an invocation in principle does not really matter, since execution of the Java program is deterministic and therefore for any literal there is exactly one clause that unifies with it at run time. Therefore, if $\mathcal{S}[\![]\!] : com \mapsto (\mathcal{D} \mapsto \mathcal{P}(\mathcal{D}))$ is the SLD semantics operator, the condition $\mathcal{S}[\![prog]\!] = \{\mathcal{C}[\![prog]\!]\}$ ensures $\mathcal{S}^*[\![prog]\!] = \mathcal{C}^*[\![prog]\!]$. Again, $\mathcal{S}^*[\![]\!] : com \mapsto (\mathcal{D}^* \mapsto \mathcal{D}^*)$ is the (collecting) abstract version of $\mathcal{S}[\![]\!]$.

This formalization is useful since it helps understanding the Java source as a set of Horn clauses (methods) composed by zero or more goals, the commands. It is also helpful because our transformation introduces new clauses such that now more than one clause might unify with a given literal. This is equivalent to saying that the execution of the transformed program on some input state might result in multiple output states, of which one is the unique state that the original program would return: $\mathcal{S}[\![prog]\!] \subseteq \mathcal{S}[\![prog_c]\!]$. An interesting property of that transformed program is that its abstract semantics $\mathcal{S}^*[\![prog_c]\!]$ still correctly approximates that of the original, i.e., $\mathcal{S}^*[\![prog]\!] \leq \mathcal{S}^*[\![prog_c]\!]$. Therefore, all we have to prove in order to show that the results of the analysis are correct is that $\mathcal{S}[\![prog]\!] \subseteq \mathcal{S}[\![prog_c]\!]$ (or $\mathcal{C}[\![prog]\!] \in \mathcal{S}[\![prog_c]\!]$) holds. Space limitations prevent us from discussing the whole transformation algorithm and providing proofs. Instead, we describe and provide a proof sketch for the case of the virtual invocation expression, which is one of the most complex operations supported.

```
staticCallSemantics(k$m(v, v_1, ..., v_n), σ)
    s = signature(call)
    body = getBody(k$m, s)
    return(bodySemantics(body, σ))

virtualCallSemantics(k?m(v, v_1, ..., v_n), σ)
    s = signature(call)
    c = lookup(runtime_class(v), s)
    return staticCallSemantics(c$m(v, v_1, ..., v_n), σ)

lookup(k, s)
    a = k
    do
        if declares(a, s)
            return(a)
        a = ancestor(a)
    while (true)
```

```
compileStaticCall(k$m(v, v_1, ..., v_n), prog_c)
    return k$m(v, v_1, ..., v_n)

compileVirtualCall(k?m(v, v_1, ..., v_n), prog_c)
    s = signature(call)
    C = resolve(k, s)
    forall c ∈ C add to prog_c the clause
        k$dyn*m(v, v_1, ..., v_n) : −
            c$m(v, v_1, ..., v_n)
    return k$dyn*m(v, v_1, ..., v_n)

resolve(k, s)
    result = ∅
    Sub = subclasses(k) ∪ {k}
    forall sub ∈ Sub
        sk = lookup(sub, s)
        result = result ∪ sk
    return result
```

Fig. 2. Standard semantics (left) and transformation (right) of method calls

3.1 Correctness of a Virtual Invocation

The description of the standard semantics in this section is a slightly simplified version of the more formal specification described in [29]. We distinguish between two different kinds of invocations: virtual and static. Assume that calls of the first type have been rewritten as $k?m(v, v_1, ..., v_n)$ and the static ones as $k\$m(v, v_1, ..., v_n)$, where k is the declared type of v. Note that we rewrote the call syntax so the invoked object v is now the first actual parameter. The main difference between the two is that while in virtual invocations we need to figure out the particular class of v through a *lookup* in the class hierarchy, that operation is unnecessary in static calls since there is only one possible receiver.

In the left column of Figure 2 we present the pseudocode for the semantics of a static call (here denoted by `staticCallSemantics`) and a virtual call (here denoted by `virtualCallSemantics`). The particular signature of the invocation has to be calculated in order to distinguish which implementation to choose, since in Java (as in the Horn clauses) there can be many methods with the same name and arity, but here they will differ in the type of at least one of the formal parameters. Also, we will assume that there exists a function `runtime_class` that returns the runtime type of the object passed as parameter.

We refer to the tuple $(v, v_1, ..., v_n)$ as *pars*. The standard semantics of the call in the original program is $C[\![k?m(pars)]\!]\sigma = C[\![c\$m(pars)]\!]\sigma$, where c is the value returned by `lookup(runtime_class(v), s)`. The SLD semantics of the transformed version is $S[\![k?m_c(pars)]\!]\sigma$, which the transformation ensures to be $S[\![k\$dyn*m (pars)]\!]\sigma = \bigcup_i S[\![c_i\$m(pars)]\!]\sigma$, where $c_i \in$ `resolve(k, s)`. The correctness condition is now reduced to proving that c is equal to some c_i. This is equivalent to showing that `lookup(runtime_class(v), s)` $\in$ `resolve(k, s)`, which can be further rewritten as `lookup(runtime_class(v), s)` $\in$ {`lookup(sub, s)` | $sub \in$ `subclasses` $(k) \cup \{k\}$}. But the runtime type of v can only be k or a subclass of it in a type safe language as Java, and therefore the condition always holds.

Example 1. Assume a hierarchy of classes like in Figure 3. The root class A declares a method foo which is further redefined (overwritten) in subclasses B,

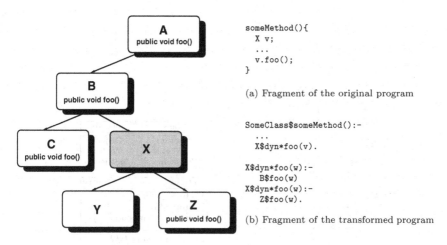

(a) Fragment of the original program

(b) Fragment of the transformed program

Fig. 3. Transformation of a virtual invocation

C, and Z. If the original program in Figure 3a) contains a virtual invocation to foo in an instance declared as being of class X, our compiler automatically transforms it into a call to a new method with two new clauses (methods) that represent all the possible receiver implementations for the call. Because X is a direct subclass of B, it can never inherit the original A implementation but only the B one, represented by the first clause of xdynfoo. Alternatively, any object of type Y and Z is also of type X and therefore we include a call to the Z version of foo in the second clause. The C implementation is discarded because of type incompatibility.

The process described has many interesting properties. First, it is based on assuming SLD resolution semantics for the transformed Horn clause program. This allows reusing existing analyzers without having to redefine the abstract unification operator in order to deal with language-dependent features, as in the case of virtual invocation. We implemented our Java analyses on top of the CiaoPP Prolog analyzer [15] without modifying its code, even when specific abstract domains and "builtin" definitions for Java language constructs had to be provided. A second strength is that correctness of the transformation depends only on showing that $\mathcal{C}[\![comm]\!] \in \mathcal{S}[\![comm_c]\!]$ holds for every command (and expression) in the source language. Although not trivial, the proof can be slightly modified for similar languages to Java, so neither the compiler nor the abstract domains need to be completely rewritten. In the case of Ciao, the proof is trivial since $prog_c = prog$.

4   Other (Meta-)Information Added by the Transformation

The addition of meta-information during the transformation, although not strictly required, can help both efficiency and full independence from the source

```
package examples;

public class Vector {

    Element first;

    public void add(int value){
        Element e = new Element();
        e.value = value;
        Vector v = new Vector();
        v.first = e;
        append(v);
    }
    public void append(Vector v){
        Element e = first;

        if (e == null)
            first = v.first;
        else{
            while (e.next != null)
                e = e.next;

            e.next = v.first;
        }
    }
}
```

```
class SubVector extends Vector{

    public void append(Vector v){
        //...
    }
}
```

class	ancestor
Vector	Object
SubVector	Vector
Element	Object

method	entry
Vector$init	y
Vector$add	y
Vector$dyn*append	y
Vector$append	y
Vector$append#1#2	n
Vector$append#3#4	n
SubVector$init	y
SubVector$append	y
Element$init	y

Fig. 4. Vector example: source code and corresponding metainformation

language. In some cases the fixpoint algorithm can be optimized if some characteristics related to the original source are known. In other cases the abstract domain can use certain information about the program not directly encoded in the Horn clauses. Both demands are solved via the addition of *metainformation* to the transformation. We illustrate this point with the example in Figure 4, which shows an alternative version of the JDK Vector class. The descendant SubVector contains an alternative version of the append method. The corresponding Horn clauses (represented as a Control Flow Graph) are shown in Figure 5. We omitted the constructor (init) clauses for simplicity.

Space reasons prevent us from listing a complete description of the metainformation; only hierarchy and method type tables are shown in Figure 4 (such tables are represented as sets of facts). In the case of the parent-child relations, the purpose is to provide the abstract domain code with access to the class tree, the more obvious application being class analysis [3]. The second table contains a classification for each method, which can be *y* (entry) or *n* (internal). It is used to optimize the performance of the fixpoint engine, avoiding *projection* and *extension* operations [5] (e.g., for blocks that share variable scope with the calling context, such as conditionals).

An *entry* method corresponds in the original program to the first clause [14] of the Java method of the same name and shares its signature, except for an extra parameter that represents the value returned. The other clauses present in the Java method are compiled into (components of) *internal* methods which share the same set of variables: all the formal parameters and local variables they reference. Examples of constructions converted into internal clauses are if, while, or for loops. In the example, we can see how the if (e==null)...else conditional in the

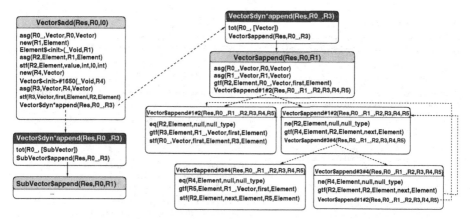

Fig. 5. Call Graph for the example in Figure 4

`Vector` implementation of **append** is converted into two different clauses, one for each branch, which actually share the same name `Vector$append#1#2` (Figure 5). In this case, the internal method is composed of two clauses which are indistinguishable from the caller's point of view, thus causing invocations to the method to be non-deterministic (i.e., causing the execution of one clause or another). Entry clauses are marked in gray, internal ones in white; dotted arrows denote non-deterministic flows while the continuous ones symbolize deterministic calls.

Another flow transformation (*extra* clauses) tries to expose the internal structure of some complex Java features, which sometimes encode sophisticated operations. That is the case of the virtual invocations studied in Section 3. Coming back to the example in Figure 4, note that the call to **append** within **add** is polymorphic: it might execute the implementation in `Vector` or the one in `SubVector`. We make this semantics explicit by inspecting the application hierarchy and replacing the virtual invocation with a set of resolved calls, one for each possible implementation. The method acting as a "hub" is called an *extra* clause; in the example we have two, `Vector$dyn*append`, marked in black. They behave in a very similar way to the conditional discussed previously, since the program flow might go through two alternative paths (clauses), one for each implementation of **append**. Each branch contains a guard (**tot**, see the first statement in each of the `Vector$dyn*append` clauses) listing the acceptable types for the callee.

It is interesting how, in an analogous way to the clause case, we introduced *extra* statements to further simplify analysis. For example, the mentioned **tot** (type of this) builtin filters the execution of subsequent statements when the class of the instance is not listed in the set of possibilities; guard statements have a similar goal in clauses that come from conditional constructions. In Figure 5 the **eq** call at the beginning of the leftmost `Vector$append#1#2` clause refers to the condition for executing the first branch, while the **ne** call contains its negated version, for the second alternative. Also, those methods that are *entry* but not *extra* contain assignments to shadow variables that simulate the call-by-reference semantics [24].

```
public class Lang{

  public void foo(Location loc){
    String lang = loc.getDefaultLanguage();
    ...
  }
}

class Location {
  public String getDefaultLanguage(){
    return "English";
  }
}

class China extends Location{
  public String getDefaultLanguage(){
    return "Mandarin";
  }
}

class Sichuan extends China{
}
```

```
Lang$foo(Res,R0,R1):-
    asg(R0_,Lang,R0,Lang),
    asg(R1_,Location,R1,Location),
    Location$dyn*getDefaultLanguage(R4,R1_),
    ret.

Location$getDefaultLanguage(Res,R0):-
    asg(R0_,Location,R0,Location),
    asg(Res,java.lang.String,"English",java.lang.String),
    ret.

China$getDefaultLanguage(Res,R0):-
    asg(R0_,China,R0,China),
    asg(Res,java.lang.String,"Mandarin",java.lang.String),
    ret.

Location$dyn*getDefaultLanguage(Res,R1_):-
    tot(R1_, [China,Sichuan]),
    China$getDefaultLanguage(Res,R1_).
Location$dyn*getDefaultLanguage(Res,R1_):-
    tot(R1_, [Location]),
    Location$getDefaultLanguage(Res,R1_).
```

Fig. 6. Transformation for dynamic dispatch in Java

5   Explicit Semantics in other OO Languages

Our framework can be adapted to other languages apart from Java (and Ciao), especially for those like C# that share similar syntax and statement semantics to Java. The examples in Figures 6 and 7 illustrate this point. In Figure 6, the value returned by the getDefaultLanguage invocation in the foo method returns English if loc has runtime type Location and Mandarin if the runtime type is China or Sichuan, since this last class inherits the implementation of getDefaultLanguage from China according to standard Java semantics [14]. The C# language is quite similar in most aspects, but polymorphic invocations have been further refined (and complicated). In Figure 7 only class China overshadows the default definition for the getDefaultLanguage method given in the superclass; HongKong inherits the Location implementation. Therefore, an invocation like (new Hong Kong()).getDefaultLanguage() returns English.

When analyzing a virtual invocation like the one in the first line of foo, we could have implemented internal mechanisms in the analyzer for differentiating the two possible interpretations that the call might have in each language. That implies an undesirable, double implementation of either the fixpoint algorithm or the abstract domains, since the analyzer would then be language-dependent. To bypass this problem, we introduce additional pseudo-builtins that contain language-dependent features. We can see in Figures 6 and 7 how the Horn clause representation is almost identical in both cases, except for the bodies of the two Location$dyn*getDefaultLanguage clauses. In the case of Java, we indicate that the first clause is executed if the runtime type of this (tot) is either China or Sichuan, while the second requires that variable to be of runtime type Location. The situation is reversed in the C# example, in which instances of Location and HongKong share the implementation Location$getDefaultLocation while invocations on objects of (exactly) class China are redirected to China$getDefaultLocation.

```
namespace Lang{

public class Lang{
  public void foo(Location loc){
    string lang = loc.getDefaultLanguage();
    ...
  }
}
class Location {
  public string getDefaultLanguage(){
    return "English";
  }
}
class China:Location{
  private string getDefaultLanguage(){
    return "Mandarin";
  }
}
class HongKong:China{}
}
```

```
Lang$foo(Res,R0,R1):-
  asg(R0_,Lang,R0,Lang),
  asg(R1_,Location,R1,Location),
  Location$dyn*getDefaultLanguage(R4,R1_),
  ret.

Location$getDefaultLanguage(Res,R0):-
  asg(R0_,Location,R0,Location),
  asg(Res,string,"English",string),
  ret.

China$getDefaultLanguage(Res,R0):-
  asg(R0_,China,R0,China),
  asg(Res,string,"Mandarin",string),
  ret.

Location$dyn*getDefaultLanguage(Res,R1_):-
  tot(R1_, [China]),
  China$getDefaultLanguage(Res,R1_).
Location$dyn*getDefaultLanguage(Res,R1_):-
  tot(R1_, [Location,HongKong]),
  Location$getDefaultLanguage(Res,R1_).
```

Fig. 7. Transformation for dynamic dispatch in C#

The abstract domain is not required to know anything about which actual language is to be analyzed but only to provide a common, correct transfer function for the tot builtin, which will return as output state the same input state if the instance happens to have a runtime type included in the list of accepted classes, and $\perp$ if not.

6   Experimental Results

We have completed a preliminary implementation of our framework within the CiaoPP preprocessor [15]. CiaoPP offers a parametric and efficient top-down analysis engine [23,16] with a good number of abstract domains, including the ones illustrated in this section. The efficiency of the algorithm relies on keeping dependencies between different predicates during analysis so that only the really affected parts need to be revisited after a change during the fixpoint process. In addition, recomputation is avoided using *memoization* [11,33,23]. Another characteristic is that it is *multivariant* (i.e., abstract calls to a given predicate that represent different input patterns are automatically analyzed separately) and follows a top-down approach, in order to allow modeling properties that depend on the data flow characteristics of the program.

We have performed two experiments with our framework using the benchmarks corresponding to the JOlden suite [31]. The first experiment is summarized in Figure 8 and shows the scalability of the transformation phase. The first three columns contain basic metrics about the application: number of classes (k), methods (m) and instructions (i). Since the latter corresponds to the bytecode representation of the source, we also list how many program points (pp) are present in the Horn clause program analyzed. This metric differs slightly from the number of instructions in the sense that extra clauses and builtins make it somewhat larger; pp also provides a better approximation of the size

name	k	m	i	pp	ct
jolden.health.Health	8	30	637	933	1.1
jolden.bh.BH	9	70	1208	1739	3.2
jolden.voronoi.Voronoi	6	73	988	1340	2.2
jolden.mst.MST	6	36	445	665	0.1
jolden.power.Power	6	32	1017	1270	2.1
jolden.treeadd.TreeAdd	2	12	193	274	2.0
jolden.em3d.Em3d	4	22	447	669	0.1
jolden.perimeter.Perimeter	10	45	543	814	0.1
jolden.bisort.BiSort	2	15	323	476	0.1
jolden.all.All	50	317	5839	7251	11.0

Fig. 8. Statistics from the transformation phase

and complexity of the program analyzed because the semantics of the object-oriented program is made explicit, as seen in Section 2. The fifth column (ct) shows the time invested (given in seconds) in transforming the input program and producing the Horn clause version and the metainformation.

The second experiment, shown in Figure 9, illustrates the scalability, efficiency, and precision of the analysis component of our framework. We first use a simple abstract domain, Nullity, capable of approximating which variables are definitely null and which ones definitely point to a non-null location. The second abstract domain is a Class Hierarchy Analysis (CHA) [3], which uses the combination of the statically declared type of an object and the class hierarchy of the program to determine the set of possible targets of a virtual invocation. The use of a CHA shows the scalability of our framework for a domain with non-linear worst-case complexity in its operations. Additionally, it also reflects the usefulness of *metainformation* files since they are required by the CHA domain in order to access the hierarchy tree. The columns labeled pp' show the number of program points reachable by the analyses. Therefore, pp' may differ from pp because the number of analyzed program points is not always the total number of program points in the program: some commands are found to be unreachable. Since our framework is multivariant and can thus keep track of different *contexts* at each program point, at the end of analysis there may be more than one abstract state associated with each program point. Thus, the number of abstract states is typically larger than the number of reachable program points. The *ast* columns provide the total number of these abstract states inferred by analysis. The level of multivariance is the ratio ast/pp', presented in the *st* columns. In general, such a larger number for *st* tends to indicate more precise results. Running times are listed in columns pt (time invested in preprocessing the program which includes the extraction of metainformation for each method in the Horn clause program and the construction of the class hierarchy) and at (analysis time); both are also given in seconds.

Both experiments have been performed on a Pentium M 1.73Ghz with 1Gb of RAM, and averaging several runs after eliminating the best and worst values. We chose to show separately the total times of the two phases (transformation and

		Nullity				CHA			
	pt	pp'	ast	st	at	pp'	ast	st	at
jolden.health.Health	2.1	921	5836	6.3	9.6	933	3542	3.8	52.1
jolden.bh.BH	2.2	1739	12384	7.1	50.1	1739	4757	2.7	59.4
jolden.voronoi.Voronoi	2.2	1277	5492	4.3	11.5	1340	5147	3.8	81.3
jolden.mst.MST	2.1	496	1503	3.0	1.1	665	1609	2.4	11.6
jolden.power.Power	2.1	1270	10560	8.3	29.9	1270	2908	2.3	32.7
jolden.treeadd.TreeAdd	2.0	274	880	3.2	0.6	274	729	2.6	6.1
jolden.em3d.Em3d	2.0	669	5565	8.3	0.9	669	3320	4.9	49.5
jolden.perimeter.Perimeter	2.1	814	2653	3.2	1.7	814	3731	4.5	25.0
jolden.bisort.BiSort	2.1	476	3353	7.0	5.8	476	1614	3.4	15.6
jolden.all.All	2.6	7188	48476	6.7	145.9	7251	29586	4.1	391.2

Fig. 9. Statistics for the Nullity and Class Hierarchy (CHA) domains

analysis) because we expect the transformation process to be fully run only once. Later executions can use incremental compilation for those files that changed, so that the overhead of the preprocessing phase should be almost negligible in medium to large programs. Although the same approach can be taken for the analysis [16], the current implementation is not incremental.

7 Related Work

Most previous research in analysis of object-oriented programs concentrates on finding new abstract domains that better approximate a particular concrete property of the program analyzed in order to optimize compilation (e.g., [4,28]) or statically verify certain properties about the runtime behavior of the code (e.g., [13,19]). In contrast there has been comparatively little work on the formal specification of the *intermediate language* to which the analyzed program is transformed or in the application of existing logic programming techniques. In [25] the authors describe how to automatically derive Prolog versions of Java programs that share the same operational semantics. However, the compilation applies to a smaller subset of Java than that supported in our work and no experimental results are provided. Also, the technique is presented from a more informal perspective and no analysis is attempted over the transformed logic programs.

More closely related to ours is the work presented in [1], which draws in part on the ideas of [26]. The authors also focus on how to reuse existing logic programming tools, in order to analyze Java bytecode. The approach is based on encoding an interpreter of the Java Virtual Machine bytecode in a logic language, Ciao [6], and then partially evaluating this interpreter with respect to the concrete program to be analyzed. This results in a *residual* program which has the same semantics as the original one but is often easier to analyze than the original set of bytecode+interpreter. As in our case, the analysis and verification experiments are performed using the CiaoPP [15] tool.

While the approach of [1] is obviously very interesting, it also has the shortcoming that it is quite dependent on the quality of the results obtained by the partial evaluator. Given the state of the art in partial evaluation, this may clearly vary significantly depending on the input program. The approach presented herein is based instead on a direct translation from the Java program into a Horn clause representation, which obviates this problem, at the cost of having to write and prove correct the transformer. Also, in this translation we do not try to mimic the operational semantics of the Java program in the Horn clause version (i.e., the resulting program if run, e.g., on a Prolog system, would not necessarily produce equivalent results to those of the Java program). Instead, the aim is to *safely approximate* the semantics of the Java program in the Horn clause representation by taking advantage of the (collecting) SLD semantics assumed by the analyzer. This allows flexibility in the translation and eliminates the burden of having to simulate exactly the operational semantics of the source language since we do not want to execute the program but only to obtain safe results by analyzing it. The flexibility and directness of this approach also allows supporting a much larger subset of the language than in [1], including exceptions, inheritance, interfaces, etc. Also, presumably because of the directness of the approach with it we have been able to analyze significantly larger programs, and in less time.

In most of the (non CLP-based) abstract interpretation frameworks for analysis of Java (e.g., [4,7]) the authors prefer to focus on particular properties and therefore their solutions (abstract domains and analysis algorithms) are tied to them, even when if they may be explicitly labeled as multipurpose [20]. In [27] the authors use a framework that is closely related to Gaia [8] (itself closely related to [23]). However, the intermediate representation is not described and the semantics of the interprocedural operations is again tied to the Java language. Also, the benchmarks used are smaller than those that we report on. The more recent Julia framework [30] is intended to be generic from the point of view of domains but once more also targets Java as unique source language. This framework is capable of analyzing large programs in a top-down way, as in our approach, the main other difference being that we support multivariance, inherited from the CiaoPP analyzer. Finally, in [22] another interesting generic static analyzer for the modular analysis and verification of Java classes is presented. The algorithm presented is also top down but is again tailored specifically to Java source.

8   Conclusions and Future Work

We have presented a transformation-based framework for analysis of object-oriented programs, which is generic in terms of the source language and abstract domain in use. The framework consists of a two-step process: a transformation of the program into a set of Horn clauses that represents a correct approximation of its standard semantics, and a mature and sophisticated fixpoint algorithm. We claim that our approach is flexible in the sense that the first phase decouples the fixpoint algorithm from any language-dependent feature. Furthermore, our experimental evaluations support the scalability of our framework showing results for medium-sized programs as well as its efficiency analyzing them in a reasonable amount of time, and precision showing high rates of multivariance.

We have performed some promising experiments on an ample subset of Java, as shown in this paper, but our aim is to support the full Java language. Also, we are currently incorporating more sophisticated abstract domains (e.g., points-to/sharing analysis). Moreover, we expect to increase the scalability of our approach, analyzing larger programs than shown in this paper. To this end, we are studying the inclusion of modular and incremental features in our fixpoint algorithm.

References

1. Albert, E., Gómez-Zamalloa, M., Hubert, L., Puebla, G.: Verification of Java Byte-code using Analysis and Transformation of Logic Programs. In: Hanus, M. (ed.) PADL 2007. LNCS, vol. 4354, pp. 124–139. Springer, Heidelberg (2006)
2. Alves-Foss, J. (ed.): Formal Syntax and Semantics of Java. LNCS, vol. 1523. Springer, Heidelberg (1999)
3. Bacon, D.F., Sweeney, P.F.: Fast static analysis of c++ virtual function calls. Proc. of OOPSLA 1996, SIGPLAN Notices 31(10), 324–341 (1996)
4. Blanchet, B.: Escape Analysis for Object Oriented Languages. Application to Java(TM). In: Conference on Object-Oriented Programming, Systems, Languages and Applications (OOPSLA 1999), pp. 20–34. ACM, New York (1999)
5. Bruynooghe, M.: A Practical Framework for the Abstract Interpretation of Logic Programs. Journal of Logic Programming 10, 91–124 (1991)
6. Bueno, F., Cabeza, D., Carro, M., Hermenegildo, M., López-García, P., Puebla, G. (eds.): The Ciao System. Reference Manual (v1.10). Technical report, School of Computer Science (UPM) (2004), http://www.ciaohome.org
7. Chang, B.-Y.E., Leino, K.R.M.: Abstract interpretation with alien expressions and heap structures. In: Cousot, R. (ed.) VMCAI 2005. LNCS, vol. 3385, pp. 147–163. Springer, Heidelberg (2005)
8. Le Charlier, B., Van Hentenryck, P.: Experimental Evaluation of a Generic Abstract Interpretation Algorithm for Prolog. ACM Transactions on Programming Languages and Systems 16(1), 35–101 (1994)
9. Cousot, P., Cousot, R.: Abstract Interpretation: A Unified Lattice Model for Static Analysis of Programs by Construction or Approximation of Fixpoints. In: Proc. of POPL 1977, pp. 238–252 (1977)
10. DeLine, R., Leino, K.R.M.: BoogiePL: A typed procedural language for checking object-oriented programs. Technical Report MSR-TR-2005-70, Microsoft Research (2005)
11. Dietrich, S.W.: Extension Tables: Memo Relations in Logic Programming. In: Fourth IEEE Symposium on Logic Programming, pp. 264–272 (September 1987)
12. Fecht, C.: Gena - a tool for generating prolog analyzers from specifications. In: Mycroft, A. (ed.) SAS 1995. LNCS, vol. 983, pp. 418–419. Springer, Heidelberg (1995)
13. Genaim, S., Spoto, F.: Information Flow Analysis for Java Bytecode. In: Proc. of VMCAI. LNCS, Springer, Heidelberg (2005)
14. Gosling, J., Joy, B., Steele, G., Bracha, G.: Java(TM) Language Specification, 3rd edn. Addison-Wesley, Professional Reading (2005)

15. Hermenegildo, M., Puebla, G., Bueno, F., López-García, P.: Program Development Using Abstract Interpretation (and The Ciao System Preprocessor). In: Cousot, R. (ed.) SAS 2003. LNCS, vol. 2694, pp. 127–152. Springer, Heidelberg (2003)
16. Hermenegildo, M., Puebla, G., Marriott, K., Stuckey, P.: Incremental Analysis of Constraint Logic Programs. ACM TOPLAS 22(2), 187–223 (2000)
17. Kowalski, R., Kuehner, D.: Linear resolution with selection function. Artificial Intelligence 2, 227–260 (1971)
18. Leavens, G.T., Baker, A.L., Ruby, C.: Preliminary design of jml: A behavioral interface specification language for java. SIGSOFT Softw. Eng. Notes 31(3), 1–38 (2006)
19. Leroy, X.: Java Bytecode Verification: An Overview. In: Berry, G., Comon, H., Finkel, A. (eds.) CAV 2001. LNCS, vol. 2102, Springer, Heidelberg (2001)
20. Lev-Ami, T., Sagiv, S.: TVLA: A system for implementing static analyses. In: Palsberg, J. (ed.) SAS 2000. LNCS, vol. 1824, pp. 280–302. Springer, Heidelberg (2000)
21. Logozzo, F., Cortesi, A.: Abstract interpretation and object-oriented languages: Quo vadis? In: Proc. of the 1st. Int'l. Workshop on Abstract Interpretation of Object-oriented Languages (AIOOL 2005). ENTCS, Elsevier Science, Amsterdam (2005)
22. Logozzo, F.: Cibai: An abstract interpreation-based static analyzer for modular analysis and verification of java classes. In: Cook, B., Podelski, A. (eds.) VMCAI 2007. LNCS, vol. 4349, pp. 283–298. Springer, Heidelberg (2007)
23. Muthukumar, K., Hermenegildo, M.: Compile-time Derivation of Variable Dependency Using Abstract Interpretation. JLP 13(2/3), 315–347 (1992)
24. Navas, J., Méndez-Lojo, M., Hermenegildo, M.: An Efficient, Context and Path Sensitive Analysis Framework for Java Programs. In: 9th Workshop on Formal Techniques for Java-like Programs FTfJP 2007 (July 2007)
25. Peralta, J., Cruz-Carlon, J.: From static single-assignment form to definite programs and back. In: Extended abstract in International Symposium on Logic-based Program Synthesis and Transformation (LOPSTR) (July 2006)
26. Peralta, J.C., Gallagher, J., Sağlam, H.: Analysis of Imperative Programs through Analysis of Constraint Logic Programs. In: Levi, G. (ed.) SAS 1998. LNCS, vol. 1503, pp. 246–261. Springer, Heidelberg (1998)
27. Pollet, I.: Towards a generic framework for the abstract interpretation of Java. PhD thesis, Catholic University of Louvain, Dept. of Computer Science (2004)
28. Ruf, E.: Effective synchronization removal for java. PLDI 2000, SIGPLAN Notices 35(5), 208–218 (2000)
29. Secci, S., Spoto, F.: Pair-sharing analysis of object-oriented programs. In: SAS, pp. 320–335 (2005)
30. Spoto, F.: JULIA: A Generic Static Analyser for the Java Bytecode. In: Proc. of the 7th Workshop on Formal Techniques for Java-like Programs, FTfJP 2005, Glasgow, Scotland (July 2005)
31. JOlden Suite, http://www-ali.cs.umass.edu/DaCapo/benchmarks.html
32. Vallee-Rai, R., Hendren, L., Sundaresan, V., Lam, P., Gagnon, E., Co, P.: Soot - a Java optimization framework. In: Proceedings of CASCON 1999, pp. 125–135 (1999)
33. Warren, R., Hermenegildo, M., Debray, S.K.: On the Practicality of Global Flow Analysis of Logic Programs. In: Fifth International Conference and Symposium on Logic Programming, pp. 684–699. MIT Press, Cambridge (1988)

Snapshot Generation in a Constructive Object-Oriented Modeling Language

Mauro Ferrari[1], Camillo Fiorentini[2], Alberto Momigliano[2], and Mario Ornaghi[2]

[1] Dipartimento di Informatica e Comunicazione, Università degli Studi dell'Insubria, Italy
mauro.ferrari@uninsubria.it
[2] Dipartimento di Scienze dell'Informazione, Università degli Studi di Milano, Italy
{fiorenti,momiglia,ornaghi}@dsi.unimi.it

Abstract. CooML is an object-oriented modeling language where specifications are theories in a constructive logic designed to handle incomplete information. In this logic we view snapshots as a formal counterpart of object populations, which are associated with specifications via the constructive interpretation of logical connectives. In this paper, we introduce the "snapshot semantics" of CooML and we describe a snapshot generation (SG) algorithm, which can be applied to validate specifications in the spirit of OCL-like constraints over UML models. Differently from the latter and from the standard BHK semantics, the logic allows us to exploit a notion of partial validation that is appropriate to encodings characterised by incomplete information. SG is akin to model generation in answer set programming. We show that the algorithm is sound and complete so that its successful termination implies consistency of the system.

1 Introduction

We are developing the <u>c</u>onstructive <u>o</u>bject-<u>o</u>riented <u>m</u>odeling <u>l</u>anguage CooML [19] (http://cooml.dsi.unimi.it), a specification language for OO systems. Similarly to UML/OCL [23], CooML provides a framework for the design of system specifications in the early stages of the development process. The language allows the user to distinguish between internally defined elements and the problem domain, which may involve loosely or incompletely defined components. This encourages the selection of the appropriate level of abstraction w.r.t. specifications.

CooML follows the spirit of lightweight formal methods [10]: it does not focus on full formalization, nor on whole system correctness, but emphasizes *partiality* in analysis and specification. In particular, in the context of OO modeling, both the validation of a specification and the check of its consistency can be achieved via the notion of *snapshot*, i.e. a population of objects in a given system state that satisfies the specification. Previous work has used snapshots for validation of UML/OCL models [8] and specifications in JML [4].

The novelty of CooML's approach resides in its semantics, which is related to the constructive explanation of logical connectives (a.k.a. the BHK interpretation [22]). Specifically, the truth of a CooML proposition in a given interpretation is explained by a mathematical object that we call an *information term*. For the time being, the latter can be visualized as a sort of *proof term* inhabiting a type/formula. The underlying logic is

King, A. (Ed.): LOPSTR 2007, LNCS 4915, pp. 169–184, 2008.
© Springer-Verlag Berlin Heidelberg 2008

characterized by how classical and constructive information co-exists, the main "entry" point being the different way in which an *atomic* formula A is given evidence (for more details we refer the kind reader to the original formulation of the logic in [15]). If we call the pair $I : P$ a *piece of information*, where P is a formula and I is its information term, then $I : P$ may be *true* or *false* in a classical interpretation w, called a *world*. Thus, we have a notion of a *model* of a piece of information based on classical logic. In particular, we use $\mathsf{T}\{F\}$ to indicate the truth of F; in fact, T does not contain evidence for F, but it yields a trivial piece of information true in all the models of F. This introduces a novel and flexible way to handle *incomplete* information, a notorious difficulty in information systems such as relational databases.

Crucially, the constructive side of the logic allows the *identification of snapshots with information terms*, thus providing a formal counterpart to the intuitive notion of object populations. We argue that CooML's proof-theoretic snapshot generation may be advantageous in comparison to a model-theoretic one, especially in cases where not all the information required to define a model is even present. The possibility of treating information in this less committed way means that we can select only the relevant information; this may have a cascade of benefits in terms of conciseness of the representation.

The contributions of this paper are twofold. First, we extend the semantics developed in purely logical terms in [15] to object oriented modeling languages. We regard an OO system specification as a CooML theory T, the system snapshots as the pieces of information $I : T$, and the related information content as a suitable set of formulae. We show that the latter can be seen as the *minimum* information needed to give evidence to snapshots and we relate that to snapshot consistency. Secondly, we describe (and implement) a snapshot generation algorithm (SGA), taking as inputs: (i) a CooML theory T, axiomatizing a set of classes in a problem domain PD; (ii) the user's generation requirements $\mathscr{G}$ – they serve an analogous purpose of domain predicates in the grounding phase of ASP's [17]. As snapshots should be consistent with respect to PD and $\mathscr{G}$, we prove that consistency checking is sound and that snapshot generation is complete, i.e. if a consistent snapshot satisfying the generation requirements exists, it will be generated. This is loosely connected to adequacy results in the theory of CLP's [7].

2   CooML Specifications

In this section we informally present the language via an example (adapted from [3]), while we defer the formal exposition to Section 2.1. The problem domain concerns a small coach company. Each coach has a specified number of seats and can be used for regular or private trips. In a regular trip, each passenger has its own ticket and seat number. In a private trip, the whole coach is rented and there may be a guide. The corresponding CooML specification is contained in the package `coachCompany` (Fig. 1). To explain our example we need to introduce CooML types system. We distinguish among *data types* (in our example, `Integer` and `Boolean`), *PD types* (`Person`), and *object types* (`Coach`, `Trip`, `Passenger`). They all inherit from the top type `Value` the identity relation and the string representation. Data types are "statically" defined, i.e., their values do not depend on the current state. CooML assumes the

```
package coachCompany;
pds{type Person;
   Integer numberOfSeats(Coach c) = (* the number of seats of c *);
   Boolean guides(Person p, Trip t) = (* p guides trip t *);
   Boolean nobooking(Passenger p, Trip t) = (* p has no booking in t *);
   Boolean vacant(Integer s, Coach c, Trip t) =
                              (* s is a vacant seat on c in t *);
   Boolean booked(Passenger p, Integer s, Coach c, Trip t) =
                              (* p has booked seat s on c in  t *);
   <constr name=bookingConstraints  language=prolog>
      false :- vacant(S,C,T), booked(_P,S,C,T).
      false :- booked(P1,S,C,T), booked(P2,S,C,T), not(P1==P2).
      false :- nobooking(P,T), booked(P,_Seat,_Coach,T).
   </constr>
   }
class Coach{
 coachPty: and{
     seats: exi{Integer seatsNr; seatsNr = numberOfSeats(this)}
     trips: for{Trip trip; trip is Trip(this) --> true} }
   Integer getSeats(){  return seats.seatNr   }
          }
class Trip{ env(Coach coach)
 TripPty: case{private: case{T{exi{Person p; guides(p,this)}}
                       T{not exi{Person p; guides(p,this)}}}
             regular: for{Integer seat; (seat in 1..coach.getSeats()) -->
                  case{vacant: vacant(seat,coach,this)
                       booked: exi{Passenger p; T{and{p is Passenger(this)
                                           booked(p,seat,coach,this)}}
      }}}}}
class Passenger{ env(Trip trip)
 PsngrPty: case{c1: nobooking(this,trip)
             c2: exi{Integer seat, Coach coach;
                     T{and{trip is Trip(coach)
                           booked(this,seat,coach,trip)}}
      }}}
```

Fig. 1. The coachCompany package

existence of an implementation that evaluates ground terms to values. A PD type extends Value with a set of problem domain functions.

Nothing is assumed about PD types; they may be characterized by a set of formal or loose properties that we call *PD constraints*, introduced by the tag <constr>.

The special subtype Obj of Value introduces object identities. Objects are created by CooML classes, which are structured in a single inheritance hierarchy rooted in Obj. The definition of a class C may depend on some *environment* parameters; namely C($\underline{e}$) is a class with environment parameters $\underline{e}$. If $\underline{e}$ is a ground instance of the environment parameters $\underline{e}$, then C($\underline{e}$) can be used to create new objects. We write "o is C($\underline{e}$)" to indicate that o has been created by C($\underline{e}$), while "o instanceof C($\underline{e}$)" means that o has environment $\underline{e}$ and has been created by a subclass C' of C. We call those *class predicates*.

In a package: (i) data types are assumed to be externally implemented; (ii) PD types are defined in the `pds` (problem domain specification) section; (iii) classes are introduced by suitable class declarations.

pds declaration and world states. The `pds` section specifies our general knowledge of the problem domain. It introduces PD types, functions and predicates using data and class types. In our example we introduce the PD type `Person` and functions `numberOfSeats`, `guides`, ... The informal descriptions ($*$...$*$) use terms of the global signature provided by the analysis phase [11]. A `<constr>` declaration introduces a set of PD constraints representing general problem domain properties that are not interpreted by CooML, but possibly by some external tool. In the example, PD constraints are expressed in Prolog assisting the SG algorithm in filtering out undesired snapshots. The class predicate "o is C($\underline{e}$)" is represented by the Prolog predicate `isOf(o, C, [`$\underline{e}$`])`, while "o istanceOf C($\underline{e}$)" is translated into `instanceOf(o, C, [`$\underline{e}$`])`. The first constraint says that a coach seat cannot be vacant and booked at the same time, the second one excludes overbooking (a seat can be booked by at most one person), while the third says that the predicate `nobooking(P,T)` holds if person P has not booked a seat on the coach associated with trip T. In this paper, we assume that the signature Σ_T of a CooML theory T (including PD types, data types and classes) is first order and that we can represent the possible states of the "real world" by *reachable* Σ_T-interpretations, dubbed *world states*. Reachability means that each element of the interpretation domains is represented by some ground terms, in our case CooML values. In a world state, PD symbols are interpreted over the external world, data types are interpreted according to their implementation, and class predicates represent the current system objects. For instance the class predicates

```
mini is Coach(),  t1 is Trip(mini),  t2 is Trip(mini),  t3 is Trip(mini),
john is Passenger(t1)
```

represent a small company with a single mini-bus `mini`, three trips `t1,t2,t3` operated by `mini` and, so far, only one passenger `john` associated with trip `t1`.

class declarations and properties. A class declaration introduces the name C of the class, its (possible) environment parameters $\underline{e}$, its property $Pty_C(\text{this}, \underline{e})$, and its methods [1]. An object **o** created by C($\underline{e}$) stores a *piece of information* structured according to $Pty_C(\mathbf{o}, \underline{e})$, and uses the methods implemented by C($\underline{e}$).

For class properties, CooML uses a prefix syntax, where formulas may be labeled. Labels are used to refer to subformulae. For example, the label `seats` is used in the `getSeats` method to refer to `seatsNr`. A *class property* P is an atomic formula over Σ_T, or (recursively) a formula of the form and$\{P_1 \ ... \ P_n\}$, case$\{P_1 \ ... \ P_n\}$, exi$\{\underline{\tau} \, \underline{x}; P\}$, for$\{\underline{\tau} \, \underline{x}; G {\rightarrow} P\}$ and T$\{P^{ext}\}$, where P^{ext} is a property that may also use negation `not` and implication `imp`. We stress that `not` and `imp` cannot be used outside T.

In CooML's semantics, a property P defines a set of possible pieces of information of the form $I : P$, where I is an *information term*, that is a structure justifying the truth of P. Each piece of information $I : P$ has an *information content*, i.e. a set of simple properties intuitively representing the minimum amount of information needed to justify P according to I. A *simple property* is either an atom or of the form T$\{P^{ext}\}$. A simple property S represents a basic information unit, i.e., it has a unique information term tt

---
[1] We use the self-reference `this` as in Java.

where `tt` is a constant. This means that the only information we have is the *truth* of S, and that the associated information *content* is simply the set $\{S\}$. Exemplifying,

```
tt : t1 is Trip(mini)
```

has information content $\{$`t1 is Trip(mini)`$\}$ and means that the trip `t1` is assigned to the coach `mini` in the current world state.

The operator `T` may enclose a complex property P and indicates that we are interested only in its truth. Let us consider

```
tt: T{exi{Person p; guides(p,t2)}}     tt: T{not exi{Person p; guides(p,t3)}}
```

The first piece of information says that `t2` is a guided trip without indicating who the guide is; the second one says that `t3` has no guide.

By default [2] the truth of a simple property S in a world state w (denoted w $\models S$) is defined as in classical logic, by ignoring `T` (i.e., w $\models$ `T`$\{P\}$ iff w $\models P$) and interpreting `case` as $\vee$, and `as` $\wedge$, `not` as $\neg$, `imp` as $\rightarrow$, `exi` as $\exists$ and `for`$\{\underline{\tau}\ \underline{x}; G(\underline{x}) \rightarrow P(\underline{x})\}$ as $\forall \underline{x}(G(\underline{x}) \rightarrow P(\underline{x}))$.

In contrast, non-simple properties are interpreted constructively, by means of information terms. A piece of information $I : P$ may have one of the following forms:

Existential. $(\mathbf{x}, I) : $`exi`$\{\tau\ x;\ P(x)\}$, where τ is the type of the existential variable x. The term $\mathbf{x}$ is a *witness* for x and the information content is the one of $I : P(\mathbf{x})$. For example,

```
(4,tt) : exi{Integer seatNr; seatNr = numberOfSeats(mini)}
```

has witness 4 and information content $\{$`4 = numberOfSeats(mini)`$\}$, signifying that our mini-bus has 4 passenger seats. Note that, differently from the case of simple properties, we know the value of x that makes $P(x)$ true.

Universal. $((\mathbf{x}_1, I_1), \ldots, (\mathbf{x}_n, I_n)) : $`for`$\{\tau\ x;\ G(x) \rightarrow P(x)\}$, where $G(x)$ is an x-*generator*, i.e. a formula true for finitely many x [3]. The information content is the union of those of $I_1 : P(\mathbf{x}_1), \ldots, I_n : P(\mathbf{x}_n)$ and of the *domain property* $\mathrm{dom}(x;\ G(x);\ [\mathbf{x}_1, \ldots, \mathbf{x}_n])$, a special simple property interpreted as $\forall x(G(x) \leftrightarrow member(x, [\mathbf{x}_1, \ldots, \mathbf{x}_n]))$. For example, the information content of

```
((t1,tt),(t2,tt),(t3,tt)) : for{Trip trip; trip is Trip(mini) → true}
```

is $\{$`dom(trip; trip is Trip(mini); [t1,t2,t3])`$\}$, showing that the domain of the `trip`-generator "`trip is Trip(mini)`" is $\{$`t1,t2,t3`$\}$. Since the atomic formula `true` corresponds to no information, it can be ignored.

Conjunctive. $(I_1, \ldots, I_n) : $`and`$\{P_1 \ldots P_n\}$. The information content is the union of those of $I_j : P_j$, for all $j \in 1..n$. For instance, a piece of information for the class property `coachPty(mini)` and the related information content IC_1 is

```
((4,tt), ((t1,tt), (t2,tt), (t3,tt))) : and{seats(mini) trips(mini)}
IC₁ = {4 = numberOfSeats(mini), dom(trip; trip is Trip(mini); [t1,t2,t3])}
```

$IC_1 = \{$`4 = numberOfSeats(mini)`, `dom(trip; trip is Trip(mini); [t1,t2,t3])`$\}$

---

[2] But one can change this, although we do not discuss it for lack of space.

[3] We omit here the precise syntax of generators.

Disjunctive. $(\mathtt{k}, I_k) : \mathtt{case}\{P_1 \dots P_n\}$. The selector $k \in 1..n$ points to the true subformula P_k and the information content is $I_k : P_k$'s. For example, if the object john with class predicate john is Passenger(t1) contains the information term (1,tt), then

$$(1,\mathtt{tt}) \; : \; \mathtt{case\{c1:nobooking(john,t1) \; c2: \; \dots\}}$$

selects the first sub-property of PsngrPty, with information content {nobooking (john,t1)}, i.e. john has no booking in trip t1 in the current state.

The information content of classes. Let $\mathtt{C}(\underline{e})$ be a class with property $Pty_C(\mathtt{this}, \underline{e})$. We associate with C the *class axiom*

$$\mathtt{clAx(C)}: \; \mathtt{for\{Obj \; this, \; \underline{\tau} \; \underline{e}; \; this \; is \; C}(\underline{e}) \; \rightarrow \; Pty_C(\mathtt{this}, \underline{e})\}$$

The corresponding pieces of information and information content are those for universal properties. The piece of information for class Coach and its information content IC_2 is:

$$((\mathtt{mini, CoachInfo})) \; : \; \mathtt{for\{Obj \; this; \; this \; is \; Coach()} \; \rightarrow \; \mathtt{coachPty(this)\}}$$
$$IC_2 = \{\mathtt{dom(this; \; this \; is \; Coach(); \; [mini]), \; 4 = numberOfSeats(mini),}$$
$$\mathtt{dom(trip; \; trip \; is \; Trip(mini); \; [t1,t2,t3])\}}$$

where CoachInfo:coachPty(mini) is defined as in the conjunctive case.

System snapshots and their information content. Let P be a package introducing a set of constraints $\mathscr{T}$ and the CooML classes $C_1, \dots, C_n$. We associate with P a CooML theory $T_P = \langle \mathtt{thAx}, \mathscr{T} \rangle$, where $\mathtt{thAx} = \mathtt{and\{clAx}(C_1) \cdots \mathtt{clAx}(C_n)\}$.

A piece of information $I : \mathtt{thAx}$ represents the information content of the whole system. We call it a *system snapshot*, to emphasise that the system may evolve through a sequence $I_0 : \mathtt{thAx}, \dots, I_n : \mathtt{thAx}, \dots$. A snapshot for our coachCompany system is of the form:

$$(I_1, I_2, I_3) \; : \; \mathtt{and\{clAx(Coach) \; clAx(Passenger) \; clAx(Trip)\}}$$

and possible information terms I_1, I_2, I_3 are

$$I_1 = ((\mathtt{mini, CoachInfo})), \quad I_2 = (((\mathtt{[john,t1], (1,tt)), ([ted,t2], (1,tt))})$$
$$I_3 = (((\mathtt{[t1,mini], (2, ((1,tt), \; (2,(john,tt)), (3,(1,tt)), (4,(1,tt)))))},$$
$$(\mathtt{[t2,mini], (1, (1,tt)))},$$
$$(\mathtt{[t3,mini], (1, (2,tt))))}$$

where [...] denote tuples. A relevant part of the information content for coachCompany is given in Fig. 2.

The above information content could be seen as an "incompletely specified" model of the coachCompany theory, where numberOfSeats, nobooking, vacant, booked and class predicates are completely specified, while for guides we have only some partial knowledge, expressed by the T-properties, and moreover nothing is said about Person. The relationship with classical models can be better explained by comparing the constructive and classical reading of CooML properties.

```
dom(o; o is Coach(); [mini]),   dom(o; o is Trip(mini); [t1,t2,t3]),
dom([o,t]; o is Passenger(t); [[john,t1],[ted,t2]]),
dom([o,c]; o is Trip(c); [[t1,mini],[t2,mini],[t3,mini]]),
4=numberOfSeats(mini),   nobooking(john,t1),   vacant(1,mini,t1),
booked(john,2,mini,t1), vacant(3,mini,t1),   vacant(4,mini,t1),
T{exi{Person p; guides(p,t2)}},   T{not exi{Person p; guides(p,t3)}}
```

Fig. 2. Part of the information content of `coachCompany`

Let $T = \langle \texttt{thAx}, \mathcal{T} \rangle$ be a CooML theory. We can switch to the classical interpretation of `thAx` simply by using the T operator, i.e. by considering the simple property $\texttt{T}\{\texttt{thAx}\}$. One can prove that $\texttt{T}\{\texttt{thAx}\}$ has a reachable model if and only if so does $\texttt{IC}(I : \texttt{thAx})$, for at least one piece of information $I : \texttt{thAx}$. Furthermore, one can prove that $\texttt{IC}(I : \texttt{thAx})$ is the minimum set of simple formulas that justifies I as an explanation of `thAx`.

In this context we are mainly interested in the notion of consistency with respect to the PD constraints, assuming that the latter can be interpreted as first order sentences. In our example, we interpret a program clause $H : -B_1, \ldots, B_n$ as the universal closure of $B_1 \wedge \ldots \wedge B_n \rightarrow H$, as usual. A system snapshot $I : \texttt{thAx}$ for a theory $T = \langle \texttt{thAx}, \mathcal{T} \rangle$ is *consistent* if its information content $\texttt{IC}(I : \texttt{thAx})$ is true in a reachable classical model of $\mathcal{T}$; T is consistent if there is a consistent snapshot for it. For example, the above snapshot (I_1, I_2, I_3) is consistent with respect to the first and second constraint of the `pds` section, but not with the third, since both `nobooking(john,t1)` and `booked(john,2,mini,t1)` belong to the information content of `coachCompany` (Fig. 2).

2.1 Formal Definitions

Let $T = \langle \texttt{thAx}, \mathcal{T} \rangle$ be a CooML theory and Σ_T the associated first order signature. The set of *information terms* for a property P, $\texttt{IT}(P)$, is inductively defined as follows, where $\underline{\mathbf{x}}$ stands for values of $\underline{x}$ of the appropriate type:

$$
\begin{aligned}
\texttt{IT}(P) &= \{\,\texttt{tt}\,\}, \text{ if } P \text{ is simple} \\
\texttt{IT}(\texttt{and}\{P_1 \cdots P_n\}) &= \{\,(I_1, \ldots, I_n) \mid I_j \in \texttt{IT}(P_j) \text{ for all } j \in 1..n\,\} \\
\texttt{IT}(\texttt{case}\{P_1 \cdots P_n\}) &= \{\,(k, I) \mid 1 \le k \le n \text{ and } I \in \texttt{IT}(P_k)\,\} \\
\texttt{IT}(\texttt{exi}\{\underline{\tau}\,\underline{x}; P\}) &= \{\,(\underline{\mathbf{x}}, I) \mid I \in \texttt{IT}(P)\,\} \\
\texttt{IT}(\texttt{for}\{\underline{\tau}\,\underline{x}; G(\underline{x}) \rightarrow P\}) &= \{\,((\underline{\mathbf{x}}_1, I_1), \ldots, (\underline{\mathbf{x}}_n, I_n)) \mid I_j \in \texttt{IT}(P) \text{ for all } j \in 1..n\,\}
\end{aligned}
$$

A *piece of information* for a closed property P is a pair $I : P$, with $I \in \texttt{IT}(P)$. A *collection* is a set of closed simple properties. The *information content* $\texttt{IC}(I : P)$ is the collection inductively defined as follows:

$$
\begin{aligned}
\texttt{IC}(\texttt{tt} : P) &= \{P\}, \text{ where } P \text{ is a simple property} \\
\texttt{IC}((I_1, \ldots, I_n) : \texttt{and}\{P_1 \cdots P_n\}) &= \textstyle\bigcup_{j=1}^n \texttt{IC}(I_j : P_j) \\
\texttt{IC}((k, I) : \texttt{case}\{P_1 \ldots P_n\}) &= \texttt{IC}(I : P_k) \\
\texttt{IC}((\underline{\mathbf{x}}, I) : \texttt{exi}\{\underline{\tau}\,\underline{x}; P(\underline{x})\}) &= \texttt{IC}(I : P(\underline{\mathbf{x}})) \\
\texttt{IC}(((\underline{\mathbf{x}}_1, I_1), \ldots, (\underline{\mathbf{x}}_n, I_n)) : \texttt{for}\{\underline{\tau}\,\underline{x}; G(\underline{x}) \rightarrow P(\underline{x})\}) &= \textstyle\bigcup_{j=1}^n \texttt{IC}(I_j : P(\underline{\mathbf{x}}_j)) \\
&\quad \cup \{\,\texttt{dom}(\underline{x}; G(\underline{x}); [\underline{\mathbf{x}}_1, \ldots, \underline{\mathbf{x}}_n])\,\}
\end{aligned}
$$

The information content $\text{IC}(I : P)$ represents the minimum amount of information needed to get evidence for P according to I. We say that a collection $\mathscr{C}$ *gives evidence to* $I : P$, and we write $\mathscr{C} \rhd I : P$, iff one of the following clauses holds:

$$\mathscr{C} \rhd \texttt{tt} : P \qquad\qquad\qquad\qquad\qquad \text{iff } P \in \mathscr{C}$$
$$\mathscr{C} \rhd (I_1, \ldots, I_n) : \texttt{and}\{P_1 \cdots P_n\} \qquad \text{iff } \mathscr{C} \rhd I_j : P_j \text{ for all } j \in 1..n$$
$$\mathscr{C} \rhd (k, I) : \texttt{case}\{P_1 \ldots P_n\} \qquad \text{iff } \mathscr{C} \rhd I : P_k$$
$$\mathscr{C} \rhd (\underline{\mathbf{x}}, I) : \texttt{exi}\{\underline{\tau}\ \underline{x}; P(\underline{x})\} \qquad \text{iff } \mathscr{C} \rhd I : P(\underline{\mathbf{x}})$$
$$\mathscr{C} \rhd ((\underline{\mathbf{x}}_1, I_1), \ldots, (\underline{\mathbf{x}}_n, I_n)) : \texttt{for}\{\tau\ \underline{x}; G(\underline{x}) \rightarrow P(\underline{x})\} \quad \text{iff } \text{dom}(\underline{x}; G(\underline{x}); [\underline{\mathbf{x}}_1, \ldots, \underline{\mathbf{x}}_n]) \in \mathscr{C}$$
$$\text{and } \mathscr{C} \rhd I_j : P(\underline{\mathbf{x}}_j) \text{ for all } j \in 1..n$$

The information content $\text{IC}(I : P)$ represents an information about the current world state. We define the information content of $\mathscr{C}$ as its closure under (classical) logical consequence, for $\mathscr{C}^* = \{P \mid \mathscr{C} \models P\}$. We say that $\mathscr{C}_1$ *contains less information* than $\mathscr{C}_2$ (written $\mathscr{C}_1 \sqsubseteq \mathscr{C}_2$) iff $\mathscr{C}_1^* \subseteq \mathscr{C}_2^*$. Intuitively, the definition of $\sqsubseteq$ is justified by the fact that an user will "trust" $\mathscr{C}^*$, whenever he trusts $\mathscr{C}$. We could use a different trust-relation, considering different logics. We only need this to hold:

(1). $\mathscr{C} \subseteq \mathscr{C}^*$;
(2). $\mathscr{C}_1 \subseteq \mathscr{C}_2^*$ implies $\mathscr{C}_1 \sqsubseteq \mathscr{C}_2$.

Using the above properties, we can establishes the minimality of $\text{IC}(I : P)$ with respect to $\sqsubseteq$:

Theorem 1. *Let $I : P$ be a piece of information:*

1. $\text{IC}(I : P) \rhd I : P$
2. For every collection $\mathscr{C}$, $\mathscr{C} \rhd I : P$ implies $\text{IC}(I : P) \sqsubseteq \mathscr{C}$.

Now we can apply the above discussion to the problem of checking snapshots against constraints. Let $T = \langle \texttt{thAx}, \mathscr{T} \rangle$ be a CooML theory. We recall that a *snapshot* for T is a piece of information $I : \texttt{thAx}$. We introduce two notions of consistency for snapshots.

- A snapshot $I : \texttt{thAx}$ is consistent with respect to the constraints $\mathscr{T}$ ($\mathscr{T}$-*consistent*) iff there exists a reachable model of $\text{IC}(I : \texttt{thAx}) \cup \mathscr{T}$.
- T is *snapshot-consistent* iff there is at least one snapshot $I : \texttt{thAx}$ such that $I : \texttt{thAx}$ is $\mathscr{T}$-consistent.

The latter definition is related to classical consistency by the following result:

Theorem 2. *Let $T = \langle \texttt{thAx}, \mathscr{T} \rangle$ be a CooML theory. T is snapshot-consistent iff there is a reachable model of $\texttt{T}\{\texttt{thAx}\} \cup \mathscr{T}$.*

3   A Snapshots Generation Algorithm and Its Theory

A snapshot generation algorithm (SGA) for a CooML theory $T = \langle \texttt{thAx}, \mathscr{T} \rangle$ takes as input the user's *generation requirements* and tries to produce $\mathscr{T}$-consistent snapshots that satisfy such requirements. Roughly, *generation states* represent incomplete snapshots, i.e. in logic programming parlance, partially instantiated terms; inconsistent attempts are pruned, when recognized as such during generation.

Consistency checking plays a central role. It depends on the PD logic and it is discussed next. In Subsection 3.2 we illustrate the use of snapshot generation for validating CooML specifications. Finally, in Subsection 3.3 we briefly outline a non deterministic algorithm based on which one may develop sound and complete implementations.

3.1 Consistency Checking

Here we briefly discuss a simplified version of consistency checking in our Prolog implementation, called SnaC. To recognize inconsistent attempts, SGA uses an internal representation of the information content of the current generation state S, denoted by INFO_S. Let P_S be the internal Prolog translation of the information content INFO_S. For this simplified version, we assume that P_S is executed by a suitable *meta-interpreter*. Without giving the formal details, we notice that INFO_S consists either of ground facts, clauses of the form H :- eq(t1,t2) or false :- B, where:

- We use eq to avoid Prolog's standard unification interfering with Skolem constants. Indeed, the latter represent unknown values originating from the translation of T{exi{...}}, where different constants may represent the same value. In this simplified account, the eq atoms are just residuated by the meta-interpreter in a list of "unsolved equations".
- The reserved atom false is adopted to detect inconsistency: its finite failure signals snapshot consistency, conversely, its success corresponds to inconsistency.

Clauses whose head isfalse are called *integrity constraints* and false may occur only as such. A SnaC representation P_S has the following property: if the meta-interpretation of a goal G succeeds from P_S with answer σ and a list L of unsolved equations, then $G\sigma$ is a logical consequence of $P_S \cup L$. Furthermore, consistency is preserved and the models of P_S are models of INFO_S (in the declarative reading of P_S, where we interpret eq as equality and false as falsehood). As an example, let us consider the SnaC representation P_{cComp} in Fig. 3 of the information content of the coachCompany package (Fig. 2).

```
isOf(mini,'Coach',[]).  false :- isOf(O,'Coach',[]), not(member(O,[mini]).
isOf(john 'Passenger',[t1]). isOf(ted 'Passenger',[t2]). ...
numberOfSeats(mini,4). nobooking(john,t1). booked(john,2,mini,t1).
vacant(1,mini,t1). vacant(3,mini,t1). vacant(4,mini,t1).
guides(P,t2):- eq(P,p0).
false :- guides(P,t3).
```

Fig. 3. The SnaC representation P_{cComp}

The facts and the constraint in the first lines come from the translation of domain properties. For example, the first row contains the translation of dom{o; o is Coach(); [mini])}. The other facts come from the translation of atoms. The clause guides(P,t2):- eq(P,p0) is the translation of

`T{exi{Person p; guides(p,t2)}}`, where p0 is a fresh Skolem constant. Finally, `false :- guides(P,t3)` is the translation of `T{not exi{Person p; guides(p,t3)}}`.

Let us analyse the three possible outcomes of consistency checking starting from the example in Fig. 3:

(a) `false` finitely fails from the program P_{cComp}. This entails that `false` does not belong to the minimum model $\mathcal{M}$ of $P_{cComp} \cup \{eq(X,X)\}$. The latter contains all the ground atoms in Fig. 3 as well as `guides(p0,t2)`. Since $\mathcal{M}$ is a model of P_{cComp}, it is also a model of the information content of the `coachCompany` package thanks to the properties of the translation.

(b) If we add to P_{cComp} the constraint

```
c1)    false :- nobooking(P,T), booked(P,_S,_C,T).
```

now the goal `false` succeeds from program $P_{cComp} \cup \{c1\}$, residuating the empty list. This implies that the snapshot corresponding to the information content of `coachCompany` is inconsistent w.r.t. `c1`.

(c) If we instead add the constraint

```
c2)    false :- guides(P,T), isOf(P,'Passenger',[T]).
```

the goal `false` succeeds from program $P_{cComp} \cup \{c2\}$, residuating `[eq(ted,p0)]`. This implies that `false` belongs to the minimum model $\mathcal{M}$ of $P_{cComp} \cup \{c2, eq(ted,p0)\}$. The equality `eq(ted,p0)` is returned to the user as a source of inconsistency.

The above discussion is reflected in the following theorem:

Theorem 3. *Let* $T = \langle \texttt{thAx}, \mathcal{T} \rangle$ *be a CooML theory,* I : `thAx` *a snapshot and* P *a program containing the translation of* $\text{IC}(I : \texttt{thAx})$ *and of the PD constraints* $\mathcal{T}$.

1. *If* `false` *finitely fails from* P, *then* I : `thAx` *is* $\mathcal{T}$-*consistent.*
2. *If* `false` *succeeds from* P *residuating a set of constraints* $\mathcal{U}$, *then* I : `thAx` *is inconsistent with respect to* $\mathcal{T} \cup \mathcal{U}$.

In the first case, SnaC accepts I : `thAx` as a $\mathcal{T}$-consistent snapshot. In the second, $\mathcal{U}$ being empty signals inconsistency. If $\mathcal{U}$ is not empty, it is returned as an answer.

A more general result can be established admitting a larger class of simple properties and PD constraints, via techniques similar to those used in CLP, such as *constraint systems* [7]. Roughly, we can consider $\mathcal{T}$ as a program of a CLP system whose calculus is an extension of the standard logic programming operational semantics and where the constraint system is the Herbrand universe under CET, modified to deal with Skolem constants.

3.2   Validating Specifications Via SG

One of the purposes of snapshot generation is understanding and validating a CooML specification. To this aim, the user can specify suitable *generation requirements* in order to reduce the number of generated examples to a manageable size and show only the aspects he is interested in. We explain the language of generation requirements and its semantics through our example. It may be helpful to keep in mind the analogy with the behaviour of an *answer set* program during grounding.

In the implementation, the number of generated snapshots can be limited by means of the the special atom `choice(A)`. This plays the role of *domain* predicates in ASP. The SG algorithm will instantiate A according to its axiomatisation. For example:

```
choice(isOf(C,'Coach',[]))  :- member(C,[c1,c2]).
choice(isOf(P,'Passenger',[T]))  :- member(P,[anna,john,ted]).
choice(isOf(T,'Trip',[C]))  :- member((T,C),  [(t1,c1),(t2,c2),(t3,c1)]).
choice(numberOfSeats(c1,3)).
choice(numberOfSeats(c2,60)).
```

instructs SG to generate one coach `c1` with 3 seats and possible trips `t1`, `t3`, and another `c2` with 60 seats and trip `t2`. The declarative meaning of `choice` is given by the axiom schema $A \rightarrow choice(A)$, which, together with the user definition of `choice`, sets up the generation requirements. The generated snapshots will satisfy the PD constraints, as well as the generation requirements.

Once the SG algorithm loads a CooML theory and the user generation requirements, it can be queried with *generation goals* (*G-goals*). A sample *G*-goal is:

$$(g1) [[3,tt], Trips] : isOf(C,'Coach',[]).$$

Since `[3,tt]:seats(C)` has information content $3 = numberOfSeats(C)$, the query looks for the information `Trips:trips(C)` for every coach C with 3 seats. More precisely, the *G*-goal includes both a generation goal ("generate all the coaches C with 3 seats that satisfy the generation requirements") and a query ("for each C, show the information on the trips assigned to it"). An answer to g1 is:

$$Trips = [[t1,tt]] \text{ and } C = c1$$

with information content

$$isOf(c1,'Coach',[]),isOf(t1, 'Trip', [c1])$$

The rest of the snapshot, including information terms for all classes in the package, is omitted for the sake of space. If the user asks for more solutions, all possible snapshots will be shown. In the above example, there are two more solutions, where `c1` has two trip assigned or none.

We now sketch some ways in which SG can be used in the process of system specification and development. This will be the focus of future work.

Validating specifications. The goal here is to show that a CooML theory "correctly" models the problem domain. Validation is empirical by nature: it relates the theory to the modeled world. The idea is to generate models that satisfy given generation requirements and check whether they match the user expectations. To this aim, it is useful to tune the generation requirements to consider separately various aspects that can be understood within a small, "human viable" number of examples, as usual in this context [8]. For instance, we may concentrate on the validation of the booking part of the

CoachCompany package. In particular, we can find some supporting evidence of the correctness of the specification in a match between the expected and actual number of snapshots, where parameters of the latter are chosen as small as possible, while preserving meaningfulness. Naturally, snapshots can be used as inputs to tools for automatic, specification-based testing generation, in the spirit of [18].

Partial and full model checking. As traditional in software model checking, here the goal is to show that, under the assumptions of the generation requirements, no snapshot satisfies an undesired property. This is obtained if the SGA finds a snapshot-inconsistency, i.e. it halts without exhibiting any snapshot. Equivalently, one can prove that every snapshot satisfies a given property by showing that its negation is snapshot-inconsistent. We call this approach *partial* model checking, because in general snapshot consistency may depend on the selection of generation requirements. We may perform full model checking if the set of generated snapshots is representative of all models of the theory w.r.t. the property under consideration.

3.3   A Schematic Algorithm

We now describe a general schema for the snapshot generation algorithm, of which SnaC is just a first rough implementation. Let $T = \langle \text{thAx}, \mathscr{T} \rangle$ be a CooML theory, where $\text{thAx} = \text{and}\{\text{clAx}(C_1), \ldots, \text{clAx}(C_n)\}$. Its information terms are represented by sets of G-goals that we call *populations*. The generation process starts from a set P_0 of G-goals to be solved, i.e. to become ground. The SGA gradually instantiates P_0, possibly generating new G-goals. It divides the population in two separate sets: ToDo, containing the G-goals not solved yet and Done, containing the solved ones. A *generation state* has the form $S = \langle \text{Done}, \text{ToDo}, \text{Closed}, \text{Info} \rangle$, where:

- Closed is a set of predicates $closed(C, \underline{e})$, which is extended when all the objects with creation class $C(\underline{e})$ have been generated. It prevents the creation of new objects of class $C(\underline{e})$ in subsequent steps.
- Info is the representation in the PD language of the information content of Done, i.e. for every $I : \text{isOf}(o, C, [\underline{e}]) \in \text{Done}$, $\text{IC}(I : Pty_C(o, \underline{e})) \subseteq \text{Info}$.

The following definitions are in order:

- A state S is *in solved form* if $\text{ToDo} = \emptyset$.
- $\text{Dom}(S) = \{ \text{isOf}(o, C, [\underline{e}]) \mid I : \text{isOf}(o, C, [\underline{e}]) \in \text{Done} \cup \text{ToDo} \}$.
- $S_1 \preceq S_2$ for $S_i = \langle \text{Done}_i, \text{ToDo}_i, \text{Closed}_i, \text{Info}_i \rangle$ iff
    1. $\text{Done}_1 \subseteq \text{Done}_2$, $\text{Dom}(S_1) \subseteq \text{Dom}(S_2)$ and $\text{Info}_1 \subseteq \text{Info}_2$;
    2. If $closed(C, \underline{e}) \in \text{Closed}_1$, then
       $\text{isOf}(o, C, [\underline{e}]) \in \text{Dom}(S_1)$ iff $\text{isOf}(o, C, [\underline{e}]) \in \text{Dom}(S_2)$.

The SGA starts from initial state $S_0 = \langle \emptyset, \text{ToDo}_0, \emptyset, \emptyset \rangle$ and yields a *solution state* $S = \langle \text{Done}, \emptyset, \text{Closed}, \text{Info} \rangle$ such that $S_0 \preceq S$; since $\text{ToDo} = \emptyset$, for every $I : \text{isOf}(o, C, [\underline{e}]) \in \text{ToDo}_0$, Done contains a ground information term $(I : \text{isOf}(o, C, [\underline{e}]))\sigma$ solving it. The algorithm computes a solution of S_0 that is minimal with respect to $\preceq$ through a sequence of *expansion steps*. The latter are triples $\langle S, I : \text{isOf}(o, C, [\underline{e}]), S' \rangle$ such that:

p1. $I : \text{isOf}(o, C, [\underline{e}]) \in \text{TODO}$ (the selected goal);

p2. $(I : \text{isOf}(o, C, [\underline{e}]))\sigma \in \text{DONE}'$ and $I : \text{isOf}(o, C, [\underline{e}]) \notin \text{TODO}'$ (it has been solved);

p3. $S \prec S'$ and, for every S^* in solved form, $S \prec S^* \preceq S'$ entails $S^* = S'$ (no solution is ignored).

The high-level code for a non deterministic SGA based on expansion steps is listed in Fig.4, where TODO_0 are the G-goals to be solved under theory $\langle \text{thAx}, \mathcal{T} \rangle$ and generation requirements $\mathcal{G}$. The SGA is a general schema, whose core is the implementation of the expansion steps, predicates $\text{error}(S)$ and $\text{globalError}(S)$. The latter are based on the ideas presented in Section 3.1. They use the integrity constraints false $:- B$ to detect inconsistency and store in the variable UC the "unsolved constraints". To ensure the correctness of SG, an implementation has to guarantee properties p1, p2, p3 of expansion steps as well as the following requirements:

(i) When new objects or new witnesses (for exi) are generated in an expansion step, they are chosen according to the generation requirements, in such a way that $\text{INFO}_S \models \mathcal{G}$ for every generated state S.

(ii) When $\text{error}(S)$ returns "true", then $\text{INFO}_{S'}$ is inconsistent w.r.t. $\mathcal{T}$ for every S' such that $S \preceq S'$ (S included).

(iii) If $\text{globalError}(S)$ returns "true", then INFO_S is inconsistent with respect to $\mathcal{T}$. If it returns "false", then either UC is empty and $\text{INFO}_S \cup \mathcal{T}$ is consistent or $\text{INFO}_S \cup \mathcal{T} \cup UC$ is inconsistent.

SG $(\langle \text{thAx}, \mathcal{T} \rangle, \mathcal{G}, ToDo_0)$

1    $Thy = \text{thAx}; PDAx = \mathcal{T} \cup \mathcal{G}; S = \langle \emptyset, ToDo_0, \emptyset, \emptyset \rangle; UC = \emptyset;$

2   **while** $ToDo \neq \emptyset$ **do**

3   **if** $\text{error}(S)$ **fail**;

4   **else** % *Generation Step:*

5   Choose $I : \text{isOf}(o, C, [\underline{e}]) \in ToDo$ and compute $\langle S, I : \text{isOf}(o, C, [\underline{e}]), S' \rangle$;

6            $S = S'$;

7   **if** $\text{globalError}(S)$ **fail**;

8   **else return** S, UC

Fig. 4. The SG Algorithm

The current implementation is essentially based on a refinement of the meta-interpreter considered in Section 3.1. It could be improved, namely in detecting more than trivial inconsistencies; indeed, no constraint simplification is supported.

To state the adequacy results, we introduce some additional notation (ITP) in order to associate a class C_j and population P with their information terms:

$$\text{ITP}(P, C_j) = [\, [\, [o_{j_1}, \underline{e}_{j_1}], I_{j_1}\,], \ldots, [\, [o_{j_k}, \underline{e}_{j_k}], I_{j_k}\,]\,]$$

$$\text{ITP}(P) = [\, \text{ITP}(P, C_1), \ldots, \text{ITP}(P, C_n)\,]$$

where, $I_{j_1} : \mathtt{isOf}(o_{j_1}, C_j, [\underline{e}_{j_1}]), \ldots, I_{j_k} : \mathtt{isOf}(o_{j_k}, C_j, [\underline{e}_{j_k}])$ are the G-goals of P with class C_j $(1 \leq j \leq n)$; if no G-goal with class C_j belongs to P, then $\mathrm{ITP}(P, C_j)$ is the empty list.

Theorem 4 (Correctness). *Let $S^* = \langle \mathrm{DONE}^*, \emptyset, \mathrm{CLOSED}^*, \mathrm{INFO}^* \rangle$ be a state computed by SG with theory $T = \langle \mathtt{thAx}, \mathscr{T} \rangle$ and generation requirements $\mathscr{G}$, and let $I^* = \mathrm{ITP}(\mathrm{DONE}^*)$ be the information term of the population DONE^*. Then, either UC is empty and $I^* : \mathtt{thAx}$ is $\mathscr{G} \cup \mathscr{T}$-consistent, or $I^* : \mathtt{thAx}$ is inconsistent with respect to $\mathscr{G} \cup \mathscr{T} \cup UC$.*

The proof follows from properties (i), (ii) and (iii).

Theorem 5 (Completeness). *Let $S_0 = \langle \emptyset, \mathrm{TODO}_0, \emptyset, \emptyset \rangle$ be an initial state of SG with theory T and generation requirements $\mathscr{G}$. If there is a state $S = \langle \mathrm{DONE}, \emptyset, \mathrm{CLOSED}, \mathrm{INFO} \rangle$ such that $S_0 \preceq S$, then the SGA reaches a state S^* in solved form such that $S_0 \preceq S^* \preceq S$.*

The proof follows from properties p1, p2 and p3.

4 Related Work and Conclusion

We have presented some features of the object-oriented modeling language CooML, a language in the spirit of UML, but based on a constructive semantics, in particular the BHK explanation of logical correctives. We have introduced a proof-theoretic notion of snapshot based on populations of objects and information terms, from which snapshot generation algorithms can be designed. More technically, we have introduced generation goals and the notion of minimal solution of such goals in the setting of a CooML specification, and we have outlined a non-deterministic generation algorithm, showing how finite minimal solutions can be, in principle, generated. We use a constraint language in order to specify the general properties of the problem domain, as well as the generation requirements. In an implementation of the SGA we assume a consistency checking algorithm, which either establishes the (in)consistency of the current snapshot, or residuates a set of unsolved constraints.

The relevance of SG for validation and testing in OO software development is widely acknowledged. The USE tool [8] for validation of UML/OCL models has been recently extended with a SG mechanism; differently from us, this is achieved via a procedural language. Other animation tools [4] are based on JML specification. In [2] the specification of features models are translated into SAT problems; tentative solutions are then propagated with a Truth Maintenance System. If a inconsistency is discovered the TMS explains the causes in view of possible model repair. Related work includes also [16], where design space specs are seen as trees whose nodes are constrained by OCL statements and BDD's are used to find solutions.

Snapshot generation is only one of CooML's aspects, once we put our software engineering glasses on and see it more generally as a *specification* rather than modeling language [12,9]. In this paper we have not considered *methods*, although the underlying logic supports a clean notion of (correct) *query* methods, namely those that do not update the system state, but extract pieces of information from it. The existence of a method M answering P (i.e., computing $I : P$) is guaranteed when P is a constructive logical consequence of thAx. Moreover, M can be extracted from a constructive proof of P. The implementation of query and update methods is a crucial part of future work.

We also plan to improve and extend the snapshot generation algorithm. There are two directions that we can pursue; first, we can fully embrace CLP as a PD logic, strengthening the connection that we have only scratched in Section 3.1. In the current prototype there is little emphasis on the simplification of unsolved constraints. This could be partially ameliorated by adopting CLP, in particular over finite domains. More in general, it is desirable to relate Theorem 3 with the notion of satisfaction-completeness in constraint systems [7]. Another direction comes from the relation between CooML's approach to incomplete information and answer set programming [1, 17], in particular disjunctive LP [13]. A naive extension of the SGA to this case would yield inefficient solutions, yet the literature offers several ways constraints and ASP may interact [14, 5]. We may explore the possibility of combining snapshot generation with SAT provers, to which we may pass ground unsolved constraints in order to check global consistency. Finally we intend to explore the more general issue of the relationships between information terms and stable models, in particular partial stable models [21]; some initial results are presented in [20].

References

1. Baral, C.: Knowledge Representation, Reasoning and Declarative Problem Solving. In: CUP (2003)
2. Batory, D.S.: Feature models, grammars, and propositional formulas. In: Obbink, H., Pohl, K. (eds.) SPLC 2005. LNCS, vol. 3714, pp. 7–20. Springer, Heidelberg (2005)
3. Boronat, A., Oriente, J., Gómez, A., Ramos, I., Carsí, J.A.: An algebraic specification of generic OCL queries within the Eclipse modeling framework. In: Rensink, A., Warmer, J. (eds.) ECMDA-FA 2006. LNCS, vol. 4066, pp. 316–330. Springer, Heidelberg (2006)
4. Bouquet, F., Dadeau, F., Legeard, B., Utting, M.: JML-testing-tools: A symbolic animator for JML specifications using CLP. In: Halbwachs, N., Zuck, L.D. (eds.) TACAS 2005. LNCS, vol. 3440, pp. 551–556. Springer, Heidelberg (2005)
5. Buccafurri, F., et al.: Strong and weak constraints in disjunctive Datalog. In: Dix et al. [6]. pp. 2–17.
6. Dix, J., Furbach, U., Nerode, A. (eds.): LPNMR 1997. LNCS, vol. 1265. Springer, Heidelberg (1997)
7. Fruewirth, T., Abdennadher, S.: Essentials of Constraint Programming. Springer, New York (2003)
8. Gogolla, M., Bohling, J., Richters, M.: Validating UML and OCL models in USE by automatic snapshot generation. Software and System Modeling 4(4), 386–398 (2005)
9. Guttag, J.V., Horning, J.J.: Larch: languages and tools for formal specification. Springer, New York, Inc., New York, NY, USA (1993)
10. Jackson, D., Wing, J.: Lightweight formal method. IEEE Computer, Los Alamitos (1996)
11. Larman, C.: Applying UML and Patterns: An Introduction to Object-Oriented Analysis and Design and Iterative Development. Prentice Hall, Upper Saddle River, NJ (2004)
12. Leavens, G.T., Baker, A.L., Ruby, C.: Preliminary design of JML: A behavioral interface specification language for Java. SIGSOFT Softw. Eng. Notes 31(3), 1–38 (2006)

13. Leone, N., et al.: The DLV system for knowledge representation and reasoning. ACM Trans. Comput. Log. 7(3), 499–562 (2006)
14. Marek, V.W., et al.: Logic programs with monotone cardinality atoms. In: Lifschitz, V., Niemelä, I. (eds.) LPNMR 2004. LNCS (LNAI), vol. 2923, pp. 154–166. Springer, Heidelberg (2003)
15. Miglioli, P., Moscato, U., Ornaghi, M., Usberti, G.: A constructivism based on classical truth. Notre Dame Journal of Formal Logic 30(1), 67–90 (1989)
16. Neema, S., et al.: Constraint-based design-space exploration and model synthesis. In: Alur, R., Lee, I. (eds.) EMSOFT 2003. LNCS, vol. 2855, pp. 290–305. Springer, Heidelberg (2003)
17. Niemelä, I., Simons, P.: Smodels - an implementation of the stable model and well-founded semantics for normal lp. In: Dix et al. [6]. pp. 421–430
18. Offutt, J., Abdurazik, A.: Generating tests from UML specifications. In: France, R.B., Rumpe, B. (eds.) UML 1999. LNCS, vol. 1723, pp. 416–429. Springer, Heidelberg (1999)
19. Ornaghi, M., Benini, M., Ferrari, M., Fiorentini, C., Momigliano, A.: A constructive object oriented modeling language for information systems. ENTCS 153(1), 67–90 (2006)
20. Ornaghi, M., Fiorentini, C.: Answer set semantics vs. information term semantics. In: Informal Proceedings of ASP 2007: Answer Set Programming: Advances in Theory and Implementation, http://cooml.dsi.unimi.it/papers/asp.pdf
21. Przymusinski, T.C.: Well-founded and stationary models of logic programs. Ann. Math. Artif. Intell. 12(3–4), 141–187 (1994)
22. Troelstra, A.S.: From constructivism to computer science. TCS 211(1–2), 233–252 (1999)
23. Warmer, J., Kleppe, A.: The Object Constraint Language: Precise Modelling with UML. In: Object Technology Series, Addison-Wesley, Reading/MA (1999)

Synthesis of Data Views for Communicating Processes

Iman Poernomo

Department of Computer Science,
King's College London, Strand, London, WC2R2LS
iman.poernomo@kcl.ac.uk

Abstract. Proofs-as-programs is an approach to program synthesis involving the transformation of constructive proofs of specification requirements into functional programs. Various authors have adapted the proofs-as-programs to other logics and programming paradigms. This paper presents an adaptation of proofs-as-programs for the synthesis of *distributed* program protocols with *side-effect-free data views*, from proofs in a constructive proof-system for Hennessy-Milner logic.

1 Introduction

System components interact with clients by two means: they expose methods to change their state, and provide side-effect-free data views of their state. Often, a system requires that such communication adheres to a protocol or order. For instance, in a banking component, the data on an account holder's bank balance should not be accessed prior to the account holder entering a correct identification code. This paper is concerned with the specification and synthesis of such data retrieval protocols.

This paper describes an augmented version of Milner's Calculus of Communicating systems for defining data retrieval protocols, a novel approach to the specification of data retrieval protocols based on traditional realizability notions and a deductive system for simultaneously deriving protocols and their specification.

We will be specifying and synthesizing the behaviour of distributed programs built on a synchronous and asynchronous messaging infrastructure. In particular, we address an important and relatively unexplored issue in the formal development of complex systems: the synthesis of complex, side-effect-free data views for distributed programs. Data views are an important aspect of all software. In object-oriented terms, they are often implemented as accessor methods that enable clients to obtain information about the state that an object encapsulates. In the case of enterprise applications, data views implement domain-specific business logic and are consequently difficult to specify and implement correctly. Our work uses proofs-as-programs techniques to specify and develop provably correct complex data views in tandem with distributed programs.

Rather than work with a specific programming language, we will consider an abstract coordination language to model distributed data retrieval protocols.

King, A. (Ed.): LOPSTR 2007, LNCS 4915, pp. 185–200, 2008.

Our coordination language consists of Milner's Calculus of Communicating Systems (*CCS*) [5] without fixed points, extended with extra constructs to denote data views that can be accessed at certain points in a system execution. Terms of our language can be easily transformed into actual systems. Basic components are modelled as *CCS* processes. *CCS* messages represent side-effect producing methods of component interfaces and data views represent side-effect-free accessor methods of interfaces. The absence of recursion corresponds to the absence of feedback loops within component architectures (the usual situation in case of enterprise systems). Synchronous and asynchronous communication between components is modelled via *CCS* message exchange. Data views of components are represented as lambda terms.

An important aspect of our language is that it supports the modelling of system protocols – the orders in which messages should be received and sent. We extend the traditional representation of a system protocol in the *CCS* to include data views. There are points in a system's execution where data views should not be accessed. For instance, as part of a security protocol, an authorizing message might need to be received to enable access to confidential data. Our language enables us to model such protocols.

We specify program behaviour as modal Hennessy-Milner formulae and provide a constructive proof system for reasoning with these specifications. Hennessy-Milner formulae are not enough to specify associated data views and the logic alone cannot be used to synthesize required views. We will define a method for data views and their dynamic behaviour with respect to system execution. We shall be able to specify two aspects of data view behaviour. *1. Functional behaviour.* We can specify what kind of values a data view should have, with respect to an associated system description. *2. Dynamic behaviour.* As a system executes, the value of a data view will evolve. The accessor method of an object will not necessarily produce the same result at different stages in the object's lifetime, as the state of the object will change. We will show how to specify modal development in data view values: requirements of data view evolution and protocols with respect to message activity. Our method adapts notions of constructive realizability to make such specifications, enabling a synthesis methodology that adapts traditional proofs-as-programs to extract data retrieval protocols from proofs of their specification.

This paper proceeds as follows. Section 2 summarizes how architectures with data views can be modelled as communicating processes using an augmented version of the *CCS*. Section 3 defines the Hennessy-Milner formulae, explaining how these formulae specify behaviour of *CCS* processes and, by extending realizability notions, data views. Section 4 presents our Hennessy-Milner logic and shows how proofs of the logic can be encoded within a logical type theory. We sketch the idea of proofs-as-distributed-programs in Section 5. We briefly review related work and provide concluding remarks in section 6.

2   Architectures with Data Views

A software architecture is generally understood to be a configuration of black-box components, connected to each other by lines of communication [4]. We will use an extension of the UML2 superstructure [6] to visually represent distributed, message-based, component-based architectures. We will then define a language that gives an operational semantics for how an architecture can behave. The language combines Milner's Calculus of Communicating Systems (*CCS*), providing concurrency and communication primitives, with a simply lambda calculus with disjoint unions and sums.

The treatment of distributed component architectures via *CCS* is well understood in the software architecture community, but an important aspect of our treatment is the explicit identification of data views.

Component architectures and data views. We review some standard concepts of system architecture design and explain how data views are to be understood.

Basic components. Basic components are the building blocks of a system architecture, designating encapsulated nodes of computation. Components can communicate in three ways: *Receiving messages.* A message is received by a component to initiate computation. Sets of messages that may be received are exposed by components as provided interfaces. *Sending messages.* A message is sent by a component to communicate with other components. Sets of messages that may be sent are exposed by components as required interfaces. *Providing data views.* The sending and receipt of messages is a way of invoking computation on components. Computation results in changes to a component's internal state. A component's state is accessed via data views, side-effect-free functions that interpret the state according to the business logic of the required system.

In UML2, basic components are visually represented as in Fig. 1(a). The lollipop denotes a provided interface. The socket denotes a required interface. We extend the UML2 with a triangle symbol to denote side-effect-free data views that are associated with component. (The triangle symbol is a superfluous extension, as it essentially corresponds to a list of the accessor methods that are associated with a UML2 component. However, for our purposes, it is useful to make data views explicit in architectural diagrams.)

For the purposes of simplicity, we will make the assumption that each interface consists of one method: a provided interface is a message that can be received and a required interface is a message that can be sent.

Protocols. A component protocol is the order in which messages may be sent and received by a component and in which data views may be invoked. In the simplest case, views can be accessed and messages can be input and output in

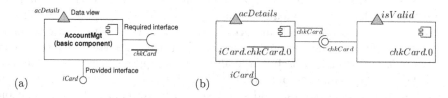

Fig. 1. (a) Visual representation of a basic component. (b) Example architecture.

any order. However, more commonly, a particular input message will result in specific output messages, and data views should be accessed at prescribed points in a computation sequence.

Example 1. Consider the banking component *AccoumtMgt* of Fig. 1 (a). The component's provided interface permits the input of a credit card number by receiving the message *iCard*. The component's required interface enables the checking of a card's validity by sending the message *chkCard*.

The data view for the program is the term *acDetails*, which outputs details about the account associated with the card. The view does not affect the state of a component. Rather, it provides information *about* the state of the component. The data view is a vital part of the component: it might be used within a larger system for displaying account details on an automated teller machine screen or on an internet banking website.

Clearly, the component should never send a request to check a card's validity without first obtaining the card's number. Also, for security purposes, account details should not be accessed via the data view before a validity check is made on the card. The protocol of the system must therefore be the following ordering:

$$iCard \rightarrow chkCard \rightarrow acDetails$$

Component communication. Synchronous communication between two components is visually represented by a connection between provided and required interfaces. The potential for asychronous communication will be denoted by unconnected, but matching, provided and required interfaces exposed by components at the same level of architectural abstraction (that is, occuring where a connection could be made).

Example 2. An example of two components in synchronous communication is given in Fig. 1(b). The left hand component is taken from Example 1. The right hand component is used to check a bank card's validity, via the provided method *chkCard*. The message *chkCard* is restricted to be synchronized between the two components.

A *system architecture* consists of a set of components with connections between them.

CCS **with data views.** We have just described how system architectures are defined according to UML2. A notation such as UML2 is useful to identify the static structure and composition of a component-based system. It is equally important to identify the dynamic behaviour of a system – e.g., how it will react to messages, what protocols are accepted, etc. A formal definition of dynamic behaviour that is compositionally associated with static system architecture descriptions is particularly useful for analysis. In our approach, we use an extension of the *CCS* to define the operational semantics of our architectures. Later we will see how logical analysis and synthesis can be developed due to this choice of formalism.

We define the set of *Actions* to consist of incoming messages m and outgoing messages $\bar{m}$ with m ranging over some set of messages. The grammar for our extension, *CCS* with data views (hereafter denoted by the overloaded *CCS*) is given as follows.

$$CCS := 0 \mid X \mid (p+q) \mid (p|q) \mid p/s \mid s.p \mid \mu X.p \mid (p \; view \; t)$$

where $p, q \in CCS$, X is ranges over a given set of variables $TVar$, s ranges over *Actions* and t is a closed lambda term for a signature $Term(\Sigma)$, now defined. Our approach is parametrized by the choice of a *many-sorted signature* $\Sigma = \langle S, TF, P \rangle$, consisting of: 1) a set S of sorts. Sorts are generated from a set of *basic sorts*, $B(S)$ according to the following inductive definition. First, $B(S) \subseteq S$. Also, if s_1 and s_2 are in S, then so are the function sort $(s_1 \rightarrow s_2)$, the product sort $(s_1 * s_2)$ and the disjoint union $(s_1|s_2)$. We assume that $B(S)$ includes a special sort, called *Unit*. 2) sorted function symbols, TF. We assume a single inhabitant () of the sort $Unit \in B(S)$. 3) sorted predicate symbols P of predicate symbols. We define the *terms* for a signature $\Sigma = \langle S, TF, P \rangle$, $Term(\Sigma)$ generated over variables from a set Var:

$$Term(\Sigma) := e \mid x \mid Inl(p) \mid Inr(p) \mid match \; p \; with \; Inl(x) => q \mid Inr(y) => r$$
$$fun \; x : s => p \mid (p \; q) \mid (p, q) \mid fst(p) \mid snd(p)$$

Terms consist of terms generated by the signature, extended to include a lambda calculus, written in an *SML* style syntax. *Inl* and *Inr* are constructors used to form disjoint unions.

Process terms form a semantics of system architectures in the following standard sense. A *CCS* process denotes the state of a distributed system in terms of its ability to perform actions and the protocol in which actions are to be performed. Actions are either sending or receiving messages or internal computation. Incoming and outgoing message actions are denoted by letters, taken from the same set, with outgoing messages marked by an overbar (¯). The τ action designates internal computation (processing that is not observable to a client). Proceses are built using the standard recursion, non-deterministic choice, parallel composition and action sequencing constructs of [5].

Terms of the calculus can be understood to directly denote compositional, behavioural specifications of the elements of system architecture that were previously described: basic components, compound components, encapsulation and architectures consisting of these elements.

The semantics of a basic component is understood as its protocol. This can be represented easily within our syntax. Required protocols are specified using the action sequencing operator, with the protocol order given by the order of actions and data views.

Example 3. For example, the protocol for the *AccountMgt* component of Example 1 is given as

$$iCard.\overline{chkCard}.(0 \; view \; acDetails)$$

The operational semantics shows this term has the required protocol: to access *acDetails*, the term must first input the card and then send a request for verification.

Parallel composition of components, permitting asychronous communication is simply achieved via the | operator. The hiding operator is understood in *CCS* to restrict communication, so that a/m means that the action m cannot communicate with terms outside of a/m, only with subterms of a. Sychronous communication corresponds to the parallel composition of terms, with the sychronized message hidden. Continuing example 3, the parallel composition $iCard.\overline{chkCard}.0|chkCard.0/chkCard$ represents synchronous communication between two components.

Data views are functions that access the state of the distributed system and provide information on it. The domain-specific function symbols of Σ provide basic data views. More complex combinations of functional views are provided as lambda terms of $Term(\Sigma)$. A data view t is associated with a process p via the constructor $(p\ view\ t)$.

Example 4. For example, the process term

$$((iCard.\overline{chkCard}.0)\ view\ acDetails)|((chkCard.0)\ view\ isValid)/chkCard$$

involves the same process constructors as the term above, but with data views inserted. The data views for the program are the domain-specific functions *acDetails* and *isValid* from Σ. The former view outputs details about the account owner associated with the card. The latter view is a boolean function whose output tells us if the card is valid or not. Note that the views do not affect the state of the system – they provide information about how the state of the system is affected by the execution of the basic distributed *CCS* terms. For instance, *acDetails* will return an error record if the *chkCard* request is made and it is determined that the card number is invalid.

In component terms, we can consider the left and right processes as states of components, and data views as side-effect-free accessor methods of component interfaces.

Operational semantics of *CCS*. The way in which *CCS* programs evaluate is given by a labelled transition system semantics. A process p can receive or send a message m, resulting in a new process p', denoted by a labelled transition $p \xrightarrow{m} p'$. The rules of Fig. 2 define when a process can make a transition to a new process in terms of possible transitions of subprocesses. All the rules except (pure) are standard and well-understood (see [5] for full motivation). For example, the rules (synch₁) and (synch₂) say that message synchronization can occur between the parallel composition of processes p and q, if one process can output a message via action m and the other can receive the message via matching action $\bar{m}$.

The (pure) rule is specific to our system. The rule says that, views can be discarded in the evaluation of a system.

The semantics of lambda terms is given by the usual reduction rules. We assume that, when a function symbol is applied to arguments of appropriate

$$\frac{}{\bar{a}.p|a.q \xrightarrow{\tau} p|q} \text{ (sync}_1\text{)} \qquad \frac{}{a.p|\bar{a}.q \xrightarrow{\tau} p|q} \text{ (sync}_2\text{)}$$

$$\frac{p_1 \xrightarrow{m} p_2}{p_1|q \xrightarrow{m} p_2|q} \text{ (conc}_1\text{)} \qquad \frac{q_1 \xrightarrow{m} q_2}{p|q_1 \xrightarrow{m} p|q_2} \text{ (conc}_2\text{)}$$

$$\frac{p_1 \xrightarrow{m} p_2}{p_1+q \xrightarrow{m} p_2} \text{ (choice}_1\text{)} \qquad \frac{q_1 \xrightarrow{m} q_2}{p+q_1 \xrightarrow{m} q_2} \text{ (choice}_2\text{)}$$

$$\frac{p_1[\mu X.p_1/X] \xrightarrow{m} p_2}{\mu X.p_1 \xrightarrow{\tau} p_2} \text{ (rec)} \qquad \frac{p \xrightarrow{m} q}{(p \text{ view } f) \xrightarrow{m} q} \text{ (pure)}$$

$$\frac{p_1 \xrightarrow{m} p_2 \quad m \text{ is not } n}{p_1/n \xrightarrow{\tau} p_2/n} \text{ (encap}_1\text{)} \qquad \frac{p_1 \xrightarrow{m} p_2 \quad m \text{ is } n}{p_1/n \xrightarrow{m} p_2} \text{ (encap}_2\text{)}$$

Fig. 2. Operational semantics for CCS programs with data views

arities and types, *within the context of a state of process evaluation*, it should always evaluate to an answer, which can be represented as another term of $Term(\Sigma)$. This assumption is formalized by means of a mapping $Eval_p$ indexed by process p, that gives the return value term for a function application, with respect to p. Given a process p, a function symbol $f \in TF_{s_1\ldots s_n,s}$ and arguments $(a_1,\ldots,a_n)$ of sort $(s_1 * \ldots * s_n)$, $Eval_p(f(a_1,\ldots,a_n))$ returns a term from $Term(\Sigma)$ of sort s.

Example 5. Consider a domain-specific API for an online romantic dating service. Users may specify desirable requirements of a date, which are then given in XML format to the system for processing. The system should recommend a date from its database that is the best match to these requirements. Depending on the state of the system (the availability of matching persons), the match might closer to or further from the requirements. The matching function is represented in Σ as a function symbol $POtoPS : XML \to XML$, which, given requirements in XML, returns a match in XML. Let o be a list of requirements that specify, say, a female nonsmoker in their 20s. The evaluation of the term $POtoPS(o))$ will have an answer that will depend on the process t under consideration. If t is a process term that denotes a state where a twentysomething female nonsmoker is available, then $Eval_t(POtoPS(o))$ will provide her as a match. However, if t is a process term that denotes a state in which there are only female smokers in their 20s, then $Eval_t(POtoPS(o))$ will provide an empty record.

For the purposes of generality, we do not explicitly define $Eval_p$ for the function symbols that occur in lambda terms. Instead, we assume that $Eval_p$ is always defined according to the domain's API specification. We assume that $Eval_p$ is so defined that repeated applications of $\triangleright_\Sigma$ always terminate. We write $\hat{\triangleright}_{\Sigma,p}$ for the transitive closure of $\triangleright_{\Sigma,p}$, and say that a *evaluates* to b if $a \,\hat{\triangleright}_{\Sigma,p}\, b$.

Definition 1. *We define the relation $\overset{m}{\Rightarrow}$ to hold between two terms a and b when b evolves from a via the action m with possibly some number of τ transitions in between:* $a = \underbrace{a_0 \xrightarrow{\tau} a_1 \xrightarrow{\tau} \ldots \xrightarrow{\tau} a_i}_{0 \leq i} \xrightarrow{m} \underbrace{b_0 \xrightarrow{\tau} b_1 \xrightarrow{\tau} b_j}_{0 \leq j} = b$

3   Specification of System Architectures

We use modal many-sorted formulae to specify and reason about two related aspects of our architectures: possible behaviours and possible data views. This understanding of formulae as specifications is key to our adaptation of proofs-as-programs. Behavioural specification is understood according to the usual semantics due to Hennessy and Milner. Data views are specified as constructive content, by adapting notions of modified realizability.

Formulae. Many-sorted formulae, $WFF(\Sigma)$, for a signature $\Sigma = \langle S, TF, P \rangle$ are constructed according to the following definition, given with respect to the denumerable set of term variables, Var_s indexed by sorts s. 1) $Q(t_1, \ldots, t_n)$ where $Q \in P_{s_1 \ldots s_n}$ is a predicate symbol in Q and every t_i ($i = 1, \ldots, n$) is a well-sorted lambda term of sort s_i. 2) If $x \in Var_s$ and A, B are in $WFF(\Sigma)$ then so are $(A \wedge B)$, $(A \vee B)$, $(A \Rightarrow B)$, $\forall x : s \bullet A$ and $\exists x : s \bullet A$. 3) If $A \in WFF(\Sigma)$ and m is a process term (with possible data views), then so is $[m]F$. 4) $\perp \in WFF(\Sigma)$. We often write $\neg A$ for $(A \Rightarrow \perp)$. (Note that we employ quantification with functional sorts. This enables us to reason with and specify typed lambda terms using our formulae.)

Behavioural specification. Possible behaviour is specified in the standard fashion for Hennessy-Milner formulae with many-sorted quantification. Properties of distributed programs are described using ordinary many-sorted formulae. For instance, consider a network containing several machines storing copies of an identical database. Assume the sort $Location$ denotes the finite number of IP addresses for these machines, and the predicate $ConnectedDB(x)$ denotes that a connection to the database has been made to the machine at IP address x. Then formula $\exists l : Location \bullet ConnectedDB(l)$ describes program behaviour in which a connection to the database at particular host has been achieved.

Definition 2. *A formula F is true of the behaviour of a term t, written $t \Vdash F$, according to the following recursive definition:*

- *If F is atomic, then $h(F, t) = True$.*
- *If $F \equiv \forall x : T \bullet G$, then for every $a : T$, $t \Vdash G[a/x]$.*
- *If $F \equiv \exists x : T \bullet G$, then there is an $a : T$ such that $t \Vdash G[a/x]$.*
- *If $F \equiv G \vee H$, then $t \Vdash G$ or $t \Vdash H$.*
- *If $F \equiv G \wedge H$, then $t \Vdash G$ and $t \Vdash H$.*
- *If $F \equiv G \Rightarrow H$, then $t \Vdash G$ entails $t \Vdash H$.*
- *If $F \equiv [m]G$, then for every u where $t \overset{m}{\Rightarrow} u$ it is the case that $u \Vdash G$.*
- *If $F \equiv \langle m \rangle G$, then there is a u such that $t \overset{m}{\Rightarrow} u$ and $u \Vdash G$.*
- *$t \vdash \perp$ is never true.*

Specification of data views. A specification of a data view defines the required behaviour of a data view function at a state in a system's execution. Data views are specified as required constructive content of formulae, in a fashion analogous to how functional programs are specified as constructive content of intuitionistic formulae in the proofs-as-programs approach. For instance, the

F	xsort(F)
$P(\bar{a})$	$Unit$
$A \wedge B$	$\begin{cases} \text{xsort}(A) & \text{if not } Harrop(B) \\ \text{xsort}(B) & \text{if not } Harrop(A) \\ \text{xsort}(A) * \text{xsort}(B) & \text{otherwise} \end{cases}$
$A \vee B$	$\text{xsort}(A)|\text{xsort}(B)$
$A \to B$	$\begin{cases} \text{xsort}(B) & \text{if not } Harrop(B) \\ \text{xsort}(A) \to \text{xsort}(B) & \text{otherwise} \end{cases}$
$\forall x : S.A$	$s \to \text{xsort}(A)$
$\exists x : S.A$	$\begin{cases} s & \text{if } Harrop(A) \\ s * \text{xsort}(A) & \text{otherwise} \end{cases}$
$\perp$	$Unit$

Fig. 3. The map xsort(F) from formulae to Σ sorts

formula $\exists l : Location \bullet ConnectedDB(l)$ can also be seen as specifying a process that *evaluates with a data view* whose content is a constructive witness for l, the location of the database which the process has connected to.

We utilize modalities to specify how a data view function might behave at some future stage in a processes's execution. For instance, the formula $\langle iCard \rangle \exists d : Account \bullet ValidDetails(d)$ specifyies a realizing a data view r of a program. The formula requires that, if the program receives a message $iCard$, then *possibly* the program provides an output data view r, acting as the witness for d, such that r is a valid account record (not an error record, when $ValidDetails(r)$ is true). The program $(iCard.\overline{chkCard}.0 \text{ } view \text{ } acDetails)$ satisifes this specification, as there are possible executions after receiving $iCard$ such that the data view $acDetails$ is a valid account record ($ValidDetails(r)$).

To formally define how to specify data views, we first need to adapt the definitions of Harrop formulae and the Skolem form to Hennessy-Milner formulae.

Definition 3 (Harrop formulae). *A formula F is a Harrop formula if it is 1) an atomic formula, 2) of the form $(A \wedge B)$ where A and B are Harrop formulae, 3) of the form $(A \to B)$ where B (but not necessarily A) is a Harrop formula, 4) of the form $(\forall x : s.A)$ where A is a Harrop formula, 5) of the form $[m]A$ where A is Harrop, or 6) of the form $\langle m \rangle B$ where B is Harrop.*

We write $Harrop(F)$ if F is a Harrop formula, and $\neg Harrop(F)$ if F is not a Harrop formula.

We use the type extraction map xsort(.) from [7], given in Fig. 3. This maps logical formulae to Σ sorts. Then we need to extend the notion of Skolem form to our modal formulae, as follow.

Definition 4 (Skolem form and Skolem functions). *Given a closed formula A, we define the Skolemization of A to be the Harrop formula $Sk(A)$ defined as follows. A unique function letter f_A (of sort xsort(A)) called the Skolem function, is associated with each A.*

- *If A is Harrop, then $Sk(A) \equiv A$.*
- *item If $A \equiv B \vee C$, then*

$$Sk(A) = (\forall x : \mathsf{xsort}(B).f_A = Inl(x) \Rightarrow Sk((B)[x/f_B]) \wedge$$
$$(\forall y : \mathsf{xsort}(C).f_A = Inr(y) \Rightarrow Sk(C)[y/f_C])$$

- *If $A \equiv B \wedge C$, then*

$$Sk(A) = Sk(B)[fst(f_A)/f_B] \wedge Sk(C)[snd(f_A)/f_C]$$

- *If $A \equiv B \rightarrow C$, then*
  - *if B is Harrop, $Sk(A) = B \rightarrow Sk(C)[f_A/f_C]$.*
  - *if B is not Harrop and C is not Harrop,*

$$Sk(A) = \forall x : s.(Sk(B)[x/f_B] \rightarrow Sk(C)[(f_A x)/f_C])$$

- *If $A \equiv \exists y : s.P$, then*
  - *when P is Harrop, $Sk(A) = Sk(P)[f_A/y]$*
  - *when P is not Harrop, $Sk(A) = Sk(P)[fst(f_A)/y][snd(f_A)/f_P]$*
- *If $A \equiv \forall x : s.P$, then $Sk(A) = \forall x : s.Sk(P)[(f_A x)/f_P]$.*
- *If $A \equiv [m]P$, then $Sk(A) = [m]Sk(P)$.*
  If $A \equiv \langle m \rangle P$, then $Sk(A) = \langle m \rangle Sk(P)$.

In a typical proofs-as-programs method such as [7], a formula A specifies a functional lambda term program p if, and only if, the program is an *intuitionistic modified realizer* of A, now defined.

Definition 5 (Intuitionistic modified realizers). *Let p be closed element of $Term(\Sigma)$. Let A be a non-modal formula. Then p is an intuitionistic modified realizer of A when $\vdash Sk(A)[p/f_A]$.*

We extend this definition to hold between process terms and formulae, to specify possible data views of processes. Data views are functional programs. So, a data view can be specified as an intuitionistic modified realizer. The presence of modal formulae permits us to formally extend the concept of realizability to specification of *possible* data views of processes. For instance, we treat modal formulae of the form $[m]B$ to specify processes whose execution of event m will result in a data view that is a Skolem formula for B.

Data views may be contained *within* process terms. This fact requires us to extend realizability to views for subterms that are contained within parallel, choice, recursion and message input or output terms. The idea is as follows. A formula can describe the view for an entire process, if such a view exists, and it can also describe visible views of subprocesses in the process. For instance, a parallel term is of the form $a|b$ or $((a|b)$ *view* $f)$. If it is the latter, then f is the data view for the process, and a formula F correctly describes this view if f is an intuitionistic realizer. If it is the former, then the term contains two data views – one for each of the subprocesses a and b. The single formula F describes this term accurately if it describes the views of both a and b as realizers.

The definition below extends these ideas recursively to all terms.

$$\frac{p \diamond A \in \mathcal{AX}}{\vdash p \diamond A} \text{ (Axiom-I)}$$

$$\frac{\vdash p^{a \diamond G} \quad \vdash q^{b \diamond G}}{\vdash \mathsf{parallel}(p,q)^{a|b \diamond G}} \text{ (parallel)} \qquad \frac{\vdash p^{a \diamond F} \quad \vdash q^{b \diamond F}}{\vdash \mathsf{union}(p,q)^{a+b \diamond F}} \text{ (union)}$$

$$\text{provided } Msg(G) \nsubseteq Msg(a) \cup Msg(b)$$

$$\frac{\vdash p^{b \diamond P} \quad a \overset{n}{\Rightarrow} b}{\vdash \mathsf{pos}(p,n)^{a \diamond \langle n \rangle P}} \text{ (pos)} \qquad \frac{\vdash p^{a \diamond P} \quad X \text{ is free in } a}{\vdash \mathsf{repl}(X.p)^{\mu X.a \diamond P}} \text{ (rec)}$$

$$\frac{\vdash p^{a \diamond P} \quad m \text{ does not occur in } P}{\vdash \mathsf{hide}(p,m)^{a/m \diamond P}} \text{ (hide)} \qquad \frac{\vdash p^{a \diamond F} \quad \vdash_{\mathsf{Int}} q^{F \Rightarrow G}}{\vdash \mathsf{cons}(p,q)^{a \diamond G}} \text{ (cons)}$$

Fig. 4. Type theoretic presentation of the structural rules of the IHM logic. The standard rules of IHM can be recovered by ignoring the proof-term subscripts, retaining only the superscript types (the program/formula pairs).

Definition 6 (Modal Realizability). *A process p is a modal realizer of a formula A, written p mr A, when the following conditions are satisfied.*

- *If A is Harrop, then $p \Vdash A$ is provable.*
- *Assume A is of the form $[m]B$. Then for all p' such that $p \overset{m}{\Rightarrow} p'$ we know that p' mr B.*
- *Otherwise,*
  - *if p is of the form $(p \text{ view } f)$, and $f \hat{\triangleright}_{\Sigma, p} answer$, then $p \Vdash Sk(A)[answer/f_A]$ holds.*
  - *If p is of the form $q|r$, then q mr A and r mr A.*
  - *If p is of the form $q + r$, then q mr A and r mr A.*
  - *If p is of the form q/m, then q mr A.*
  - *If p is of the form $\mu X.q$ then $q[\mu X.q/X]$ mr A.*

4   Deductive System

Hennessy-Milner logics are formal systems for simultaneously reasoning about and constructing *CCS* programs. A sequent-based Hennessy-Milner logic was first described in [8]. We shall employ a simpler, constructive, natural deduction version of that logic, called Intuitionistic Hennessy-Milner logic (IHM), for reasoning about and synthesizing provably correct *CCS* programs with views.

Calculus. The logic manipulates theorems, which consist of pairs of programs and formulae of the form $p \diamond F$, where the left hand side of the diamond is a process, and the right hand side is a specification of the process's behaviour.

Our system is defined with respect to a separate logical subsystem. For purposes of adapting proofs-as-programs, we take this subsystem to be intuitionistic logic, as presented in [7]. The rules of IHM can be obtained from Fig. 4. We motivate each rule as follows. 1) The (parallel) rule tells us that, if G is a property shared by two programs a and b, then G is also true of their parallel composition $a|b$. 2) The (union) rule says that, if G is a property shared by two programs a

and b, then G is also true of their nondeterministic choice composition $a + b$. 3)
The rule (pos) asserts that, if process a can possibly evolve to b by performing
action m (and possibly some internal actions), and A is known to hold over b,
then $\langle m \rangle A$ holds for a. 4) The (repl) rule says that if P is known for a then it is
known for the replication of a. 5) The (hide) rule says that if P is true of a and
does not involve a statement about m, then P is still a true statement about
a/m. 6) The (cons) rule permits us to use intuitionistically derived inferences to
conclude new things about the same process.

There is an axiom introduction rule in both subsystems Int and IHM that
allow us to develop proofs from a domain specific theory given by a set $\mathcal{AX}$ of
axioms. We assume the axioms represent a consistent and true theory of domain
specific truths about processes.

One of the important properties of the calculus is that, given a proof of a theorem $p \diamond F$, the formula F is a correct behavioural description of the process p.

Theorem 1 (Behavioural soundness). *If $\vdash p \diamond F$ then $p \Vdash F$.*

Proof. By induction on the length of the derivation $\vdash p \diamond F$.

This theorem shows that a proof of a theorem F will result in an accompanying
process that satisfies F as a behavioural specification. However, it says nothing
about the satisfaction of F as a data view specification.

We consider a process p to satisfy a process/formula pair $q \diamond A$ when 1) the
formula is true of the behaviour of p, 2) the formula correctly specifies a possible
data view of p as a modal realizer and 3) p and q are identical, modulo differences
in data views. When this is the case, we say that p is a *process realizer* of $q \diamond A$,
and we write p pr $q \diamond A$. The calculus alone is not enough to produce process
realizers. We need to employ program extraction techniques to do this. The next
step in providing such an adaptation is to define the logic as a type theory, to
encode proofs for eventual transformation.

Type-theoretic presentation. Our calculus forms a *logical type theory, LTT*,
with proofs represented as terms (called proof-terms), program/formula pairs
represented as types, and logical deduction given as type inference. The proof-
terms use a grammar similar to that of standard proofs-as-programs approaches
for denoting proofs in Int, but extended with new terms to incorporate the structural rules of the IHM. Because of the (cons) rule, proof-terms corresponding to
structural rule applications can involve proof-terms corresponding to intuitionistic logic rule application. Type theoretic presentations of Int and IHM are given
in [7] and Fig. 4, respectively. (It is important to note that this LTT is a lambda
calculus that is separate and distinct from the lambda calculus that is used for
data views.)

5   Extraction

We now outline our process of extracting process realizers from proofs of specifications. We define an extraction map extract : $LTT \rightarrow CCS$, from the terms of

$p^{w \diamond P}$	eview$(p^{w \diamond P})$
any proof-term with $H(P)$	()
Axiom$((w \ view \ f) \diamond P)$	f
cons$(q^{a \diamond A}, r^{A \Rightarrow C})$	$\begin{cases} (\text{extract}_{\text{Int}}(r) \ \text{eview}(i)) & \text{not } H(A) \\ \text{extract}_{\text{Int}}(r) & H(A) \end{cases}$

Fig. 5. View extraction, defined over non-structural proof-terms. $H(A)$ means A is a Harrop.

$p^{w \diamond P}$	extract$(p^{w \diamond P})$
any proof-term with $H(P)$	w
Axiom$((w \ view \ f) \diamond P)$	$(w \ view \ f)$
cons$(q^{a \diamond A}, r^{A \Rightarrow C})$	$(a \ view \ \text{eview}(p))$
parallel$(p^{a \diamond A}, q^{b \diamond B})$	extract(p)|extract(q)
union$(p^{a \diamond A}, q^{b \diamond B})$	extract(p) + extract(q)
pos$(q^{a \diamond A}, m)$	m.extract(q)
hide$(q^{a \diamond A}, m)$	extract$(q)/m$
repl$(X.q^{a \diamond A})$	μX.extract(q)

Fig. 6. The extraction map

the logical type theory, *LTT*, to processes of *CCS*. Our map is an extension of the usual intuitionistic extraction map extract$_{\text{Int}}$ from Int proof-terms to modified realizers, as presented in [7]. The map is extended for IHM proof-terms in Figs. 5 and 6.

We assume that the intuitionistic extraction map always takes axiom introduction proof-terms (of the form Axiom$_{\text{Int}}(A)$) to modified realizers (lambda terms that realize A). Also, we assume that each IHM axiom introduction rule is with a proof-term of the form Axiom$((l \ view \ f) \diamond A)$ such that f is a modified realizer of A and $(l \ view \ f)$ is a process realizer of A. This assumption means that axioms that specify processes and views are always transformed into programs that satisfy these specifications.

We have the following soundness result for intuitionistic extraction.

Theorem 2 (Soundness of intuitionistic extraction). *Take any intuitionistic proof, represented in the LTT as $\vdash_{\text{Int}} p^P$ Then* extract$_{\text{Int}}(p)$ *will produce a modified realizer of $P \vdash_{\text{Int}} Sk(P)[\text{extract}_{\text{Int}}(p)/f_P]$.*

Proof. The proof proceeds according to the usual proofs of extraction soundness for intuitionistic logic. The presence of modal formulae does not affect the proof.

We wish to derive a similar result for the extraction map over IHM proof-terms. However, the proof is not as straightforward as the intuitionistic case. We require the following definition of *modular* proof-terms. These are proof terms in which applications of intuitionistic reasoning never occur after (are "modular" with respect to) process building rules (parallel) or (union) for a non-Harrop formulae.

Definition 7. *A proof-term t is modular if, and only if, it does not contain subterms of the form* $\mathsf{cons}(a, b^{C \Rightarrow D})$ *where C is non-Harrop and a contains subterms of the form* $\mathsf{parallel}(p, q)$ *or* $\mathsf{union}(p, q)$.

Soundness of extraction is provable for modular proofs.

Theorem 3 (Soundness of modular proof extraction)
Consider any modular proof $\vdash r^{g \diamond G}$. *It is true that* $\mathsf{extract}(p)$ *mr* $a \diamond G$.

In general Theorem 3 does not hold. To see this, consider the following example.

Example 6. Recall the online dating example (Example 5) above. Let $PO(x)$ and $PS(y)$ be predicates over XML sheets holding, respectively, when x is a list of requirements specifying a female nonsmoker in their 20s, and when y is the best match for the user requirements. Take the proof (we omit proof-terms for the sake of space) where the all subtress are modular:

$$
\cfrac{\cfrac{\vdash (p\ view\ a) \diamond \exists x : XML \bullet PO(x) \qquad \vdash (q\ view\ b) \diamond \exists x : XML \bullet PO(x)}{\vdash (p\ view\ a)|(q\ view\ b) \diamond \exists x : XML \bullet PO(x)}\ (parallel) \qquad \cfrac{}{\vdash_{\mathsf{Int}} \exists x : XML \bullet PO(x) \Rightarrow \exists y : XML \bullet PS(y)}}{(p\ view\ a)|(q\ view\ b) \diamond \exists y : XML \bullet PS(y)}\ (cons)
$$

The process $(p\ view\ a)|(q\ view\ b)$ is not a realizer of $\exists y : XML \bullet PS(y)$, because the views a and b are, by assumption of proof modularity, witnesses for the requirements list x in $\exists x : XML \bullet PO(x)$, and the fact that the XML schema for a requirements list is different from that of a matching date.

By intuitionistic extraction, the proof of the intuitionistic inference corresponds to a function f that transforms a list of requirements into a matching date. The required process can be obtained by applying the matching function $POtoPS$ repeatedly to the two inner views a and b. This yields the correct process realizer

$$(p\ view\ POtoPS(a))|(q\ view\ POtoPS(b))$$

This can be obtained by the IHM extraction $\mathsf{extract}$ map and Theorem 3, if we first transform the proof-term for the above proof into a form where all applications of (cons) occur prior to application of (parallel), where A stands for $\exists x : XML \bullet PO(x) \Rightarrow \exists y : XML \bullet PS(y)$:

$$
\cfrac{\cfrac{\vdash (p\ view\ a) \diamond \\ \exists x : XML \bullet PO(x) \qquad \vdash_{\mathsf{Int}} A}{\vdash (p\ view\ a) \diamond \exists y : XML \bullet PS(y)}\ (cons) \qquad \cfrac{\vdash (q\ view\ b) \diamond \\ \exists x : XML \bullet PO(x) \qquad \vdash_{\mathsf{Int}} A}{\vdash (q\ view\ b) \diamond \exists y : XML \bullet PS(y)}\ (cons)}{\vdash (p\ view\ a)|(q\ view\ b) \diamond \exists y : XML \bullet PS(y)}
$$

If we have a systematic way of transforming non-modular proof-terms into equivalently typed modular proof-terms, then we can use the extraction map and Theorem 3 to obtain correct processes from proofs. This transformation is done via a normalization strategy that moves all applications of the (cons) rule up a derivation, before applications of other structural rules, in the fashion of our example. The strategy is given by a normalization relation $\rhd$, as defined by

$$
\begin{aligned}
&\mathsf{app}(\mathsf{abstract}\ X.\ a^{(A\Rightarrow B)}, b^A) && \rhd\ a[b/X]^B \\
&\mathsf{specific}(\mathsf{use}\ x:s.\ a^{\forall x:s\bullet A}, v:s) && \rhd\ a[v/x]^{A[v/x]} \\
&\pi_1(\langle a,b\rangle^{(A\wedge B)}) && \rhd\ a^A \\
&\pi_2(\langle a,b\rangle^{(A\wedge B)}) && \rhd\ b^B \\
&\mathsf{case\ inl}(a)^{A\vee B}\ \mathsf{of\ inl}(x^A).b^C,\ \mathsf{inr}(y^B).c^C && \rhd\ b[a/x]^C \\
&\mathsf{case\ inr}(a)^{A\vee B}\ \mathsf{of\ inl}(x^A).b^C,\ \mathsf{inr}(y^B).c^C && \rhd\ c[a/y]^C \\
&\mathsf{select}\ (\mathsf{show}(v,a)^{\exists y:s\bullet P})\ \mathsf{in}\ z.x^P[z/y].b^C && \rhd\ b[a/x][v/z]^C \\
&\mathsf{cons}(\mathsf{parallel}(p^{a\diamond A}, q^{b\diamond A}), r^{A\Rightarrow C}) && \rhd\ \mathsf{parallel}(\mathsf{cons}(p,r),\mathsf{cons}(q,r))^{a|b\diamond C} \\
&\mathsf{cons}(\mathsf{union}(p^{a\diamond A}, q^{b\diamond A}), r^{A\Rightarrow C}) && \rhd\ \mathsf{union}(\mathsf{cons}(p,r),\mathsf{cons}(q,r))^{a+b\diamond C}
\end{aligned}
$$

Fig. 7. The reduction rules that define $\rhd$

the rules in Fig. 7. This is the usual normalization relation (β reduction) adapted to our lambda calculus of proof-terms and to moving structural rules.

The strong normalization property tells us that the normalization process over a calculus will always terminate. To show that this property holds over our calculus, we need to show that the proof-terms are strongly normalizable, posessing only finite reduction sequences that result in normal, irreducible proof-terms.

Lemma 1. *After normalization, all proof-terms are modular.*

Then, by Theorem 1, Lemma 1 and Theorem 3, we can normalize proof-terms and then apply extract to obtain required process realizers from any proof of a specification.

6 Related Work and Conclusions

There are a number of UML-based approaches to developing distributed systems – see, for example [1,2]. However, while all such systems also involve development of data views, these approaches do not accommodate explicit data view specification. At best, any UML-based approach permits data view specifications to form part of a distributed interaction protocol specification, which could be interpreted in our version of the *CCS*.

Very few attempts exist that adapt proofs-as-programs methods to distributed systems synthesis. Stirling presents a constructive version of Hennessy-Milner logic in [9], but did not use its constructive properties for program synthesis. A similar calculus is used in [3] for this purpose, but, rather than using a transformative extraction mapping, they directly take the modal proofs as distributed programs. Proof-terms for the various modalities are understood as remote procedure calls, commands to broadcast computations to all nodes in the network, commands to use portable code and commands to invoke computational agents. An important difference between our approach and these methods is that they are not concerned with data view synthesis, while this is our primary focus. To the best of our knowledge, proofs-as-program style synthesis has never been adapted for synthesis of distributed programs with data views, nor to the case of assertion generation.

Our results show a successful and practical approach to merging constructive proofs-as-programs with a Hennessy-Milner logic. We retain the advantages of both methods, using them to target their concerns separately. Hennessy-Milner logic is retained to reason about and develop the behaviour of processes. Constructive realizability is adapted to reason and develop functional views of processes. Throughout the extraction process, programs with both aspects are synthesized from proofs.

References

1. Apvrille, L., de Saqui-Sannes, P., Lohr, C., Snac, P., Courtiat, J.-P.: A new UML profile for real-time system formal design and validation. In: Gogolla, M., Kobryn, C. (eds.) UML 2001. LNCS, vol. 2185, Springer, Heidelberg (2001)
2. Gomaa, H.: Designing concurrent, distributed, and real-time applications with UML. In: ICSE 2001: Proceedings of the 23rd International Conference on Software Engineering, pp. 737–738. IEEE Computer Society Press, Los Alamitos
3. Jia, L., Walker, D.: Modal proofs as distributed programs (extended abstract). In: Schmidt, D. (ed.) ESOP 2004. LNCS, vol. 2986, pp. 219–233. Springer, Heidelberg (2004)
4. Medvidovic, N., Taylor, R.N.: A classification and comparison framework for software architecture description languages. IEEE Transactions on Software Engineering 26(1), 70–93 (2000)
5. Milner, R.: Communication and Concurrency. Prentice-Hall, Englewood Cliffs (1989)
6. OMG.UML Superstructure v2.0. Technical report, Object Management Group (2003), http://www.omg.org/cgi--bin/doc?ptc/2003-08-02
7. Poernomo, I., Crossley, J., Wirsing, M.: Adapting Proofs-as-Programs: The Curry-Howard Protocol. In: Monographs in Computer Science, Springer, Heidelberg (2005)
8. Simpson, A.K.: Compositionality via cut-elimination: Hennessy-milner logic for an arbitrary gsos. In: LICS 1995, Proceedings 10th Annual IEEE Symposium on Logic in Computer Science, San Diego, California, USA, 26-29 June 1995, pp. 420–430. IEEE Computer Society Press, Los Alamitos (1995)
9. Stirling, C.: Modal logics for communicating systems. Theoretical Computer Science 49, 311–347 (1987)

Action Refinement in Process Algebra and Security Issues[*]

Annalisa Bossi[1], Carla Piazza[2], and Sabina Rossi[1]

[1] Dipartimento di Informatica, Università Ca' Foscari di Venezia, Italy
{bossi,srossi}@dsi.unive.it
[2] Dipartimento di Matematica e Infomatica, Università di Udine, Italy
carla.piazza@dimi.uniud.it

Abstract. In the design process of distributed systems we may have to replace abstract specifications of components by more concrete specifications, thus providing more detailed design information. In the context of process algebra, this well-known approach is often referred to as *action refinement*. We study the relationships between action refinement and security properties within the Security Process Algebra (SPA). First we formalize the concept of action refinement as a structural inductive transformation. Then we prove several compositional results which can be exploited in the stepwise development of processes. Finally, we consider information flow security properties for SPA processes and define a decidable class of secure processes which is closed under refinement.

1 Introduction

In the development of a complex system it is common practice first to describe it succinctly as a simple abstract specification and then to stepwise refine it towards a more concrete implementation. This hierarchical specification approach has been successfully developed for sequential systems where abstract-level instructions are expanded until a concrete implementation is reached (e.g., [28]).

In the context of process algebra, the refinement methodology amounts to defining a mechanism for replacing abstract actions with more concrete terms. We adopt the terminology *action refinement* [16] to refer to this stepwise development of systems specified as terms of a process algebra. In the literature, action refinement is also referred to as *vertical refinement* as opposed to *horizontal refinement* indicating any transformation of a system making it more nearly executable, for instance more deterministic, without adding new actions or expanding sub-computations. The latter is usually expressed in terms of pre-orders such as trace inclusion or simulation. We studied the relationships between this second form of refinement and information flow security in [3]. However, we cannot use the results obtained in [3] to deal with vertical refinement since the two forms of refinement provide orthogonal mechanisms for program development.

---

[*] Supported by the MIUR projects 2005015785 "Fondamenti Logici dei Sistemi Distribuiti e Codice Mobile" and 2005015491 "Vincoli per la programmazione con insiemi, l'analisi di sistemi con automi, il ragionamento su intervalli e la bioinformatica".

In process algebra, action refinement is usually defined in languages including a sequential composition operator ";" that allows one to syntactically substitute a process for an action. So, for instance, the refinement of r in the process $a; r; b; \mathbf{0}$ with the process F can be defined as the process $a; F; b; \mathbf{0}$. This is the most followed approach (see, e.g., [1,15]). However, many process algebras, e.g., CCS, do not include the sequential composition operator. Thus in order to support action refinement, action-prefixing is usually replaced by sequential composition. As noticed in [1] this modification requires to introduce a suitable notion of termination and to consequently adapt the semantic equivalences.

Here we follow a different approach and instead of modifying our language, we define action refinement as a structural inductive transformation. We model action refinement as a ternary function Ref taking as arguments an action r to be refined, a system description E on a given level of abstraction and an interpretation of the action r on this level by a more concrete process F on a lower abstraction level. The refined process, denoted by $Ref(r, E, F)$, is intended to be obtained from E by expanding each occurrence of r in E through F. We assume that the process F indicates its termination by a distinguished label $\overline{\text{done}}$, i.e., following Milner's terminology (see [20]), F is *well-terminating*. The refined process is obtained by applying a structural inductive transformation based on the *Before* operator defined in [20] as:

$$Before[F, E] \stackrel{\text{def}}{=} (F[\overline{f}/\overline{\text{done}}] | f.E) \setminus \{f\}.$$

For instance, if E is the process $r.a.\mathbf{0}$ where r is the action we intend to refine by the process $F \stackrel{\text{def}}{=} b_1.b_2.\overline{\text{done}}.\mathbf{0}$, the refined process, denoted by $Ref(r, E, F)$, will be the process $Before[F, E] \stackrel{\text{def}}{=} (b_1.b_2.\overline{f}.\mathbf{0} | f.a.\mathbf{0}) \setminus \{f\}$ which corresponds to the sequential composition of processes F and $a.\mathbf{0}$, and hence it models the substitution of the action r in E with F. In practice we follow the static syntactic approach to action refinement (see, e.g., [22]).

The main motivation behind our approach is that of studying the relationships between action refinement and security. Indeed, in system development, it is important to consider security related issues from the very beginning. Considering security only at the final step could lead to a poor protection, or, even worse, could make it necessary to restart the development from scratch. On the other hand, taking into account security from the abstract specification level, better integrates it in the whole development process, possibly driving some implementation choices. A security-aware stepwise development requires that the security properties of interest are either preserved or gained during the development steps, until a concrete (i.e., implementable) specification is obtained.

In this paper we consider *information flow security* properties [11,14,18,23], i.e., properties that allow one to express constraints on how information should flow among different groups of entities. These properties are formalized by considering two groups of entities labelled with two security levels: *high* (H) and *low* (L). The only constraint is that no information should flow from H to L. In [2] we studied persistent information flow security properties for the *Security Process Algebra* (SPA) introduced in [11]. These properties are obtained as instances of a *generalized unwinding condition* which requires that each high level action is "simulated" in such a way that it is impossible for the low level user to infer which high level actions have been performed. This general framework allows us to uniformly deal with some decidable subclasses of the well-known *NDC* and *BNDC* properties for SPA processes defined in [11]. The fact that we do not modify our language to introduce action refinement allows us to reason on the relationships between action refinement and the security properties of SPA processes. In particular, we study the conditions under which our notions of security are preserved under action refinement.

The paper is organized as follows. Section 2 introduces the SPA language. In Section 3 we formalize the notion of action refinement and provide some compositionality results. In Section 4 we introduce our information flow security properties and define decidable classes of secure processes which are closed under action refinement. Finally, in Section 5 we discuss some related work. The proofs of the results presented in this paper are reported in [5].

2   The SPA Language

The *Security Process Algebra* (SPA) language [11] is a variation of Milner's CCS [20] where the set of visible actions is partitioned into two security levels, high and low, in order to specify multilevel systems. The SPA syntax is based on: a set $\mathcal{L} = I \cup O$ of *visible* actions where $I = \{a, b, \ldots\}$ is a set of *input* actions and $O = \{\bar{a}, \bar{b}, \ldots\}$ is a set of *output* actions; a special action τ which models internal computations, not visible outside the system; a function $\bar{\cdot} : \mathcal{L} \rightarrow \mathcal{L}$, such that $\bar{\bar{a}} = a$, for all $a \in \mathcal{L}$. $Act = \mathcal{L} \cup \{\tau\}$ is the set of all *actions*. The set of visible actions is partitioned into two sets, H and L, of high and low security actions such that $\bar{H} = H$ and $\bar{L} = L$. The syntax of SPA *terms* is as follows[1]:

$$T ::= \mathbf{0} \mid Z \mid a.T \mid T + T \mid T|T \mid T \setminus v \mid T[f] \mid recZ.T$$

where Z is a variable, $a \in Act$, $v \subseteq \mathcal{L}$, $f : Act \rightarrow Act$ is such that $f(\bar{l}) = \overline{f(l)}$ for $l \in \mathcal{L}$, $f(\tau) = \tau$, $f(H) \subseteq H \cup \{\tau\}$, and $f(L) \subseteq L \cup \{\tau\}$. We apply the standard notions of *free* and *bound* (occurrences of) variables in a SPA term. More precisely, all the occurrences of the variable Z in $recZ.T$ are *bound*; while an occurrence of Z is *free* in a term T if it is not bound. A SPA *process* is a SPA term without free variables. We denote by $\mathcal{E}$ the set of all SPA processes, ranged over by $E, F, G, \ldots$ We introduce also a notion of *bound* and *free* actions. We say that an action a is *bound* in a term T if it belongs to a restriction, i.e., $\setminus v$ occurs in T and $a \in v$, or is used in a relabelling operator, i.e., f occurs in T and $f(a) \neq a$ or $f(b) = a$ for $b \neq a$. We identify SPA terms up to α-conversion, thus we can assume that a bound action can occur only in a restriction or a relabelling operator or in their scopes. Hence, the set of actions occurring in a term T can be split into two disjoint sets: the set $bound(T)$ of actions which are bound in T and the set $free(T)$ of actions which are not bound in T.

---

[1] Actually in [11] recursion is introduced through constant definitions instead of the *rec* operator.

Prefix	$$\overline{a.E \overset{a}{\to} E}$$

Sum

$$\frac{E_1 \overset{a}{\to} E_1'}{E_1 + E_2 \overset{a}{\to} E_1'} \qquad \frac{E_2 \overset{a}{\to} E_2'}{E_1 + E_2 \overset{a}{\to} E_2'}$$

Parallel

$$\frac{E_1 \overset{a}{\to} E_1'}{E_1|E_2 \overset{a}{\to} E_1'|E_2} \qquad \frac{E_2 \overset{a}{\to} E_2'}{E_1|E_2 \overset{a}{\to} E_1|E_2'} \qquad \frac{E_1 \overset{l}{\to} E_1' \quad E_2 \overset{\bar{l}}{\to} E_2'}{E_1|E_2 \overset{\tau}{\to} E_1'|E_2'}$$

Restriction

$$\frac{E \overset{a}{\to} E'}{E \setminus v \overset{a}{\to} E' \setminus v} \quad \text{if } a, \bar{a} \notin v$$

Relabelling

$$\frac{E \overset{a}{\to} E'}{E[f] \overset{f(a)}{\to} E'[f]}$$

Recursion

$$\frac{T[recZ.T[Z]] \overset{a}{\to} E'}{recZ.T[Z] \overset{a}{\to} E'}$$

with $a \in Act$ and $l \in \mathcal{L}$.

Fig. 1. The operational semantics of SPA terms

The operational semantics of SPA processes is given in terms of *Labelled Transition Systems* (LTS). In particular, the LTS $(\mathcal{E}, Act, \to)$, whose states are processes, is defined by structural induction as the least relation generated by the axioms and inference rules reported in Figure 1. The operational semantics for an agent E is the subpart of the SPA LTS reachable from the initial state E.

Intuitively, **0** is the empty process that does nothing; $a.E$ is a process that can perform an action a and then behaves as E; $E_1 + E_2$ represents the nondeterministic choice between the two processes E_1 and E_2; $E_1|E_2$ is the parallel composition of E_1 and E_2, where executions are interleaved, possibly synchronized on complementary input/output actions, producing the silent action τ; $E \setminus v$ is a process E prevented from performing actions in v; $E[f]$ is the process E whose actions are renamed *via* the relabelling function f; if Z is a free variable in T, then $recZ.T[Z]$ is the recursive process which can perform all the actions of the process obtained by substituting $recZ.T[Z]$ to the place-holder Z in $T[Z]$.

We will use the following notations. If $t = t_1 \cdots t_n \in Act^*$ and $E \overset{t_1}{\to} \cdots \overset{t_n}{\to} E'$, then we write $E \overset{t}{\to} E'$ and we say that E' is *reachable* from E, also denoted by $E \rightsquigarrow E'$. We denote by $Reach(E)$ the set of all processes reachable from E. We also write $E \overset{t}{\Longrightarrow} E'$ if $E(\overset{\tau}{\to})^* \overset{t_1}{\to} (\overset{\tau}{\to})^* \cdots (\overset{\tau}{\to})^* \overset{t_n}{\to} (\overset{\tau}{\to})^* E'$ where $(\overset{\tau}{\to})^*$ denotes a (possibly empty) sequence of τ labelled transitions. If $t \in Act^*$, then $\hat{t} \in \mathcal{L}^*$ is the sequence gained by deleting all occurrences of τ from t. As a consequence,

$E \stackrel{\hat{a}}{\Longrightarrow} E'$ stands for $E \stackrel{a}{\Longrightarrow} E'$ if $a \in \mathcal{L}$, and for $E(\stackrel{\tau}{\to})^* E'$ if $a = \tau$ (note that $\stackrel{\tau}{\Longrightarrow}$ requires at least one τ transition while $\stackrel{\hat{\tau}}{\Longrightarrow}$ means zero or more τ transitions).

The concept of *behavioral equivalence* is used to establish equalities among processes and it is based on the idea that two processes have the same semantics if and only if their behavior cannot be distinguished by an external observer. We recall here the definition of *strong bisimulation* [20], which equates two processes when they are able to mutually simulate their behavior step by step.

Definition 1 (Strong Bisimulation). *A symmetric binary relation* $\mathcal{R} \subseteq \mathcal{E} \times \mathcal{E}$ *over processes is a* strong bisimulation *if* $(E, F) \in \mathcal{R}$ *implies, for all* $a \in Act$, *if* $E \stackrel{a}{\to} E'$, *then there exists* F' *such that* $F \stackrel{a}{\to} F'$ *and* $(E', F') \in \mathcal{R}$.

Two processes E *and* F *are* strongly bisimilar, *denoted by* $E \sim F$, *if there exists a strong bisimulation* $\mathcal{R}$ *containing the pair* (E, F).

A SPA term with free variables is called *context*[2]. If $C[Y_1, \ldots, Y_n]$ is a context with free variables $Y_1, \ldots, Y_n$, then we denote by $C[T_1, \ldots, T_n]$ the term obtained from $C[Y_1, \ldots, Y_n]$ by simultaneously replacing all the occurrences of $Y_1, \ldots, Y_n$ with the terms $T_1, \ldots, T_n$, respectively. For instance, if $C[X] \stackrel{\text{def}}{=} h.0|(l.X + \tau.0)$ and $D[X, Y] \stackrel{\text{def}}{=} (l.X + \tau.0)|Y$ are contexts, then the notation $C[\bar{h}.0]$ stands for $h.0|(l.\bar{h}.0 + \tau.0)$, while the notation $D[\bar{h}.0, \bar{l}.0]$ stands for $(l.\bar{h}.0 + \tau.0)|\bar{l}.0$.

Finally, observe that our calculus does not provide a sequential composition operator. However, following Milner [20], we can define it by introducing the convention that processes indicate their termination by a distinguished label $\overline{\text{done}}$.

Definition 2 (Strongly Well-terminating process). *Let* F *be a SPA process.* F *is* strongly well-terminating *if for every* $F' \in Reach(F)$ *it holds:*

(1) $F' \stackrel{\text{done}}{\to}$ *is impossible;*
(2) *if* $F' \stackrel{\alpha}{\to} 0$ *then* $F' \sim \overline{\text{done}}.0;$
(3) *if* $F' \stackrel{\overline{\text{done}}}{\to}$ *then* $F' \sim \overline{\text{done}}.0.$

Our definition is a slight variation of Milner's notion of well-termination. The latter simply consists of points (1) and (3) above (point (2) is omitted) and thus it models the class of processes which *may* indicate their termination but they may also not indicate it. Although the theory developed in this paper holds also for Milner's definition, we prefer to adopt the strong notion of well-termination since it leads to a more meaningful notion of refinement.

When F is strongly well-terminating, the sequential composition of processes F and E can be defined through the operator *Before* introduced by Milner in [20].

Definition 3 (Before operator). *Let* E *be a SPA term and* F *be a SPA process such that* F *is strongly well-terminating.*

$$Before[F, E] \stackrel{\text{def}}{=} (F[\bar{f}/\overline{\text{done}}]|f.E) \setminus \{f\}$$

where $\bar{f}/\overline{\text{done}}$ *denotes the relabelling function replacing* $\overline{\text{done}}$ *with a new name* $\bar{f}$.

---

[2] Notice that a SPA term denotes either a process or a context.

3   Action Refinement

It is standard practice in software development to obtain the final program by first defining an abstract, possibly not executable, specification and then refining it until one arrives to a concrete specification that can directly be implemented. Abstract operations are replaced by more detailed programs which can possibly be further refined. In the context of process algebra, this stepwise development amounts to interpreting actions on a higher level of abstraction by more complex processes on a lower level. This is obtained by introducing a mechanism to transform actions into processes. There are several ways to do this. Here we follow a syntactic approach defining the refinement as a syntactic process transformation.

3.1   Action Refinement for SPA Processes

To define action refinement we need to specify (1) which are the processes F that can be used to refine a process E and (2) which are the actions r refinable in E. A process F can be used to refine a process E only if the free actions of E do not occur bound in F, and vice-versa. Notice that this condition is not restrictive since, by α-conversion, we can always assume that the two processes do not share bound actions. Moreover, we require that F is different from $\mathbf{0}$ and that it is strongly well terminating. In this case we say that F is *pluggable* in E.

Definition 4 (Pluggable terms). *Let E be a SPA term and F be a SPA process. F is pluggable in E if*

(a) $bound(E) \cap free(F) = bound(F) \cap free(E) = \emptyset$;
(b) F is not the process $\mathbf{0}$;
(c) F is strongly well-terminating.

Notice that in the above definition E is a SPA term, i.e., it may have free variables. This is necessary to allow us to define the notion of refinement by structural induction on E.

If F is pluggable in E, then an abstract action r occurring in E is refinable with F if r is not bound in E and it does not occur in F otherwise we would enter into an infinite loop of refinements. All these requirements are formalized in the following notion of refinability.

Definition 5 (Refinable actions). *Let E be a SPA term, F be a SPA process, and $r \in \mathcal{L}$. The action r is said to be refinable in E with F if:*

(a) F is pluggable in E;
(b) $r \notin bound(E)$;
(c) r does not occur in F.

Example 1. Consider the process $E \stackrel{\text{def}}{=} (r.a.\mathbf{0}|\bar{a}.b.\mathbf{0}) \setminus \{a, \bar{a}\}$ and the process $F \stackrel{\text{def}}{=} c.d.\overline{\text{done}}.\mathbf{0}$. In this case the action r is refinable in E with F.

Consider now the process E as above and $F_1 \stackrel{\text{def}}{=} (b.\overline{\text{done}}.\mathbf{0} + c.d.\overline{\text{done}}.\mathbf{0}) \setminus \{b\}$. In this case condition (a) of Definition 4 is not satisfied since $bound(F_1) \cap$

$free(E) = \{b\} \neq \emptyset$. Hence r is not refinable in E with F_1. However, it is immediate to see that we can exploit α-conversion and transform F_1 into $F_2 \stackrel{\text{def}}{=} (e.\overline{done}.0 + c.d.\overline{done}.0) \setminus \{e\}$. Now, r is refinable in E with F_2.   □

The intended meaning of the refinement of an abstract action r in a process E with a refining process F is that of expanding each occurrence of r in E by F. In order to support action refinement, in the literature the prefixing operator is usually replaced by sequential composition ";" [1,15]. Here we follow a different approach and model sequential composition by using a construction based on *well-terminating* processes and the *Before* operator as suggested in [20].

Let r be an action refinable in E with F. To define the refinement of E with F we replace each occurrence of r in E through the *Before* operator having F as first argument and the subprocess of E which follows r as second argument. Thus, for instance the refinement of r in $E \stackrel{\text{def}}{=} a.r.b.0$ with $F \stackrel{\text{def}}{=} c.d.\overline{done}.0$ is obtained by replacing $r.b.0$ with $Before[F, b.0]$, i.e., it is $a.Before[c.d.\overline{done}.0, b.0]$ that is exactly $a.(c.d.\overline{done}.0[\bar{f}/\overline{done}] | f.b.0) \setminus \{f\}$.

The notion of *action refinement* is defined by structural induction on the term to be refined as follows:

Definition 6 (Action Refinement). *Let E be a SPA term and F be a SPA process such that r is an action refinable in E with F. The refinement of r in E with F is the term $Ref(r, E, F)$ inductively defined as follows:*

$$(1) \quad Ref(r, 0, F) \stackrel{\text{def}}{=} 0$$
$$(2) \quad Ref(r, Z, F) \stackrel{\text{def}}{=} Z$$
$$(3) \quad Ref(r, r.E_1, F) \stackrel{\text{def}}{=} Before[F, Ref(r, E_1, F)]$$
$$(4) \quad Ref(r, a.E_1, F) \stackrel{\text{def}}{=} a.Ref(r, E_1, F), \ if \ a \neq r$$
$$(5) \quad Ref(r, E_1[f], F) \stackrel{\text{def}}{=} Ref(r, E_1, F)[f]$$
$$(6) \quad Ref(r, E_1 \setminus v, F) \stackrel{\text{def}}{=} Ref(r, E_1, F) \setminus v$$
$$(7) \quad Ref(r, E_1 + E_2, F) \stackrel{\text{def}}{=} Ref(r, E_1, F) + Ref(r, E_2, F)$$
$$(8) \quad Ref(r, E_1 | E_2, F) \stackrel{\text{def}}{=} Ref(r, E_1, F) | Ref(r, E_2, F)$$
$$(9) \quad Ref(r, recZ.E_1, F) \stackrel{\text{def}}{=} recZ.Ref(r, E_1, F)$$

Point (3) of the above definition deals with the basic case in which we replace an occurrence of r with the refining process F. If $E \stackrel{\text{def}}{=} r.E_1$ and r is the only occurrence of r in E, then $Ref(r, E, F) \stackrel{\text{def}}{=} Before[F, E_1] \stackrel{\text{def}}{=} (F[\bar{f}/\overline{done}] | f.E_1) \setminus \{f\}$ representing the process which first behaves as F and then, when the execution of F is terminated, proceeds as E_1. In all the other cases the refinement process enters inside the components of E. This is correct also when restriction or relabelling operators are involved: indeed, condition (a) of Definition 4 ensures that undesired bindings of actions will never occur, while condition (b) of Definition 5 guarantees that we never refine restricted or relabelled actions. Point (c) of Definition 5 is useful to prevent infinite loops of refinements.

Point (b) of Definition 4 requires that F is not the empty process. This choice is motivated by the fact that in the literature there is no general agreement on what an empty refinement, i.e., the refinement of an action into the empty process, should be. In [25] actions refined into the empty process are simply erased (*forgetful refinements*), while in [10] those actions are deadlocked since the empty refinement is interpreted as an erroneous step in the top down development procedure. In many other works the empty refinement is simply ignored in order to avoid technical problems (see [1]). Here we follow this approach and assume that the refining process is always non empty.

Finally, point (c) of Definition 4 requires that the refining process F is strongly well-terminating. This allows us to define the sequential composition of SPA processes in the spirit of [20]. In the literature, the sequential composition operator ";" is just added to the language in order to allow, for instance, the refinement of $E \stackrel{\text{def}}{=} r.a.\mathbf{0}$ with $F \stackrel{\text{def}}{=} b.\mathbf{0}|c.\mathbf{0}$ obtaining the refined process $(b.\mathbf{0}|c.\mathbf{0}); a.\mathbf{0}$. Using our definition, F is not pluggable in E since it is not well-terminating. Notice that we cannot simply replace the $\mathbf{0}$'s of F with $\overline{\text{done}}.\mathbf{0}$, since the resulting process would not be well-terminating. However, following Milner [20], we can define the *strongly well-terminating* parallel composition operator:

$$P \; Par \; Q \stackrel{\text{def}}{=} (P[\bar{f_1}/\overline{\text{done}}] \mid Q[\bar{f_2}/\overline{\text{done}}] \mid (f_1.f_2.\overline{\text{done}}.\mathbf{0} + f_2.f_1.\overline{\text{done}}.\mathbf{0})) \setminus \{f_1, f_2\}$$

The process $P \; Par \; Q$ is strongly well-terminating and performs an action $\overline{\text{done}}$ when and only when both component agents have terminated. Thus, in the above example, we can use the well-terminating process $b.\overline{\text{done}}.\mathbf{0} \; Par \; c.\overline{\text{done}}.\mathbf{0}$ to refine the action r in $E \stackrel{\text{def}}{=} r.a.\mathbf{0}$.

Example 2. Let $E \stackrel{\text{def}}{=} r.a.\mathbf{0} + b.\mathbf{0}$ and $F \stackrel{\text{def}}{=} c.\overline{\text{done}}.\mathbf{0} + d.\overline{\text{done}}.\mathbf{0}$. It is immediate to observe that r is refinable in E with F. By applying Definition 6 we get:

$$
\begin{aligned}
Ref(r, E, F) &\stackrel{\text{def}}{=} Ref(r, r.a.\mathbf{0}, F) + Ref(r, b.\mathbf{0}, F) \\
&\stackrel{\text{def}}{=} Before[F, Ref(r, a.\mathbf{0}, F)] + b.\mathbf{0} \\
&\stackrel{\text{def}}{=} Before[F, a.\mathbf{0}] + b.\mathbf{0} \\
&\stackrel{\text{def}}{=} (c.\overline{\text{done}}.\mathbf{0} + d.\overline{\text{done}}.\mathbf{0}[\bar{f}/\overline{\text{done}}]|f.a.\mathbf{0}) \setminus \{f\} + b.\mathbf{0} \\
&\sim c.\tau.a.\mathbf{0} + d.\tau.a.\mathbf{0} + b.\mathbf{0}.
\end{aligned}
$$

$\square$

Example 3. Let $E \stackrel{\text{def}}{=} (a.r.b.\mathbf{0}) \setminus \{b\}$ and $F \stackrel{\text{def}}{=} c.d.\overline{\text{done}}.\mathbf{0}$. Since $bound(E) = \{b\}$ and b does not occur in F, we have that r is refinable in E with F. Indeed:

$$
\begin{aligned}
Ref(r, E, F) &\stackrel{\text{def}}{=} (Ref(r, a.r.b.\mathbf{0}, F)) \setminus \{b\} \\
&\stackrel{\text{def}}{=} (a.Ref(r, r.b.\mathbf{0}, F)) \setminus \{b\} \\
&\stackrel{\text{def}}{=} (a.Before[F, Ref(r, b.\mathbf{0}, F)]) \setminus \{b\} \\
&\stackrel{\text{def}}{=} (a.Before[F, b.\mathbf{0}]) \setminus \{b\} \\
&\stackrel{\text{def}}{=} (a.(c.d.\overline{\text{done}}.\mathbf{0}[\bar{f}/\overline{\text{done}}]|f.b.\mathbf{0}) \setminus \{f\}) \setminus \{b\} \\
&\sim (a.c.d.\tau.b.\mathbf{0}) \setminus \{b\}.
\end{aligned}
$$

Notice that, our notion of refinability does not allow us to directly refine r in E with $F_1 \stackrel{\text{def}}{=} b.d.\overline{\text{done}}.0$. However, we can first apply an α-conversion transforming E into the equivalent process $E_1 \stackrel{\text{def}}{=} (a.r.e.0) \setminus \{e\}$ and then refine r in E_1 with F_1 getting, as expected, the refined process which behaves as $(a.b.d.\tau.e.0) \setminus \{e\}$.   □

Example 4. Let $E \stackrel{\text{def}}{=} a.r.b.0 | r.c.0$ and $F \stackrel{\text{def}}{=} c.d.\overline{\text{done}}.0$. By applying our definition and by the example above we get:

$$Ref(r, E, F) \stackrel{\text{def}}{=} Ref(r, a.r.b.0, F) | Ref(r, r.c.0, F)$$
$$\stackrel{\text{def}}{=} (a.(c.d.\overline{\text{done}}.0[\bar{f}/\overline{\text{done}}] | f.b.0) \setminus \{f\}) \;|$$
$$(c.d.\overline{\text{done}}.0[\bar{f}/\overline{\text{done}}] | f.c.0) \setminus \{f\}$$
$$\sim a.c.d.\tau.b.0 | c.d.\tau.c.0.$$

As expected, the two occurrences of r in E are replaced by two copies of F.   □

From now on when we write $Ref(r, E, F)$ we tacitly assume that r is refinable in E with F. Notice that if r is refinable in E with F and E is strongly well-terminating then also $Ref(r, E, F)$ is strongly well-terminating.

3.2   Compositionality

At any fixed level of abstraction during the top-down development of a program, it is unrealistic to think that there is just one action to be refined at that level. Compositional properties of the refinement operation allow us to do not care about the ordering in which the refinements occur.

First we show that our refinement can locally be applied to the subcomponents in which the actions to be refined occur.

Lemma 1. *Let $C[Z_1, \ldots, Z_n]$ be a SPA context, $E_1, \ldots, E_n$ be SPA terms, F be a SPA process, and $r \in \mathcal{L}$ be refinable in $C[E_1, \ldots, E_n]$ with F. Then*

$$Ref(r, C[E_1, \ldots, E_n], F) \stackrel{\text{def}}{=} Ref(r, C, F)[Ref(r, E_1, F), \ldots, Ref(r, E_n, F)].$$

In particular, if C is a context with no occurrences of r, the above lemma ensures that $Ref(r, C[E_1, \ldots, E_n], F) \stackrel{\text{def}}{=} C[Ref(r, E_1, F), \ldots, Ref(r, E_n, F)]$. Therefore, if we consider a process E of the form $E_1 | E_2 | \ldots | E_n$ and an action r occurring only in E_i for some i, then it is sufficient to apply the refinement to E_i to obtain $Ref(r, E, F) \stackrel{\text{def}}{=} E_1 | \ldots | Ref(r, E_i, F) | \ldots | E_n$.

If we need to refine two actions in a term E, they can be swapped in the following sense.

Lemma 2. *Let E be a SPA term, F_1, F_2 be SPA processes, r_1 and r_2 be actions refinable in E with F_1 and F_2, respectively. If r_1 does not occur in F_2, then*

$$Ref(r_2, Ref(r_1, E, F_1), F_2) \stackrel{\text{def}}{=} Ref(r_1, Ref(r_2, E, F_2), Ref(r_2, F_1, F_2)).$$

In particular, if also r_2 does not occur in F_1, then

$$Ref(r_2, Ref(r_1, E, F_1), F_2) \stackrel{\text{def}}{=} Ref(r_1, Ref(r_2, E, F_2), F_1).$$

4   Preserving Security Properties under Refinement

In this section we first present some information flow security properties for SPA processes. Then we investigate conditions under which our notions of security are preserved under action refinement.

4.1   Security Properties

Information flow security in a multilevel system aims at guaranteeing that no high level (confidential) information is revealed to users running at low security levels [13,19], even in the presence of any possible malicious process (attacker).

In [11] Focardi and Gorrieri introduce the properties *Non-Deducibility on Compositions (NDC)* and *Bisimulation-based Non-Deducibility on Compositions (BNDC)* in order to capture every possible information flow from a *classified (high)* level of confidentiality to an *untrusted (low)* one. The definitions of *NDC* and *BNDC* are based on the basic idea of Non-Interference [14]: "No information flow is possible from high to low if what is done at the high level *cannot interfere in any way with the low level*". More precisely, a system E is secure if what a low level user sees of the system is not modified by composing any high process Π to E. The concept of *low observation* is expressed in terms of an *equivalence relation on low level actions* between processes. The idea is that two systems cannot be distinguished by a low level observer if and only if they are equated by an equivalence relation considering low level actions only. The two properties *NDC* and *BNDC* differ only on the low level observation equivalence they consider. *NDC* is based on *trace equivalence on low actions*, denoted by $\approx^l_T$, while *BNDC* considers the notion of *weak bisimilarity on low actions*, denoted by $\approx^l_B$.

The definition of *weak bisimilarity on low actions* (*trace equivalence on low actions*) is the same as the definition of weak bisimilarity [20] (trace equivalence) except that low and silent actions only (belonging to the set $L \cup \{\tau\}$), instead of all actions (belonging to the set Act), are considered.

Weak bisimilarity on low actions equates two processes if they are able to mutually simulate their low level behavior step by step. Moreover, it does not care about internal τ actions.

Definition 7 (Weak Bisimulation on Low Actions). *A symmetric binary relation $\mathcal{R}$ over processes is a* weak bisimulation on low actions *if $(E, F) \in \mathcal{R}$ implies, for all $a \in L \cup \{\tau\}$, if $E \xrightarrow{a} E'$, then there exists F' such that $F \xRightarrow{\hat{a}} F'$ and $(E', F') \in \mathcal{R}$.*

Two processes $E, F \in \mathcal{E}$ are weakly bisimilar on low actions, *denoted by $E \approx^l_B F$, if there exists a weak bisimulation on low actions $\mathcal{R}$ containing (E, F).*

Trace equivalence on low actions equates two processes if they have the same sets of low traces, again, without considering the τ actions.

Definition 8 (Trace Equivalence on Low Actions). *The set of traces $T^l(E)$ associated with a process E is defined by: $T^l(E) = \{t \in (L \cup \{\tau\})^* \mid \exists E' : E \xRightarrow{t} E'\}$. Two processes E, F are* trace equivalent on low actions, *denoted by $E \approx^l_T F$, if $T^l(E) = T^l(F)$.*

Trace equivalence on low actions is less demanding than weak bisimilarity on low actions, hence if two processes are weakly bisimilar on low actions, then they are also trace equivalent on low actions.

Properties $BNDC$ and NDC are thus formally defined as follows:

$$E \in BNDC \text{ if for all high processes } \Pi, \ E \approx_B^l (E|\Pi)$$
$$E \in NDC \text{ if for all high processes } \Pi, \ E \approx_T^l (E|\Pi).$$

Since weak bisimilarity on low actions is stronger than trace equivalence on low actions, it holds that $BNDC$ implies NDC.

Properties NDC and $BNDC$ are difficult to use in practice: NDC is not decidable in polynomial time, while the decidability of $BNDC$ is still an open problem. In [12], Focardi and Rossi introduce the property *Persistent BNDC* (P_BNDC) which is a natural persistent extension of $BNDC$ (i.e., a system E is P_BNDC if every state E' reachable from E is $BNDC$) and it is a sufficient condition for $BNDC$. They show the decidability of P_BNDC by exploiting a bisimulation based characterization. Other persistent security properties have been later introduced, e.g., the properties *Persistent NDC* (P_NDC) in [4] and *Compositional P_BNDC* (CP_BNDC) in [2].

All the *persistent* properties mentioned above can be defined as instances of a *generalized unwinding condition* [2] which requires that each high level action is "simulated" in such a way that it is impossible for the low level user to infer which high level actions have been performed. The generalized unwinding condition is parametric with respect to two binary relations on processes: an equivalence relation on low actions, $\sim^l$, which represents the low level view, and a transition relation, $\dashrightarrow$, which characterizes a local connectivity.

Definition 9 (Generalized Unwinding). *Let $\sim^l$ be an equivalence relation on low actions and $\dashrightarrow$ be a binary relation on processes. The unwinding class $\mathcal{W}(\sim^l, \dashrightarrow)$ is defined as*

$$\mathcal{W}(\sim^l, \dashrightarrow) \overset{\text{def}}{=} \{E \in \mathcal{E} \mid \forall \ F, G \in Reach(E)$$
$$\text{if } F \overset{h}{\to} G \text{ then } \exists G' \text{ such that } F \dashrightarrow G' \text{ and } G \sim^l G'\}.$$

It holds that P_NDC coincides with $\mathcal{W}(\approx_T^l, \overset{\hat{\tau}}{\Longrightarrow})$ [4], P_BNDC coincides with $\mathcal{W}(\approx_B^l, \overset{\hat{\tau}}{\Longrightarrow})$ and CP_BNDC coincides with $\mathcal{W}(\approx_B^l, \overset{\tau}{\Longrightarrow})$ [2]. Moreover, $P\_NDC \subseteq NDC$ and $P\_BNDC, CP\_BNDC \subseteq BNDC$.

Example 5. Let $l \in L$ and $h \in H$. The process $h.l.h.\mathbf{0} + \tau.l.\mathbf{0}$ is P_BNDC. The process $h.l.\mathbf{0}$ is not P_BNDC. □

Example 6. Let us consider a distributed data base (adapted from [16]) which can take two values and which can be both queried and updated. In particular, the high level user can query it through the high level actions qry_1 and qry_2, while the low level user can only update it through the low level actions upd_1

and upd_2. Hence $qry_1, qry_2 \in H$ and $upd_1, upd_2 \in L$. We can model the data base with the SPA process E defined as

$$E \stackrel{\text{def}}{=} recZ.(qry_1.Z + upd_1.Z + \tau.Z + \\ upd_2.recW.(qry_2.W + upd_2.W + \tau.W + upd_1.Z)).$$

The process E is P_BNDC. Indeed, whenever a high level user queries the data base with a high level action moving the system to a state X then a τ action moving the system to the same state X may be performed, thus masking the high level interactions with the system to low level users. $\square$

4.2   Classes of Secure Processes Closed under Action Refinement

In this section we investigate conditions under which our notions of security are preserved under action refinement. In particular, we are interested in the definition of classes of processes satisfying an instance of $\mathcal{W}(\sim^l, \dashrightarrow)$ and closed under action refinement.

We first introduce the concept of $(\mathcal{P}, r)$-refinable contexts, where $\mathcal{P}$ is a process property and r is an action. Intuitively, a class of contexts is $(\mathcal{P}, r)$-refinable if all processes in it satisfy $\mathcal{P}$ and it is closed under refinement of the action r.

Definition 10 ($(\mathcal{P}, r)$-refinable contexts). *Let $\mathcal{P}$ be a class of processes and r be an action. A class $\mathcal{C}$ of contexts is said to be $(\mathcal{P}, r)$-refinable if:*

- *if $E \in \mathcal{C}$ and E is a process, then $E \in \mathcal{P}$;*
- *if $E, F \in \mathcal{C}$ and r is refinable in E with F then $Ref(r, E, F) \in \mathcal{C}$.*

We introduce a parametric definition of classes of contexts. Given a sequence $s = s_1, s_2, \ldots, s_n$ of actions, we denote by $s.E$ the process $s_1.s_2.\ldots s_n.E$. Moreover, given a set v of actions we denote by $s \cap v$ the set of actions occurring both in s and in v, while, given a relabelling f we denote by $f[s]$ the set $\{s_i \mid f(s_i) \neq s_i\}$. A relation $\circ$ over terms is a *congruence* if $C_1[Z] \circ C_2[Z]$ and $E_1 \circ E_2$ imply $C_1[E_1] \circ C_2[E_2]$.

Definition 11 ($\mathcal{C}(\asymp, s)$). *Let $\asymp$ be a reflexive congruence over SPA terms and s be a sequence of actions. $\mathcal{C}(\asymp, s)$ is the class of contexts containing: the process $\mathbf{0}$; Z, where Z is a variable; $l.C_1$, $h.C_1 + s.C_1'$, $C_1 \setminus v$, $C_1[f]$, $C_1 + C_2$, $C_1|C_2$, and $recZ.C_1$, with $l \in L \cup \{\tau\}$, $h \in H$, $C_1 \asymp C_1'$, $s \cap v = \emptyset$, $f[s] = \emptyset$, and $C_1, C_1', C_2 \in \mathcal{C}(\asymp, s)$.*

Let $\dashrightarrow$ be a binary relation on processes, we say that s *entails* $\dashrightarrow$ if $E \stackrel{s}{\rightarrow} E'$ implies $E \dashrightarrow E'$. Let $\asymp$ be a binary relation on terms, we say that $\asymp$ is *preserved under refinement* of action r if $E \asymp E'$ implies $Ref(r, E, F) \asymp Ref(r, E', F)$.

The following theorem provides sufficient conditions to ensure that all the processes in the class $\mathcal{C}(\asymp, s)$ are secure and the class itself is closed under refinement of r.

Theorem 1. *Let* $\mathcal{W}(\sim^l, \dashrightarrow)$ *be an unwinding condition. If* $s \in (L \cup \{\tau\})^*$ *is a sequence of low and silent actions which entails* $\dashrightarrow$, r *is an action which does not occur in* s, $\asymp$ *is a reflexive congruence preserved under refinement of* r, *and* $\asymp \cap (\mathcal{E} \times \mathcal{E}) \subseteq \sim^l$, *then the class* $\mathcal{C}(\asymp, s)$ *is* $(\mathcal{W}(\sim^l, \dashrightarrow), r)$-*refinable.*

Moreover, under the above conditions, if E *and* F *are two processes such that* $E, F \in \mathcal{C}(\asymp, s)$ *and* r *is a refinable action in* E *with* F, *then* $Ref(r, E, F) \in \mathcal{W}(\sim^l, \dashrightarrow)$ *and* $Ref(r, E, F) \in \mathcal{C}(\asymp, s)$.

Let $\equiv$ denote the syntactic equality between SPA terms. It is immediate to see that $\equiv$ is a reflexive congruence preserved under refinement and it is included in $\sim^l$ for each binary relation $\sim^l$ over SPA terms. We can then instantiate the above theorem with $\equiv$ as the relation $\asymp$, obtaining the following corollary.

Corollary 1. *Let* $\mathcal{W}(\sim^l, \dashrightarrow)$ *be an unwinding condition. If* $s \in (L \cup \{\tau\})^*$ *is a sequence of low and silent actions which entails* $\dashrightarrow$, r *is an action which does not occur in* s, *then the class* $\mathcal{C}(\equiv, s)$ *is* $(\mathcal{W}(\sim^l, \dashrightarrow), r)$-*refinable.*

Moreover, under the above conditions, if E *and* F *are two processes such that* $E, F \in \mathcal{C}(\equiv, s)$ *and* r *is a refinable action in* E *with* F, *then* $Ref(r, E, F) \in \mathcal{W}(\sim^l, \dashrightarrow)$ *and* $Ref(r, E, F) \in \mathcal{C}(\equiv, s)$.

Example 7. Consider again the abstract specification of the distributed data base represented through the SPA process E of Example 6. The process E belongs to the class $\mathcal{C}(\equiv, \tau)$ of Definition 11. In fact, $C_1 \stackrel{\text{def}}{=} qry_2.W + upd_2.W + \tau.W + upd_1.Z \in \mathcal{C}(\equiv, \tau)$, and then $C_2 \stackrel{\text{def}}{=} recW.C_1 \in \mathcal{C}(\equiv, \tau)$. Hence, $C_3 \stackrel{\text{def}}{=} qry_1.Z + upd_1.Z + \tau.Z + upd_2.C_2 \in \mathcal{C}(\equiv, \tau)$. Therefore $E \stackrel{\text{def}}{=} recZ.C_3 \in \mathcal{C}(\equiv, \tau)$.

We can refine the update actions by requiring that each update is requested and confirmed, i.e., we refine upd_1 with $F_1 \stackrel{\text{def}}{=} req_1.cnf_1.\overline{done}.0$ and upd_2 with $F_2 \stackrel{\text{def}}{=} req_2.cnf_2.\overline{done}.0$, where $req_1, cnf_1, req_2, cnf_2$ are low security level actions. We obtain:

$$Ref(upd_2, Ref(upd_1, E, F_1), F_2) \stackrel{\text{def}}{=}$$
$$Ref(upd_2, Ref(upd_1, recZ.(qry_1.Z + upd_1.Z + \tau.Z +$$
$$upd_2.recW.(qry_2.W + upd_2.W + \tau.W + upd_1.Z)), F_1), F_2) \stackrel{\text{def}}{=}$$
$$recZ.(qry_1.Z + (req_1.cnf_1.\overline{done}.0[\bar{f}/\overline{done}] \| f.Z) \setminus \{f\} + \tau.Z +$$
$$(req_2.cnf_2.\overline{done}.0[\bar{f}/\overline{done}] \| f.(recW.(qry_2.W +$$
$$(req_2.cnf_2.\overline{done}.0[\bar{f}/\overline{done}] \| f.W) \setminus \{f\} +$$
$$\tau.W + (req_1.cnf_1.\overline{done}.0[\bar{f}/\overline{done}] \| f.Z) \setminus \{f\})) \setminus \{f\} \sim$$
$$recZ.(qry_1.Z + req_1.cnf_1.\tau.Z + \tau.Z +$$
$$req_2.cnf_2.\tau.recW.(qry_2.W + req_2.cnf_2.\tau.W + \tau.W + req_1.cnf_1.\tau.Z)).$$

Since F_1 and F_2 are in $\mathcal{C}(\equiv, \tau)$ and τ entails $\stackrel{\hat{\tau}}{\Longrightarrow}$, by applying Corollary 1 we have that the process $Ref(upd_2, Ref(upd_1, E, F_1), F_2)$ is in $\mathcal{W}(\approx^l_B, \stackrel{\hat{\tau}}{\Longrightarrow})$, i.e., it is *P_BNDC*. $\square$

Another binary relation over SPA terms, which can be used to find sufficient and decidable conditions for proving both *P_NDC* and *P_BNDC* is the relation $\asymp$ defined as follows: $E_1 \asymp E_2$ if and only if $E_1 \equiv E_2$ or $E_1 \sim E_2$ and E_1, E_2

are high level processes (i.e., they have neither variables nor low level actions) or $E_1 \equiv D_1[E_1']$ and $E_2 \equiv D_2[E_2']$, with $D_1[Z] = D_2[Z]$ and $E_1' = E_2'$.

By instantiating $\asymp$ with $=$ and s with τ we obtain the class $\mathcal{C}(=, \tau)$ which is decidable with the proof system presented in the Appendix. By exploiting Theorem 1, we can prove that the class of secure processes $\mathcal{C}(=, \tau)$ is closed under refinement of low level actions, as stated by the following corollary.

Corollary 2. *The class* $\mathcal{C}(=, \tau)$ *is both* (P_NDC, r)-*refinable and* (P_BNDC, r)-*refinable, for all low level actions* $r \in L$.

The proof follows from the fact that P_NDC coincides with $\mathcal{W}(\approx_T^l, \overset{\hat{\tau}}{\Longrightarrow})$, P_BNDC coincides with $\mathcal{W}(\approx_B^l, \overset{\hat{\tau}}{\Longrightarrow})$, and τ entails $\overset{\hat{\tau}}{\Longrightarrow}$. In order to prove that $=$ is preserved under refinement we exploit Lemma 1.

Notice that we can obtain the same result by replacing $\sim$ (strong bisimulation) in the definition of $=$ with any congruence included in $\approx_B^l$. For instance we can use the weak progressing bisimulation defined in [21].

5   Conclusions and Related Works

In this paper we study the relationships between action refinement and information flow security within the Security Process Algebra (SPA).

Action refinement has been extensively studied in the literature. There are essentially two interpretations of action refinement: *semantic* and *syntactic* (see [15]). In the semantic interpretation an explicit refinement operator, written $E[r \rightarrow F]$, is introduced in the semantic domain used to interpret the terms of the algebra. The semantics of $E[r \rightarrow F]$ models the fact that r is an action of E to be refined by the process F. In the syntactic approach, the same situation is modelled by syntactically replacing r by F in E. The replacement can be *static*, i.e., before execution, or *dynamic*, i.e., r is replaced as soon as it occurs while executing E. In order to correctly formalize the replacement, the process algebra is usually equipped with an operation of sequential composition (rather than the more standard action prefix), as, e.g., in ACP, since otherwise it would not be closed under the necessary syntactic substitution. Our approach to action refinement follows the static, syntactic interpretation. The use of the *Before* operator to realize the refinement allows us to keep the original SPA language without introducing a sequential composition operator for processes.

In [1] Aceto and Hennessy introduce a static syntactic notion of action refinement on a variation of CCS in which action-prefixing is replaced by sequential composition and neither recursion nor relabellings are allowed. The semantics of this language is expressed as a strong bisimilarity extended with a condition on the termination of processes. Instead of extending the language, we follow Milner's approach and implement sequential composition by context operations. This allows us to consider the full language with recursion and relabelling.

Action refinement is also classified as *atomic* or *non-atomic*. Atomic refinement is based on the assumption that actions are atomic and their refinements should in some sense preserve this atomicity (see, e.g.,[9,6]). As an example, consider the processes $E \stackrel{\text{def}}{=} r.0|b.0$ and $F \stackrel{\text{def}}{=} a_1.a_2.\overline{\text{done}}.0$. The atomic refinement of r in E with F should be a process where r is replaced by F and the execution of $a_1.a_2$ is non-interruptible, i.e., action b cannot be executed in between the execution of a_1 and a_2. On the other hand, non-atomic refinement is based on the view that atomicity is always relative to the current level of abstraction and may, in a sense, be destroyed by the refinement (see, e.g., [1,10,26]). Unfortunately, the standard behavioral equivalences of CCS, such as strong and weak bisimulation and trace equivalence, are not preserved under non-atomic refinements. In the literature different equivalences based on non-interleaving semantics which are preserved under refinement have been studied (see, e.g., [7,27]). In this paper we follow the *non-atomic* approach. Actually, this approach is on the whole more popular than the former.

Recently in [24], Seehusen and Stølen addressed the problem of preserving trace-based security properties under transformations from an abstract specification to a concrete one. The particular transformations they deal with may be understood as a special case of action refinement where the concrete specification is generated automatically from the abstract specification. The information flow security framework presented in the paper is inspired by [18] and is based on the composition of basic security predicates. This approach is quite simple and allows one to capture many trace-based properties expressed over event systems. Following Jacob's observations [17], the authors notice that information flow properties are in general not preserved by the standard notions of refinement. As argued by Jacob, the problem originates from the inability of most specification languages to distinguish between the two sources of nondeterminism, named, underspecification and unpredictability. The authors then propose to refine the notion of refinement and that of secure information flow such that this distinction is taken into consideration. Based on this approach they propose quite *ad hoc* conditions under which transformations maintain security.

In the literature the term *refinement* is also used to indicate any transformation of a system that can be justified because the transformed system implements the original one on the *same* abstraction level, by being more nearly executable, for instance more deterministic. The implementation relation is expressed in terms of pre-orders such as trace inclusion or various kinds of simulation. Many papers in this tradition can be found in [8]. The relations between this form of refinement and information flow security have been studied in [3]. Although both action refinement and the refinement considered in [3] aim at transforming a system specification into a more executable one, the principles behind the two kinds of transformations are completely different, and thus a comparison is not meaningful.

Acknowledgments

We would like to acknowledge the anonymous referees of the preliminary version of the paper for their useful comments and suggestions.

References

1. Aceto, L., Hennessy, M.: Adding Action Refinement to a Finite Process Algebra. Information and Computation 115(2), 179–247 (1994)
2. Bossi, A., Focardi, R., Macedonio, D., Piazza, C., Rossi, S.: Unwinding in Information Flow Security. Electronic Notes in Theoretical Computer Science 99, 127–154 (2004)
3. Bossi, A., Focardi, R., Piazza, C., Rossi, S.: Refinement Operators and Information Flow Security. In: Proc. of the 1st IEEE Int. Conference on Software Engineering and Formal Methods (SEFM 2003), pp. 44–53. IEEE Computer Society Press, Los Alamitos (2003)
4. Bossi, A., Piazza, C., Rossi, S.: Modelling Downgrading in Information Flow Security. In: Proc. of the 17th IEEE Computer Security Foundations Workshop (CSFW 2004), pp. 187–201. IEEE Computer Society Press, Los Alamitos (2004)
5. Bossi, A., Piazza, C., Rossi, S.: Action Refinement in Process Algebra and Security Issues. Technical Report CS-2007-8, Dipartimento di Informatica, Università Ca' Foscari di Venezia, Italy (2007)
6. Boudol, G.: Atomic Actions. Bulletin of the EATCS 38, 136–144 (1989)
7. Bravetti, M., Gorrieri, R.: Deciding and axiomatizing weak ST bisimulation for a process algebra with recursion and action refinement. ACM Transaction on Computational Logic 3(4), 465–520 (2002)
8. de Bakker, J.W., de Roever, W.-P., Rozenberg, G. (eds.): REX 1989. LNCS, vol. 430. Springer, Heidelberg (1990)
9. de Bakker, J.W., de Vink, E.P.: Bisimulation Semantics for Concurrency with Atomicity and Action Refinement. Fundamenta Informaticae 20(1), 3–34 (1994)
10. Degano, P., Gorrieri, R.: A Causal Operational Semantics of Action Refinement. Information and Computation 122(1), 97–119 (1995)
11. Gorrieri, R., Focardi, R.: Classification of Security Properties (Part I: Information Flow). In: Focardi, R., Gorrieri, R. (eds.) FOSAD 2001. LNCS, vol. 2171, Springer, Heidelberg (2001)
12. Focardi, R., Rossi, S.: Information Flow Security in Dynamic Contexts. Journal of Computer Security 14(1), 65–110 (2006)
13. Foley, S.N.: A Universal Theory of Information Flow. In: Proc. of the IEEE Symposium on Security and Privacy (SSP 1987), pp. 116–122. IEEE Computer Society Press, Los Alamitos (1987)
14. Goguen, J.A., Meseguer, J.: Security Policies and Security Models. In: Proc. of the IEEE Symposium on Security and Privacy (SSP 1982), pp. 11–20. IEEE Computer Society Press, Los Alamitos (1982)
15. Goltz, U., Gorrieri, R., Rensink, A.: Comparing Syntactic and Semantic Action Refinement. Information and Computation 125(2), 118–143 (1996)
16. Gorrieri, R., Rensink, A.: Action Refinement. Technical Report UBLCS-99-09, University of Bologna (Italy) (1999)
17. Jacob, J.: On the Derivation of Secure Components. In: Proc. of the IEEE Symposium on Security and Privacy (SSP 1989), pp. 242–247. IEEE Computer Society Press, Los Alamitos (1989)
18. Mantel, H.: Possibilistic Definitions of Security - An Assembly Kit -. In: Proc. of the IEEE Computer Security Foundations Workshop (CSFW 2000), pp. 185–199. IEEE Computer Society Press, Los Alamitos (2000)
19. McLean, J.: Security Models and Information Flow. In: Proc. of the IEEE Symposium on Security and Privacy (SSP1990), pp. 180–187. IEEE Computer Society Press, Los Alamitos (1990)

20. Milner, R.: Communication and Concurrency. Prentice-Hall, Englewood Cliffs (1989)
21. Montanari, U., Sassone, V.: CCS Dynamic Bisimulation is Progressing. In: Tarlecki, A. (ed.) MFCS 1991. LNCS, vol. 520, pp. 346–356. Springer, Heidelberg (1991)
22. Nielsen, M., Engberg, U., Larsen, K.S.: Fully Abstract Models for a Process Language with Refinement. In: de Bakker, J.W., de Roever, W.-P., Rozenberg, G. (eds.) Linear Time, Branching Time and Partial Order in Logics and Models for Concurrency. LNCS, vol. 354, pp. 523–548. Springer, Heidelberg (1989)
23. Sabelfeld, A., Myers, A.C.: Language-Based Information-Flow Security. IEEE Journal on Selected Areas in Communication 21(1), 5–19 (2003)
24. Seehusen, F., Stølen, K.: Maintaining Information Flow Security Under Refinement and Transformation. In: Dimitrakos, T., Martinelli, F., Ryan, P.Y.A., Schneider, S. (eds.) FAST 2006. LNCS, vol. 4691, pp. 143–157. Springer, Heidelberg (2007)
25. van Glabbeek, R.J., Goltz, U.: Equivalence Notions for Concurrent Systems and Refinement of Actions. In: Kreczmar, A., Mirkowska, G. (eds.) MFCS 1989. LNCS, vol. 379, pp. 237–248. Springer, Heidelberg (1989)
26. van Glabbeek, R.J., Goltz, U.: Refinement of Actions and Equivalence Notions for Concurrent Systems. Acta Informatica 37(4/5), 229–327 (2001)
27. van Glabbeek, R.J., Vaandrager, F.W.: The Difference between Splitting in n and n+1. Information and Computation 136(2), 109–142 (1997)
28. Wirth, N.: Program Development by Stepwise Refinement. Communications of the ACM 14(4), 221–227 (1971)

Author Index

Lecture Notes in Computer Science

Sublibrary 1: Theoretical Computer Science and General Issues

For information about Vols. 1– 4618
please contact your bookseller or Springer

Vol. 4739: R. Moreno Díaz, F. Pichler, A. Quesada Arencibia (Eds.), Computer Aided Systems Theory – EUROCAST 2007. XIX, 1233 pages. 2007.

Vol. 4736: S. Winter, M. Duckham, L. Kulik, B. Kuipers (Eds.), Spatial Information Theory. XV, 455 pages. 2007.

Vol. 4732: K. Schneider, J. Brandt (Eds.), Theorem Proving in Higher Order Logics. IX, 401 pages. 2007.

Vol. 4731: A. Pelc (Ed.), Distributed Computing. XVI, 510 pages. 2007.

Vol. 4728: S. Bozapalidis, G. Rahonis (Eds.), Algebraic Informatics. VIII, 291 pages. 2007.

Vol. 4726: N. Ziviani, R. Baeza-Yates (Eds.), String Processing and Information Retrieval. XII, 311 pages. 2007.

Vol. 4719: R. Backhouse, J. Gibbons, R. Hinze, J. Jeuring (Eds.), Datatype-Generic Programming. XI, 369 pages. 2007.

Vol. 4711: C.B. Jones, Z. Liu, J. Woodcock (Eds.), Theoretical Aspects of Computing – ICTAC 2007. XI, 483 pages. 2007.

Vol. 4710: C.W. George, Z. Liu, J. Woodcock (Eds.), Domain Modeling and the Duration Calculus. XI, 237 pages. 2007.

Vol. 4708: L. Kučera, A. Kučera (Eds.), Mathematical Foundations of Computer Science 2007. XVIII, 764 pages. 2007.

Vol. 4707: O. Gervasi, M.L. Gavrilova (Eds.), Computational Science and Its Applications – ICCSA 2007, Part III. XXIV, 1205 pages. 2007.

Vol. 4706: O. Gervasi, M.L. Gavrilova (Eds.), Computational Science and Its Applications – ICCSA 2007, Part II. XXIII, 1129 pages. 2007.

Vol. 4705: O. Gervasi, M.L. Gavrilova (Eds.), Computational Science and Its Applications – ICCSA 2007, Part I. XLIV, 1169 pages. 2007.

Vol. 4703: L. Caires, V.T. Vasconcelos (Eds.), CONCUR 2007 – Concurrency Theory. XIII, 507 pages. 2007.

Vol. 4700: C.B. Jones, Z. Liu, J. Woodcock (Eds.), Formal Methods and Hybrid Real-Time Systems. XVI, 539 pages. 2007.

Vol. 4699: B. Kågström, E. Elmroth, J. Dongarra, J. Waśniewski (Eds.), Applied Parallel Computing. XXIX, 1192 pages. 2007.

Vol. 4698: L. Arge, M. Hoffmann, E. Welzl (Eds.), Algorithms – ESA 2007. XV, 769 pages. 2007.

Vol. 4697: L. Choi, Y. Paek, S. Cho (Eds.), Advances in Computer Systems Architecture. XIII, 400 pages. 2007.

Vol. 4688: K. Li, M. Fei, G.W. Irwin, S. Ma (Eds.), Bio-Inspired Computational Intelligence and Applications. XIX, 805 pages. 2007.

Vol. 4684: L. Kang, Y. Liu, S. Zeng (Eds.), Evolvable Systems: From Biology to Hardware. XIV, 446 pages. 2007.

Vol. 4683: L. Kang, Y. Liu, S. Zeng (Eds.), Advances in Computation and Intelligence. XVII, 663 pages. 2007.

Vol. 4681: D.-S. Huang, L. Heutte, M. Loog (Eds.), Advanced Intelligent Computing Theories and Applications. XXVI, 1379 pages. 2007.

Vol. 4672: K. Li, C. Jesshope, H. Jin, J.-L. Gaudiot (Eds.), Network and Parallel Computing. XVIII, 558 pages. 2007.

Vol. 4671: V.E. Malyshkin (Ed.), Parallel Computing Technologies. XIV, 635 pages. 2007.

Vol. 4669: J.M. de Sá, L.A. Alexandre, W. Duch, D.P. Mandic (Eds.), Artificial Neural Networks – ICANN 2007, Part II. XXXI, 990 pages. 2007.

Vol. 4668: J.M. de Sá, L.A. Alexandre, W. Duch, D.P. Mandic (Eds.), Artificial Neural Networks – ICANN 2007, Part I. XXXI, 978 pages. 2007.

Vol. 4666: M.E. Davies, C.J. James, S.A. Abdallah, M.D. Plumbley (Eds.), Independent Component Analysis and Signal Separation. XIX, 847 pages. 2007.

Vol. 4665: J. Hromkovič, R. Královič, M. Nunkesser, P. Widmayer (Eds.), Stochastic Algorithms: Foundations and Applications. X, 167 pages. 2007.

Vol. 4664: J. Durand-Lose, M. Margenstern (Eds.), Machines, Computations, and Universality. X, 325 pages. 2007.

Vol. 4661: U. Montanari, D. Sannella, R. Bruni (Eds.), Trustworthy Global Computing. X, 339 pages. 2007.

Vol. 4649: V. Diekert, M.V. Volkov, A. Voronkov (Eds.), Computer Science – Theory and Applications. XIII, 420 pages. 2007.

Vol. 4647: R. Martin, M.A. Sabin, J.R. Winkler (Eds.), Mathematics of Surfaces XII. IX, 509 pages. 2007.

Vol. 4646: J. Duparc, T.A. Henzinger (Eds.), Computer Science Logic. XIV, 600 pages. 2007.

Vol. 4644: N. Azémard, L. Svensson (Eds.), Integrated Circuit and System Design. XIV, 583 pages. 2007.

Vol. 4641: A.-M. Kermarrec, L. Bougé, T. Priol (Eds.), Euro-Par 2007 Parallel Processing. XXVII, 974 pages. 2007.

Vol. 4639: E. Csuhaj-Varjú, Z. Ésik (Eds.), Fundamentals of Computation Theory. XIV, 508 pages. 2007.

Vol. 4638: T. Stützle, M. Birattari, H. H. Hoos (Eds.), Engineering Stochastic Local Search Algorithms. X, 223 pages. 2007.

Vol. 4630: H.J. van den Herik, P. Ciancarini, H.H.L.M.(J.) Donkers (Eds.), Computers and Games. XII, 283 pages. 2007.

Vol. 4628: L.N. de Castro, F.J. Von Zuben, H. Knidel (Eds.), Artificial Immune Systems. XII, 438 pages. 2007.

Vol. 4627: M. Charikar, K. Jansen, O. Reingold, J.D.P. Rolim (Eds.), Approximation, Randomization, and Combinatorial Optimization. XII, 626 pages. 2007.

Vol. 4624: T. Mossakowski, U. Montanari, M. Haveraaen (Eds.), Algebra and Coalgebra in Computer Science. XI, 463 pages. 2007.

Vol. 4623: M. Collard (Ed.), Ontologies-Based Databases and Information Systems. X, 153 pages. 2007.

Vol. 4621: D. Wagner, R. Wattenhofer (Eds.), Algorithms for Sensor and Ad Hoc Networks. XIII, 415 pages. 2007.

Vol. 4619: F. Dehne, J.-R. Sack, N. Zeh (Eds.), Algorithms and Data Structures. XVI, 662 pages. 2007.